'... this intimate, eminently readable biography ... was assembled with love, respect and reverence without losing its sense of balance and accuracy ... painted in full and vibrant hues, giving short shrift neither to Ellington's inestimable importance as a musician nor his fascinating personality and character. Highest recommendation.' SAN DIEGO UNION TRIBUNE

'Nicholson ... successfully brings a humanness and warmth to America's finest composer ...' LIBRARY JOURNAL

'... a genuinely innovative contribution to Ellington studies ... one of the most approachable and easily digestible ways to come to terms with the mythic proportions of this most inescapable figure.'
Colm O'Sullivan, SUNDAY TRIBUNE (Dublin)

'Like the Ellington suite for which it is named, Stuart Nicholson's copiously researched appreciation of Duke Ellington's life and art is a work of unobtrusive joy ...' NEWSDAY

'... [This] affectionate but honest portrayal doesn't shy from Ellington's earthy sensuality, his superstition, drinking, gambling and use of crude language ... And thanks to Nicholson's sensitive editing, it preserves all of its speaker's dignity and humanity. There is no meanness or smallness anywhere in this portrait.' CHRISTIAN SCIENCE MONITOR

'Fascinating ... thoroughly researched, highly readable' BOSTON GLOBE

'Rich in personal anecdote and period detail ... Nicholson's prodigious ... archival research and his thoughtful orchestration of source material let him combine accessibility with scholarly authority. The book's title comes from a 1934 number Ellington penned to mourn the death of his mother; it sums up the sweetly nostalgic mood this richly deatiled biography creates.'
PUBLISHERS WEEKLY

'A Portrait of Duke Ellington is an ambitious, compelling and wonderfully realized exploration of a great man's life. The Duke deserved a handsome memorial on his centenary, and Stuart Nicholson has provided it.'
YORKSHIRE POST

'... far from being a conventional biography ... intimate ... rounded'
WESTERN MAIL (Cardiff)

'Parts of the Ellington personality remain in the shadows because no one was ever allowed to get too close. But in these pages Stuart Nicholson comes as near as anyone has ever done.' HERALD (Glasgow)

'... one of the most enjoyable and riveting books on the subject you'll ever read.' JAZZ JOURNAL INTERNATIONAL

A PORTRAIT OF

DUKE ELLINGTON

REMINISCING IN TEMPO

STUART NICHOLSON is the only European jazz writer to have
received two Notable Book of the Year commendations from
The New York Times Review of Books, for his biographies of
Ella Fitzgerald and Billie Holiday. Praised for his 'scholarship
and musical insight' (*Observer*), 'impressive knowledge of jazz'
(*Sunday Times*) and 'clear-eyed intelligence' (*New York Times*),
these are now widely regarded as the definitive works on the
legendary singers. Stuart Nicholson is also the author of *Jazz:
The 1980s Resurgence*, described by BBC Radio 4 as 'one of the
essentials of any jazz library' and now considered the standard
work on what was an important renascent decade for jazz; and
A History of Jazz-Rock, the first of its kind, and praised by *Kirkus
Review* for its 'impeccable musical scholarship'.

By the same author:

Jazz: The 1980s Resurgence
Ella Fitzgerald
Billie Holiday
Jazz-Rock: A History

A PORTRAIT OF

DUKE ELLINGTON

REMINISCING IN TEMPO

STUART NICHOLSON

PAN BOOKS

To Marsha and Bob Dennis

First published 1999 by Sidgwick & Jackson

This edition published 2000 by Pan Books
an imprint of Macmillan Publishers Ltd
25 Eccleston Place, London SW1W 9NF
Basingstoke and Oxford
Associated companies throughout the world
www.macmillan.co.uk

ISBN 0 330 36732 3

Copyright © Stuart Nicholson 1999

The right of Stuart Nicholson to be identified as the
author of this work has been asserted by him in accordance
with the Copyright, Designs and Patents Act 1988.

1 3 5 7 9 8 6 4 2

A CIP catalogue record for this book is available from
the British Library.

Typeset by SetSystems Ltd, Saffron Walden, Essex
Printed and bound in Great Britain by
Mackays of Chatham plc, Chatham, Kent

CONTENTS

CONTENTS

FOREWORD

I met Duke Ellington once. I was a gauche young teenager asking for his autograph. Ellington graciously obliged, and moved on to sign another jostling fan's concert programme. There were a lot of concert programmes that night. Chewing gum, rhythmically, remorselessly, he patiently autographed about fifty or sixty of them. He, of all people, didn't have to be doing this at his age. Not simply a jazz musician, not simply a band leader, he was an internationally famous star who had been celebrated by royalty, heads of state and the rich and famous. Yet he diligently attended this simple public relations task just as he had done every night of his performing career since the 1920s. This elderly, dignified man could have retired years before and lived off the royalties from his thousands of compositions, one of which is still broadcast every minute of every day somewhere around the globe – 'Satin Doll', 'Caravan', 'C Jam Blues', 'Perdido', 'Sophisticated Lady', the list goes on and on. I was struck by his eyes – kind, baggy and oh-so-weary. He was much taller than I expected, his blue satin jacket was not just blue, it was electric blue and he had let his hair grow down the back of his neck on to his shoulders. Strange this, I remember thinking, since everyone knew he had a personal hairdresser among his entourage. Earlier, he had been roaring, growling and 'Y-e-e-e-e-s'-ing his road-weary band into ever greater deeds of derring-do. They gradually responded, albeit with studied nonchalance, and after about an hour they were firing on all cylinders. This was band *leading*, I thought, as he imposed his personality on to this bunch of disparate characters that comprised his famous orchestra. Another day, another city, this time somewhere in Britain on a windy, wet February night. He conducted, danced a few steps, pounded a grand piano with ear-to-ear chords and charmed his audience into submission. When it was all over everyone rose as if directed by some unseen hand and applauded and applauded. Ellington smiled and thanked us for inspiring him and his orchestra. He told us we were all very beautiful, very sweet, very gracious and I think we all believed him. And, he said, he loved us madly. Backstage he seemed much older. I was bursting to ask him about the Harlem jazz scene of the 1920s, Bubber Miley, the Cotton Club, the Swing Era and the 1940s band with Jimmy Blanton. And that was just for starters. I didn't, of course, and it was just as well. Little did I know that years before he had decided he was born in 1956 and talking about the past was just about the last thing he liked to do.

When he died in 1974, Duke Ellington still had a long career ahead of him as a cultural icon. His music showed that America, particularly black America, had had enough of European values and attitudes. Here was someone different, American classiness that was classless and it came out in his music, which was as rich and varied as anything to be found in jazz. He called it Negro music, since he felt the term jazz was narrow and limiting, and the sounds he conjured from his imagination were unique even in a music where individuality was once prized above all. Acutely aware of image, he understood it wasn't enough to be regarded as a jazz composer. He projected himself as a serious jazz composer because that was what he was and it turned out to be his best weapon against racial prejudice. Yet as a black musician amid the lowlife of Prohibition America he also realized he could not improve his status without becoming a celebrity. It was a role he had prepared himself for since childhood. Charismatic, eloquent, he came to epitomize black dignity, yet beneath the sophisticated façade which the public saw were countless Duke Ellingtons that together comprised a personality as rich and as complex as his music.

When he arrived in New York in the 1920s it was the so-called 'jazz age' of Scott Fitzgerald, the point at which alcohol, dance and music intersected, creating a dangerous and liberating aura that appealed to white socialites. Back then the term jazz was used very loosely, it could have meant anything from Ragtime to Eliot's *Waste Land*, the product of Tin Pan Alley to the real thing proposed by a Jelly Roll Morton, a King Oliver or a Louis Armstrong. As the decade wore on one thing became clear, if the 1920s was indeed the Jazz Age, then the music of that age was black. But while jazz provided the energy that symbolized the decade, it was Ellington who gave it eloquence. Yet it was not until he had reached New York that he discovered what it was he wanted to express. It was something that came in response to events that were shaping his life, the unfathomable process of being in the right place at the right time providing the forum for his untried talent to flourish. The nightly grind and daily practice inspired his creativity, the greater the one, the greater became the other, not just in the 1920s but throughout his life. By the time he died in 1974, jazz had acquired a stature far beyond its folk origins or dance crazes like the Charleston, and while Ellington may not have been entirely responsible for its cultural elevation, he was the first person everybody cited for bringing it about. His very numerous compositions from 'Soda Fountain Rag' to 'The Three Black Kings' made the case for his genius; his recordings confirm it.

From my brief meeting I wanted to know more about this charismatic man and the tensions within his life that gave force to such creativity. Still in school, I bought Ellington biographies when I saw them in book sales, auction lists and in second-hand book stores and I saved for a copy of his autobiography *Music*

Is My Mistress. But getting a handle on Ellington's real life history was not as straightforward as I had initially imagined. Ellington knew that the price of fame meant he was fair game for the prying eyes of the media to whom scandal was news, so he controlled his story. He took out expensive advertisements in the press to make them think twice about offending a paying customer, he paid off gossip columnists (some were added to his payroll) and he even fed the press tit-bits of scuttle-butt to keep them on-side.[1] The ploy was largely successful; when a fire broke out in an apartment block where he was spending the night with one of his lady friends the building was evacuated, but Ellington's presence on the sidewalk in a dressing gown alongside his similarly clad companion failed to hit the gossip columns.

Flaubert maintained that an artist should manage to make posterity believe he never existed but Ellington was of course too large a figure to elude posterity entirely so he did the next best thing. For all his outgoing charm, he gave posterity only that part of him which was necessary to achieve his ends. The rest he kept under wraps, an intensely private person who restricted his innermost thoughts to a close circle of intimates. It is now his music that commands our attention, as it should do, but this has left a void where his life used to be. And this cannot quite be filled by discussion, debate and musical analysis – whether this or that period of his recordings was best, the extent to which his longer works should be valued or whether his Sacred Concerts should be considered jazz. To me it seems the more that has been written about Ellington, the faster and further he has receded into legend. Gradually he has been claimed by 'the closed shop of university research where only tenured academics are allowed near [him]',[2] so great has his stature grown in the intervening years since his death. Today he appears a distant, remote icon who only comes to life on recordings, yet Ellington was a larger than life personality with all the quirks and foibles that so often accompany genius.

To separate art from the artist fails to situate the art in its time or acknowledge the competing forces, both internal and external, that shaped the artist's life. That is why audiences are so interested in the details of an artist's biography. Yet as Max Harrison has said, the more we scrutinize an artist's life, no matter how exemplary the achievement, the more does that life take on human shape – only human, all too human. And so biographies are not advisable reading for those who seek heroes, as most jazz fans do. Mindful that Ellington is quite obviously the music's finest composer, reference to his voracious sexual appetite, for example, invites resentment in the mistaken belief that such allusions demean his artistic achievements. This in stark contrast to the classical masters such as Bach, Mozart, Beethoven and Wagner who have been the subject of much closer scrutiny – thus only Christ and Napoleon have been the subjects of more books than Wagner. Yet their place in cultural history is permanently established no matter what their human frailties, hence the sublime elevation of Mozart's finest music is in no way questioned by the schoolboy scatological preoccupations of some of his letters.

Maybe this unease in discussing Ellington's sex life reflects the saddest part of Freud's legacy, that no-one can talk about sex without offending someone, or perhaps it has its roots in America's traditional insecurity when confronted with European culture, something that today has been taken over by jazz fans and aficionados in both America *and* Europe who are uncomfortably aware that their music, even as the twentieth century draws to a close, remains uncomfortably close to its vernacular origins. In balancing the claims of a new tradition in the making against the long established values of European culture, jazz becomes extremely self-conscious. It is an art form that is not at peace with itself, which is perhaps how it should be. It is, after all, in flux, growing and developing still, with all the tensions and controversies that implies.

To me there seemed an overwhelming need to re-engage with Ellington as a man, rather than as musical polymath. To achieve this I felt it was time to view his biography from a new perspective. The portrait that follows is an oral history which I hope gives immediacy to a life which, like all lives, had its share of happiness, sadness and drama. Whether we like it or not we live in a soundbite era, and I was greatly attracted by the immediacy of the recollections gathered for this centennial celebration which are intended to lend events in Ellington's life real meaning.

It was an approach that occurred to me only after I had completed my biographies of Ella Fitzgerald and Billie Holiday. In both studies I made frequent use of interview material, including a description of Billie Holiday first singing 'Strange Fruit' in Cafe Society recounted to me by her bass player, the late John Williams. This gave me a clue. Here was an authenticity that no biographer, however gifted, could replicate. For a couple of paragraphs at least, I was in that Cafe Society audience in 1939.

It took me back to the first book on jazz I ever purchased, *Hear Me Talkin' to Ya* by Nat Shapiro and Nat Hentoff, an oral history of jazz. I had read it even before my brief encounter with Ellington and to me it conveyed a romance and excitement more formal studies of jazz lacked. It made me wonder whether a similar approach might work in a biographical context, constructed in a way that might have value to established Ellington fans as much as those coming to his life story for the first time. Certainly the Ellington we encounter today in broadsheets, academic journals and history books allows little of the compelling weave of complexities and contradictions of the inner man to surface. And while his life has been told many times before, it seemed to me that perhaps here was a way of presenting a portrait of him that might have an authenticity others lacked.

What interested me in this approach was the amount of detail it is possible to reveal through the particularization of an interviewee's recollections. The challenge was, of course, in maintaining a narrative flow while using juxtaposition to illuminate events within the normal ebb and flow of biography. Also, I wanted to probe Ellington's life for access points to his music. Ultimately, it is often our subjective response to events in his real-life history that lends meaning to his music, especially since so much of that music is either bound up in impressionistic portraits of people and places, or in the powerful imagery of his works of social significance, such as the extended composition *Black, Brown and Beige* or the musical revue *My People*.

Since Ellington, and more particularly Sonny Greer, had remarkable memories, there was a solid foundation from which to begin. Greer, for example, used to amaze Ellington by recalling the names and home towns of fans they had met on their interminable one-night stands through America maybe ten or fifteen or even twenty years earlier. Since it has been my experience when interviewing artists that time and place often blur one into another, leaving the luckless interviewer to try to unravel this historical sequence, I was surprised and delighted by Ellington and Greer's often precise chronology. Equally, my main concern was to obtain new material that would, in my view, present a fresh perspective on Ellington's life. This meant hunting out Ellington's FBI file, for example, documents which, if nothing else, provide a running commentary on the paranoid politics of an era. I was able, through film-maker Don McGlynn, to use a lengthy, unpublished interview with Ellington's manager Irving Mills, and Donald L. McCathran provided me with an hour-long interview with Otto Hardwick. The late Leonard Malone and Don McGlynn allowed me use of interviews from their substantial holdings, including many interview out-takes the world has never seen. The archives I cite below provided me with many contemporaneous clippings, and Annie Kuebler of the Smithsonian Institution provided me with access to interview material from which hitherto only small extracts had been taken. The sheer size of what she made available for me to use in this book, I think, daunted many researchers because of the hours and hours needed to sift through it all to find anything substantive.

As my research gradually accumulated I realized I needed perhaps twice and three times as much as would have been needed for an orthodox biography (I wish I had realized this *before* I began . . .). There was, of course, a tale to tell, and much material had to be abandoned if it did not fit into the overall flow of the text. Sometimes I was spoilt for choice, sometimes I searched weeks for just one snippet to drive the narrative forward in the way I wanted, but fortunately only rarely was I forced to resort to using the standard Ellington reference works. Consequently a lot of what follows is new to the published Ellington canon, and that which is not I hope is given greater meaning presented in this new context.

One of my concerns was to use material either from Ellington's own mouth or from people close to him – his family, close friends, band members and business associates best placed to observe him at close quarters. That way the reader can be confident that whoever's voice it is, it will be speaking from the perspective of knowing Ellington well. Invariably, the relationship of these voices to Ellington emerges in the text, so I have not provided a *dramatis personae* which would be distracting (the temptation to flip backwards and forwards irresistible, I always find). I have, however, tried to keep the reader aware of the chronological context of events so their significance in Ellington's story is understood. Throughout, I have tried not to intrude, but to gently guide the reader through the various recollections in the hope that their significance gradually emerges. In the same way a newspaper photograph is composed of countless tiny dots that in isolation mean little, it is my hope that when taken together, these recollections will provide a portrait of Ellington that would have been impossible to achieve through an orthodox biography.

When I described in some detail how I intended to approach this telling of Ellington's life to Annie Kuebler of the Duke Ellington Collection, Archive Center, NMAH, in the Smithsonian Institution, Washington D.C., she guided me through the enormous Ellington holdings to provide me with access to material that was suitable for my purposes. Not only did she give me much background information about the Ellington resources, but she was keen to see it play a prominent role in an Ellington biography as a way of publicizing the importance and extent of the Smithsonian holdings. That I am happy to do. In an age of government cutbacks and increasing scrutiny on the public purse, we all must be vigilant in ensuring that this important collection remains available to teach and inspire future generations about Ellington's legacy.

Annie also put me in touch with Donald L. McCathran, who kindly gave me access to an interview with Otto Hardwick by Felix Grant of Radio WMAL on 29 April 1964, for which I am most grateful. Larry Appelbaum made me most welcome in the Library of Congress in Washington D.C., and guided me around their holdings, including the Jerry Valburn Collection. He insisted I join the twentieth century and get hooked up to e-mail when I returned to the UK, for which I am grateful. From time to time he tracked down elusive cuttings and interview snippets, tasks which impinged on his very busy schedule, yet he always found time to provide answers to my questions. His knowledge of jazz is huge, and I am in his debt for the time and trouble he took on my behalf.

Once again I am grateful for the resources that were made available to me at the Institute of Jazz Studies at Rutgers University by Dan Morgenstern. Without his guidance, suggestions and advice this book would not have assumed the shape it has. In what is, unquestionably, the most important resource in jazz, I was allowed untrammelled access to its every corner, for which I am grateful. My comments earlier about government funding for public institutions apply equally to the Institute, which deservedly has a worldwide reputation, built up over the years by its dedicated staff. To me it remains one of the seven wonders of the world. Also, I would like to acknowledge the assistance of the New York Public Library Schomburg Center for Research in Black Culture and the New York Public Library Performing Arts Research Center at Lincoln Center.

In the United Kingdom I am grateful to Andrew Simon and Paul Wilson for the help and facilities made available to me at the National Sound Archive of the British Library: Andrew for making possible a transatlantic inter-library loan and Paul for helping me track down endless cuttings from the incredible array of publications and periodicals the Archive holds. Grateful thanks for the assistance of David Nathan at the National Jazz Archive at Loughton Library, Professor Dennis McCalvin and Dr Lindsay M. Newman curators of the Jack Hylton Collection at Lancaster University, the British Library Newspaper Library, Dave Bennett, Darryl Sherman, Harold 'Bob' Udkoff and Loren Shoenberg whose generous assistance in all my books to date is greatly appreciated. Thanks also to Adam Seiff and Sharon Kelly at Sony Jazz for their support, Kerstan Mackness and Steve Sanderson at New Note Records, and special thanks to Ellington expert Max Harrison for his thoughts and welcome advice in completing this Foreword.

Very grateful thanks to film-maker Don McGlynn, the producer and director who has brought us some of the finest music documentaries ever made, including *Art Pepper: Notes from a Jazz Survivor*, *The Mills Brothers Story*, *The Soundies*, *Glenn Miller: America's Musical Hero*, *The Spike Jones Story*, *Techno: Lost In Bass*, *Dexter Gordon: More Than You Know* and *Charles Mingus: Triumph of the Underdog*. In 1984–5 he was involved in an as yet uncompleted documentary on the life of Irving Mills and kindly gave me access to both the edited film and a full transcript of a detailed Mills interview that hitherto has not been in the public domain. He also made available to me countless interviews from his huge video and audio library as well as providing stimulating company when I visited with him in Copenhagen. There he introduced me to Leonard Malone, the distinguished journalist and writer, who co-produced the documentary film *A Duke Named Ellington* from which interview extracts and out-takes are quoted in the text. Leonard also gave me access to much radio interview material from his collection. Little did I realize that within just a few weeks of meeting him his battle with cancer would end. A wonderful man, I do wish I had had the opportunity to get to know him better.

I doubt whether this book would have been possible without the help and hospitality of Marsha and Bob Dennis, my dear friends in New York, who, aware of the impecunious plight of this writer, threw their home open to me (again) so that I could work on my research under Marsha's careful guidance. Marsha is the long-serving President of the New York Jewish Genealogical Society and her knowledge of New York's public records is second to none. The warmth of their welcome on my visits to New York is something I treasure, and it is to them this book is dedicated.

My wife Kath has once more put up with the long hours to see this project through to completion and to her my love. My mother, my in-laws, Eileen and Jim, have kept me smiling, while my brother Malcolm's unfailing good humour, despite being recently claimed by marriage, always lifts my spirits. My thanks to Gordon Wise, my editor who has been a model of support and patience in seeing this project through and providing me with valuable suggestions in structuring the book – even though at the time I was reluctant to accept them. Finally, thanks to Mandy Little, my literary agent, for her continued support.

STUART NICHOLSON
WOODLANDS ST MARY, BERKSHIRE
OCTOBER 1998

I'm just an up and coming musician struggling to find another new note.[1]

Duke Ellington[1]

PROLOGUE

1840 was the year Queen Victoria of Britain married Prince Albert of Saxe-Coburg-Gotha, Nelson's column was erected in Trafalgar Square, the Penny Post was instituted, Britain's Opium War with China began and Robert Browning wrote 'Sordello'. They were all events that still have, in some way, shape or form, resonance over a century and a half later, but they meant nothing to James Ellington, a Carolina cotton picker born that year. Like almost everyone else who was black in America then, he began his life as a slave. James, later known as Jim, entered the world in North Carolina[1] and the 1870 Census reveals him to have been a 'mulatto', suggesting he may have had a white father or grandfather, and a check of census records reveals most people with an Ellington surname in North Carolina at that time were white.[2] Jim was shown as a farm labourer living with his wife Emma (née Walker, b. circa 1844) and their seven children in Ironton Township, Lincoln County, North Carolina. Emma had given birth to her first child as a teenager – the 1870 Census says she was fourteen at the time, the 1880 census says she was sixteen – and she and all her children were noted in the 1870 Census as being 'black' except their seven-year-old daughter Ella, who was also shown as a 'mulatto'. Their first born, Jerry, was already a farm labourer at the age of twelve. The 1880 Census shows Jim to be paralysed, suggesting an accident sustained during his labouring job, and also reveals his father to have been born in North Carolina

1

and his mother in Virginia, a question not asked in the earlier census. By then Emma had given birth to a further five children, the youngest of whom was James Edward, one year old, and recorded by the census taker simply as a 'male infant'. James Edward, who would later acquire the nicknames 'JE' and 'Uncle Ed', was born on 15 April 1879. By the time of the 1900 Census, Jim and Emma Ellington had moved with several of their family to 'Washington City, District of Columbia', and were in rooms at 2129 Ward Place. Jim was shown as 'Head of the Family', had no occupation, while Emma was shown as a 'Laundress'. Their son James Edward, then twenty-one, had his occupation described as a 'Driver for Doctor'. Also living in the household were two of Jim and Emma's daughters, their youngest son George, then eighteen and a printing office porter, and James Edward's wife Daisy. Daisy Ellington (née Kennedy), whose date of birth is shown as 'January 1878',[3] was the daughter of James William Kennedy, one of only forty black police officers in Washington, and Alice Williams, of mixed Indian and Negro descent. One of five sisters and three brothers, Daisy had married James Edward on 3 January 1898 and had recently given birth to a young son, who was also recorded in the neat handwriting of the census taker. His name was shown as Edward K. Ellington and his date of birth was given as April 1899.

CHAPTER ONE
FLAMING YOUTH

When Edward Kennedy Ellington was born on 29 April 1899, Washington D.C. was then the largest black urban community in America. It was a city rigidly divided by segregation, but the divisions in society did not end there. The members of the black community were further divided by caste and by class. Such a social environment provided strong character-forming experiences. Yet despite being a city riven by social divisions – white society was equally riddled with class barriers – Washington D.C. was considered a leader in the education of Afro-Americans. In 1864 a law was passed that required the city to provide a black public-school system and in the aftermath of the Civil War Howard University, quickly recognized as black America's seat of learning, was established in 1867. By the early 1900s, Washington Afro-American society boasted the highest standards of culture enjoyed by black people anywhere in America, prompting Langston Hughes to observe, 'Never before, anywhere had I seen such persons of influence – men with some money, women with some beauty, teachers with some education – quite so sure of their own importance and their high places in the community.'

While Ellington's family did not move in the highest circles, their circumstances were economically secure and their values imbued with those of the black middle-class society around them. They were a part of a social group whose morals were steadfastly Victorian and often puritanical in outlook and who shared a

3

genteel interest in the arts and expected their children to aspire to the highest standards of education and deportment.

From the start, Ellington was encouraged to become an achiever, and was taught pride in his race and a duty to represent it well. His role model was his father, James Edward Ellington, who throughout his life aspired to the values of a gentleman. His mother Daisy Ellington doted on her son: 'You're blessed,' she told him, and he believed her.

DUKE ELLINGTON: Once upon a time a very pretty lady and a very handsome gentleman met, fell in love and got married, and God blessed them with this wonderful baby boy. They held him in the palm of their hand and they nurtured him until he was eight years old and then they put his feet on the ground. He ran out of the front door, out across the street and somebody said, 'Hey, Edward, up this way.' The boy was me, incidentally. He got to the next corner and somebody says, 'Hey, Edward, up there and turn left, you can't miss it.' And it's been going on ever since.[1]

DUKE ELLINGTON: You know, my mother played music. She played those beautiful piano things written by Carrie Jacobs Bond, who wrote some pretty delicate music – it was so pretty that when my mother played, I used to cry – it was so pretty. My father played by ear, some of the old standard operatic things.[2]

RUTH ELLINGTON: My mother was absolutely puritanical; she wore nose glasses and she didn't even wear lipstick because she thought that a woman should not be attracting another man.[3]

Ellington's sister Ruth was born in August 1915.

DUKE ELLINGTON: I was terribly spoiled as a youngster.[4]

DUKE ELLINGTON: My mother started telling me about God when I was very young. There was never any talk about red people, brown people, black people, or yellow people, or about the differences that existed between them.[5]

DUKE ELLINGTON: She never went anywhere without me, she go to a dance and take me to the dance and dress me up and sit me up on the bandstand, next to the musicians. I'd sit there and watch them ... it's a thing that had some fascination for me, but it was a thing I never had any hope of doing.[6]

RUTH ELLINGTON: My mother was not a social butterfly, she was very staid and stayed at home.[7]

DUKE ELLINGTON: My father had a good job, he was a butler and he was a great provider. Then he quit that job, and in the First World War, rented a big house down on K Street – a big fashionable neighbourhood – for all these women war workers, high salaries, and he was a caterer. He did well until the war ended, that was the end of that, then he got a job blueprinting in the Navy yard.[8]

RUTH ELLINGTON: [He] was a Chesterfieldian gentleman who wore gloves and spats, and very intellectual. Self-educated. My father came from a family of ten, and he arrived in Washington from North Carolina – Lincolnton, where he was born – at the age of seven. He had not more than a third grade education, but by the time he reached teens he was hired by a doctor in Washington, a Dr [Middleton F.] Cuthbert, who brought him up, taught him how to drive the first horseless carriage, which was an electric car. Dr Cuthbert had a magnificent library from floor to ceiling with big old leather chairs – I used to go there in later years and see this library – and my father, as a teenager, read omnivorously from this library. So had you talked to my father by the time he was forty – and then he'd read the newspapers and read everything – he was a well-educated man, but he had done it through this doctor. This doctor stayed close to us all the time. When I was born, for instance, he was the one who put my mother in hospital where I was born and he was the one took care of me until I was a big girl all through my mumps, and measles and all that. This doctor took care of me, and when he finally died, just before we came to New York, he left my father $3,000. He still remembered him, we were always close. And I'm sure he supervised Edward's surgery too, in Washington, with the hernia.[9]

Dr M. F. Cuthbert lived at 1462 Rhode Island Avenue, Washington D.C.

DUKE ELLINGTON: My father was a great man. He knew all the right things to tell me, how to be a fine, upright, clean-living gentleman, be a credit to the family, and I know all of them, and I know exactly what to tell any young man what to do – but I didn't do them all.[10]

RUTH ELLINGTON: I don't want to say [my father was] stern, I don't want to say [he was] dictatorial, but his language was quite precise and sharp and he was an authority figure and Edward always respected and loved him so much. My father had this insatiable love of people. Duke, I think, was a little more reserved, more like the Kennedys.[11]

DUKE ELLINGTON: There was so much education around Washington, that you got a little bit of everything. It was not a case of conservatory music being some strange factor because you had to go to these damn concerts whether you liked it or not, recitals and so forth, they'd bring in guest stars, people in the concert field.[12]

DUKE ELLINGTON: Ragtime was way back when I was a child, I heard the word ragtime, I didn't know what it was about. As I grew up I heard these 'piano plunkers', they used to call them.[13]

DUKE ELLINGTON: [My lessons] were enough to make Mrs Clinkscales' first recital. Mrs Clinkscales was my music teacher.

Half the time she'd come around and I'd be out there playing baseball or something, my mother had to pay her off. She wanted me to be something. But I was too wild, running the street.[14]

Ellington attended the Garnet Elementary School between 1905 and 1908, and during this period he received piano lessons from Mrs Marietta Harvey (née Clinkscales).

DUKE ELLINGTON: There was no connection between me and music, until I started fiddling with it myself. As far as anyone teaching me, there was too many rules and regulations, and I just couldn't be shackled into that. As long as I could sit down and figure it out for myself, then that was all right.[15]

DUKE ELLINGTON: In the schools in Washington, when I was in school here, they had separate schools, coloured schools and white schools, and it was a very good thing for the negro. What used to happen was that they were concerned with you being a representative of a great and proud race. This was it, when you walked out of this place and went out on to the street you are a representative and your behaviour is what the race depends upon to command respect. Which is very important – they used to pound it into you, you go to the English class, that was more important than the English.[16]

Ellington's English teacher at Garrison Junior High School was Miss R. A. Boston (1913–14).

RUTH ELLINGTON: Coming out of Washington where you grew up in a segregated society, where the black American middle class which he grew up in was very proud and very well informed and it was expected of you to be well informed, go to college, get a degree and to be proficient in the arts. That was the norm for that black American middle class.[17]

DUKE ELLINGTON: I don't know how many castes of Negroes there were in the city at that time, but I do know that if you decided to mix carelessly with another you would be told that one just did not do that sort of thing.[18]

DUKE ELLINGTON: By the time I was eleven or twelve years old I had read Sherlock Holmes, Cleek of Scotland Yard and Arsène Lupin.[19]

DUKE ELLINGTON: I had piano lessons like all children do, like everybody did. But this had nothing to do with the thing that followed when I was fourteen.[20]

DUKE ELLINGTON: I decided to go adventuring when I was fourteen years old. I left my home in Washington D.C. and went to Asbury Park, New Jersey. I had no real reason for going. My people were very good to me, but I just wanted to get out and try my wings. I thought it would be easy for me to land a job. I thought I was a pretty good man at that time. Of course I did not know how to do anything well. I was getting pretty hungry too, about this time. I saw a coloured boy, and asked him if he knew where I could find a job. Asbury Park, as you know, is a seaside resort and many coloured boys were used there in the hotels and cafes. The boy sent me to a hotel, telling me that they needed a bus boy. I hurried to the place only to find that the job had been filled. 'But,' said the manager, 'Ve neet von fer der dishes.' Now, if ever there was a task I hated with perfect hatred, it was washing dishes. Pangs of hunger overcame my distaste for dishwashing so I took the job. I held it too, until the fall term of school began. So I went back home, not as a penitent, prodigal son, but as a young man on his own with a supply of good clothes and some money saved up.[21]

MAURICE ZOLOTOW: He went to Asbury Park to work as a dishwasher in a summer hotel and here he heard his first ragtime composition, played on a piano roll. It was Harvey Brooks's 'Junkman Rag'.[22]

DUKE ELLINGTON: I cannot tell you what that music did to me. It was different from the average piano selection. The individuality of the man showed itself in the composition as he played it. I said right then, 'That's how I would like to play a piano, so without being told, everybody would know I was playing.'[23]

MAURICE ZOLOTOW: He was set on fire by the rolling rhythm and the entrancing tremble of ragtime. He sought out Mr Brooks and pleaded to be taught a few simple progressions.[24]

DUKE ELLINGTON: Harvey was not selfish. When I told him about my resolve he encouraged me and taught me many of the short cuts he had figured out, to successful playing. I was eager to learn and I lived at the piano. It wasn't very long before I could hear a tune and after a few moments I could reproduce it, often adding different variations.[25]

DUKE ELLINGTON: Then I was confined to the house for weeks, because of some cold or something, and so I started picking at the piano and I picked out a thing we called 'Soda Fountain Rag' – my first composition. In those days I used to stand over the piano players for hours and hours and hours just watching and listening.[26]

DUKE ELLINGTON: I used to go to the Howard Theatre almost every day to hear good music and one of the greats to appear there was Luckeyeth Roberts. His hands were so spread out he could stretch a 12th (feat) in either one.[27]

DUKE ELLINGTON: I think I knew about two full numbers, and one night somebody very desperately came to me and said they needed a piano player to come up to Room Five [at True Reformers Hall in Washington] and play. Well, not only was it a very, very bad piano, but I had to play it from eight to one and at the end of the night I got 75 cents, and this was my first gig and I ran home like a thief with that money. It was like stealing it because I would play these numbers over and over, but I would change the tempos and play them in different styles, I think that was my first experiment in rhapsodizing or developing a theme.[28]

DUKE ELLINGTON: Soon I began to play for small dances and house parties. Sometimes I would be fortunate to get another boy to play with me, either on a saxophone or banjo.[29]

DUKE ELLINGTON: My father said something about playing that old ragtime music, or something like that, but I never had no real resistance against what I was doing.[30]

RUTH ELLINGTON: I loved Edward. Everything he did was wonderful, because that was the way I was brought up. Everybody in the whole family, aunts, uncles, cousins, everybody adored Edward. So whatever he did was marvellous, whatever he played was wonderful.[31]

DUKE ELLINGTON: [Uncle Ed] sort of talked me out of childhood. He'd say there's other things besides baseball. You couldn't miss him, his immaculate attire.[32]

Uncle Ed was Ellington's father's nickname.

DUKE ELLINGTON: I was trying to fuck ever since I was six years old. I wasn't doing very much of it, but I was tryin' and it felt pretty good, whatever it was. I finally got it in when I was around about twelve years old, I guess, out in a field someplace, I don't know where it was, I don't know who it was.[33]

RUTH ELLINGTON: I know my mother said [Edward] took me home in his arms out of the hospital and when it was time for me to walk, he took me by my top braid and guided me around the room. I remember as a little girl, him squeezing me so tight and he was always very protective.[34]

OTTO HARDWICK: I first met Duke in school, Duke was going to Armstrong at the time, Armstrong High School, I was going to Dunbar, but more or less we were neighbours, Duke lived in one block, I lived in the other, Duke lived at 1212 T Street Northwest, I lived in 1345 T Street so automatically we just saw each other every day, and became great friends.[35]

Otto Hardwick was born in Washington D.C., 31 May 1904. Ellington attended the Samuel H. Armstrong Technical High School between 1914 and 1917.

EDNA THOMPSON: It was at Armstrong that Ellington and I fell in love. He had just learned the difference between girls and boys.[36]

Edna Thompson was born in Washington D.C. on 4 August 1898.

DUKE ELLINGTON: We'd get girls, all the same social clique, and go down the reservoir, get in somebody's car or even walk up to the reservoir, they would line up there, everybody had his own girl, of course, and we'd be in hearing distance, you couldn't look, you'd be in hearing distance and the object was to see who did the greater job as a man. If the girl's reaction was greater, then he was a great fucker, because this chick was hollering and screaming, 'Hello Daddy!' 'Oh, baby, I'm coming!' and all that shit, and we found out some of the cats were cheating. Some of them were pinching the chicks to make them holler, and we found one cat whose old man had a taxi cab company was slipping the chick quarters! It's always been competitive, all the way along the line![37]

DUKE ELLINGTON: I got a job as a soda jerker to make some money for college . . . my job was in a place called *The Poodle Dog*.[38]

DUKE ELLINGTON: There was a *great* pianist there, Lester Dishman. *Wonderful*. I learned an awful lot just watching him. And sometimes I recall some of his devices in my playing. He was a man who sometimes indulged himself – going around from one place to another. People before they went to work would often stop at somebody's house and just play the piano. Then go somewhere else, you know. And as they went along – I mean, naturally the people would serve refreshments. So by the time he got to work he was full of refreshments.[39]

• DUKE ELLINGTON: When he wasn't able to sit up at the keyboard any longer I filled in, still improvising, composing or otherwise making free use of some basic melody. One day while playing my original 'Soda Fountain Rag', doing it in a different tempo each time I played it, Oliver 'Doc' Perry heard me and began coaching me for one of his orchestras.[40]

REX STEWART: There was a lot of music and bands around Washington at that time. Some of the better known were Doc Perry (whose piano man was Eddie Ellington – before he was called Duke), Elmer Snowden, Sam Taylor and Gertie Wells. Professor Miller had the best doggone military band outside of the US Marine band. Then there was Cliff Jackson, Emory Lucas, the Elgin Brothers, Tommy Miles, Jim Blair and Caroline Thornton … Nor shall I forget the Washington Bell Hops, Mose Duncan's Blue Flame Syncopators and Ike Dixon out of Baltimore.[41]

Rex (William, Jr) Stewart was born in Philadelphia on 22 February 1907, but moved to Washington D.C. as a young child with his mother Jane Johnson Stewart.

DUKE ELLINGTON: There was Doc Perry, Lester Dishman, Louis Brown, 'Sticky' Mac, Clarence Bowser, half of them were conservatory men, the other half couldn't read, but they had terrific left hands. I wanted to sound like they sounded.[42]

DUKE ELLINGTON: This is the school I was raised in, being a parlour piano player.[43]

DUKE ELLINGTON: Then there was a man named Grant. Henry Grant. He was the supervisor of music in Washington schools. He said he would teach me harmony. I had a kind of harmony inside me, which is part of my race, but I needed harmony that has no race at all but is universal. So you see, from both these men I received freely and generously, more than I could have ever paid them for. I repaid them as I could; by playing for Mr Perry, and by learning all I could from Mr Grant.[44]

DUKE ELLINGTON: I really studied piano at that time. Russell Wooding was then directing a jazz concert orchestra of sixty pieces in a Washington theatre, and, against his better judgement, he gave me a job as one of his five pianos. All went well until I came to a pause. Instead of remaining silent, as the score directed, I broke into a typical Ellington improvisation. Mr Wooding very properly fired me.[45]

DUKE ELLINGTON: There was a guy named 'Swifty' Carruthers, he couldn't play much piano like half a dozen cats I knew around Washington. 'Swifty' would come in, his entrance was a bitch. He would come in, when he sat down he was *sharp*. His collar was high, tie neat as a pin. He'd sit down and his hands were manicured, you thought God was going to say something, you know![46]

DUKE ELLINGTON: In high school in Washington, my pal Edgar McIntree decided since I was a pretty fancy guy, I was eligible for his constant companionship, I should have a title, so he called me 'Duke'.[47]

REX STEWART: The corner of Seventh and T streets was *the* hangout for Washington musicians. By tagging along, I got to see all the local big-timers – Doc Perry, Elmer Snowden, Sam Taylor, Gertie Wells, Claude Hopkins and many others. Eddie Ellington had already acquired the nickname 'Duke' by this time and he too hung out on the corner. In fact, he had the added distinction of being 'king' of Room 10 in True Reformers Hall, which stood on the same corner. Room 10 was where the teenagers held their get-togethers. I can still see the young Ellington playing the piano and fixing that famous hypnotic smile on the nearest pretty girl.[48]

DUKE ELLINGTON: Rex and I were very much alike in many ways. Rex was from Washington too, Rex's mother was a piano player, good piano player. She used to play at the Blue Mouse Theatre. Rex was one of these nervous cats, like me.[49]

DUKE ELLINGTON: My first on-stage appearance was selling 'Peanuts-Popcorn-Chewing-gum-Candies-Cigars-Cigarettes-and-Score-Cards' at the ball park! When I became more sophisticated, I was promoted to selling cold drinks. I was completely terrified at the Washington Ballpark, it was like going on stage, stage fright. Everybody in the park was looking at me! All I wanted to see was the baseball game.[50]

Ellington's job was at the Griffith Stadium, Washington D.C.

DUKE ELLINGTON: We used to play baseball at an old tennis court on Sixteenth Street. President [Teddy] Roosevelt would come by on his horse sometimes, and stop and watch us play. When he got ready to go he would wave and we would wave at him.[51]

EDNA THOMPSON: I taught Ellington ... how to read music. Ellington would be out behind the YMCA playing football and basketball when he should have been studying. We were going to Armstrong High School then. Duke wanted to be a commercial artist. I wanted to be a music teacher.[52]

DUKE ELLINGTON: I was originally going to be an artist. I was a good artist. I could paint, draw and all that. And that's what I was majoring in in high school, I won a scholarship to Pratt Institute, but by that time I was involved in j-a-z-z. I was coming up with jazz. I was making a lot of money while I was in high school, I was a professional musician when I was sixteen.[53]

Ellington won a scholarship sponsored by the National Association for the Advancement of Coloured People (NAACP) to Brooklyn's Pratt Institute, but turned it down.

DUKE ELLINGTON: I never did make chemistry or French in high school, I never did make those subjects. I had one point to go before I graduated high school but then I quit. I went to high school in 1914. Finally, when I started getting work [in music], I was working, there was numbers I had to learn, you know? I couldn't even read, I had to get the music in the afternoon, and take it home, and memorize it, and then I'd bring it out at night, set it up on the piano, the other guys sittin' around, they were reading it, [but not me].[54]

• DUKE ELLINGTON: I got my first break when I was about seventeen years old, and Louis Thomas sent for me to play piano one night. Thomas was the leader of a society band whose only competition was Meyer Davis. I was to get a chance to play in his band on the condition I learned how to play 'Siren Song' well enough to perform that night. I spent the whole day learning the tune. Then I arrived on the job and found the band was a legitimate one, they wouldn't take any 'jumps'. The musicians started talking to me about correct chords and in a few minutes I knew I'd be sunk. Then somebody requested 'Siren Song' and in great relief I started plunking out the number. I had often watched Luckey Roberts who had come down from New York to play the Howard Theatre. He had a flashy style and a trick of throwing his hands away from the piano. It occurred to me that I might try doing what he did. Before I knew it the kids around the band were screaming with delight and clapping for more. In two minutes the flashy hands had earned me a reputation and after that I was all set.[55]

REX STEWART: At Odd Fellows Hall in Georgetown there was always a dance on a Saturday night. A lot of us youngsters used to hang around the hall, peeping in the windows at the dancers and musicians. This particular Saturday night there was a quartet working that sounded great to us kids because they played the popular tunes of the day . . . we gaped over the fence, suddenly I yelled to my buddy, 'Hey, that guy playing the piano – I know him. That's Eddie Ellington!'[56]

DUKE ELLINGTON: During the war, the First World War, I was just a yearling. Meyer Davis and Louis Thomas were the two society bands, Louis Thomas was coloured and Meyer Davis was white, and they sent out bands. They had one-inch ads in the telephone book. Well, during the war, all these strange people from all over the country they wanted music, they'd look in the telephone book, 'Music Furnished for All Occasions', and I used to work in Louis Thomas's fifth band, I didn't know nothing about music, I was just bullshitting, and Louis would send me out on jobs, me and a drummer.[57]

DUKE ELLINGTON: [Thomas] sent me to Ashland Country Club, fabulous place for millionaires, and he told me to collect $100 and give him $90, and I woke up and I said, 'What's happening here?' That's when I woke up and got into business for myself.[58]

EDNA THOMPSON: Shortly before we were twenty we got married [on 2 July 1918] and before we were twenty-one Mercer came [on 11 March 1919]. Ellington was working in music then and he was a messenger in the Treasury Department. He also painted backdrops for the Howard Theatre. Those were hard days. But even then he had hitched his wagon to a star. He knew he would be great.[59]

Edna and Edward 'Duke' Ellington set up home together at 1955 Third Street, NW, Washington D.C.

DUKE ELLINGTON: In 1918 I was deeply involved in music. I got married, had a son – tremendous responsibilities. Bought a house, automobile, worked around Washington as a musician, played a lot of society parties around Washington during the World War Number One.[60]

By now Ellington was earning enough to buy a Chandler – then between $1,800 and $2,500 – and move to a house at 2728 Sherman Avenue, NW, Washington D.C.

EDNA ELLINGTON: Then the second baby came. It was too close to the first and died.[61]

OTTO HARDWICK: At the time Duke was playing and I was aspiring to be a musician; although at the time I was just a pupil of music I wanted to get out into the band business, and Duke offered me my first opportunity, says, 'C'mon, let's play with me.' I said, 'I don't think I'm good enough.' He said, 'Who is good enough? C'mon, just bring your horn!'[62]

DUKE ELLINGTON: Otto Hardwick, or 'Toby' as we call him, was just growing up at that time . . . he was playing bass fiddle with Carroll's Columbia Orchestra and he was so small his father used to carry his bass to work for him. I, considering myself a veteran, decided I would break Toby in. He got himself a saxophone, in those days it was a C-Melody.[63]

OTTO HARDWICK: Well, he had a drummer, Lloyd Stewart, and I think it was a banjo player, his name was White, Philly White, and they added a sax – they didn't know whether they were going to get a good one or not, I was the fourth man![64]

DUKE ELLINGTON: I got him a job, and later on I used to send him out on jobs and pretty soon he got to be known as one of the best saxophone players in town. [Trumpeter] Artie Whetsol used to work with us sometimes too.[65]

OTTO HARDWICK: Every man in his band had the freedom of expression as far as the music was concerned. We would have an arrangement, but if there was something you felt you wanted to put in it, you were free to do it, privileged to make suggestions, just spontaneously burst out with it, and if he liked it, or if he didn't, he'd go along with it anyway.[66]

DUKE ELLINGTON: Toby had a weakness for $90 suits, and he ended up buying himself a Pullman automobile. We called the car 'Dupadilly'. You always had to push to start it and it didn't have a crankhandle. It inevitably stalled on a hill. One day it stopped and somewhere and we got out and left it and that was the end of Dupadilly. Before that though ... Claude Hopkins had a car and I had a Chandler and Toby and Felix and Bill used to race our two cars and the Dupadilly. After work we'd set out, going nowhere and as fast as we could. We didn't bother about street crossings or anything else. I don't know why we never cracked-up.[67]

OTTO HARDWICK: We had fun, excitement and extra cash in those days.[68]

DUKE ELLINGTON: Toby was always a guy who enjoyed having a ball, he had us all laughing.[69]

REX STEWART: Whenever that old gang that used to hang around True Reformers Hall in Washington would meet anywhere in the world, the 'remember whens' would always get around to Otto and the gang's adventures with Dupadilly, as Toby's old wreck of an auto was called. Although that was kid stuff, it was still colourful enough to become part of the Hardwick legend.[70]

OTTO HARDWICK: All of a sudden we began to get a lot of 'dicty' jobs. We would all pile into my Pullman automobile, the 'Dupadilly', and Duke would direct me to drive to an embassy, ministry or private mansion ... This was all Meyer Davis territory and none of us were able to figure out how Ellington was muscling in on all these fine gigs. Sometimes he had two or three jobs going at the same time and would rush around to make an appearance with each group he'd sent out.[71]

DUKE ELLINGTON: The reason why I was so successful, I imagine, was because I put a one-inch ad in the telephone book alongside Meyer Davis and Louis Thomas who were the only other bands who advertised in the telephone book, so I too was sending out several bands every night, very lucrative business.[72]

DUKE ELLINGTON: Whenever anyone wanted anything in Washington, they looked in the phone book. Especially so where bands were concerned. If somebody wanted to hire some music and didn't know what musicians they wanted, I figured they were just as likely as not to pick the biggest name in the book.[73]

IRRESISTIBLE JASS
FURNISHED TO OUR SELECT PATRONS
The Duke's Serenaders
COLORED SYNCOPATERS
E. K. ELLINGTON, Mgr.
2728 SHERMAN AVE. N. W. Phone Columbia 7842

DUKE ELLINGTON: This happened at the time of the First World War. And I began to get engagements. People started to call me up – a lot of war workers in Washington. They were all strangers who didn't know Louis Thomas from Meyer Davis, Duke Ellington or anybody else. When they wanted a party they'd look in there and see who played music and call up and say they wanted a band. So I was sending bands out too. And of course, every time you'd book another band the price would go up.[74]

SONNY GREER: In 1918 I came down for three days from Asbury Park, N.J., my home, and stayed on. I didn't tie up with Ellington immediately . . . I worked for three years in the pit of the Howard Theatre, playing shows. All the guys were Puerto Rican but me. It was at the Howard I met Juan Tizol. After I had hung out with Toby for a while, Duke and I met.[75]

William 'Sonny' Greer was born in Long Branch, N.J., on 13 December c. 1895.

DUKE ELLINGTON: [Sonny] was supposed to be a very fly drummer and anybody from New York had the edge on us. But maybe, we thought, he wasn't all that he was cracked up to be. We watched him work in the pit [of the Howard Theatre], and he used a lot of tricks. He was flashy but our minds weren't made up. We decided to give him the works and find out just what sort of guy he was, maybe he hadn't done any more than just pass through New York. We stood on the street corner and waited for him. Everybody used to stand on the street corners then and try and look big-time. 'Whatcha say?' we ask him. I take the lead in the conversation because I'm sure I'm a killer with my new shepherd plaid suit, bought on time. Sonny comes back with a line of jive that lays us low. We decide he's OK.[76]

SONNY GREER: [When] I met Duke he wasn't thinking about being no professional musician. You know how guys stand on the corner, him and Claude Hopkins, Toby 'Otto' Hardwick, standing on the corner, they was talking some jive, they started talking about New York. He said, 'Sonny can tell you about New York. He's from New York.' So I come in there and started that jive talk, that funny old talk, telling them cats about New York, painting a glorious picture about New York, and right away them cats were on me like white on rice.[77]

OTTO HARDWICK: When Sonny came to Washington, we asked him into the band. Mr Stewart our drummer had another field he wanted to go into. Sonny Greer came into Washington and he was sensational. He was from Long Branch and we used to call him 'Little Willie from Long Branch', he was very sensational, he was a good drummer, he did tricks with his sticks, and things and he was our first contact from New York, he had been in New York for some time and he was quite flashy and everyone took a liking to him, there was a lot of Sonny Greer influence at that time, a lot of Sonny. I mean the popularity [of the Duke's Serenaders] began to grow with Sonny Greer and that was it.[78]

SONNY GREER: I was a charter member [there and] then and Duke played piano, but he [was] a commercial illustrator, you know, paint them pictures, and he wasn't thinking of becoming no professional. He used to play around house parties, and clubs or something like that.[79]

DUKE ELLINGTON: I kept my painting for a while, I kept it up to about after I got married, I did a little painting and it finally dwindled off. The enthusiasm lingered on for a while, we'd buy a lot of paint, crayon. I had a sign shop in Washington.

Ellington's sign-writing business was in a basement in Third Street, Washington D.C.

DUKE ELLINGTON: If you wanted to give a dance you came to get the sign painted at my place and I asked, 'Who's playing the music?' and I get the music job, and if they came to book the band I'd ask, 'Who's painting your signs?' I was a smart kid.[80]

RUTH ELLINGTON: He would paint signs in the day and play music at night. He was always ambitious and needed very little sleep.[81]

DUKE ELLINGTON: Juan Tizol came into town that year too. He was with a band from Puerto Rico that Marie Lucas brought back to play in the pit at the Howard. We had to acknowledge that was a hell-fired band, all the musicians in it could switch instruments and at that time that was extraordinary.[82]

JUAN TIZOL: I met Duke when I was down at the Howard Theatre, with Marie Lucas. We play anything over there – overtures. We got to be friends at the Howard Theatre, not too much, but he knew about me, you know? He had heard about me when I played in the pit band ... [At the time] Duke Ellington was playing this particular box with five musicians and he was the piano player with this jazz band.[83]

JERRY RHEA: On many occasions I went along to take care of the vocal choruses [for Ellington]. I'll never forget the weekly Sunday supper shows at the Howard Theatre. There used to be as many as five bands competing at the theatre between 5pm and 6.30pm. There was an orchestra in each box and one in the pit. The bands alternated and each unit gave out their version of popular tunes of the day like 'Rose of the Rio Grande' or 'Ten Little Fingers and Ten Little Toes'. The idea was to see what band got the most applause and Duke's Serenaders won a good share of the times. The customers got all the fine music during these supper stanzas for an eleven cent charge.[84]

DUKE ELLINGTON: Later on I got hot down in Virginia, down with the very rich people, the people who ran the horse shows, and I used to play the horse show dances. And you'd go down to Virginia, you stay there, and do a whole week of horse shows, you go from one place to the other all around there, [just] four pieces.[85]

OTTO HARDWICK: Other times we drove out to Manassas, Warrenton or Orange in Virginia to play a horse show, a fancy ball or a big reception.[86]

DUKE ELLINGTON: One of these society people down in Warrenton, Virginia, or some place – he had a barn and he decided to give a barn dance. He put in a hardwood floor especially for this barn dance. He told me he wanted four pieces that night and he said: 'You have *got* to be there yourself.' I said: 'All right, sure. This'll be so much money and so forth. Fine.' That's all settled. The day before the dance the man called up and he says: 'Duke, do you know what I did?' I says, 'What did you do?' He says: 'We put the hardwood floor in but we forgot to put a piano up there. What are we going to do?' I says, 'Well, don't worry about a thing, because I play guitar too!'[87]

OTTO HARDWICK: One time we played in a hayloft and had to climb up a ladder to the bandstand. They couldn't get a piano up there so Duke played banjo all night. There was another job we played in the open air for a horse show in Orange. In those days there was no such thing as a sound system. We were all sure that no one could hear the band and that made us afraid we wouldn't get paid – but we did![88]

DUKE ELLINGTON: [My father] used to walk around and brag, 'Well, he picked up the piano by ear and now he's making more money than I am.' That's the attitude they had.[89]

SONNY GREER: [Duke] was sharp as a Gillette blade. His mother and father drilled that into him – Uncle Ed and Aunt Daisy we used to call them. His father was a fine-looking man, *polished*. Duke learned his way of talking from Uncle Ed.[90]

MERCER ELLINGTON: The way the table was set was just like those at which my grandfather had butlered. This, you might say, is where the dukedom began.[91]

The 1920 Census shows James and Daisy Ellington and their daughter Ruth residing in James Kennedy's home at 2147 L Street, Washington D.C., Ellington senior's job described as 'Butler – private Family'.

Rex Stewart: Washington D.C., in 1921, was the right time and the right place for me to hear music. I don't think there were many towns with more dance halls than Washington ... [and] there was a dance somewhere every night ... One of the features at these halls was the battle of the bands ... [and] my first awareness of this delightful phenomenon was at the Lincoln Colonnades. There were three bands, but the main battle was between Doc Perry and Sam Taylor. The third outfit was only a pick-up group with Duke Ellington on piano ... there were others in the band but I don't remember their names or faces ... Doc, as I remember, had Artie Whetsol on trumpet and rarely had I heard a sweeter tone ... Doc Perry had the best musicians, but old Sam Taylor had that beat.[92]

Duke Ellington: Band contests were very popular in those days, and one that I remember was arranged between Elmer Snowden's eight-piece band with Artie [Whetsol] and Toby and our three pieces ... the next contest was with Blind Johnny's band. Johnny played a whole lot of piano and won that one.[93]

Duke Ellington: For a long time I had been rehearsing a riff to make the piano sound like Jimmy Johnson. Everybody was trying to sound like the 'Carolina Shout' that Jimmy had made on a piano-player roll. I got it down by slowing the roll. I had it so close that when Jimmy came into town to play one night, they made me get up on stage to cut him.[94]

The occasion when Ellington was persuaded to play 'Carolina Shout' for Johnson was probably after 'The Twentieth Century Jazz Revue' held at Washington's Convention Hall on 25 November 1921.

Duke Ellington: He was wonderful. He told me I was coming along, I followed him around all night. As a matter of fact I showed him where all the joints were, where to go so he wanted to hang out all night drinking booze, I took him all down the South-West, to all the buffet flats, after-hour joints.[95]

SIDNEY BECHET: I met Duke Ellington in Washington the time I was there in *How Come*. He was hanging around the stage door then, coming in all the time we were doing our rehearsals and asking to play the piano. He played it in James P. Johnson fashion back then. At that time, 1922, he ... had a band together called the Washingtonians and we hung out some; we were good buddies for hanging out together. Duke was a fine man to be with, an easy man in himself.[96]

DUKE ELLINGTON: Things were swell for two or three years and after a while I was averaging about $150 to $200 a week. By around 1922, I had myself a pretty good band. The Miller brothers were with me, they were three low-down musicians who came from one of those musical families where everybody plays some instrument. There was Bill Miller, Brother and Felix. Being all of twenty or so they were sophisticates and imbibed corn whiskey and gin heavily, either one serving as a chaser to the other.[97]

DUKE ELLINGTON: Everybody in our band at that time was a juice-hound, juice meaning any kind of firewater. We all thought we were extra special, and liked to smoke big cigars and look like Stuart Holmes in the movies.[98]

DUKE ELLINGTON: Sometimes ... you had a real big band, like a thirty-piece job, you'd have a couple of bass fiddles, five pianos, ten banjorines and nine C-Melody saxophones, they all played the same goddamned thing, they all played the same part, just had to have the music for them![99]

DUKE ELLINGTON: After work, musicians usually gathered at the Industrial Cafe, where they would hold a general gab-fest and jam session. Every guy would try to tell a bigger lie than the last one, and that's where Sonny showed us what he was made of, he always carried off all the honours.[100]

DUKE ELLINGTON: At that time I had a sign shop. When I got ready to go to New York, Ewell Conway came in with me and I left him there. I was a hell of a poster man, that was my talent.[101]

MERCER ELLINGTON: Conway was one of the guys who helped him get started and was in the business of sign painting. They continued their friendship.[102]

Conway, and later his son, remained in business into the 1960s.

DUKE ELLINGTON: Before I left Washington, every week I used to have to participate in a [piano] contest: Claude Hopkins and I a couple of times, Blind Johnny and I a couple of times.[103]

DUKE ELLINGTON: After local success, the whirl of New York. Always that clamouring for more music, always remembering I could play with music as long as I wanted because anything that happened was a bonus, you know. I was no musician, my real talent was art. Anything I got out of music I always figured was a gift, something like a prize, I never thought that this was my talent.[104]

CHAPTER TWO

JUNGLE NIGHTS IN HARLEM

In February 1923, veteran vaudeville bandleader Wilbur Sweatman contacted Sonny Greer with an offer of employment in New York City, having earlier heard him play in the pit band of the Howard Theatre. By then the clique of Greer, Hardwick and Ellington had become a tight one. Greer accepted, on the understanding Sweatman find a place for Hardwick and Ellington as well.

What made Ellington leave a successful business, a young wife and child can be stated fairly simply. It was the lure of Harlem, then fast coming into vogue with a rich surge of arts, music and letters that in 1925 would prompt The New York Times to observe, 'We are on the edge, if not in the midst, of what might be called a Negro Renaissance.'

As Negro Renaissance gave way to Harlem Renaissance, black people at last found prominent Afro-American figures in all areas of culture and the performing arts they could look up to. From the moment Ellington and Greer had met, Greer was always extolling Harlem's virtues, and stories were rife among the black community of its better employment prospects and its vibrant night life. It was the age of the house-rent party, events originally held by the residents of Harlem's Valley community for the purpose of raising money for the exorbitant weekly rent they were charged. These funky, down-home affairs often began around midnight and continued until dawn, a blur of marijuana, booze, collard greens and *hot piano playing. The music was provided by Harlem's stride pianists, honing their styles and working out ideas for more formal public performance. Egged on by their peers, these pianists were regarded as celebrities within their community. The best of them enjoyed a considerable following, so ensuring the success of any party they were booked to play and, as a result, they were able to command good pay for their services.*

Almost at once Ellington and his chums were plunged into a romantic world quite unlike anything they had experienced in Washington. For Ellington the experience would be a defining one. As he got to know the piano greats of the day came the opportunity to learn more and more about his craft as a musician. With it came the realization that New York, and more particularly Harlem, was where his destiny lay.

DUKE ELLINGTON: In 1923 I came to New York to join Wilbur Sweatman's band – he was the man who played three clarinets at one time – a top vaudeville artist. This lasted a couple of months but this wasn't one of Sweatman's better years.[1]

Their first engagement opened the week of 5–12 March 1923 at Harlem's Lafayette Theatre.

SONNY GREER: We come to New York, so me and Duke had a room together. I had an aunt in New York, got a room. I think I was giving her $3.00 a week. We had adjoining rooms for $3.00 a week. Duke ain't never been to New York. He ain't never seen no building as tall as that in his life. Wilbur Sweatman had this engagement at the Lafayette Theatre and so I got the gig for us, we played around New York, in New Jersey but we worked on Keith's Circuit too, but it was just four of us on stage and he played clarinet, three of them at one time. Stage setting, he had a beautiful stage setting, whole lot of drapes . . . he had an engagement in Chicago or somewhere, but we wouldn't go. Said no, we ain't leaving New York, so he got somebody else.[2]

DUKE ELLINGTON: We went off in the evening regardless of whether we had any money or not and we met all the hip guys. I got a big thrill when I strolled into the Capitol Palace at 140th and Lenox, down in the basement found 'The Lion' working there.[3]

WILLIE 'THE LION' SMITH: I had a band at the Capitol Palace, Duke came around to the Capitol Palace and I had a West Indian band, most of them were West Indian authentic. That time he came around to the Capitol Palace it was at 140th Street and Lenox Avenue, beautiful place owned by the name of Johnny Powell.[4]

DUKE ELLINGTON: My first impression of the Lion – even before I saw him – was the thing I felt as I walked down those steps. A strange thing. A square fellow might say, 'The joint is jumping,' but to those who had become acclimatized – the tempo was the lope – actually everything and everybody seemed to be doing whatever they were doing in the tempo the Lion's group was laying down. The walls and furniture seemed to lean understandingly – one of the strangest and greatest sensations I ever had. The waiters served at that tempo; everybody who had to walk in, out or around the place walked with a beat.[5]

WILLIE 'THE LION' SMITH: This good-looking guy walked up to me and said, 'Hello there, Lion. I'd like to sit in with the boys.'[6]

DUKE ELLINGTON: The Lion extends a hand and says, 'Glad to meet you, kid' – and looking over his shoulder – 'Sit in there for me for a couple of numbers. D-flat.'[7]

WILLIE 'THE LION' SMITH: At that time, Duke and his pals weren't doing so well. They used to come into the Capitol and sit down and listen to me and my band rip. When Duke came in, I used to set him down to play. He was always a good looking, well-mannered fellow; one of those guys you see him, you like him right away; warm, good natured. I took a liking to him and he took a liking to me. I introduced him, and all the girls took a liking to him too.[8]

DUKE ELLINGTON: Every night we would dress up and go down and see 'The Lion', acting like some big-time Charlies . . . 'The Lion', he loved us, like for instance, 'You need a haircut. Here's fifty cents, go to Morrow's get your hair cut.'[9]

DUKE ELLINGTON: We went the rounds every night, looking for piano players. We didn't have any gold, but then Sonny was good at that sort of thing. He would stride in, big as life, and tell the man . . . 'Hello, Jack, I'm Sonny. I know so-and-so, and he told me to look you up. Meet my pals, Duke and Toby.' Then the man would hear that Duke played a whole lot of piano. I'd sit down after the Lion, and then Fats Waller would sit down after me. Fats used to follow Jimmy Johnson around, and the Lion used to say of him, 'Yeah, a yearling, he's coming along. I guess he'll do all right.' Jimmy Johnson used to get all the house-rent parties to play. There were so many of them he turned a lot over to Lippy. Lippy had heard so much piano that he couldn't play any more. He only thought piano. Lippy would give a lot of piano players work, then he'd remember me. One time things were so bad that even Sonny took a job playing piano. Lippy knew every piano and piano player in town. He used to walk around all night long with James P., the Lion, Fats and myself.[10]

BEN WEBSTER: That was New York style. If you didn't drink you were out, you couldn't join the crowd. Piano players ran in what you called packs, like a pack of wolves, you know, and they drank, to see who could drink the most, stay up the longest – two, three, four days – and still play. So that was New York style.[11]

WILLIE 'THE LION' SMITH: Our wandering gang back in those days included the Duke and his pals; James 'The Brute' Johnson, looking like a bear in his racoon coat; Corky Williams who was the first person to sing 'Christopher Columbus' with its original bawdy lyrics; Alberta Simmons, the dark-skinned pianist, who could drink and pound the piano like a man; and Raymond 'Lippy' Boyette. My boy Fatso (Waller), or Filthy as I called him, was always tagging along. We didn't give him much of a chance to play back then. I'd tell Duke, 'Yeah, he's a yearling, he's coming along and will do all right one of these days.'[12]

DUKE ELLINGTON: I was one of the main hangers-on. Lippy would walk up to any man's house at any time of night. He'd ring the doorbell. Finally somebody would wake up and holler out of the window about who it was and who was making all the disturbance. Lippy would answer: 'It's Lippy and James P. is here with me.' These magic words opened anybody's door and we would sit and play all night long.[13]

BENNY CARTER: Sometimes it would take place in the clubs, and sometimes it would take place in homes, there used to be a place on 131st Street near Seventh Avenue called Rubin's, if I remember correctly, it might have been a home or it might have been an after-hours spot, you know, where they used to go. I think it might have been down a basement, but they would all congregate there, there was always a friendly jousting thing, a pianist would play, the other would stand over him and all of a sudden he would get up and the other would take over, one right after the other, you know. Always challenging.[14]

DUKE ELLINGTON: I've heard the great things between 'The Lion' and James P. Johnson – battles, real gladiator stuff.[15]

SAM WOODING: Duke wasn't considered in those days, Ellington wasn't [considered] a great pianist. He wasn't a piano player at all. The real piano players were the Harlem stride geniuses, men like James P. Johnson and Willie 'The Lion' Smith.[16]

DUKE ELLINGTON: 'The Lion' used to sit down and play for me, I'd take him home and sit a bottle on the piano, and 'The Lion' would sit down and play and it was real wonderful because he would explain the way so-and-so played, this was way back, people he had heard when he was a kid, 'Dollar Bill' and 'Blackjack' and all sorts of weird names. And he was just a great piano player, because he was a real two-fisted piano player.[17]

MERCER ELLINGTON: He always had the greatest regard for Willie. If anybody taught Ellington theory it was Willie. He taught him things pianistically and he taught him things instrumentally.[18]

DUKE ELLINGTON: 'The Lion' was my strongest influence. 'The Lion' was a lot of people's strongest influence. He was Fats

[Waller's] influence, and as big and as important and as great as James P. Johnson was, he was strongly influenced by 'The Lion'. And even [Art] Tatum – he came to New York and heard 'The Lion' and for the next two years you could hear it all over his playing.[19]

DUKE ELLINGTON: It wasn't long after that I found fifteen dollars in an envelope in the street. It bought me a new pair of shoes, paid Sonny's and my rent and the fare back to Washington for us.[20]

DUKE ELLINGTON: We got to Washington on a Sunday morning. Otto went to his home, because he lived in Washington, and Sonny came home with me. I still remember the smell of hot biscuits when we walked in. There was butter and honey. My mother broiled six mackerel. There was lots of coffee. Uncle Ed got out the old decanter and we lay there drinking corn in the sunshine. It was nice.[21]

DUKE ELLINGTON: When I finished eating that first breakfast, I made up my mind I'd put up for a while and organize another band.[22]

DUKE ELLINGTON: That was the beginning of the five-piece band – Whetsol, Greer, Toby, Snowden and me, it was a sort of co-operative organization, nobody was really the leader, I think Snowden was really the front. We would just sit down at the piano and we'd say you take this and you take that.[23]

ELMER SNOWDEN: I had just about the most popular band in town, in my band was Otto Hardwick, Art Whetsol, Eddie Ellington . . . we played all of the dance halls and worked almost every night.[24]

DUKE ELLINGTON: After [we had] stayed [in Washington] for a while, Fats Waller came through town with a burlesque show. [Garvin] Bushell was with the band too, and Clarence Robinson and Bert Adams were the feature dance team with the show. Sitting in my house, eating my chickens by the pair, Fats told me they were all going to quit; that we'd better come on up to New York and get the job.[25]

GARVIN BUSHELL: Adams and Robinson were a dance team, and their agent talked them into getting a band because they could make more money: put it in vaudeville and make it a big headline act. Bert Adams was the piano player and Clarence Robinson was the dancer and singer (he also produced a lot of the floor shows around New York). They got Seymour Irick on trumpet, Lew Henry on trombone, Mert Perry on drums and myself [on saxes]. We didn't have any bass. Now, one night some fellow fought Bert Adams in the park and shot him. He got killed. So we had to revise the act and got Fats Waller on piano. We put Katie Crippen into the act as singer. One of the agents downtown thought up a name: Liza and her Shuffling Sextet . . . On a trip to Washington, D.C., a few of us went to hear a band in a little backstreet place. This group was headed by Elmer Snowden, the banjo player. There was a youngster playing piano named Duke Ellington, Toby Hardwick was on saxophone, Schiefe [Arthur Whetsol] on trumpet[26] and Sonny Greer on drums. After we heard the band, Clarence and I got into a terrific argument and we decided to split up. So Clarence went to Snowden and said, 'I've got a job for you.' I kept the original band with Fats on piano. In the meantime, we had six and a half more weeks booked with the act on the Politime. Clarence figured he could take this new band and do the gigs, but I decided to beat him to the punch. Early Monday morning I went into the Palace Theatre office in New York. I said, 'Clarence and I split up, and he's bringing in a strange band. I have the original one. Now, I could get a new dancer, or what do you want to do?' They got leery and cancelled the whole six and a half weeks. So when Clarence arrived in New York with

Snowden, Duke and that bunch, they didn't have any work –
I'd cancelled all their jobs.[27]

DUKE ELLINGTON: Then there was a wire from New York saying
Fats had decided not to leave, so Artie Whetsol, Sonny, Toby
and Snowden went up alone. Then they sent for me; everything
had been fixed, the job was a cinch for me![28]

OTTO HARDWICK: Fats Waller was supposed to play with us
when we came to New York with Elmer Snowden but Fats
wouldn't stoop to play with greenhorns and didn't even show
up. Then Duke was persuaded to join us.[29]

DUKE ELLINGTON: By the time I got back to New York, that
[job] had petered out. I was depending on a job on arrival,
coming up from Washington, first class style, big dinner in the
dining car, then from Pennsylvania Station up to 125th Street I
had a taxi ride and after paying that I had about a dollar left.
Sonny Greer met me at the kerbstone and said, 'Give me some
money.' I said, 'I thought we were working?' He says no. He
says, 'It blew.' So there we were. We went from there.[30]

OTTO HARDWICK: The first thing we wanted to do when he got
here was to see Coney Island. With a couple of bucks between
us, Sonny, Duke, Whetsol and I subwayed out there and spent
our dough on hot dogs and just watched the fun. We came on
a fortune teller and stood on the fringe of the crowd to listen.
Suddenly he called to us. We shook our heads in unison, moving
back a step. He shouted: 'I know you haven't got any money,
but I want to tell you something anyway. You're thinking of
going back home, don't do it. Something's going to break for
you in three days and you fellows will work together for the rest
of your lives and never have to look for a job again!'[31]

DUKE ELLINGTON: So we started from scratch. It was summertime, it was hot as hell and we used to have to ride that subway

every morning to go downtown and audition down in the Strand Building, that's where most of the agents were at that time.[32]

RUTH ELLINGTON: When Edward came to New York from Washington, Edna followed soon after, and because there was no place to keep a baby, she left Mercer with my mother as a kind of temporary measure I think.[33]

EDNA ELLINGTON: We were very young then. Kids really. I think we both thought Mercer was a toy. We left Mercer in Washington and went to New York.[34]

MERCER ELLINGTON: I was strongly disciplined by my grandfather up to the age of about fourteen until I finally grabbed him instead of him grabbing me and he decided that was over with . . . children were just not allowed to do certain things, lest ways I wasn't, and as a result we were inhibited.[35]

EDNA ELLINGTON: I was one of Ellington's show girls, though really all I had to do was walk around and lend an atmosphere. Those were the days when we lived in one room and beans were only five cents a can. Some days we didn't have five cents.[36]

MERCER ELLINGTON: It wasn't at all easy for my parents when they first moved to New York. All they had was a room in the house of Leonard Harper, a choreographer and producer at Connie's Inn.[37]

The 1924 New York Directory shows Ellington residing at 2067 Seventh Avenue. The 1925 Census reveals Edward and Edna Ellington and Otto and Gladys Hardwick as lodgers at the same address, shown as the home of Leonard and Arsciola Harper.

WILLIE 'THE LION' SMITH: Things were so tough that they had about decided to go back to Washington. But I said, 'Why go back to Washington when I'm doing all right? Let's stick it out. You've gone this far.' I was a guy who was handling a few bucks

County **New York**

Enumeration of the Inhabitants of Block No. 2, Election District

Town _____, Assembly District No. 19

Name of Institution _____

PERMANENT RESIDENCE		NAME of each person whose usual place of abode on June 1, 1925, was in this family. Enter surname first, then the given name and middle initial, if any. INCLUDE every person living on June 1, 1925. Omit children born since June 1, 1925.	RELATION Relationship of each person to the head of the family	COLOR, SEX AND AGE		
Street.	House Number.			Color or Race.	Sex.	Age at last birthday.
1		2	3	4	5	6
Seventh Av	2067	Fastle Gloria F	Lodger	B	F	15
Seventh Av	2067	Harper Leonard	Head	B	M	27
Seventh Av	2067	Harper Arociola	Wife	B	F	26
Seventh Av	2067	Ellington Leonard	Son	B	M	26
Seventh Av	2067	Ellington Edna	Lodger	B	F	26
Seventh Av	2067	Hardwick Otto	Lodger	B	M	21
Seventh Av	2067	Hardwick Gladys	Lodger	B	F	20
Seventh Av	2067	Duckiff Harvey	Lodger	B	M	24
Seventh Av	2067	Craig Beatrice	Head	B	F	32
Seventh Av	2067	Smith Benjamin	Lodger	B	M	54

then and was always willing to split it down with them. We'd stand on street corners and I'd give them lectures each morning. I'd lecture to them on the ladies. There was no way for them to miss.[38]

DUKE ELLINGTON: We had people who were looking out for us like 'The Lion' – Willie Smith. He would let us come in and sit in for him on two or three numbers while the girls were singing, and at the end of each number they would split the tips and this gave us a springboard for the next day, which we would usually invest in the six-ball game at the pool room.[39]

REX STEWART: Oh yes, there was a five-piece band from my home town of Washington, who, rumour said, existed on the earnings of its pool-hustling drummer, Sonny Greer, because they worked so very little.[40]

MERCER ELLINGTON: For the most part Sonny was really the stalwart of the life support, because when they were without jobs Sonny used to go down with George Raft and shoot pool downtown and hustle the extra money they needed for beans.[41]

EDNA ELLINGTON: You know, Ellington loved baked beans. Not the kind you get anywhere, but the old fashioned kind that take a long time to cook.[42]

DUKE ELLINGTON: We kept right on auditioning but nothing ever happened. There was no work. Then Brick-Top came along, she saved the day for us. I'd worked with Brick-Top – the famed Brick-Top of Montmartre, Paris – at the Oriental in Washington. Barron's was then a very popular spot and she knew Barron very well. She got him to let his band go and hire us instead. We'd scuffled for five weeks and here at last we were to go to work.[43]

The five weeks without work Ellington refers to were probably early July to August 1923. Ada 'Brick-Top' Smith (1894–1984), a red-haired singer who had earlier toured the vaudeville circuits with Florence Mills and Cora Green as the Panama Trio when Ellington probably first met her, moved to Paris the following year and rose to fame at Le Grand Duc in Paris, which was adopted by Cole Porter and the smart set, before opening her own club, Bricktop's, on the Rue Pigalle. Over the years various editions of the club became the haunt of royalty, society and leaders in the arts. Barron D. Wilkins had previously run 'The Little Savoy' in New York's midtown tenderloin district – West 35th Street – before moving up to Harlem in 1915 to open Barron's at 2259 Seventh Avenue at West 134th Street, one of the first big Harlem night clubs. Among those he had employed in the past were Sam Wooding and his Society Syncopators, Mamie Smith, James P. Johnson and Willie 'The Lion' Smith.

SONNY GREER: Barron Wilkins had a basement club. It was a popular club. But the guys didn't really start hanging out there in a bunch until we came because he had never heard anybody like us. So the word spread and they come down there. The place was so packed they couldn't accommodate all the musicians trying to come in. And a one-set rule that we had at the time, we were paid for entertaining so we couldn't let just anybody walk in and play. Bricktop ... was the hostess there. She got us the job in June [*recte* July] and the business tripled overnight. It got to be one of the clubs. So all the musicians, our friends, they'd come in. He never turned them away but as far as playing, they come to listen. All of them come to listen, the white musicians, coloured musicians.[44]

DUKE ELLINGTON: We were only five but we had arrangements for everything and it was what we've now named conversation music, kind of soft and gut-bucket.[45]

SONNY GREER: Everything we played was so close together, but other small bands, they just played hurdy-gurdy, they wasn't together, they never heard nobody that played like us. Six pieces sounded like twelve, and we played so smooth, we were never loud, very soft, beautiful. We went down there in July and stayed the whole summer.[46]

DUKE ELLINGTON: Luckey Roberts liked what we were doing with our five-piece band at Barron's – as a matter of fact he liked it so much he gave us his time – like he would come over to Barron's in the afternoon when we were rehearsing and give us question-and-answer lecture demonstrations – he said it was fun for him too (and vitally instructive to us) to go through the musical possibilities of a five-piece band.[47]

DUKE ELLINGTON: There were lots of 'Mr Gunions' who came into Barron's. A 'Mr Gunion' is anybody with lots of money. We used to make $30 a week and tips ran to $20 a piece per night. There were nine of us who had to split, the four entertainers and ourselves. We used to see fellows throwing $20 in halves on the floor.[48]

DUKE ELLINGTON: We were Toby, Whetsol, Sonny, Snowden and we let Snowden handle the business. I didn't have my mind on leadership. But then Snowden got a raise and we didn't know till later.[49]

TOM WHALEY: So Sonny, you know how Sonny talk, and says, 'Man, when you going to give us a raise?' And the man said, 'I just raised you.' He had raised Elmer, give Elmer the raise and Elmer didn't give it to the guys, so they fired Elmer and Sonny was supposed to take the job, Sonny said, 'No, I don't want the job. Give it to Duke.'[50]

SONNY GREER: It didn't take long before we thrust leadership on Duke. He didn't want it, but his disposition was better balanced than ours. He could keep us in line without doing much. We were a pretty wild bunch in those days, myself in particular.[51]

DUKE ELLINGTON: It was after Snowden left that we got Freddy Guy . . . it was funny the way it came about. We used to hang out a lot at a spot called the Orient. Earl Dancer ran the place, and Freddy had the band. But Earl owed Freddy so much money that Freddy was practically the owner. Fats Waller was working for him there and when we first walked in, Freddy big-timed us, asking Fats who we were. Fats spoke his little piece, and we were all relieved when Freddy OK'd us. Later on we got to be good friends, and Freddie liked our band so much that when Snowden quit, he decided to come with us.[52]

SONNY GREER: Out of the whole aggregation, whole band, Freddy was the sensible one. He didn't have no wild traits like the musicians like us. He was a Rock of Gibraltar, steady. He was the mainstay of the band, he was a lady's man. Nice-looking guy.[53]

FREDDY GUY: Fats was in a little band I was playing banjo with and one night Duke and the boys came to hear us. Everybody heard everybody else in those days. Fats looked over his shoulder, pointed Duke out to me and asked if I knew him. I said I didn't. As the night went on, Duke asked if I'd play a number or two with his men. He said he didn't have any music, but would call the chords. I said that was fine. We had a pretty good session that night.[54]

SONNY GREER: Barron Wilkins, a very unassuming man. But when he said something he meant it. He was high with the syndicate. But he was stubborn, that's how he got killed, he was very stubborn. He was shot by a guy named Yellow Charleston. He didn't try and run away, it was one of those things, from high up it got pinpointed.[55]

WILLIE 'THE LION' SMITH: Yellow Charleston doubled as a dope peddler working out of Barron Wilkins' place and he was also employed by the Owney Madden gangsters; when Madden decided to get rid of Barron it was little tubercular Yellow Charleston who stabbed him to death one night as he was leaving the club. It wasn't hard for Yellow to do because he was always hopped-up on opium.[56]

COUNT BASIE: I once played in a little group Otto [Hardwick] had while the Washingtonians were sort of laying off. That was the time I got a chance to work in Barron's. I also know that this was while Bricktop was still working in Barron's, because that was where I first met her. It was while I was in Barron's club with Otto's group that Duke got his band back together. People thought the Washingtonians had broken up for good, but I knew different. I do know that it was when some show job came up that those guys began to get back together.[57]

DUKE ELLINGTON: In September 1923 we landed a job through Leonard Harper at the Hollywood Café at [203 West] 49th Street and Broadway. Harper had the revue there, and it was a hot show.[58]

THE CLIPPER: The Hollywood, a comparatively new Times Square basement cabaret (it opened 1 September last), is on West 49th Street. The band is the sole feature up to midnight, when Harper's Dixie Revue goes on, repeating again at 2 a.m. The boys can seemingly satisfy without exerting themselves ... they disclose painstaking rehearsal, playing without music.[59]

FREDDY GUY: The style of music that began to develop was different from anyone else's. Duke worked largely from head arrangements and he insisted everyone memorize their parts. He thought you couldn't get inside a piece of music if you were busy keeping up with the charts.[60]

OTTO HARDWICK: The Hollywood was quite a spot. Jimmy and Tommy Dorsey, Bing, Whiteman, Joan Crawford, well, today's headliners crowded the place.[61]

DUKE ELLINGTON: It was patronized by the whole Broadway set. Ours was a late-hour place. Everybody used to come when they got through working their regular gig, like Paul Whiteman, Lopez, the California Ramblers, and all of the show stars and all of those people. This was a place that had new acts there. This is where I found out that you really had to learn to read music. Not only that, I had to play the bass, strong bass, on the piano. This is before we had a bass in the band.[62]

OTTO HARDWICK: We wanted to add a few more pieces, but the bandstand was so small, that's how Bass Edwards came to play with us. We had to find a man with an instrument to fit the stand, and Bass played an upright recording tuba.[63]

SONNY GREER: This Bass Edwards, he took a waiter's tray this big. And he had a light in the bell. He'd take the tray and fan, like a trumpet player play, and play ten choruses like on the trumpet and he always had a cigar, never take it out of his mouth. That was his trademark. Bass Edwards, he was something else![64]

FREDDY GUY: I finally went with the band in February 1924, just in time for the downtown opening at the Kentucky Club – I even took a cut in pay to join.[65]

DUKE ELLINGTON: Later the name was changed to the Kentucky Club. We did well there and our run lasted well into five years. During that time, Sonny's drums got burned-up three different times, because of the club's periodic fires. Station WHN was just opening up around then and they started broadcasting us every night after two a.m. All that air-time helped build up our name. The Kentucky Club definitely became the place to go.[66]

The name of the Hollywood was changed to the Club Kentucky, or Kentucky Club as it became known, in March 1925.

SONNY GREER: We had all kinds of people coming into the Kentucky Club – entertainers, racketeers, socialites, the good and bad. Because I knew so many characters and had a great memory, no one could get a drink in the place unless I gave the nod. We worked until 11 in the evening until after the sun came up. Then we went out on the town.[67]

DUKE ELLINGTON: During my first few months in NY I found out that anybody was eligible to take songs into the music publishers on Broadway. So I joined the parade and got myself teamed up with a nice guy named Joe Trent. He was experienced in this routine. He liked my music and he was a good lyricist. So he took me by the hand and guided me around Broadway. We wrote several songs together and auditioned every day in one publisher or another and as was normal, we had practically no success til one day we took a song in and demonstrated it for Fred Fisher, publisher and a great song writer himself. He listened, said I like it, I'll take it, so Joe said, 'You know of course that we want $50 advance.' F.F. said OK, give me a lead and I'll sign the contract. Joe turned to me and said, 'Give the man a lead sheet' – UHG! I had never made a lead sheet or tried to write music of any kind. But it was 4.30pm and I knew that the check book would be closed at 5pm. So in spite of the ten pianos in ten booths banging away I sat down and made a lead sheet and satisfactory too! We got the money, split the money, and then split the scene. I had broken the ice and at the same time gotten hooked on writing MUSIC.[68]

DUKE ELLINGTON: Late in the evening, after you get through peddling songs up and down Broadway and get refused, there was always one haven: the last minute you needed some small change, a half dozen of the song writers would get together somewhere and whip up some blues, each one would have his blues in his hand and we would go over to Irving Mills, he would buy them for $15–$20 outright. But he bought the same goddamned tune over and over so many times it wasn't funny – he didn't know though. Just change the name of it, switch the first line and the second line, the blues are all the same anyway! And a couple of times Irving would take these damn things and get them recorded and they would make money![69]

This early meeting with Irving Mills, in the music publishing business with his brother Jack who owned Jack Mills, Inc., which they formed in 1919, would be the precursor of a gradual association between the two men that would see them recording a test pressing for Gennett Records together in 1925 (with Mills as vocalist) and the Washingtonians recording a song published by Jack Mills on their first Gennett recording session in April 1926 (a record date probably set up by Mills).

DUKE ELLINGTON: Will Marion Cook was one of the great masters. He was a great musician, originally from Washington D.C., my home, and he went to Europe and he was a great violinist and did a lot of wonderful writing, he associated with a lot of the serious musicians and writers of Europe, Paris, he was a real master. He had this white mane of hair, he would come down Broadway in the days when we were trying to sell songs to the publishers and we would go to the publisher and often we would meet him in the publishers because the publishers all knew he was a great musician. He never wore a hat, it was hot summertime and I'll never forget one day Jack Robbins says, 'Will, you should put a hat on your head walking about in the sunshine, you'll get sunstroke.' 'I don't need a hat.' He says, 'Here's twenty dollars, go get yourself a hat.' We came out of Robbins', went downstairs and got in a taxi cab, and we rode up through the park, in the taxi cab and we would discuss music. And I would get my lessons, I would ask questions and get my education.[70]

Will Marion Cook (1869–1944) went to Oberlin Conservatory at thirteen to study violin. Three years later he won a scholarship to study with Joseph Joachim at the Hochschule in Berlin. On his return he studied at the National Conservatory of Music under John White and Anton Dvorák. He enjoyed a successful songwriting career and in 1918 organized the New York (later American) Syncopated Orchestra which gave a command performance at Buckingham Palace in 1919. A well-schooled musician and an excellent teacher, around the time he met Ellington he was conducting the Lafayette Theatre production of 'Negro Nuances' (1924), written by and featuring his wife, the soprano Abbie Mitchell.

DUKE ELLINGTON: I'd been doing a bit of writing . . . and had scored the show *The Chocolate Kiddies* in 1924. Joe Trent was the lyric writer and Robbins had the score. At the time, Robbins was on Broadway with only one small room.[71]

DUKE ELLINGTON: Sometimes you attempt a melody or tune that's worthy of somebody you love. A tune I wrote for my mother, it later got words put to it and was called 'It's You'. That was way back, before I left Washington, and I put it in a show that went to Europe, *The Chocolate Kiddies* . . . it went to Germany, stayed for two years, I never saw the show, they rehearsed it in New York – Josephine Baker was a chorus girl in it, and Adelaide Hall was in it, Sam Wooding's band.[72]

SAM WOODING: It wasn't a legitimate show; it was a revue and people all used their own music. Bobby and Babe Goins, Johnny Hudgins, Greenlee and Drayton, they all had their own music and all I had to do was play that music. We had our own arrangements [for the band], that's what made it a novelty, the Europeans liked the Negro's style of jazz better than Paul Whiteman's.[73]

Chocolate Kiddies *was a 1925 revue designed to give European audiences a sampling of black entertainment from Harlem. Sam Wooding and his Orchestra from the Club Alabam was the featured band and the company included more than thirty singers and dancers. The evidence suggests Ellington and Trent contributed songs to the show, but as presented in Europe it did not have a full score by them. A copy of the programme from a summer 1925 engagement in Sweden gives general composer credits to Ellington and Trent but there are only three songs listed in the programme by them, 'Deacon Jazz', 'Jim Dandy' and 'With You' (sic).*[74]

DUKE ELLINGTON: 'The Bird of Paradise', that's a thing I wrote in 1924, I think it was published by Robbins. It was the day of the – people used to talk about the bulldykers, you know what they are? They're lesbians. They were girls who fucked girls, butches. My little piece was about the two of them, the bulldyker and the straight girl. That was what it was supposed to be, then finally it ends up so peaceful. [It was recorded by Jimmie Lunceford], he liked it, Robbins most likely talked him into doing it! It was a piano piece, as far as I'm concerned, it was conceived for my kind of piano playing, and when the band became 'my instrument', I found to interpret these piano pieces with the band was a real rough job [so I never recorded it], it was simpler to write a new number. I'm really not the most ambitious man in the world![75]

DUKE ELLINGTON: Then Whetsol left us, went back to Howard University to finish studying medicine. Bubber Miley was still young then, but we had him join. Our band changed its character when Bubber Miley came in. He used to growl all night long, playing gut-bucket on his horn. That's when we decided to forget all about sweet music.[76]

OTTO HARDWICK: Bubber was unpredictable. Do you know we had to shanghai him into the band? Whetsol went back to

Howard University and we needed a good man. We wanted Miley. Even then, we had a reputation for sticking together and Bubber knew this. He was playing at a little place uptown and was happy there, so he stalled us off, thinking that when Whetsol came back, we'd let him go. One night when we finished work, we went up to Harlem, got Bubber stiff, and when he came to he was in a tuxedo growling at the Hollywood, on Broadway. We also added a trombone, Charlie Irvis. He was strictly a gutbucket trombonist ... the word gutbucket must have stemmed directly from Irvis's style and his use of a real bucket for a mute. He was a growler, too, but not like Miley. However, he and Bubber got together on duets after growling at each other for a few days, and thus set the style of the band.[77]

DUKE ELLINGTON: Nobody really picked up on Charlie Irvis ... he got a great, big, fat sound at the bottom of the trombone – melodic, masculine, full of tremendous authority. There was a kind of mute they built at that time to go into a trombone to make it sound like a saxophone, but he dropped his one night and the darn thing broke into a million parts. So he picked up the biggest part that was left and started using it. This was his device and it was greater than the original thing.[78]

LAWRENCE BROWN: [In the early days] there seemed to be two or three influences that were the strongest, and one of those influences was a trumpet player by the name of Bubber Miley and the other a trombone player by the name of Charlie Irvis. Bubber Miley was a person who played with a plunger and different mutes and got different effects. And Irvis did the same on trombone, the two of them were like a duo, and it sort of developed that they were a jungle-istic type of music. The band became the accompaniment to this music.[79]

SONNY GREER: He never thought about writing compositions in the Kentucky Club. We just took stocks and changed them around and made them a little different and sound different. Because all the bands of that time, they – you know the publishers, song publishers, would take a song and bring them to the club and you'd play them just like they're written. But special arrangements, they didn't have that, we were one of the first who had that, you know.[80]

DUKE ELLINGTON: [The Kentucky Club] show was great vaudeville acts at that time. Some white, some coloured – they had a coloured chorus, about six girls, all pretty chicks. Clarence Robinson was the producer, who incidentally was the guy who had the act in the burlesque show who we were supposed to join in Fats Waller's place when we came back to New York the second time! Bert Lewis was the comedian, great comedian, Ina Heywood was an operatic soprano, Sally Fields – wonderful soul ballad singer. Who else? They had two or three dance acts. We stayed there four years.[81]

AMERICAN AND ORIENTAL CUISINE

CLUB KENTUCKY

203 WEST 49TH STREET, NEW YORK
BERT LEWIS AND HIS HOSPITALITY GANG

| SALLY FIELDS | ANN ALLISON |
| HANLEY SISTERS | RIGELOW & LEE |

MUSIC BY DUKE ELLINGTON'S WASHINGTONIANS

| OPEN AT 10 P.M. | DIMINE CIRCLE 71573 |
| Proprietor (Management) | LEO BERNSTEIN |

Computer Reconstruction of Original Advertisement from 'Variety' held by Smithsonian Institution[82]

DUKE ELLINGTON: This was a great spot for us ... the band would play all night, we'd play a show and play some dance music. Late at night we'd send the band home and Sonny Greer and I would work the floor, take one of those little pianos and push it around the floor from party to party and answer requests, sob songs, popular songs, dirty songs, all sorts of songs. Anything the customer wanted he had to have; he was expected to put $20 a song. If business was slow we even knew the boss's song, 'My Buddy from Heaven'. Then we'd go uptown and make a round of all the juice joints, and come home busted.[83]

FREDDY GUY: Once you put your horn to your mouth, you didn't take it out until you quit. Until period. You started at [eleven] and played *until*.[84]

SONNY GREER: We didn't go to work till 11.00 and we stayed open till 7.00 in the morning. Our club was a little small place and after 3.00 in the morning you couldn't get a seat. They'd stand around and it got so popular, we were packed and jammed. Paul Whiteman would bring all his friends and band down there.[85]

DUKE ELLINGTON: Paul Whiteman was known as the 'King of Jazz' and no one as yet has come anywhere near carrying that title with more certainty and dignity. (Forsook his 1st violin chair in the Denver Symphony to organize a class jazz band.) There are those who have come onto the scene, grabbed the money and ran off to plush boring life of boredom. But nobody held onto their band always adding interesting musicians to the payroll with no regard to their behaviour. All he wanted was to hear these great cats blow and they blew up a storm. Then, as we said in *Drum is a Woman*, 'Dressed her in woodwinds and strings and made a lady out of jazz.' We knew way back when we were in the Kentucky Club, the K.C. stayed open as long as the cash register rang and Whiteman and his men and many others like Cal. [California] Ramblers [space] I remember the first night Bix Beiderbecke came to New York to join P.W. at the Palais Royale – because after their gig they all came down to the KC to listen to our 6 pce band and we must have been saying something because they kept coming back. PW in his most gracious manner would always slap me a $50 bill to cut up with my cats.[86]

SONNY GREER: The Club Kentucky was something and the money was flying. Money is flying. You better believe it. Now that was in the twenties when a dollar was a dollar. We had all the gangsters, all the big gangsters you read about, Legs Diamond, Lucky Luciano and all the Brooklyn gang. They'd rendezvous.[87]

EDNA ELLINGTON: Like all things, times began to get better. But I was young and jealous and didn't want to share [Duke] with the public. I couldn't stand around waiting until the public had their fill of him before he could give me some time. If there was something important I wanted to say to him, I wanted to rush up and tell him then.[88]

MERCER ELLINGTON: My relationship with my parents was rather remote except during the summers, when I would go to New York for about two or three months.[89]

WILLIE 'THE LION' SMITH: Some nights before it was time for me to report for work I'd go down to Times Square to catch the first show at the Kentucky Club ... Two of my good drinking companions were still in the group – Sonny Greer and saxophonist Otto Hardwick. It was another basement joint like the clubs uptown and the bandstand was up under the sidewalk in the corner. The bandsmen had to walk three stone steps to get on the stand. Their dressing rooms were like the Black Hole of Calcutta. The stand there at the Kentucky Club only held six men and Duke had to play the piano from the dancefloor. If you worked up on the deck long enough, you wound up with hunched shoulders because the stand was about five-and-a-half feet from the glass grill up in the sidewalk.[90]

VARIETY: CLUB KENTUCKY. Not strictly a sawdust place ... the $1.50 couvert draws a mixed drop-in trade of some of the 'wise mob' and others ... Bert Lewis is the master of ceremonies. He does the introducing in fly fashion ... The coloured band, Duke Ellington's Washingtonians is a wow. They give forth plenty of torrid jazz and are trojans for hard work. The accompaniment is equally expert for the dance music. The Kentucky is a great drop-in place for a few laughs and a few times around the floor. Sans attempts at any particular atmosphere or 'front', the fornier has built itself up with a cosmopolitan following ... as a result the house counts up consistent profits weekly.[91]

DUKE ELLINGTON: Sometimes somebody would come in from some place that didn't particularly – wanted to let his hair down, and he would forget and say something ugly to one of the coloured fellows in the band. And Bubber would call Mr Bernstein on his trumpet, and he'd put his mute in and say, 'Mr Bernstein' on the trumpet, and Bernstein would come over with his cigar and say, 'What's the matter?' And [Bubber] says, 'That man over there said something ugly to us!' And he'd say, he'd walk up to the party, and say, 'I'm Leo Bernstein, I own the joint, how are you? I'm very happy to have you, have a drink on the house.' He'd call the waiter and the guy who said the dirty word, he point to him like this, meaning to give him a Mickey!'[92]

JOE 'TRICKY SAM' NANTON: When Duke came and asked me to play in the band I didn't want to go because he was offering me my friend's [Charlie Irvis's] job. 'He'll be back next week,' I said. Duke insisted. I promised to join him, but I didn't show up. The following night Duke came by and asked why I didn't come in. This time he waited until I got dressed and TOOK me with him.[93]

Nanton joined Ellington in June 1926.

DUKE ELLINGTON: Bubber and Tricky were the first to get really wide recognition for the plunger thing. They had such beautiful teamwork together. Everything they played represented a mood, a person, a picture.[94]

LAWRENCE BROWN: Tricky was a man that had m ₋ ; talents, and most of his talents he was unconscious of. His playing was one talent and he had a natural gift for being funny. You'd just look at Tricky Sam and his big eyes, and he was funny. And his music backed up his being funny too. He had a way of phrasing his music that was – I don't think anyone has ever picked up on that. And it's just lost because no-one even tried to catch the true meaning of his music. His parents were from the West Indies, and that West Indian influence was kept in his playing. And everything he played, you could tell that was Tricky Sam because of the growl. He was a very nice fellow ... everybody loved Tricky Sam. He and Bubber Miley were the basis of the band in the early days.[95]

JOE 'TRICKY SAM' NANTON: Bubber was an idea man. For instance we'd have a printed orchestration and Bubber would always have some stuff of his own and soon we'd have a trio or quartet on the part and if one of us didn't know the chorus the others would tell us what to play.[96]

DUKE ELLINGTON: Bubber and I, we used to do a lot of wonderful things. He'd come up with a lick, three or four bars, eight bars or something, make a number out of it. He was completely soul.[97]

JOE 'TRICKY SAM' NANTON: What a loveable guy [Bubber Miley was]. Even rival trumpet players loved him. He was loaded with personal magnetism and dominated any situation. His ideas were more or less the backbone of the band. His ideas and tunes he wrote set the band's style. 'East St Louis Toodle-Oo' and certain parts of 'Black and Tan Fantasy' (except my contribution), some parts of which we used to play when we were running around together before we joined the band.[98]

DUKE ELLINGTON: We were very playful in those days; one night up in Newport, Rhode Island, we were playing up there, and we stayed there that night, up drinking all night long, and Tricky went to sleep, and we were walking around, because Tricky had been asleep about ten or fifteen minutes, it was just daylight, dawn beginning to break, so we get the hot idea to wake up Tricky and tell him, 'Come on man, you know what time it is, it's six o'clock in the evening!' And he looks up and he says, 'Man, I sure had a good sleep.' And we got two blocks from the place until it got daylight before he realized, 'This ain't sun-down, this is sun-up!' And went back to bed! That was the night after the woman came, we had played a dance there, a woman came in a wheelchair and she listened to the music all night and at the end of the dance she got up and ran to the bandstand and thanked us all, said, 'You have given me something!' And she didn't realize she was standing up, she had left her wheelchair, no kidding! That was before Harry Carney, that was 1926. She said the music had gotten into her soul, into her bones![99]

During the summer months, the Club Kentucky would close its doors and the band picked up whatever work they could.

DUKE ELLINGTON: Buddy Bolden, King Oliver, Louis Armstrong, and the greatest, I think, of all of them was [the soprano saxophonist and clarinettist] Sidney Bechet, who I thought was the symbol of the whole thing because I thought he was completely independent of any influence, he influenced a lot of people, nobody influenced him. He played from an artist's perspective, I don't think he made a fortune or anything like that, but he was a pure artist all the way through.[100]

DUKE ELLINGTON: Bechet played with us in 1926, and I had Bechet and Bubber in the band at the same time. Bechet had a dog called 'Goola', a big one, nice one, a collie. Those times Charlie Shribman, one of the great men of the band business, he's really one of the great humanitarians. I met Charlie Shribman – the first time was through a phone call. You see, when I was working at the Kentucky Club, 49th and Broadway, after the Christmas holidays and they've got the New Year's Eve money, they always had a fire in the Kentucky Club, burn up Sonny Greer's drums in the place and they had to buy him a new set of drums. This is a wonderful place! So after one of these fires, I got a call from Charlie Shribman sayin', 'Hey, I've been looking for a band, can I get you to come up and work for me, for a couple of weeks?' I said, 'Well, yeah!' This cat had heard about us, because all the musicians who worked downtown used to hang out in our joint when they got off of their jobs, like the California Ramblers, the Whiteman band, the Lopez band, and they would all come down there, Charlie knew all these people and word got to him.[101]

OTTO HARDWICK: We had so many people that would come into the night club where we played, and everyone wanted us to go first one place then the other. But it was more or less like a family, even the people we worked for, we didn't want to leave them. It was like tearing yourself away from one of the family, that's not an easy thing to do. Money had nothing to do with it.[102]

DUKE ELLINGTON: When [Shribman] found a band wasn't doing anything he'd take them to Salem, put them in a hotel, they'd live there and they'd work out of Salem. We were driving around in one of them Model T Fords with the side things on, driving around in the snow in January, and having a ball, and then we'd go back in the summertime.[103]

SONNY GREER: One time we played a gig for Charlie Shribman in the summertime, we'd go up to Salem Willows for the summer because the club had closed, sort of house band for him, one night Bubber Miley and Bechet they wanted to go, I forget where in Massachusetts, it cost $35 one way in a cab. Them cats got drunk up there and kept the cab driver. The bill was a hundred and some dollars. Kept him there all night in the whorehouse, brought him back so Charlie Shribman paid and the cab driver had such a good time he gave Bechet half the money back. Bechet was – everybody loved him. Even Duke loved him. He was a fun-loving man. He lived. He was beautiful.[104]

DUKE ELLINGTON: It was on one of these trips up to New England when Bechet was in the band. He was in the band a whole season. In those days it was the guy who blew the horn was like a gladiator and he'd go out and blow and the next guy to follow him had to beat what he did, it was always the spirit of the challenge at all times, and Bechet and Bubber Miley, they used to do this thing and both of them used to drink a little bit, but Bechet and Bubber they would growl at each other something awful, Bechet would go out and play ten choruses and Bubber would play ten choruses, and while one was playing the other was back there taking nips! Then Bechet would come out and say 'I'm going to call Goola [his dog]: Goola, Goola.' It was a gas, man.[105]

SONNY GREER: Bechet and Tricky and Bubber, every night was a jam session. We play our stuff but for an added attraction all them musicians was coming and hanging out. Bechet would take a napkin off the table and put it in his teeth and hide his hands underneath and drive you crazy, Tricky would take a plunger, he had an old tomato can bent up. He'd make it sound like a bass, drive you crazy, play two notes, send you wild.[106]

DUKE ELLINGTON: Mal Hallett had a band up in New England, and you had to play alongside him. The big dance territories were in Massachusetts and Pennsylvania. Charlie Shribman put on dances and they'd have battles of music ... We had a six piece and we used to play [Hallett] contrast wise. He'd know we were coming on, and he'd blow up a storm and lift the roof off. Then we'd crawl in there with our six pieces and begin slowly and develop it, so that when we did play loud it would seem as though we were playing louder than we actually were.[107]

CHICAGO DEFENDER: This week this writer is pleased to let the Musical Bunch throughout the country know about Duke Ellington and his band who have invaded the New England territory and stormed it with their great orchestral ability ... To tell about this famous band we must first go back some five years when Mal Hallett and his crack outfit made their initial appearance in this territory.... From the very start Hallett and his band was a knockout.... The news of Hallett's success had hardly reached New York, it seemed, before New England states were flooded with New York orchestras.... But ... there is one organization that now holds its head high in the air, proud and mighty, Duke Ellington and his Washingtonians.[108]

SIDNEY BECHET: We made some records, too, while we were together, but for some reason, I don't know, they were never released. I feel real sad about that because they were good records and now there's no trace of them ... At that time Otto, Duke and myself used to go over to Duke's place to fool around on the piano, talk how we were going to build this thing with all the band. Duke, he'd be making arrangements for the band – not the kind of hit parade arrangements ... but a kind of dividing of the piece, placing its parts. What we were after, it was to get the feeling for the band, playing together. That way the music was working for itself. The arrangements, they came out of that. And that was good times in Duke's apartment.[109]

DUKE ELLINGTON: Practically every afternoon we'd go to one of the movie houses where they had a symphony orchestra in the pit, they had many of them on Broadway – the Paramount, the Tivoli, the Capitol, the Roxy, about seven or eight of them, and every one of them had a symphony orchestra. They had the big regular symphonic work as the overture, and they would do a presentation with a small group or large group, depending on which theatre it was, and you'd sit and you would listen to the symphony through two or three shows and you'd go to the Kentucky Club and try and make your six-piece band sound like the symphony. Of course, you didn't have any success, but it was a lot of fun.[110]

SONNY GREER: I always dug colour and the drummers who knew how to use it. There were these percussionists at the old Capitol Theatre on Broadway. Billy Gladstone was one of them. Duke and I would go by and see a picture. But it was the show that interested me. Those cats could play. They didn't realize it, but I took some of their stuff and used it in my own way, particularly [later] during the Cotton Club shows.[111]

DUKE ELLINGTON: Mexico was our dear friend who retired from the army, he was a professional soldier, and opened a juice joint in 133rd Street in the year of 1923 or 4, he went to Mexico [in World War I], he was a professional soldier down there, his name was George Jamés [pronounced Ha-mez], he used to say he was the only Mexican from North Carolina! Mexico was great, a wonderful cat.[112]

JUAN TIZOL: Mexico used to take care of Duke, clothes and stuff like that, and drive him around. He was with Duke almost all the time.[113]

DUKE ELLINGTON: Mexico, he ran the hottest gin-mill on 133rd Street. We used to hang-out at his place, drinking up the booze.

We called it 99% – one more degree either way and it would bust your top, we said.[114]

DUKE ELLINGTON: In those days the amount of liquor one drank determined your status and of course there were many who had the reputation ... liquor drinking among the musicians was done from the Gladiator perspective just the same as playing of his instrument. So there were many challenges and contests ... now there are certain things that a contestant does and certain things a contestant does not do. After finishing the whole half pint [of liquor] the contestant does not make a fall nor does he take a chaser. He smiles cordially and possibly reaches for a cigarette, always smiling like he just had a saucepan of milk.[115]

WILLIE 'THE LION' SMITH: One New Year's Eve, there was a big party for Ellington and his band at Mexico's after working hours. Around dawn the buzzer sounded. In rushed the racket squad, knocking down the doors with their axes ... Mexico must have gotten behind in protection payments because raids like this didn't happen very often.[116]

DUKE ELLINGTON: Every Wednesday night [Mexico] used to have a battle of some specific instrument and of course, all the performers of that particular instrument were invited to partici-pate in the contest. They had trumpet nights and they had alto sax nights, they had tenor sax nights and I shall never forget the night they had the tubas' battle of music! And of course this was just a small house and the joint was in the basement, and you had to make a turn to get into the door on the upstairs steps and naturally only one bass player – the joint was only big enough to allow one bass player in at a time – and the rest had to stand out on the kerb and wait their turn to come in![117]

JOE 'TRICKY SAM' NANTON: We'd take the whole brass section out and sit in with other bands and jam. We'd just tell the brass section to lay out and we'd take over and play the parts we'd worked out. Have a drink, tear out and go to another place. Our pet spots were Charlie Johnson's and Small's Paradise.[118]

Edwin A. Smalls, a former elevator boy from South Carolina, opened Small's Paradise at 2294 Seventh Avenue on 22 October 1925.

DUKE ELLINGTON: Small's was the place to go, the one spot where everybody'd drop in. And a lot of musicians from Downtown too; Jack Teagarden used to bring along his horn, and Benny and Harry Goodman, Ray Bauduc and a gang of others. Then on Sundays, Small used to hire a guest band, the best he could get, and there'd be a regular jamboree. Matinees on Sunday were something too. Elmer Snowden did the hiring for a while, and all kinds of musicians worked that job. Johnny Hodges and guys from Chick [Webb's] band, and a lot of others. There was always plenty of whiskey around those places, and the music would jump and everything else besides.[119]

SONNY GREER: Smalls. The Sunday breakfast dances attracted show people from one end of the city to the other. Charlie Johnson led the band. Jabbo Smith was featured trumpet man. All kinds of cats sat in ... Bix Beiderbecke and the Whiteman boys ... 'Bean' [Coleman Hawkins] and the Henderson bunch, including that great drummer Kaiser Marshall. Chick Webb showed up quite a bit too. There were so many marvellous mornings in Harlem, it was like another world.[120]

DUKE ELLINGTON: Mr Braud. Oh yes, Wellman Braud. That's another first, it was tubas up until then, tubas were the thing. We started out with this string bass, and it turned out pretty good. All these New Orleans fellas were there, we had the real 'N'awlins' music – you have to know how to say it, it's 'N'awlins!' I saw him first at the Howard Theatre in Washington, in a show. Braud was a wonderful influence, a great 'flavour'.[121]

Wellman Braud [pronounced Bro] joined the band in June 1927. He played both tuba and string bass, but soon specialized in string bass. Along with the Jean Goldkette Orchestra, Ellington was one of the first bands to make the move from tuba to string bass.

SONNY GREER: We had something special going in the old band. The flavour was a once in a lifetime thing. We worked as one man. Duke was the brains, always prodding us to do better, showing kindness and understanding. He was always *with* his men. While working on new things, he might be a bit distant. But then, after putting his thoughts down on paper, Ellington would come out with us after the job a few nights running. He'd listen to the guys and get an idea of what they were thinking.[122]

DUKE ELLINGTON: The band had been at the Kentucky Club about three and a half years when I first met Irving Mills. We were playing the 'St Louis Blues', and he asked what it was. When I told him he said it sure sounded nothing like it. So maybe that gave him ideas.[123]

CHAPTER THREE
COTTON CLUB STOMP

*Hand in hand with the Harlem Renaissance came an unpre-
cedented interest in Harlem's speakeasies and cabarets on the part
of the white leisure classes, in part stimulated by Carl Van
Vetchten's fifth novel,* Nigger Heaven *(1926). The subject of
strenuous controversy, denounced by W. E. B. Du Bois as 'a
blow in the face', but praised as a great achievement by Alain
Locke, James Weldon Johnson and Charles S. Johnson, it described
some of the more exotic activities taking place uptown, helping
stimulate interest in Harlem's cabarets among well-to-do white
downtowners. 'Slumming' in Harlem became a fad, where they
could enjoy black entertainment without appreciably crossing the
colour line and consume bootleg liquor in relatively unhindered
circumstances.*

*With bootleg liquor came the gangsters, 'The Mob', who catered
for the high-living white downtowner – and in some instances
black clientele who could afford their prices – with clubs that
featured increasingly sophisticated black floorshows that exploited
the negro/bootleg entertainment vogue. 'Throughout the speakeasy
era . . . the pleasure lovers rarely considered an evening's excitement
exhausted unless the night, or rather the early post-midnight hours
were topped off with a journey to Harlem,' wrote Louis Sobol in*
The Longest Street. *Cabarets like Small's Paradise, Pod & Jerry's,
the Nest, Connie's Inn and the Cotton Club were able to boast
they brought 'Broadway to Harlem and Harlem to Broadway' with*

shows that featured singers, dancers, novelty acts and dance music. These cabarets were no mere hole-in-the-wall joints, but sophisticated night clubs.

In 1925 the gala opening of Small's Paradise attracted more than 1,500 guests, for example, while the Cotton Club could seat up to 700 patrons. The bands that played for these cabarets were no longer the small ad hoc combos that played for neighbourly house rent parties and parlour socials, or provided background music in the speakeasies and other night spots, but ensembles capable of playing for the complicated routines of chorus lines, singers and entertainers as well as dance music for the patrons who crowded the dancefloors in between showtime. It brought the need for increasingly sophisticated arrangements for enlarged ensembles of two and three trumpets, one and two trombones and three and four saxophones plus a rhythm section. It was the arrangements that defined a band's personality; setting the pace was Charlie Johnson's band at Small's Paradise, Billie Fowler at the Club Alabam, Don Redman at Connie's Inn, Luis Russell at the Nest and, the doyen of the Harlem bandleaders, Fletcher Henderson at the downtown Roseland Ballroom. Landing a job at one of these plumb night spots meant security of employment and something more: recognition.

IRVING MILLS: I [started out] as a songplugger. A songplugger had to report to the five-and-ten cent stores and sing from 9.30 in the morning until 5.30 at night, not only the songs the publisher he was representing was featuring, but any request the people wanted before they bought these ten-cent copies. There was no radio, and so we had to 'make' the songs, and the songpluggers were known by the amount of business they did that week to get additional booking. The company I was working for broke up, McCarthy and Fisher, and my brother, who was head of the contracts in the same company, decided if we published our own songs, I can get the demonstrations in the stores. And so we did, and we took offices on 45th Street and Broadway. It was one flight up, we had five piano rooms. When we first started we were very disappointed when we started in business we couldn't get the writers we planned on to get people's songs, because getting all signed up with different publishers they had exclusive contracts, so we had to resort to freelance writers ... I was in Chicago on a plugging tour and I enquired in one of the music shops what was selling, and they told me about a coloured star, doing a lot of business, there was a lot of demand for that, that was Alberta Hunter. And they told me they had this company, so I got on the train and I went out there and I met these people, they didn't know anything about the record business ... I bought the company and I had Alberta come to New York. I had to have an accompaniment for these artists and so about Fletcher Henderson being the best arranger and writer, and conductor. I formed a company called the Down South Music Company and I opened up in the Roseland building and Fletcher Henderson was to conduct all these dates set up for the race records. But I had to fire Fletcher Henderson, he was either late with the arrangements, for the recording date, he wasn't serious, or he'd change the men or he'd change the arrangements, I needed somebody I could rely on more and I was looking for someone else to take over that department, when I went down to the Kentucky Club one night to talk about a little revue we were going to put in there, and I heard a new band, and the boss said they had just come in from Chicago and wanted my opinion on this orchestra. I listened to this orchestra and said this was the type of combination I needed to replace Henderson. And so after listening to Duke Ellington, this little combination at the Kentucky Club, I had him up to my office, had a talk with him, told him exactly what I needed and how reliable he has to be in order to be prompt on the recording dates.[1]

Mills' reference to a Chicago date is puzzling, unless the band

*played there during the summer months when the Kentucky Club
annually closed its doors.*

DUKE ELLINGTON: He talked to me about making records.
Naturally I agreed, and we got together four originals. They
were for the Vocalion and Brunswick labels, and we made 'East
St Louis', and 'Birmingham Breakdown' for the first.[2]

*The company ledger notes that the session took place in the
'P.M.' of 29 November 1926, and lasted three hours.*

DUKE ELLINGTON: In 1927 Clarence Robinson came up again,
he had a show [*Jazzmania*] in the Lafayette Theatre in Harlem,
we played with the show around Philadelphia, Washington,
Harlem, various places in New York.[3]

*Jazzmania opened at Harlem's Lafayette Theatre on 10
October 1927. Its star was the singer and dancer Adelaide Hall.*

ADELAIDE HALL: I was standing in the wings and he started
playing all these beautiful tunes. When it came to 'Creole Love
Call' – the melody – I said, 'Oh, it's so beautiful, isn't it?' And I
started humming a counter melody, and he said, 'Adelaide,
that's what I've been looking for! That's just what I want for
this record.' I said, 'What?' He said, 'What you've been doing
there, what you've been humming.' I said, 'I wouldn't know
how to go over that again.' He said, 'Yes, you could do it. Try.'
He said, 'I'll start it again from the chorus, see if you can.' I
said, 'I'll try.' And with that he went out, stood in front of the
orchestra and started it again, and I started this humming and
at the end of the chorus he said, 'That's what we're going to do
when we record that in a few days!' I said, 'I don't see how we
can, Duke, because I don't know what I'm doing.' He said,
'Leave it to me!' And that's how it was done.[4]

*Adelaide Hall was never a member of the Ellington organiza-
tion, but recorded 'Creole Love Call' with them on 26 October
1927 and became forever after associated with him.*

IRVING MILLS: Because of my activity in making all these race records, I spent a lot of time up in Harlem and I went into these little cafés and saw great talent. I had seen many of the Ziegfeld shows and I figured they had no story in Ziegfeld shows, it was strictly a revue with great songs, with beautiful costumes, beautiful girls, good dancing and I figured these race . . . these black people, can do it better. If I could only put these things together, get these dancers and great singers and co-medians – which I loved in those days – I could put on my own black revue and it was a case of finding a spot where to do it, and I tried several places until I hit the Cotton Club, it was called the Cotton Club at that time, and they had just had an orchestra and three acts, a dance team, a comedian and a singer. But they had a place upstairs where the gangsters used to have a separate entrance, it was an evening place where the betting went on. I met Herman Stark, the manager, and I said, 'How would you like to have a little revue on there, with a chorus, beautiful girls, put a whole production together?' and he said, 'You have to take it up with Frenchy [George 'Big Frenchy' DeMange], the boss,' and he said, 'Would you do it?' What was involved in there, they weren't out to spend a lot of money, they didn't understand putting a show on in a club, and I talked with Frenchy and he said, 'We'll try one.'[5]

DUKE ELLINGTON: Irving Mills manoeuvred it – Irving Mills and Jimmy McHugh – Jimmy McHugh was writing the shows for the Cotton Club.[6]

Jazzmania at the Lafayette was replaced by Clarence Robin-son's new production Dance Mania *in mid-November 1927. It is possible that the Cotton Club manager Herman Stark heard the Ellington band – now described in the* New York Age *as 'Famous'[7] – in the Lafayette's new production and decided to sign them.*

FREDDY GUY: Right next to the [Lafayette] Theatre there was a tavern and the contract was signed there. I was with Duke all night. The next day we had to leave for a date in Philadelphia for a week, which gave us no time between our return and our opening. When we got back, we had to rehearse the entire show, routines all afternoon and night, literally up to showtime.[8]

RALPH COOPER: Duke's band had a commitment to play a date in Philadelphia when the Cotton Club gig was offered. Clarence Robinson, who would later work at both the Cotton Club and the Apollo Theatre, was producing at the Philadelphia theatre. Clarence refused to release Ellington's band from its contract until he received a suggestion he couldn't ignore from Madden's associates. 'Be big,' Clarence was told, 'or be dead.'[9]

Robinson's Dance Mania *troupe that included the Ellington band were booked for two weeks commencing 21 November 1927 at Philadelphia's Standard Theatre.*

SONNY GREER: Owney Madden. Owney Madden owned the Cotton Club. He was over Dutch Schultz, Al Capone and all of them. He wasn't a – a little, tiny guy. Talked like a girl. Never raised his voice. When he said something that was it.[10]

Madden, who when he died in 1965 owned a casino in Hot Springs, Arkansas, was born in England. In his youth he had been a sadistic killer in New York, but he emerged in the 1920s as a sophisticated racketeer who moved as an equal among the crooked politicians and major crime figures along the East Coast. He was not seen regularly at the Cotton Club, his energies devoted to operating the Phoenix Cereal Beverage Company on West 25th Street where his bootleg beer found its way into many of the bars and clubs in New York City.

DUKE ELLINGTON: We opened at the Cotton Club 4th December in 1927. Jimmy McHugh and Dorothy Fields had scored the show, and Jimmy had been instrumental in getting us the booking.[11]

IRVING MILLS: Well, there were so many people available we just had to weed them out, you know, all the girls that can dance good, and I got hold of a fella named [Clarence] Robinson who put the routines together, that was the first show. And we rented the costumes and it was good music, you know, that Jimmy [McHugh] wrote.[12]

JIMMY MCHUGH: It so happened that this particular show which I had written for the Cotton Club was enhanced with the introduction of the great talent of Miss Dorothy Fields. It was our first collaboration and it was the first time I had orchestrations written by the conductor-pianist Duke Ellington which I paid him $50 per song.[13]

SONNY GREER: [It was] the first time we had a regular Broadway production up there [in Harlem]. We rehearsed the show, we were playing there, but we wasn't playing the show. The new show had about three weeks after we come in there, so we just played entertainment while they were rehearsing, but opening night, everybody in New York was there. Sensation.[14]

VARIETY: COTTON CLUB (NEW YORK) – Aida Ward ... is a charming song saleswoman and the particular luminary of the proceedings ... The big attraction, of course, are the gals, 10 of 'em, the majority of whom in white company could pass for Caucasians. Possessed of the native jazz heritage, their hotsy-totsy performance if working sans wraps could never be parred by a white gal. The brownskins' shiveree is worth the $2 couvert alone. In Duke Ellington's dance band, Harlem has reclaimed its own after Times Square accepted them for several seasons at the Club Kentucky. Ellington's jazzique is just too bad.[15]

DUKE ELLINGTON: Originally I had engaged a violinist who was accustomed to conducting shows, and all the – that was a normal picture in those days, the violinist is standing up, conducting the orchestra for the show, and I found out that I was more familiar with shows with my experience at the

Kentucky Club than he was, so I put the piano around in the middle, conducted from the piano.[16]

BARNEY BIGARD: This prima donna, Aida Ward was her name, the prima donna of the show, and she was trying to get the band fired because the band they had before, she was going with one of the guys in the band. So Duke had to hire a fiddle player to lead her tunes, you know. And the manager of the Cotton Club kept telling her, he says, 'If I were you, I wouldn't bother the band. You're making yourself being hated. Why don't you leave the band alone?' 'No,' says Aida, 'They can't play for me, they're just ruining my songs.' So then that new show come in because of the new band. So her part, she come out, she's got to have a big obbligato in front, you know, just she and the fiddle. So Otto Hardwick says, 'We got her now!' So just before showtime the guy left the fiddle on the piano, Otto Hardwick got some soap and dampened it and soaped the bow, you know, and soaped the bow up good. So when she came out to sing and starts that falsetto and the fiddle player's supposed to back her up with some little obbligato, there ain't nothing coming out. And she sings, and he's just going like mad and he can't get a thing, and she's looking back to see what's happening and we're just sitting there laughing like mad until she got so that she had to walk off the stage crying. So the manager said, 'I told you, I told you, you mess with the band and now see what they're doing!' From then on, boy, she was just as sweet as a pie. She thought the band was the greatest band in the world.[17]

DUKE ELLINGTON: We got Barney from King Oliver's band, before that it was Rudy Jackson – we were on the New Orleans clarinet-playing kick! They had an entirely different character, these New Orleans players, during the heyday of the clarinet they began to sound like whistles, they lost the wood, the timbre, but most of these New Orleans cats have that wood sound. And the guy who had the most wood I ever heard on clarinet was [Sidney] Bechet. Which I love, and I think is the greatest, there ain't nothing like wood when playing a clarinet.[18]

Barney Bigard joined Ellington in early January 1928. He had been with King Oliver from 1925 to 1927, and had been with Luis Russell for eight weeks prior to joining Ellington.

BARNEY BIGARD: I joined Duke in '27 (*recte* 1928) I was working with Luis Russell at a place called the Nest. Helen Morgan and all of those kind of people used to come there. And they'd have a ball – sometimes I wouldn't get home till 12 noon. But I had me about $40 or $50 in my pocket [a night] and the job only paid me about $75 [a week]. And I left all that to go with Duke. After I got to working in the big band, I kind of liked it, and [Wellman] Braud kept telling me, 'Millet, this guy's going to go places. We're going to make some money. Stay. Don't leave. Stay.' And I stayed and we did make some money. He told me right.[19]

OTTO HARDWICK: Then came the better era, we enlarged the band, with the same principle, every man had freedom of expressing his own ideas, and it went for a good thing, because no one man could say, 'This is it, this is the way I want to hear it.' The band wasn't built like that.[20]

SONNY GREER: I objected to making the band larger, but that's what THEY wanted.[21]

JOE 'TRICKY SAM' NANTON: When we went into the Cotton Club we only had one trumpet, Bubber. Then we added Louis Metcalf.[22]

Metcalf had previously recorded with Ellington in 1926 and 1927.

LOUIS METCALF: During my last month with Sam Wooding I got the opportunity to double with Duke in regular engagements at the Cotton Club. This was the time Duke increased his personnel from his original six.[23]

BENNY WATERS: Ellington came [from] the Kentucky Club with just a six-piece band. Good, too. Then his big band was formed right at the Cotton Club. He was a little rusty at that period. And our band [Charlie Johnson's] had been well established at Small's Paradise. So we had the lead on him. Of course it didn't take him long to get straight.[24]

NED E. WILLIAMS: I first heard the Ellington band in 1927, which was the year it made its debut at the famous Cotton Club ... I can't say I was too much impressed with the Ellington crew on that visit. It definitely didn't have the form and polish that it acquired later.[25]

Williams had recently joined Mills Artists Inc., as Irving Mills's assistant.

IRVING MILLS: The first show was kind of weak, but it was an entirely different kind of show than just having vaudeville acts, you know, you had a girlie revue. Well, the next one we knew what to add, to elaborate on it. And there was a man by the name of Frenchy – the mob had different people who took care of different places. They were all very nice, gentlemanly people ... so the second show was a vast improvement. Now we made our own costumes to order. We didn't rent costumes on the second show. And Frenchy and I had a handshake. He liked what I was doing and he said go ahead and do anything I wanted. And I was the boss of the whole thing, from the beginning, I don't know, I think we did twenty-four shows [by the time the Cotton Club eventually closed].[26]

LOUIS METCALF: The Cotton Club was a class house and, considering that Duke was still organizing his band, the fact that we were makin' about seventy-five a week with him showed how much he was thought of. But, believe me, Duke had to

fight every inch of the way to get what he wanted. Some of the guys used to tell him he was a fool to give in so much to management, but Duke knew what he wanted, and I guess to get what you want, you have to compromise.[27]

SPIKE HUGHES: The Cotton Club was Harlem's most famous nightspot. It was expensive and exclusive; it cost you the earth merely to look at the girl who took your hat and coat as you went in; it was run by a white man for white patrons who sincerely believed that when they visited the place they were seeing Harlem at its most authentic. The talent, like the waiters and the girl who checked your hat, was coloured, and occasionally the best coloured talent money could buy.[28]

IRVING MILLS: We found the best talent of black always was available to us because there was no other big, high spots to play. And to play the Cotton Club was like playing the Ziegfeld Theatre or playing the Palace Theatre for the blacks, and so we had more people than we could possibly use.[29]

DUKE ELLINGTON: You went up a long set of stairs upstairs, turn right and you'd be facing across the dancefloor, and if you went across to the middle of the dancefloor and turned left, you'd be facing the bandstand. They probably had a cover charge of $4–$5, depending on what night it was – night club business in those days didn't depend on large crowds, all they needed was one good party and then they'd make it because one good party would spend more money than a whole house full of people who were economizing, a house full of thrifty people.[30]

SPIKE HUGHES: But it was not Harlem, for no Negroes were permitted to enter the Cotton Club's doors. If you were very famous, like Ethel Waters or Paul Robeson, then the management would allow you to show your coloured face inside the door; but you had to be tucked away discreetly in an inconspicuous corner of the room.[31]

SONNY GREER: We had coloured people come up there, but the prices were so high. The average coloured person back off. They could go to Small's Paradise and them clubs, but when you come to the Cotton Club, you sit down, you're going to spend a lot of money. Of course them coloured guys in the rackets, they associated like working for the guys, they'd come up and sit down and spend money and have a ball. They put out the red carpet for Bill Robinson, he was a big star. They put out the red carpet for him, but the ordinary layman out there – porter, them carrying bricks and working, it was too much pressure – he couldn't stand that.[32]

MERCER ELLINGTON: One of the fallacies was the racial aspect. What separated the men from the boys in the Cotton Club was purely the dollar. I remember seeing lines of limousines stretching five blocks – that was the type of clientele. White, black or blue, if you didn't have the money to pay the cover charge you didn't get in.[33]

DUKE ELLINGTON: By this time ... we'd just hired Carney. Carney was only a kid at the time, and we had to tell him everything. He wanted to know what the money was, and when we told him $75, he could hardly credit his ears.[34]

Harry Carney had toured briefly with Ellington in New England in the summer of 1926 and recorded with the band in December that year, finally joining the band on a full-time basis in June 1927 for a summer tour of New England.

IRVING MILLS: By now Duke had expanded the orchestra to ten pieces and I gladly contributed the salaries of the additional musicians out of my share of the project, because this was obviously more than the mere launching of a dance orchestra or show band. In those days it was necessary for a bandleader to play shows and for dancers.[35]

SONNY GREER: Carney came down with his clarinet in a paper bag. Young kid. And played! So Duke latched on to him.[36]

HARRY CARNEY: I didn't first go to work with Duke when I arrived in New York. I went to New York originally on [my school] holidays. I had been working – playing – in Boston. And through Johnny Hodges I got a job at the Savoy Ballroom, one night they had a masquerade ball and they had a relief band. And Johnny Hodges got me the job with the relief band. In the band was a guitar player who had a job coming up and invited me to join his group. We were playing at a place called the Bamboo Inn and during the course of the time we were there, Duke would come on his night off at the Kentucky Club. And I guess that's where he paid attention to my playing, my enthusiasm – a young kid – and the place burned down after being there for three months and I met him on the street and he enquired as to what I was doing, and I told him just gigging around, so he invited me to go to New England with him.[37]

DUKE ELLINGTON: He was a good musician, had very good training. He came with us when he was seventeen years old – we used to call him 'Youth', he didn't have enough seniority to object![38]

HARRY CARNEY: It was during the summer we were playing in the New England area, in Massachusetts. My being from Massachusetts, it was very nice for me to be in Massachusetts, showing off in front of all my friends playing with Duke Ellington – I was seventeen at the time. Well, we travelled ... by automobile ... our headquarters was Salem, Mass. – we could leave in the afternoon, and travel and make the date on time.[39]

HARRY CARNEY: When I got to New England my mother wanted me to return to school, you see I was a drop-out in third year high school; I promised her, since I was doing so badly the semester before, if I could quit and could return during the fall, that I would go back to school, make a fresh start.[40]

OTTO HARDWICK: We had to have the permission of his mother that we would see that he was taken care of . . . We had to go to his mother to make sure we were going to take care of him as long as he was with the band.[41]

HARRY CARNEY: After the season in New England with Duke, they were returning to New York, and that's when he talked to my mother, influenced my mother to allow me to go back to New York with him. Then we went into the Cotton Club.[42]

IRVING MILLS: The first thing I did was to get a wire into the Cotton Club – radio. And that took off and he became an overnight sensation, so much so that the theatres requested a performance of Duke Ellington, and he became known all over the United States.[43]

DUKE ELLINGTON: Here was the real springboard because we were on the radio from the Cotton Club practically every night and we did so well on WHN, that Columbia Broadcasting System came over and we went on the entire Columbia trans-continental network. Ted Husing was the principal announcer. Broadcasting in those days was a little different because you didn't have to clear numbers in front and Ted would get on the microphone and say, 'Well, Duke, what's next?' and I would say, 'Well, let's see, I tell you what, we recorded a number today, let's hear what it sounds like on the radio.'[44]

VARIETY: One of the hottest bands on the air is Duke Ellington's from the Cotton Club Monday midnights. One torrid trumpeter brays and blares in lowdown style that defies passiveness on hearing it.[45]

DUKE ELLINGTON: Harlem had a tremendous reputation, everyone expected blaring trumpets, squirming girls, every night was Saturday night and everybody had rhythm, all that sort of thing. Everyone who came to New York had to come to Harlem, on Sunday night in the Cotton Club it was a night of introducing celebrity after top celebrity for the entire evening.[46]

SPIKE HUGHES: The Master of Ceremonies behaved as though the whole concern was being broadcast all the time (which it might well have been), and there was incessant spotlighting of celebrities. The purely obscure who had paid their cover charge were apparently delighted to have their attention diverted from their food and look up from their plates to realize they were in such distinguished company as (quote) None Other Than That Great Hollywood Actor and Personality Who Needs No Introduction (pause) Freddy (pause) FISH!!! (unquote – applause). Mr F. would then rise gracefully and bow in the spotlight to the acclamation of the audience and the delight of the blondes who shared his free table and had been out of work even longer than he had. From one None-Other-Than the spotlight would move to another – to a little-read Broadway columnist, and on to an obscure song-writer known personally to the Master of Ceremonies, but whose name the audience can never have heard in its life before. Occasionally, if the Master of Ceremonies was lucky, he would have the spotlight directed on to a couple of members of British Peerage – an Earl with an American mother. The presence at the Cotton Club of the British aristocracy invariably inspired more applause than anything else revealed by the roving spotlight: the open mouthed astonishment of the New Yorkers was exceeded only by that of the British members of the audience, who had never previously heard of the noble lords either.[47]

RUTH ELLINGTON: I'll never forget the first time I heard Edward's music. Of course we'd heard it at home, playing ragtime, but here he was playing his own music with his own band on the radio from New York, coming out of this old-fashioned horn-speaker. I think radio had just about been invented . . . or at least just launched commercially. It was quite a shock. Here we were, my mother and I, sitting in this very respectable Victorian living room, my mother so puritanical she didn't even wear lipstick, and the announcer from New York tells us we are listening to 'Duke Ellington and His Jungle Music!'[48]

SONNY GREER: I don't know whether it was Paul Whiteman, because he idolized Duke, or Gershwin. He was a steady customer at the Cotton Club. They used to be in awe of the things Duke used to do, so they were sitting up at the Cotton Club and George Gershwin says to Paul, 'I know what that is, that's Jungle Music.' And it stuck with us.[49]

BARNEY BIGARD: A lot of people don't know that Gershwin wanted to collaborate with Duke years ago in the Cotton Club. George Gershwin. Duke didn't want to. Duke wanted to do it all by himself, but Gershwin wanted to be a partner with Duke.

And that would have been terrific, you know? But no, he didn't want to. And at that time, I mean, a mixture like that would have been fantastic.[50]

LOUIS METCALF: It was the days of those lovely tunes, such as 'Black Beauty', 'The Mooche', 'Swampy River' and the swinging 'Jubilee Stomp'. I was lucky enough to record with them and am on most of those arrangements. Now, I'll tell you something you may not know. There was a clause in our contract and every composition that Duke or any of the band wrote had to be sold outright for twenty-five dollars to his manager [Irving Mills]. So for many years all those wonderful compositions which everyone knows and loves brought Duke and his musicians practically nothing. In those days we were glad to get twenty-five. How were any of us to know that they would one day become classics?[51]

DUKE ELLINGTON: I tried desperately to try and sound like Fletcher Henderson. I could only do it as far as the musicians' limitations would allow. If for instance there was something I wanted to do that had some sort of Henderson influence, and it wasn't a thing my people leaned to or felt sympathetic about, then I had to readjust, and in this way I developed. I think all writing is much more interesting when it is more personalized, when it is individual or personally tailored to the musicians going to do the playing.[52]

MERCER ELLINGTON: When he was in the early Cotton Club, and he had to write the shows, he didn't necessarily know how to write too well himself at that point, but he'd sit there at the piano and run through these things, say, 'OK, you play this,' and they'd play that part, and he'd say, 'You play this here.' And he would write the arrangement horizontally, I've only known a few people in the course of my life who could write like that . . . If some song happened to be very popular and he'd gotten quite a bit of requests for it, in those days he'd go down to some bar or whatever and with a fistful of nickels and keep on playing the same song on the jukebox and keep on playing it until he heard the arrangement and as he listened to it he wrote out the parts one at a time.[53]

BARNEY BIGARD: It was like a tradition of the band, Tricky and Bubber, they made duets together, like on 'Black and Tan Fantasy', where they would growl on the horn. That was an identification of Ellington's band.[54]

IRVING MILLS: Now they were so satisfied with the policy of a production in the Cotton Club because it brought a lot more people to the club ... I had to have assurance that they're not going to switch, the Mob would switch, to somebody else who could come in and try and put on a better show or something, you know? And so I formed a corporation immediately and became president of Cotton Club Productions.[55]

SONNY GREER: We really played what you would call a stage production, we had a natural Broadway show. Them girls stopped the show. Oh, the girls, the chorus. Stopped them cold. Sixteen of them, they were hand-picked, like you pick a beauty contest. The prettiest coloured girls in the world. They looked pretty on the stage and when they were on the street, down on Broadway shopping, people would turn around and look at them. They never seen nobody like that. That was the Cotton Club girls. Famous.[56]

NED E. WILLIAMS: I was bewildered by the elaborate floor revue at the Cotton Club, even then comparable with the top Broadway musicals and fascinated by the dispatch and lack of commotion with which a belligerent drunken guest was subdued and evicted by club attachés.[57]

DUKE ELLINGTON: The great thing about it was when the show was on – they did have a wonderful show – no one was allowed to talk during the show. I'll never forget, some guy would be juiced, and talking, and the waiter would come around, 'Sir would you please . . .' and the next thing the captain would come over, 'Sir,' and so forth, and the next thing the head waiter would come and then next thing, the guy would just disappear![58]

SONNY GREER: [Owney Madden] loved Duke because him and Duke used to sit up and play 'Grits' and all that, 'Coon Can' all night long after the club closed. Me, I'm ready to run. When the last note hit, I'm gone. He loved Duke and he loved me. And his influence was so powerful that we was always in the clear.[59]

MERCER ELLINGTON: I met some of the gangsters – Madden and those people; they were just guys out to make a living, a night-club to them was a bit like a car, it was a status symbol; also it was a way to turn the money over, a good front. The one thing I remember is Pop playing bridge every night with the others for a dollar a point – that was big money in those days, we're talking thousands of points![60]

BARNEY BIGARD: Now, when I joined Duke I used to have a lot of fuss with him at first. I'd ask him if he was making the right arrangement in the chords, and we'd have fusses all the time. I remember he would say, 'Well, Barney, just sit and play what I've put in front, that's it. Don't worry about it.' Then I gradually got acquainted with the sounds of the band, with its harmonies, and then I loved the music.[61]

OTTO HARDWICK: To us, at first, things sounded quite weird. We found out first before the average fans found out, it's something that actually had to grow on you. And it had to grow on us first before we could really put into it what it deserved.[62]

Louis Metcalf: With the increased personnel the band had a wonderful sound. Ellington was very futuristic and way ahead of his time.[63]

Duke Ellington: Arthur Whetsol ... would speak up in a minute on the subject of propriety, clean appearance and reliability. If and when any member of our band made an error in grammar he was quick to correct him. He was aware of all Negro individuals who were contributing to the cause by *commanding respect.* He knew all about Negro colleges and he also knew all the principal scholastic and athletic leaders personally.[64]

Whetsol rejoined Ellington in mid-March 1928, bringing the trumpet section of Louis Metcalf and Bubber Miley up to three.

Joe 'Tricky Sam' Nanton: Whetsol was a truly great trumpet player ... [he] had a brilliant mind and was extremely adaptable, complete master of his horn. His ideas for obbligato were astounding, had lots of soul.[65]

Duke Ellington: Whetsol. He was a great man. He was a great man, organization man. He was a man who was not a disciplinarian, but if a guy wasn't dressed properly or his behaviour was just a little short of what it should be, he could take a cigarette and flick the ash on it and give him a look to the point where everybody would straighten up. He was a great organization man. We had fines in the band for coming late, and dressing, of course, that was the thing. Whetsol was too much and his tonal character has never been duplicated, it was such a fragile thing, nobody has really had his gentility, fragility. Wonderful man. He was part of the backbone of that whole set-up. Whetsol, Greer and Braud, in his way. These cats – a guy would do something that was a little bit off as far as behaviour was concerned and they'd eat his ass out, each one in his own way. Wonderful cats.[66]

BARNEY BIGARD: Otto Hardwick, he wouldn't show up some-times for two and three nights and I always wondered what he was doing. I knew he was a heavy drinker. So one night I decided I'm going to hang out with him and find out what he's doing, you know. Then he called me, 'Let's go make bouzan.' I taught him to say that, bouzan. Let's go have a ball with drinking. He said, 'You going to make bouzan with me tonight?' and I said, 'Yeah, I'm with you.' All he did was run from apartment to apartment, all of his friends, lady friends, apart-ment to apartment, drinking and drinking until he got stoned. He got me so stoned I missed the night. I says, 'Oh, no.' I couldn't believe it, but that's what he used to do for no rhyme or reason. He'd just go out.[67]

DUKE ELLINGTON: Toby was in and out, and in and out, and in and out – Toby did a lot of living! Now and then he would get a chick that would take care of him and he would submit.[68]

REX STEWART: When Harry Carney joined Duke in 1927 ... [he] was playing alto and clarinet ... I've wondered if perhaps Harry was hired to replace Toby on one of the sudden self-declared vacations Toby had a tendency to take? And then, when Toby returned, Harry switched over to baritone.[69]

Hardwick left the band shortly after a recording session on 26 March 1928 to visit Europe, where he became a fluent French speaker during his stay in Paris, playing with Noble Sissle and with his own group at Bricktop's. Although he returned to New York the following year he did not return to Ellington's band until 1932.

MERCER ELLINGTON: Otto was very highly educated – a very sharp mind.[70]

HARRY CARNEY: There were quite a few good baritone players in those days. Sonny Adams. Willie Grant. Joe Garland. Foots Thomas with the Missourians. As a matter of fact, all the bands used a baritone if the band was over a certain number of pieces. The average nine or ten piece would have baritone or someone who doubled baritone. I continued with alto, to about '32.[71]

DUKE ELLINGTON: Chick [Webb] was always dogged by bad luck and never managed to hold a band steady for long. But every time he'd get a job he could always hire first-rate musicians. Then the band would have a lay-off and some of the guys would have to take work somewhere else. Johnny Hodges came over to me in 1928.[72]

Hodges joined Ellington on 18 May 1928.

DUKE ELLINGTON: We had a meeting in the band whether to get Buster Bailey or J. H. [Johnny Hodges] – Barney voted Buster out, so we sent for the new blood.[73]

JOHNNY HODGES: I'd been with Chick Webb. You see, Duke started Chick, gave Chick his first band. Duke was working at the Kentucky club, six pieces. Another club opened on 50th Street and Seventh Avenue. It wanted a band just like Duke's. So he asked me to have a band and I didn't want any part of having a band. He asked Chick. We got together six pieces and tried to make it sound like Duke. We did pretty good until we had a fire. During that time fire was common in clubs. We went up to the Savoy [Ballroom] for two weeks and stayed about six months. I left and started gigging with a fellow named Luckey Roberts. The bread was good. Thought it would last forever. So I kept gigging and gigging. Meanwhile, Otto Hardwick had an accident, went through the windshield of a taxicab. Had his face all cut up and I had to go to work for him. Duke offered me a job. I still wouldn't take the job, kept putting it off and putting it off. Everybody was trying to talk me into it.[74]

JOHNNY HODGES: I joined Duke in '28. It was my sister's birthday, May 18th, which is also my son's birthday, a day to remember. I replaced Otto Hardwick, 'Professor Booze' they called him. He was terrific. There was no man in the world who could master the high notes like him. In those days ... I very seldom played anything slow. They were all fast, peppy tunes ... so what happened was Duke threw it all on me and I had to rehearse this thing and try and get as close to .[Otto] as I possibly could. He was first alto.[75]

JOHNNY HODGES: I used to stay out of school to listen to [Bechet], stayed away so often the truant officer was looking out for me. But they never could catch me – I'd go too fast. That's why I'm called Rabbit, I'd run on fast, like a rabbit.[76]

JOHNNY HODGES: Sidney Bechet gave me one of his sopranos in 1925. He used to teach me many things – and I was willing to learn. A lot of credit is due to him.[77]

JOE 'TRICKY SAM' NANTON: [Then] Metcalf quit because he felt he wasn't getting enough solo parts and that's when Freddie Jenkins came into the band.[78]

Jenkins joined Ellington in the fall of 1928, replacing Louis Metcalf who had left to join Jelly Roll Morton at the Dreamland on 125th Street and Seventh Avenue.

FREDDIE JENKINS: For the first two days I mostly sat around with my horn on my knees. I think Duke felt sorry for me because occasionally he call for some standard like 'Tishimingo', and I'd be able to jump in and swing on it. After another couple of days I got a little more used to Ellington numbers, but they were still hard for me. I could read the score all right, but improvising was something else. So, I told Duke that I didn't think I'd be able to make it. Duke asked if I was giving him notice and when I said yes, he reminded me that it had to be a two week notice and suggested I stick around and see if I felt that way after two weeks. If I did I could quit, but if I wanted to stay the notice would be out the window.[79]

SONNY GREER: Freddie Jenkins was a master showman. He played the trumpet left-handed, he idolized Louis Armstrong. Freddie Jenkins, he was a picture, he would hit them high notes and twirl that horn someway with his left hand. Perfect showman and the people loved him because he was tiny. They called him 'Posey', he was a knockout.[80]

FREDDIE JENKINS: When I was a little boy my hand was cut pretty bad and they had to cut the finger tips off ... [so] I started playing the trumpet with my left hand. With Duke, you were in show business and show business meant just that. You're there to perform and nothing must interfere with the enjoyment of your patrons. You must try to hide any deformity you have which might divert attention from what you are doing. You don't want them feeling sorry for you. You want them to enjoy your music ... as far as I know I was the only left-handed trumpet player at the time.[81]

JOE 'TRICKY SAM' NANTON: Jenkins used to sit in the middle [of the trumpet section] and Bubber was always scolding him for 'posturing and posing'. Miley switched him to the end chair so he couldn't be seen as well. But it didn't work. Freddy pulled more tricks than ever. So we all gave up. We found, though, the public had caught on and liked his antics ... and soon he was the spark plug of the band with his comedy routines.[82]

LAWRENCE BROWN: He just fit, everything just fit in like a puzzle in this odd picture. Little Posey would pose, you know, everything with him was a picture, very pleasant-natured little fellow, and that's why they called him Little Posey. He was small and everything he did was posed, in a pose.[83]

DUKE ELLINGTON: It was still too early for fellows to get real big time about money ... a lot of the guys liked to play so much that in spite of being on a regular job, they'd still hire out to work matinees, or breakfast dances. The gin-mills were wide-open at that time and there weren't any restrictive regulations about closing hours, nobody went to bed at nights and round three or four in the mornings you'd find everyone making the rounds bringing their horns with them.[84]

DUKE ELLINGTON: I once heard Coleman Hawkins and Sidney Bechet tie up in the Cotton Club all night, or early Sunday morning, and when I say tie up, I mean hour after hour of blowing back at each other; these are great moments.[85]

IRVING MILLS: I was making records with the Victor company with Duke Ellington and I thought in order to make a 12-inch record and have a record of production, like the Red Seals, that I would add the Hotsy Totsy Gang and I would put the white band and the black band together as one, we would have twenty-four pieces, only to get a call a few days later from Victor, they had a big problem, and the problem was that I ought to know better than to put a black and white band together – how are they going to list the record? Under the black label or under the white label and whose names are going to be on it? And so I said, 'Is that what I came here for? Is that the big problem?' I said, 'I'm glad you brought that up because I have a mind to tell you as long as Duke Ellington is on a black label and it's under the counter when they want it on Broadway instead of being on the bulletin and he's a big hit on radio, that it's time he's on the white label and unless he's not on the white label we won't make any more records.' And the record was released and it was on the white bulletin.[86]

Warren Mills and his Blues Serenaders, one of Irving Mills's many pseudonyms for various groups he assembled, was in fact the session Mills refers to. On 20 December 1928 Ellington's band, a white group led by Matty Malneck and ten members of the Hall Johnson Choir recorded 'St Louis Blues' coupled with 'Gems from Blackbirds 1928'. Variety[87] stated the score for 'St Louis Blues' was that used in the finale to the revue 'Blackbirds of 1928'.

DUKE ELLINGTON: Bubber was very temperamental and liked his likker, he used to get under the piano and go to sleep when he felt like it. In fact all our horn-blowers were lushies, and I used to have to go around and get them out of bed to see that they got to work.[88]

MERCER ELLINGTON: [Bubber] was a very warm person, probably impractical because I got along with him so well and he was a sort of person who could easily live in a kid's world and make you feel he was one of you, you know? And as a result, I think this is one of the things that led to his demise, he really didn't care too much how he handled himself.[89]

COOTIE WILLIAMS: The reason why [Duke] fired Bubber Miley was every time some big shot come up to listen to the band, there wasn't no Bubber Miley. And the whole band had been built around Bubber Miley. And maybe he decided, he says, 'Well, this man has got to go. I have to let him go and get somebody' . . . After Duke fired Bubber Miley, Johnny Hodges said to him, 'Why don't you get Cootie?' But I had never played no music like that. [Johnny] heard me with Fletcher [Henderson's] band, maybe, and heard me down at the Bandbox. And so I left Fletcher and went up there with Duke. And I used to laugh when Tricky would start blowing, you know. It sounded funny to me.[90]

Bubber Miley left the band in February 1929 and was subsequently replaced by Williams after much lobbying by Johnny Hodges on his behalf.

MERCER ELLINGTON: Cootie will readily admit that when he came into the band he thought it was crazy to be going around doing this [growling]. It took him, well, some time to begin to realize he was in the midst of something that was very constructive.[91]

COOTIE WILLIAMS: [Duke] didn't say nothing till it come to me, sitting up there playing, it come to me and I said, 'Well, this man hired me to play like that.' So I kept on listening to Tricky. One night I had the plunger and I said, 'Wah, wah!' And I woke everybody up, and they said, 'That's it. That's it. Keep on. That's it.'[92]

DUKE ELLINGTON: He caught onto a lot from Tricky Sam and before you knew it everybody was saying nobody could work with a plunger like Cootie.[93]

PITTSBURGH COURIER: FLETCHER HENDERSON REPLACES DUKE ELLINGTON – Because of some misunderstanding between Vincent Youmans and Irving Mills, the latter manager of Duke Ellington, Duke and his orchestra will not open with Vincent Youmans' *Horse Shoes* [later renamed *Great Day*], the musical show now in rehearsal until June 2, and has been replaced by Fletcher Henderson and his orchestra from the Roseland.[94]

REX STEWART: [A] great rivalry developed between Ellington and Henderson ... the story is frequently told that Fletcher replaced Duke in *Great Day*. That is just not the way it happened. Irving Mills tried his best to keep Smack [Henderson] out of *Great Day* so that he could build Ellington, but it was Vincent Youmans himself who chose Henderson.[95]

Henderson himself was replaced by Paul Lannin in early July 1929. After touring out of New York, Great Day *lasted just 37 performances on Broadway, closing on 16 November 1929.*

MERCER ELLINGTON: [1929 was] the year of the Wall Street crash ... Nobody seems to have even suspected the possibility of a crash, but suddenly the whole thing flopped and banks began to fold. So Pop was back at the bottom again, supposedly an important man, but without money.[96]

IRVING MILLS: We weathered the storm all through that whole 1929 period, I didn't have any money, I was out thousands of dollars before anything ever developed. I dressed up the band, I wanted the boys to feel like they were the tops of the whole black set. I didn't know where the money was coming from, I didn't make any money in the Cotton Club. You know I was a music publisher, I was glad to get my songs plugged and I was glad to have a home for the band to have it together for the records.[97]

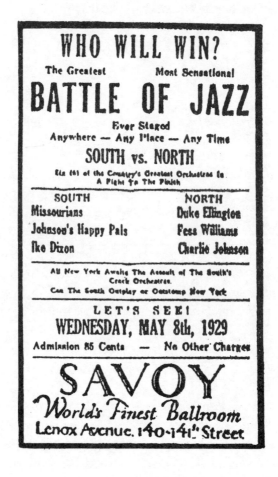

CHAPTER FOUR

HIGH LIFE

Ellington quickly adapted to the requirements of the Cotton Club floorshows, and became a focal point of their elaborate productions. Following the December 1927 revue, he was featured in The Cotton Club Show Boat *that opened on 1 April 1928,* Hot Chocolate *that opened on 7 October 1928,* Springbirds *that opened on 31 March 1929 and* Blackberries *that opened on 29 September 1929. A common thread that ran through all these productions were the speciality numbers by Jimmy McHugh and Dorothy Fields, but it was Ellington, of course, who arranged these tunes for his band. It was just one of many duties he performed as musical director, including contributing the music for up to a dozen speciality acts that filled out each revue, providing original compositions for dancers, the chorus line, his own feature spots and dance music for the Cotton Club clientele who took over the dancefloor in between showtime.*

Every few months a new production was mounted that might depict jungles in darkest Africa, scenes from the Deep South or the Wild West that provided a backdrop against which the Cotton Club dancers, clad in skimpy costumes, strutted their stuff. These cameos imposed a huge creative burden on Ellington to provide suitable musical correlation to the exotic visuals enacted by the dancers and singers, and he responded with remarkable imagination and creativity to the diversity of musical situations the producers dreamed up.

The Cotton Club environment was quite different from those of the great dance bands led by the likes of Fletcher Henderson or Chick Webb, who enjoyed long residences at the Roseland Ballroom and the Savoy Ballroom respectively. There they conformed to the expectations of a dance-going public, playing waltzes, tangos, two-steps as well as plenty of rhythm numbers for the dance-crazy Lindy Hoppers to enact out their courtship rituals. Consequently these bands were not challenged to provide music as rich and varied as Ellington's striking accompaniment for the Cotton Club productions with its dark, mysterioso saxophones, growling trumpets and trombones. Quickly dubbed 'Jungle Music', it took Ellington deeper and deeper into the realms of unusual tone colours, of ingenious part writing that combined unorthodox combinations of instruments, into compositions that explored theme and development to an extent that was unusual in jazz of the period and into integrating soloist and orchestration in such a way that one complemented the other (rather than the usual practice of presenting the 'hot' solo as an end in itself that may or may not relate to the thematic material at hand).

Within this unique musical laboratory, Ellington flowered as a composer and arranger, his work extending to claim the attention of those in the classical field such as Percy Grainger, then Head of Music at New York University, Basil Cameron, conductor of the Seattle Symphony Orchestra, and Leopold Stokowski, then conductor of the Philadelphia Symphony Orchestra. However, on 29 October Wall Street laid its famous egg, and Depression gripped America. Ellington would later say, 'Our plaintive little sound seemed to fit the times.'

Despite massive unemployment, people seemed determined to survive, and survive with dignity. The music of Duke Ellington and his nightly broadcasts from the Cotton Club on an NBC wire epitomized the pride of black America, poignant yet vibrant sounds that gave voice to their dreams, creating a demand far beyond Harlem for his music.

DUKE ELLINGTON: We played Ziegfeld's *Show Girl* while we were playing at the Cotton Club, that's the show George Gershwin introduced 'An American in Paris', the ballet. I think the show opened a little after Al Jolson married Ruby Keeler, he was there opening night and he sang 'Liza' to her. Tore it up.[1]

Ziegfeld's Show Girl *opened Tuesday 2 July at the Ziegfeld Theatre at 54th Street and Sixth Avenue but closed prematurely after 111 performances on Saturday 5 October 1929. Meanwhile, on 29 September 1929, Ellington opened* Blackberries, *his fifth successive Cotton Club revue.*

FREDDIE JENKINS: Though most people didn't know it then, Ruby Keeler was married to Al Jolson, and one night he dropped in to see the show. Of course they turned the spot on him right away and the applause was so loud that it stopped the show. Nick Lucas [one of the cast] was right in the middle of a solo but Jolson kept right on down the aisle and up on the stage and took over. Nick sure was embarrassed! For this show we were on stage during the whole performance, located on an elevator platform at the back, surrounded with a beautiful setting and there was a regular orchestra in the pit. On some numbers with the full cast on stage we couldn't hear the pit band or see the director and sometimes we'd finish a little early or a little late. So Sonny just pretended to play the drums in our band and the pit drummer played loud so we could catch the beat. And the way Sonny went through the motions was something to see.[2]

DUKE ELLINGTON: When Mrs Clinkscales came to New York, I was in Ziegfeld's *Show Girl*, and I came on and I could see her up in the balcony, up in the mezzanine, waving a handkerchief.[3]

FREDDIE JENKINS: We'd play a night show at the Ziegfeld, be back at the Cotton Club at eleven and play until four a.m. In

the recording studios at seven a.m. and record until noon. In the afternoon we were making movie shorts or doing a matinee at the Ziegfeld or rehearsing![4]

DUKE ELLINGTON: WV [Will Vodrey] got us the gig in Z [Ziegfeld's] *Show Girl* with Ruby Keeler and Jimmy Durante. Gershwin score. During the rehearsal there was an abrupt change in the music going from one key to another. WV picked up the parts one at a time and distributed a 12 tone chord (without) a score that was the most consonant 12 tone chord I have ever heard. Boss musician baby![5]

Ellington would later say he had 'valuable lessons in orchestration' from Vodrey.

FLO ZIEGFELD: It was probably foolish of me, after spending so much money on a large orchestra, to include a complete band in addition, but the Cotton Club Orchestra, under the direction of Duke Ellington, that plays in the cabaret scene, is the finest exponent of syncopated music in existence. Irving Berlin went mad about them, and some of the best exponents of modern music who have heard them during rehearsal almost jumped out of their seats with excitement over their extraordinary harmonies and exciting rhythms.[6]

SONNY GREER: Ziegfeld, he glamorized the American woman. We done a Ziegfeld show, next to last show, *Show Girl*, with Ruby Keeler. Next to last show he ever done. We were still at the Cotton Club, we were doubling. 'An American in Paris', from the Ziegfeld show, 'Liza' that all the bands played, was from that show. We played it. We were the first to play a Ziegfeld show. Never had no coloured band play it.[7]

DUKE ELLINGTON: In 1929 we made it a twelve-piece band, we brought Tizol up from Washington.[8]

Joe 'Tricky Sam' Nanton: By this time Tizol had almost put music aside. He was playing a valve trombone and nobody wanted a valve trombone and, too, he was a legit man.[9]

Duke Ellington: Whetsol was telling us about Tizol, 'Oh, you've got to have Tizol on the band.' All the time the payroll was going up! But we brought him in, still playing at the Cotton Club and doubling at Ziegfeld's *Show Girl*.[10]

Juan Tizol: One day the telephone rang and it was Duke Ellington asking me to come over and join the band, because that particular time he said, 'I need you in the band because I'm getting to go with the *Ziegfeld Follies*.' And in that show, called *Show Girl*, was Ruby Keeler and that comedian, Schnozzola – Jimmy Durante . . . When he got the show in the *Ziegfeld Follies*, then he knew he could afford to have me in the band . . . he knew about my reputation for reading and so forth. So I joined the band and we used to play in the Ziegfeld show at night, and after the show we would get in two taxicabs and run right over to the Cotton Club until three o'clock. We had two shows and he gave me $125 a week, which was a lot of money at that particular time.[11]

   Tizol had earlier played on some of Ellington's broadcasts from the Cotton Club, but joined the band permanently in July 1929 during Show Girl.

Barney Bigard: This guy was Duke's bodyguard. He'd go get Duke from the theatre with his machine gun between his legs, and they had bullet-proof glass. You see there were two factions. The big one in New York was Owney Madden and the other one was Capone. They were like that, you know, so they had to protect their men from each other. And brother, that was something. And poor Duke, he used to be so glad when that man would bring him back. I said, 'That's what you get for being so smart!'[12]

IRA GERSHWIN: There was much musical entertainment in *Show Girl*. Of the twenty-seven items we wrote, fourteen were used. Then there was the ballet in 'American in Paris', which opened the second set and ran at least fifteen minutes. Then there was a scene in which Duke Ellington and his band played a couple of numbers ... Everything considered, I wouldn't be surprised if *Show Girl* set a record for sparseness of dialogue in a musical.[13]

One reason, perhaps, that during its run it only averaged $35,000 a night in a theatre that could do $55,000. Featuring five principals, which was a first for a Broadway show, its overheads and costs were too high to break even.

MERCER ELLINGTON: The big thing I went to was the *Ziegfeld Follies*, when he played there. All I knew was this was something that had a tremendous effect. I didn't know why in those days, what the glory of being involved in a Ziegfeld production meant.[14]

In the second week of August 1929, Ellington and his band filmed and recorded Black and Tan *at RCA's Gramercy Studios in New York. Released on 29 October 1929, the film includes an elaborate presentation of 'Black and Tan Fantasy' with the Hall Johnson Choir as well as performances of 'The Duke Steps Out', 'Black Beauty', 'Cotton Club Stomp' and 'Flaming Youth' with dancing by the Five Hot Shots and the star Fredi Washington.*[15]

BILLBOARD: A short subject that is artistic, beautifully done, well played and will fit nicely into any programme.[16]

EVENING GRAPHIC: [Duke Ellington's] motion picture short *Black and Tan Fantasy* has attracted more attention from audiences and film critics than many feature pictures.[17]

EDNA ELLINGTON: Then came the big break-up. Ellington thought I should have been more understanding of him. I guess I've regretted it. I *know* I've regretted it. You see, I'm still hooked on Ellington. Why didn't we divorce after the break-up? I love Ellington and I'm going to stick my neck out and say I don't think he hates me. I was hurt, bad hurt when the break-up came, but I have never been bitter. Any young girl who plans to marry a man in public life – a man who belongs to the public – should try to understand as much about the demands of show business first and not be like I was. Above all, she should remember not to cook until she sees the whites of their eyes. They're never on time.[18]

MERCER ELLINGTON: The cause of my parents splitting had really been a torrid love affair Pop had with a very talented and beautiful woman, an actress. I think this was a genuine romance, that there was love on both sides, and that it amounted to one of the most serious relationships of his life.[19]

The actress was Fredi Washington (b. 23 December 1903), the beautiful star of Black and Tan. *In August 1933, trombonist Lawrence Brown would marry Washington, a marriage that would last until 1948. Ellington's affair with Washington was something Brown never managed to forgive Ellington for.*

LAWRENCE BROWN: Something happened between [Ellington] and his wife [Edna] and he's been terrible with women ever since. I mean, like he's always trying to make somebody's wife, because somebody made his wife and they got in such a fight, that slash he has on the side of his face, she cut him while he was sleeping, with a razor.[20]

BARNEY BIGARD: [Edna] cut him ... He was living on Seventh Avenue somewhere around there, in one of those apartment buildings ... that big scar on the side of his face? His wife did that to him ... But then I know she used to – I heard. I don't like to mention names but he was quite a figure in the music world. That's all I'll say, and a real gentleman. And I imagine Duke heard about it and got after her and they had a big argument and she waited till he went to sleep and slit him on the face with a razor blade.[21]

Quite what story is correct is impossible, of course, to verify, but certainly in the movie short Black *and* Tan, *a long scar running the length of Ellington's left cheek is plainly visible, particularly in the final scene.*

MERCER ELLINGTON: He probably hadn't come home for two or three days and he and mother got into a tremendous fight, in the course of which she got hold of this knife and slashed him across the face.[22]

BARNEY BIGARD: [Edna] was an evil ... Mildred was a cute little gal. She's cute. She was real nice. She used to dance with a fellow called Henri Wesson [at the Cotton Club]. She saved Duke. Duke used to gamble, you know, and sometimes he didn't have enough money to pay off the boys in the band and she'd give him her salary to pay off. And he treated her badly.[23]

Ellington appears to have broken with his wife Edna in 1929, moving in with Mildred Dixon at an apartment at 381 Edgecombe Avenue.

EDNA ELLINGTON: I didn't want a divorce and neither did he. We're proud of the way we get along. He has always provided for me through the years. I see Ellington sometimes. Whenever anything happens he'll call me or I'll call him. He'll open up when he gets angry. But Duke, and Mercer takes after him in this respect, is a lonely man. He masks his emotions. Never wants you to know how he actually feels. Ellington's music is nostalgic. The break-up helped Ellington in many ways, it challenged him to create.[24]

RUTH ELLINGTON: Duke wrote to my mother that he had rented a five-room apartment at 381 Edgecombe Avenue, and he would like us all to come to New York to live. Of course, he was the apple of [his mother's] eye, and the minute he said that she said, 'Of course, we'll just let Ruth finish up junior high school and the next day we'll go to New York!' Mercer was about ten, I was fourteen, about three and a half years the difference between us ... I remember my father was resisting, because he felt he was being put out to pasture at such a tender age of forty-nine! And the day we were moving all the furniture, he sat in the back room, closed himself off – we lived in one of those three-storey bay window brick houses, at 1212 T Street, North Washington, those with the lace curtains – and he closed himself in the smallest back room of the house and said, 'I'm not going to New York.' And the furniture was going out and we were packing and we *were* going to New York. We went on ahead, because we had to be registered in school almost the next day and he stayed on to dispose of the house.[25]

DUKE ELLINGTON: [By] 1930 I was beginning to make a bit of a reputation, my mother had been up to stay with me all summer and she liked it, she had asthma when she was in Washington, she used to suffer all summer, and she stayed with me in 1930. Nothing ever happened, never came back. I said you should stay up here. She stayed up here, never had asthma.[26]

RUTH ELLINGTON: Now, we all know since then asthma is an allergy that could be psychosomatic and maybe it was just the move to New York, I think in 1930, to live with Edward, that cured her of asthma. I don't know. We came to New York and she didn't have another attack of asthma. It stopped, she didn't have medication.[27]

RUTH ELLINGTON: We got to New York, everybody settled down, Mercer went to school, he was fifth grade, I went to Wadley High School, my mother immediately discharged the houseman that Duke had, because my mother said nobody was going to clean her house or cook! She had done it in a three-storey house in Washington and she certainly could handle a small five-room apartment, so she fired everybody and began to cook and clean herself, and Duke was as happy as he could be ... I remember when Duke used to go to the Cotton Club and he would come home three and four o'clock in the morning and I would be going to High School and sleeping in the room right next to him he would be playing the piano softly all night long, I would get up at eight o'clock in the morning to go to High School, he would still be up, because he had only come in two or three hours before and he would be composing softly on the piano.[28]

MERCER ELLINGTON: This is a man who came in at three or four o'clock in the morning and sat religiously at the piano and composed. At nine that's all I knew, listening to Duke Ellington writing and playing.[29]

RUTH ELLINGTON: He always came in and kissed us all and tucked us in – you'd wake up and feel him tucking you in, he was very very tender, very careful. He would go out and say kiddingly, 'Mother, I've come home to dine!' And she would pile his plate up with all this wonderful food. He loved to eat, rich, rich food, tremendous amounts of rich food. So, we had a very warm home life.[30]

MERCER ELLINGTON: In 1929 [*recte* 1930] we moved permanently to New York. Pop would send my mother an allowance and all that, and I would split my time. I would live in part of town with Pop and then I'd go and live in another part of town with my mother.[31]

RUTH ELLINGTON: [Mildred] lived with us too. My mother did not care for it at all. [Here's this man] who adored his mother, and who had this terrific complex, but what he tried to do, he roomed Mildred upstairs, but she just kept appearing, you know? Until finally she was kind of there. She was a dancer in the Cotton Club – posh. [She was in the picture] before we came to New York.[32]

MERCER ELLINGTON: Pop was always girl conscious and would have preferred a daughter. As a result my hair was kept long in braids so he would tolerate my presence.[33]

DUKE ELLINGTON: We played, while playing the Cotton Club ... Maurice Chevalier's first personal appearance in New York at the Fulton Theatre.[34]

*From 30 March to 14 April 1930, before their nightly appear-
ances at the Cotton Club, Ellington played a prestigious two weeks
at the Fulton Theatre at 46th Street, west of Broadway, with
Maurice Chevalier, then making his US debut.*

SONNY GREER: It was done through our manager Irving Mills's
connection. We played it. We played the first half of the show
on stage, just us. No women in the show. Us and the Berry
Brothers, that's a trio. In the second part, when he come on, we
played the pit. Man, I remember opening night, Maurice Chevalier, you know, he's a Frenchman didn't speak no English at
the time. Man, we opened for him, opened up the band and
tore them down. We were on the stand playing and this cat was
getting dressed to go, didn't have his pants on, just his shirt, he
tried to run on stage, so much commotion in the audience. We
were tearing them up, people screaming and hollering, he had
never heard that. They had to hold that cat, man. He laughed at
it when we saw him in Paris, when we went to Europe in 1933,
he laughed about it. But we played his American debut. That's
right! We had a lot of firsts.[35]

DUKE ELLINGTON: My first *real* conducting job was not at the
Cotton Club. It was when I picked up a baton when we were
playing the Maurice Chevalier personal appearance.[36]

HERALD TRIBUNE: One of the suavest and most agreeable entertainments in town, where Mr Dillingham presented Maurice
Chevalier for a fortnight's entertainment with Duke Ellington's
extraordinary orchestra – Mr Ellington's share in the entertainment is no inconsiderable one. Of all our band leaders he best
succeeds in making jazz seem an end in itself and not merely an
invitation to dance. The quality of his orchestration is exciting
and varied: his bandsmen unerring in their technique.[37]

MERCER ELLINGTON: The next big thing I saw involving Pop
was when he was the person and orchestra to play on the same

show as the initiation of Maurice Chevalier to New York. This was a phenomenal thing [for a black band].[38]

DUKE ELLINGTON: Good luck is about being at the right place at the right time doing the right thing before the right people. If the four points don't meet, forget it.[39]

DUKE ELLINGTON: We started doing theatres and neighbourhood houses, like the Audubon, the Bronx Crotona, the Broadway and the Brooklyn.[40]

DUKE ELLINGTON: When you played a stage show with a band in those days you were right behind the big vaudeville period, and of course nobody would use music racks on the stand, the pit orchestra would use music racks but to go up on the stage and use music was just too 'square' to be heard of, and so I found the simplest way to make guys memorize quickly was to just give them their notes aurally and we'd find that we'd have a rehearsal, and they run one number, and I would give each man a note until you'd get a phrase, no specific length, whatever was convenient for memory purpose, it might be a phrase of two bars, a phrase of four bars, or eight bars, with repeats and so forth and so on, and you'd give this man this note, this man this note and this man this note and we found by investing a couple of hours like that at night we could come in next morning and play it for a show. There was no problem, everybody knew their parts.[41]

FREDDIE JENKINS: [One] time we worked five hours on a passage using seven different relative keys. We didn't know what that was about at the time, but . . . it worked.[42]

DUKE ELLINGTON: We'd been playing a three day run at the 58th Street Theatre when along comes a guy and says we open at the Palace the following day. Situated at 46th Street and Broadway, the Palace was the big thing at the time.[43]

Ellington's excursion into the unfamiliar world of vaudeville at the Palace Theatre took place on 16–29 May 1930 (he had previously played one engagement there on 21 April 1929).

DUKE ELLINGTON: I'd known people working twenty years had never made the Palace. I was terrified and stiff and scared.[44]

DUKE ELLINGTON: I nearly had to get down on my knees to get the boys to play at all. They were too scared at first.[45]

BARNEY BIGARD: We were all set to open and we had on our new white ties and tails, but most of the guys were real nervous because this was such a biggie. There was just two shows a day and if the public liked what you did, and you got those first edition notices, then you would work fifty-two weeks of a year automatically. This being at stake, we were shivering with apprehension in the dressing room. We knew all the critics and Broadway 'big wigs' were out there.[46]

DUKE ELLINGTON: They told us it was necessary for me to M.C.! I didn't know the first thing about how to M.C. and the thought of it half scared me to death. Then we were on the stage.[47]

BARNEY BIGARD: We took the stand behind the curtain. Then they pulled the curtain and we like froze. Out came Duke and took his bow. He turned to us and waved his baton to get us to hit that great big chord that would start our show. Down came the baton ... nothing. Nobody moved or blew a note. Duke's eyes were blazing at us all but he turned and smiled sweetly to his audience just as if he were conducting a tea dance. He turned back to us, still smiling, and said in a loud voice, 'Play, you bastards!' We got through that first week somehow and I'll never know how, but we got good press.[48]

VARIETY: The hit of the show ... his standing among the coloured race in modern music is relative to that of the late Jim Europe.[49]

Originally booked for one week, Ellington was held over for a second.

RUTH ELLINGTON: Edward was extremely protective of me, but in such a wonderful, sweet, luxurious way that one doesn't know one is being protected. One loves riding around at sixteen with a mink coat but one doesn't know one is a prisoner, in effect.[50]

IRVING MILLS: I wanted Duke to do an Amos 'n' Andy picture. Bill LeBaron, who was head of RKO, he liked the black talent and every time he came to New York I took him to the Cotton Club, and they were doing a picture and I said, 'Gee, it would be nice to have Duke in that.'[51]

DUKE ELLINGTON: In 1930 we went to California to make a picture there, an Amos 'n' Andy picture, and in order to get out of my obligations to the Cotton Club, I had to pay Cab Calloway's band to work for us while we were gone, that was the beginning of Calloway's tremendous career.[52]

CAB CALLOWAY: Moe Gale booked us into a club called the Crazy Cat at the corner of 48th Street and Broadway. Man, we were back in the mainstream again. It wasn't a big club, but it catered to the Broadway after hours clientele, mainly white. We were the house band for dancing and a variety show ... We weren't in there a couple of weeks, though, when a peculiar thing happened. One night after our last show the headwaiter came over to me and said, 'Cab, there's some guys here who want to talk to you.' 'Who the hell are they?' I asked. 'I'm beat and I don't want to see no-one.' 'You better see them Cab.' So I walked across the room to a table in the corner. The club was empty by then and four guys were sitting there with their coats and hats on. I could tell from the look of them they were from the mob. Wide-brimmed hats, long cloth coats, one of them had shades. They were all white guys. I tried to be cool, but inside I was scared to death. 'Who's booking you?' one of them asked. 'Moe Gale.' 'Yeah? Well you tell Moe Gale that we want you and your band to come into the Cotton Club.' 'But Duke's in there.' 'He's going on the road to make a film and do a tour. We need a replacement and we want you. Be up at the club tomorrow afternoon to rehearse the show.' The Cotton Club mob had just bought out my contract and the Missourians' contract the easy way. Pure muscle.[53]

FREDDIE JENKINS: [Our] first trip out [to Hollywood] was for the Amos and Andy film *Check and Double Check*. They came up to the Cotton Club one night to see our show and Irving Mills made a deal with them. We played one nighters clear across the country and back on that trip. We had some real good scenes in that film. The big hit song in the show was 'Three Little Words', and we were in that scene. Incidentally, while we were out there we recorded that number with Bing Crosby and the Rhythm Boys – they were a lot of fun to work with.[54]

DUKE ELLINGTON: They wrote 'Three Little Words' for Sonny to sing, because he was a singing drummer in those days. We got to Hollywood, and he got mike fright, light fright, Hollywood fright and all sorts of funny things, and he said, 'Man, I can't sing, I'm not a singer, I'm a drummer,' and he was just scared to death. So we said, 'Well, tell you what we'll do, let's go over and get Bing.' So we went over to the Cocoanut Grove and got Bing and he made the track. The next day the director heard the record – the track – and he says, 'This guy can't sing a note by himself,' he says, 'Go get the three of them.' So then we went back and got the three guys and brought them back over there, and they made the track – The Rhythm Boys made the track – and they photographed it as our three trumpet players singing [for the film].[55]

Ellington recorded 'Three Little Words' in Hollywood for RCA Victor, first with a vocal by Jimmy Miller and again with Emmanuel Hall's Quintet, on 20 August 1930, but the results were rejected. Just under a week later, on 26 August, came the version with the Rhythm Boys (Bing Crosby, Al Rinker and Harry Barris), released three months later. For the film Check and Double Check, *the song had a brief run through during the ballroom sequence, and although the on-screen visuals show the trumpet section singing the lyrics through megaphones, it was the Rhythm Boys who provided the vocals for the film soundtrack.*

SONNY GREER: We stayed in California making pictures about three months, Man, we had a whole dressing room, place – a stage, where we rehearse for the picture. Them actors got a break where we were playing. They would come over and say, 'Sonny, play – Duke, play your original compositions.' We would. We would have a jam session every time we got a break, the place was full of guests and visitors, and they stayed so long and the man had to come there and say, 'Stop playing so them actors can get back over here on the set and do their thing.'[56]

JUAN TIZOL: They make me and Barney [Bigard] a lot darker and they gave us the cold cream and so forth, when we were through, to go there and wash it off and take all that stuff off. Oh, it was awful.[57]

Ellington spent the final days of July, all of August and the first couple of days of September 1930 on the RKO set filming Check and Double Check. *On 6 September the band was back in New York, before going out on tour.*

RUTH ELLINGTON: We would go to the Paramount Theatre and sit there and applaud and after a couple of thousand people finish applauding, my mother was still applauding![58]

The New York premiere of Check and Double Check *was on 31 October 1930.*

FREDDIE JENKINS: Duke developed his own technique and styles mainly by utilizing the band. He used to set us on the stand and pay us union scale, maybe for four or five hours, just to help him formulate chords. He'd assign different notes to every instrument and say, 'Play that, B–a–a–m!' and it might produce a big C13th, what we call a Christmas chord. Then he'd take those same notes and switch them to different instruments and while you'd still have a big C13th, it would sure sound a lot different. Sometimes he'd do that three or four times until he found the combination he wanted. One thing among many he discovered was that if you get sounds pitched very close together they would produce a mike-tone. Like a trumpet, upper register trombone and lower register clarinet would produce a mike-tone that would sound almost like a fourth instrument.[59]

DUKE ELLINGTON: What we actually attempted to do at that time, the two instruments we were using with the mutes and plungers, when we used that combination in 'Black and Tan Fantasy' we had a lot of trouble with mike, and in spite of the fact we made many good takes they kept throwing them out, because of the mike-tone, so I figured if I put a low clarinet down at the bottom, it would centralize that mike-tone and I think that's what happened. And so then we did 'Mood Indigo' with the clarinet at the bottom, and the mike-tone centred it simply, somewhere or other – it's a tone that's not there, it's an illusion of a tone, this is how this came about.[60]

That unique 'mike-tone' was a feature of 'Mood Indigo', first recorded 14 October 1930 on the Okeh label with a small band and recorded twice more during the month for Brunswick and again for Okeh.

DUKE ELLINGTON: [Originally] we had a small-band record date one afternoon for Okeh Records, and we made a thing

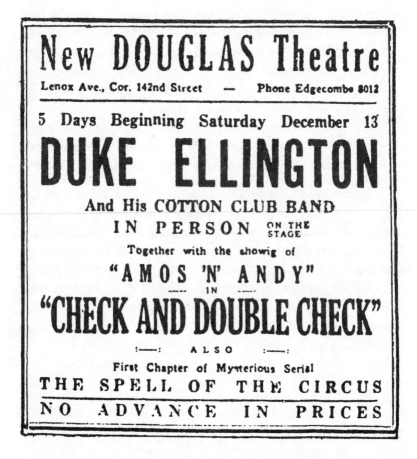

called 'Dreamy Blues', I wanted to call it 'Mood Indigo', but Irving said that wasn't commercial enough! We'll call it 'Dreamy Blues'. That night we came [to broadcast] and Ted Husing was announcing, he says, 'Duke, what you got tonight? What you gonna put in here? Let's play something new tonight.' I said, 'OK. I just recorded a thing today called "Mood Indigo".' And so we played it and next day we were swamped with mail about it, and so that's how it kept its name, 'Mood Indigo'.[61]

DUKE ELLINGTON: This was our first big hit.[62]

DUKE ELLINGTON: We were the first band around the Paramount Publix circuit, that started a whole new thing. All these bands came up behind us.[63]

DUKE ELLINGTON: We went to Chicago about this time to play the Paramount circuit and they [Mills] wanted us to have a girl singer. It was a toss-up whether it should be Ivie Anderson or Mae Alix. They both being good singers, it didn't make any difference, but Ivie got the job.[64]

Ellington opened a tour of the Balaban & Katz movie theatre circuit (Paramount Publix Theatres) at the Metropolitan Theatre, Boston, on 6–12 February 1931, followed by a week at the Chicago Oriental, opening on Friday 13 February 1931.

SONNY GREER: Irving Mills says, 'We should have a female vocalist for this engagement.' And Mae Alix was real fair, real fair, but she had been in New York and we used to go and see her at the cabaret, so Irving Mills – he liked Mae Alix because she was hell of an entertainer – so he asked Duke and he asked me, he say I can get Mae Alix for you, so we say all right. So we lived in a hotel right next door to the Grand Terrace in Chicago, so I'm a cabaret man and I went next door and [Ivie Anderson] was in a show there, and Fatha Hines had the band there. I saw this girl, a cute brown-skinned girl. Really something, so the

Duke say, 'What do you think? What do you think of her?' I say, 'Man, that's the girl.' Now we are going to play these days. Mae Alix looks too white. I say, 'You don't want somebody that look like a white girl in front of the band,' I say, 'Look at this girl!' So sure enough, he like her and say, 'Yeah, I think you're right.' So the next day we open at this theatre in Chicago [with her].[65]

SONNY GREER: In the meantime at the Cotton Club, I used to do a lot of talking back to Ethel Waters. She was in the show at the Cotton Club. She used to sing different songs and I would do a lot of ad-lib conversation with her and it was a terrific hit, you know, so we went down and did the first show with Ivie and she got a nice sympathetic hand, nothing spontaneous. So she came off and she was crying and Irving Mills, he was very understanding. So when I come off stage, he say, 'Sonny, why don't you talk back to her like you used to do with Ethel Waters at the Cotton Club? The next show, I think this would be fine, but I don't tell her because it would look like it was rehearsed. Just make the ad-lib. Just say anything.' So the second show when she come out, she was singing a song, I recall, real good, 'I'm a Little Blackbird Looking for a Bluebird Too', that was the opening number. She came out there and she sing 'I'm a Little Blackbird Looking for a Bluebird Too', and in the back of all them drums I raised up and say, 'Don't look no further, baby, I'm right here!' And the house caved. It shocked her so much she almost forgot the lyrics, so the house caved in and from then on she never looked back. Standing ovation. You know, each show was different. I never said the same thing twice. It wasn't no set routine. I said anything that come into my mind, you know to fit the thing. And she was so surprised, Irving Mills was surprised and it was a feature, the people ate it up, and from then on we were like ham and eggs, Ivie and I.[66]

DUKE ELLINGTON: We opened the Oriental Theatre in Chicago, and broke all records there, and we played there I think two weeks and then we played the uptown Paradise, and then we came back to the Oriental and broke that record again. And she became a part of the organization, we liked her, we added her to the band, that was before Mildred Bailey went with Whiteman – that was another of those firsts.[67]

At the end of a four-week tour of B&K Theatres, Ellington invited Anderson to become the band's regular vocalist. An immense asset to the band in public performances, she remained until 1942.

REX STEWART: Ivie fit Duke's band to perfection, so much so that her spot has never been filled adequately by anyone else in my opinion. Sonny Greer, who was Ivie's stage partner, was one of the wittiest impromptu jesters in music. Together, Ivie and Sonny were a great team.[68]

IVIE ANDERSON: When I first started out with Duke I used to wear coloured dresses. When he suggested I wear only white, I tried it out and found it so effective that I've been doing it ever since. And for another thing, Duke helped me tremendously in moulding my style of singing. When I joined him I was just an ordinary singer of popular songs. Duke suggested I find a 'character' and maintain it. What's more he's a leader who believes in taking a lot of time and trouble for his singer. He's always supplied me with ideal accompaniment ... the first one I sang was 'Minnie the Moocher', when the boys in the band worked out the idea of talking back to me while I was singing.[69]

DUKE ELLINGTON: That summer we played out at the Lincoln Tavern, and 'Don't Mean a Thing If It Ain't Got That Swing', wrote that out there.[70]

IRVING MILLS: We were booked into a café in Chicago, and of course everybody wanted to come because they were crazy about the Ellington band, they had heard it on radio, and they heard

the records but had never seen him in person. But before that I had taken six weeks away from the Cotton Club to play in the [movie] theatres. And when you play in the theatres, four or five shows a day, you get very 'stagey'. You start playing for an audience and you don't see any dancing in front of you, like you do in a café, so when we opened in this café we noticed the people were not dancing properly, and they were all looking at the band and were out of step. Something wrong with the band, they were playing the kind of music that they were playing in the theatres for the six weeks, the tempo wasn't there, I missed it and I was very annoyed, I couldn't wait until that set was over so I can get back to Duke and tell him that he's got to think more of the rhythm on account of what's happening on the floor. I said, 'Duke, it don't mean a thing if it ain't got that swing, the people aren't dancing properly, they're all out of step there, you're playing more for stage than you are for dancing.' And he said, 'What did you say?' 'It don't mean a thing if it ain't got that swing!' He said, 'That's a good idea.' He had a good sense of humour, Duke, and he said, 'Go on, continue, that.' And the first thing you know he had a melody all ready for it. 'It Don't Mean A Thing If It Ain't Got That Swing', it talked for itself. So Ivie Anderson said to write it out, so I made up a chorus, I made it up right there. Then the boys gave it the rhythm now, and they realized they had to get back into the tempo like the Cotton Club, and it didn't take long, after two or three sets they were back in the groove again.[71]

The Ellington band left the Cotton Club 6 February 1931 for an extended tour of theatres heralded by a full page ad in Variety *on 28 January. Beginning with the tour of the Paramount Publix circuit, theatre engagements dominated their itinerary until the Lincoln Tavern booking in Chicago from 12 July–13 August, where Ellington played for dancers. 'It Don't Mean a Thing (If It Ain't Got That Swing)' was subsequently recorded in New York, 2 February 1932.*

DUKE ELLINGTON: Every once in a while, you'll notice that I drop out of vaudeville for a week or a few weeks and play dance engagements. That wakes up the boys and they get back into form. When they see people moving around the floor, they've got to put snap and ginger into their work.[72]

IRVING MILLS: We had no problem with bookings. But we always saw to it that they had the right publicity, that they were well behaved, that nobody fooled around with any whites – at those times it was dangerous, you know? And of course Fletcher Henderson had that reputation, and he got mixed up in Chicago. So [James] Petrillo [the Musicians' Union boss in Chicago] thought that I booked him in there, at the time, and I had nothing to do with that. And he didn't want any more black bands in Chicago. He told me off, on that thing.[73]

SONNY GREER: I'm the last one off the stage because I had all the equipment, I had to check to see all that. So I come off and standing in Duke's dressing room was two big cats. I come off, I'm going in the room. And one guy, he stopped me, 'You can't go in there, Mr Petrillo's in there, you can't go in.' So I brushed past him and went in. So this cat Petrillo was standing up there, man, and these guys were his bodyguards. He was standing up there, talking to Duke, pointing his finger, 'You can't do this, you can't do that.' So I say to Duke, 'What's the matter, man?' He say, 'This guy's trying to give me a hard time.' They don't know Owney Madden is our boss. I say, 'Get on the phone, call this number.' We had to get a private number. So Petrillo say, 'Who are you calling?' I say, 'The man who owns our band.' And he knew, he knew the number. So Owney answered; said, 'Put him on.' What he said – no more trouble.[74]

IRVING MILLS: We wanted Duke to be recognized as someone more important, and of course I was criticized by a lot of people, they looked down on me because I was a jazz fiend, and so we encouraged him to write more serious works, and little by little he started to get a lot better, bigger arrangements and tunes made.[75]

Creole Rhapsody Parts 1 & 2 *was recorded on 11 June 1931.*

WASHINGTON, D.C. NEWS: DUKE ELLINGTON MEETS HOOVER – Duke Ellington, America's coloured King of Jazz, called to meet President Hoover [yesterday].[76]

According to the press, Ellington was presented to President Hoover on 1 October 1931, but Hoover's private papers cast doubt on whether this meeting took place.[77] Accompanying Ellington on his visit to the White House were Mrs E. F. McCarroll, Elrita Skinner, Mrs Eloise Skinner, Rev. J. C. Olden, J. A. G. Lavalle and James Mills.

DUKE ELLINGTON: By 1931 [Bing] was the biggest thing, ever. [We made 'St Louis Blues' together] in 1932, about three o'clock in the morning, up at 1776 Broadway, Brunswick Records.[78]

LAWRENCE BROWN: Irving Mills hired me, when Duke was appearing at the Orpheum Theatre. The first time I saw [Duke] was the next day, which was Wednesday, I went down. And he says, 'I never knew you,' Duke says, 'I never knew you, I never met you, I never heard you. But Irving says get you, so that's that.' So well, 'How much you paying?' So I started with Duke Ellington for $70 a week. Of course, that was the beginning of many, many surprises. The first one was that I didn't know – I thought when you joined a band of that calibre, you made your salary plus expenses, plus you made it every week, work or play. I didn't know that you made that $70 the days you worked, and only got paid for – like if you worked three days, you got three-sevenths. And all the expenses were on you. I didn't know that, so that started my real, real life.[79]

Between 11 March and 1 April 1932 Ellington played the Los Angeles Orpheum. Brown, who at the time had been playing Frank

*Sebastian's Culver City Cotton Club, brought Ellington's trombone
section up to three.*

DUKE ELLINGTON: Lawrence Brown was playing out in Culver
City at the Cotton Club, Frank Sebastian's joint, he had been
with Les Hite; Hampton, Lionel Hampton was in that band,
Marshal Royal too. [Lawrence] was a crooner, a trombone
crooner. That's what he used to do out there. He used to walk
around the tables and play tunes, requests, he knew everything.[80]

MERCER ELLINGTON: Lawrence Brown was formally and highly
educated.[81]

LAWRENCE BROWN: When I came from the coast, we went to
Hartford, Connecticut, where we rehearsed. I didn't play with
the band up there. I didn't play with the band at first because I
was the thirteenth man. And there was so much – what do you
call it – superstition, that, oh, no, not thirteen men. Had to wait
for the fourteenth man. And the fourteenth man was Otto
Hardwick, and at the time he was working somewhere in
Washington, doing something and didn't come until later. So
my first actual date of playing was at a theatre, and of all the
numbers I was playing this solo on 'Trees'.[82]

*Otto Hardwick returned to the reed section for a series of one-
nighters beginning 23 May 1932 in Nuttings-on-the-Charles, Wal-
tham, Mass. Since returning from Paris in 1929, he joined Chick
Webb's band before forming his own group to play the Hot Feet
Club in Greenwich Village, and we have Hardwick's uncorrobor-
ated assertion that this band defeated Ellington's group in a battle
of music. He rejoined Ellington after a short stint in Elmer
Snowden's band.*

OTTO HARDWICK: When I rejoined the band it was just like I'd
never left. Except this way, maybe. It wasn't *our* thing any
longer. It had become Ellington's alone.[83]

DUKE ELLINGTON: You take Lawrence Brown, he's a guy who's very staid, a little stuffy really, and he plays all kinds of music. Low gut-bucket music and he plays pretty too, but the little he has to say personally in his conversation – he is agreeable conversationally and all that – he is not what you would say is a guy who has a lot to say, but he has a lot to play.[84]

LAWRENCE BROWN: There were no third trombone parts, so I had to sort of compose my own parts. Then as the new numbers came out they started arranging for third trombone. All bands at that time were most ear bands. Whatever you heard you'd pick up a place to fit in, a part to fit in. Whatever you heard was missing, that's where you were.[85]

LAWRENCE BROWN: The first recording [with Duke] I made was 'The Sheik' in New York. They sort of considered me a new addition, a new funny sound, so I was soloing from the beginning almost.[86]
Brown's solo on 'The Sheik of Araby', recorded 16 May 1932, was widely admired by musicians at the time.

JOHNNY HODGES: 'The Sheik of Araby' made in 1932, on which I played soprano. Bechet taught the band that. He played that for us, and Tizol put it down.[87]

DUKE ELLINGTON: We stayed at the Cotton Club alternating with Calloway, six months in, six months out.[88]

BARNEY BIGARD: Calloway used to fill the place when we'd go on the road from the Cotton Club and there was a manager there called Herman Stark. The day of the opening of the new show, Calloway was betting him that we wouldn't be able to open the show because the music wasn't complete. So Stark says, 'Don't you worry.' He says, 'It'll open and it'll be complete by that time.' So Calloway said, 'No, I bet you.' So they made a wager. And sure enough Duke – we rehearsed that evening and

Duke wasn't writing anything down. He'd get on the piano and whatever rhythm he wanted he'd give you the rhythm, then he'd give each individual musician his notes. Now, you had to memorize that, you see. And when he'd given everybody their note, then they would start playing it with the rhythm that he wanted, and it came out beautiful. But nobody knew that, the people. If somebody didn't [memorize it], why, he used to write it down on an empty sheet of music that wasn't anything on it. And he'd just put it in front of them. You know, play it two or three times, well, you knew it. So Calloway says, 'I should go shoot myself. That man is phenomenal. He's something else.' So Stark says, 'I told you.' He said, 'I never worry about him at all.'[89]

FREDDIE JENKINS: I think that was because everyone in the band was endowed with so much natural talent. We didn't have to pray over anything and write it out. Duke would just set down a background to give us the chord level and the general idea and that only took about ten minutes. Then Johnny Hodges, or someone, would start some figure like ba–da–ta–ta–ta–ta–ta–ba–da and bing, that was it. Everyone would hear his own part in his own ear and we'd set it up and do it that way.[90]

NED E. WILLIAMS: Then there was that night at the Cotton Club when the entire brass section of the Ellington band arose and delivered such an intricate and unbelievably integrated chorus that the late Eddie Duchin, usually a poised and dignified musician, literally rolled on the floor under his table in ecstasy.[91]

IRVING MILLS: I kept changing from show to show the different talent and the different songwriters, and it gave me an excuse for new records for Duke Ellington to record and to have new songs all the time.[92]

MERCER ELLINGTON: The demand was so great and the amount of arrangements that had to be provided for each show, you know. They changed each production, I'd say on the average of every six months, and new materials had to be gotten, new songs written for it.[93]

RUTH ELLINGTON: Every time there was a new show [at the Cotton Club], the whole family was allowed to go one of the nights to see the new show. It was really glamorous, even though the inside decor was that of a log cabin, when you got inside and saw all the girls, bangles and feathers and beads, all these beautiful girls and they put a gold light on so they all appeared to be gold in colour. It was incredible. I've never seen anything like it, ever.[94]

MERCER ELLINGTON: The great service they had there. I remember the rum punch with all the cherries in them, I had never seen that done before.[95]

BARNEY BIGARD: This is at the Cotton Club and this gangster did time for one of the big bosses there. And, oh, he's a big rugged Irishman. Bad, real bad. So he came in there and the day they brought him to the Cotton Club they'd got him a big Lincoln limousine, bought him that, gave him money, and got him a beautiful blonde gal. So he came in there – so he dances like them old Bowery boys, you know. Real stiff and everything. So he gets around to the piano and said, 'Hey, fella, will you play "Singing In The Rain?"' Duke, 'Yeah, that's "Singing In The Rain".' Another set come on, no 'Singing In The Rain'. The third set come on, he comes around there and he grabbed Duke by the neck, 'I asked you to play "Singing In The Rain" God damn it!' So Herman Stark, the manager, had to run up and grab this guy and talk to him away from Duke. And Herman Stark came back and said, 'Duke, are you crazy?' He said, 'He asked me for "Singing In The Rain". I'm going to play it.' He said, 'Yeah, you're going to play it. When?' He said, 'Pretty soon, yeah.' He said, 'Do you know that guy?' He said, 'He just did a stretch for Frenchy for killing . . .' Duke said, 'Huh?' 'For killing, for killing!' 'He did?' We played 'Singing In The Rain' for an hour![96]

MERCER ELLINGTON: Stravinsky used to come by and sit and listen to the band from time to time in the Cotton Club days. They got to know each other pretty well. And Orson Welles used to sit on the bandstand and write his scenarios. He used to like to sit right in the brass section and write while the band was playing. Nobody ever knew he was there, you know. He'd be sittin' there in between the two rows between the trumpets and trombones.[97]

LAWRENCE BROWN: Oh, Sonny Greer, the personality kid of the band. The drummer – very flashy! He had the most beautiful sets of drums in the business when I joined in 1932. And he took great pride in polishing them and keeping them. He had a complete set including timpanis and vibraphones and all kinds of drums and cymbals. He really dressed up the band with his outfit, in the centre, way up high.[98]

IRVING MILLS: You had to have a showpiece when you got to the theatres. Big drum sets because everything was elevated and the drum set was on top and it had to be as wide as the stage there. And I remember buying the first drum set, I had never seen so many drums and equipment with bells and everything. We finally wrote a song called 'Ring Them Bells'.[99]
   'Ring Dem Bells' was recorded twice in 1930.

SONNY GREER: I used a lot of equipment – tymps, bells, chimes in addition to the drum set and cymbals – during my years with Duke. When the curtain broke in a theatre, you really saw a conglomeration of class! Yet that wasn't the point of it; I wanted to create all kinds of sounds and give Ellington's music what I felt it needed. I always dug colour.[100]

IRVING MILLS: I went into hock with the drummer, to get the best drum set. I didn't have any money.[101]

In later years Greer would act as consultant to the Leedy Drum Co, and receive his instruments free.

LAWRENCE BROWN: Always jovial, a member that perfectly fit the organization. [Sonny] could remember names from years before and would surprise any number of people when they'd come up and he'd call their name right off.[102]

ROGER PRYOR DODGE: The last time I saw Bubber Miley was at the Lafayette Theatre in Harlem ... Backed by Irving Mills, Bubber was enabled to build his own orchestra. He secured the services of Gene Anderson, piano, and Zutty Singleton, drums. The band was placed in a show called *Harlem Scandals*. They opened at the Lincoln Theatre in Philadelphia and subsequently played at the Lafayette. But in Philadelphia Bubber had been running a high fever and at the Lafayette he was obviously an ill man ... Aside from an engaging solo on a piece called 'Angel' he seemed to have lost his original force and vitality. It wasn't long after this I got a letter from his mother, telling me he was sick. I went to see him. He had dwindled to 76 pounds – a little shrivelled old man. This seems hardly believable, but on entering his mother's cold-water flat I asked this little huddled old man if I might see Bubber! It seems as if he had tuberculosis for some time. Later I got another letter telling me to come to Bellevue. Now he was James Miley and only his relatives remembered him. His mother told me he was to be taken to Welfare Island. I missed the visitor's hour when I went to see him there, and a few days later was shocked to hear he was dead. He was 29 years old. My wife and I went to his funeral. It was held in what looked more like a white-washed shack than anything else. Apparently there were no musicians there although there was a large wreath of flowers from Duke Ellington. The mourners were out of his mother's tenement life. Was this the funeral of one of the greatest artists of our time?[103]

Bubber Miley died 20 May 1932.

EVENING GRAPHIC: REMINISCING WITH DUKE ELLINGTON – If you should ask [Duke], Paul Whiteman is his favourite musician.[104]

LAWRENCE BROWN: ['Sophisticated Lady'], that's one of those everybody jumps in and helps out, but mainly I had the theme which I played all the time which is the first eight bars. And Otto Hardwick played the release and I went back to the first eight bars. That was the basic tune of 'Sophisticated Lady', see no-one knows what's going to happen. You never know when you have a coming number on your hands. We were just doing something we wanted to do.[105]

One of Ellington's most famous numbers, 'Sophisticated Lady' was first recorded 15 February 1933. The composer credits originally showed Ellington, Hardwick, Brown and Mills.

OTTO HARDWICK: ['Sophisticated Lady'] – me and Lawrence Brown. We used to call ourselves 'the co-writers'.[106]

BARNEY BIGARD: That's the only thing I didn't like about Duke. He never gave the boys in the band the credit they deserved. Like Otto Hardwick and Lawrence Brown wrote 'Sophisticated Lady' but their names are not on it. It wouldn't cost him nothing to credit them – he was a genius.[107]

DUKE ELLINGTON: The last show we played [at the Cotton Club] was with Ethel Waters. Then we played the Capitol Theatre (we'd played the Paramount in 1930–31) ... Around this time, you get yourself geared up to go out on the road.[108]

The 22nd Cotton Club Revue opened 16 April 1933 where Ellington remained until the end of May. Ethel Waters had a huge hit in the revue singing 'Stormy Weather', described by

Variety *as 'the biggest song hit in the last ten years'.*

JUAN TIZOL: The time Ethel Waters opened at the Cotton Club, he did the music for the whole show, he wrote the music, and I did all the extractions. He'd do the score and I'd take it home or go to his house with him.[109]

REX STEWART: [Tizol] was truly an important cog in the Duke's wheel, because he did all the extractions of Duke's voluminous writing efforts. This was no easy chore, as oft times Duke would attempt to write things that couldn't be written! Then Juan would scribble a facsimile and spend hours interpreting what the boss intended.[110]

JUAN TIZOL: He used to have a system that in the Cotton Club after we got through, we both go to Duke Ellington's house and while he was writing I would start extracting for the whole band. Like writing on one staff, he'd write for the four saxophones and three trumpets and three trombones and I got to go there and I would extract them and transpose the whole thing for the band. And I would stay there sometimes until, oh gosh, eight or nine o'clock in the morning writing.[111]

A thoroughly schooled musician, Tizol acted as Ellington's music copyist throughout his tenure with the band. Even in the '60s, after he had left Ellington, he was called upon to assist on Ellington's score for the 1966 film Assault on a Queen.

NED E. WILLIAMS: Then there was that unforgettable night when Ethel Waters stood in the spotlight, with the Ellington band pulsating behind her, and sang, for the first time in public, a song by Harold Arlen and Ted Koehler called 'Stormy Weather'.[112]

IRVING MILLS: I needed a big number for Ethel Waters, she can't go out and sing anything, she's got to have a big [feature]. So we wind up with 'Stormy Weather'.[113]

SONNY GREER: Ethel Waters ... very hard to get along with. She was going with Eddie Mallory then. She didn't take no back-talk off nobody. I got along with her good because when she started to get tight with me, I would dummy up and say nothing. You had to know how to handle her and stay a little ahead of her. And she sang 'Stormy Weather' like nobody. But Ivie could sing it like her. I don't know who sang it the best, her or Ivie. Ivie picked it up and sang it [with the band]. Beautiful. But every time she sang it, it rained![114]

One reason why Greer might have found Waters 'very hard to get along with' was her bisexuality. Although well known, even notorious in her day, he refrains from commenting on this although her rival Alberta Hunter was more forthcoming, making a pointed allusion to Waters' self-destructive, rude and lesbian side (although without acknowledging she herself was gay) in Alberta Hunter: A Celebration in Blues.[115]

DUKE ELLINGTON: At first I was happy. There were lots of pretty women and champagne and plenty of money ... [But then] I'd see people writing little pop numbers that were going over big. I didn't see why I should try and do something good. I thought I'd stop writing. Music publishers would come around with little tunes and say, 'If you put your name on it, we'll make it our Number One plug.' If something bad was plugged, it would go over better than something good that wasn't. I felt it was all a racket. I was on the point of giving up.[116]

CHAPTER FIVE

THE DUKE STEPS OUT

After leaving the Cotton Club in early 1931, Ellington capitalized on the national popularity his regular radio broadcasts had brought him by extensive touring. In those pre-television days, exposure on the radio – which by 1930 was a fixture in over one third of American homes – brought enormous publicity.

As the decade progressed, it became the norm for bandleaders to play at a loss at venues with a radio wire in the sure knowledge that their asking price would rocket when they went out on the road, and any losses they had incurred could be quickly turned around into big profits. During 1931, for example, Ellington played the huge 3,200-seat Oriental Theatre in Chicago five times, grossing almost $50,000 a week and beating all previous box office records. Equally his exposure in a Ziegfeld production, and his role in Maurice Chevalier's successful American debut, represented unprecedented recognition for a black band within a white entertainment infrastructure, bringing him enormous prestige. Forty years later, Ellington still spoke of these achievements with great pride in interviews. Equally, his extended run at the Palace Theatre was another event whose lustre seems to have been dulled by the passage of time, but whose importance cannot be overstated as Ellington's career gathered momentum.

Ellington's popularity, underlined by his suave appearances in motion pictures and concert-style appearances in movie houses across America, was reinforced by an end-of-year readers' poll to find the most popular band, conducted by the Pittsburgh Courier *in 1931.*[1] *Ellington won by a substantial margin.*

By now, Ellington's standing had become something akin to that of a pop star, and even though he was unable to command the same money as top white bands, he was nevertheless described by the Evening Graphic *in 1932 as 'one of the outstanding stage attractions in the country'.*[2] *Yet that same publication pointed out that Ellington was unable to secure a radio sponsor, white business not caring to associate themselves with a black band, however successful it might be. Even so, by early 1933, forty-five radio stations across America were broadcasting Ellington's live performances without sponsorship.*

On 9 March 1933, Ellington had returned to the Cotton Club for one of the most successful revues they ever mounted, Cotton Club Parade, *starring the singer Ethel Waters. It represented another triumph for Ellington, who recorded the big hit from the show, Harold Arlen's 'Stormy Weather', with an Ivie Anderson vocal, and followed it up with a movie short (shades of today's music marketing with a record release supported by a video). Yet despite the success of the record, Ellington had become disenchanted with the music business, even entertaining dark thoughts of abandoning his career. But on 2 June 1933 he boarded the S.S.* Olympic *bound for Southampton, and although he didn't know it at the time, his self-esteem was about to receive a boost that would sustain him through the ups and downs of the '30s and beyond.*

DUKE ELLINGTON: I shall never forget [1933]. We were just finishing a very successful three months run at the Cotton Club when we heard the European bookings were set. That was the year of 'Sophisticated Lady' and the big hit, 'Stormy Weather'. We sailed on the *Olympic* directly following a record breaking week at the Capitol Theatre. John Hammond came to see us off with bon voyage presents: phonograph, camera, records – all very good, nothing but the best, just like the man who gave them to me.[3]

After playing the Capitol Theatre from 26 May to 1 June 1933, Duke Ellington and his Famous Orchestra sailed for England on 2 June aboard the S.S. Olympic, *seen off at the quayside by the Mills Blue Rhythm Band playing 'Stormy Weather'.*

IRVING MILLS: Well, we got on the boat, and it was during the Economic Conference that England gave every four years where all the heads of all the colonies of England came to London. A lot of them were on the boat at that time. I didn't know too much of what was going on, but we were requested to give a concert on the boat, which we did.[4]

MELODY MAKER: As this issue of *The Melody Maker* is published, Duke Ellington and his orchestra are on board the *Olympic* en route for England, and in a few days time will be commencing a flying tour of the country with a debut at the London Palladium. Ever since Jack Hylton took courage in his hands and backed his belief in the Ellington proposition to the tune of an enormous guarantee, musicians, fans and the general public have gone Ellington mad.[5]

Hylton's personal guarantee was £40,000.

DUKE ELLINGTON: We were met at Southampton by Jack Hylton. There was a lot of photographing and then on to London on the train. And the train is where I got my first taste of gin and tonic. It was a terrible thing. I had never acquired a taste for that. Then off the train in London.[6]

BARNEY BIGARD: The most impressive thing I ever remember is when we were getting off the train in London and all the people turned up at the station. As we stepped off the train they were calling everybody by their names: 'Here's Barney, here's Hodges, here's Cootie, here's Tricky Sam.' They recognized everyone. That was a surprise to me.[7]

DUKE ELLINGTON: Out of the station to the hotel – the Dorchester House – where I very hurriedly made a quick change and over to Jack Hylton's for a cocktail party. There I met all the principals in all the lines that were in any way associated with what we were doing: critics, columnists, musicians, heavy conductors. There was an editor from the *Daily Express* (Tommy Driberg) and I hardly had a chance to get my first cocktail down. I hardly had a chance to get seated, when he asked me this question: 'What is hot?' I told him something about a tree, a long drawn out thing. It was too early in my trip to England to give him anything definite so that I gave him something drawn out like: 'Hot is a part of music, like a root is part of a tree, and the twigs and the leaves and the trunk. Hot is to music as a root, a trunk, a leaf is to a tree.' Hot at the moment was really the blossom or the fruit, because it had no real – what was hot to one person wasn't hot to someone else. I was kidded about Tommy Driberg's editorial in Lord Beaverbrook's paper, the *Daily Express*, saying I was a good sample of somebody to send to the House of Commons to represent the colonies. Why in England, 'Mood Indigo' was hot.[8]

OTTO HARDWICK: The records were being played over there and we didn't know anything about it. We were popular over there before we even had the slightest idea.[9]

THE PEOPLE: LIES . . . Oh, and all the stories of Duke Ellington being thrown out of hotels are lies. His rooms were booked at the Dorchester two days before he arrived. He is occupying a suite there.[10]

DUKE ELLINGTON: The hotel we stayed at was too overserviced – it took them from four o'clock in the morning until seven o'clock that evening to find out I had moved out of my room . . . We went into the hotel in the morning and they didn't have a suite like we wanted so we took these separate rooms. I sat up until quite late until the suite was available and then I went there and went to bed. So they still had me registered in the other room.[11]

NEWS OF THE WORLD: So much has been written and said of Duke Ellington and his Negro band, which will make its first appearance in England at the Palladium tomorrow, that considerable interest has been aroused by its engagement to play in London.[12]

DUKE ELLINGTON: Then we opened at the Palladium. The first show was at seven o'clock – actors don't work in the daytime in England – that's really living, you have all day to get high and then the night to make your living. I came into the first show in time to make the bow! The show was a great success. They not only applauded loudly; I thought they would do like they do in America – you know, after you step to the microphone and thank them kindly, it dies down in a minute – but here it went on for about five or ten minutes – I didn't know what to do – I'm scared to death every time I've ever walked onto a stage anyway, I'm no showman at all. But I stumbled through something. That enthusiastic audience had everybody scared to death.[13]

JUAN TIZOL: Oh! You've got to be nervous with those kind of people out there. They are expecting so much from you and when we first started and opened the curtain and announced Duke Ellington, the applause lasted so long, you know it's gonna shake you up.[14]

DUKE ELLINGTON: Ivie got up to sing 'Stormy Weather' and started crying in the middle of it. The man who was managing the show was terribly impressed. He said the idea of letting a great artist like that sing a hot song after that! – after 'Stormy Weather' she should take a bow, that's all. He thought the tears were planted.[15]

SONNY GREER: I'll never forget it. We closed the first half of the programme and we opened the second half. All the others were English acts, so this big lady, she's a big star and I forget her name, she was in the middle of her song doing her act, so we were backstage chasing, in the dressing room, all you had to do was ring the bell and the waiter would come back and serve you, anything you wanted. That's the first time I ever saw that. Them European acts were terrible. They was dead. So the guys were nervous, the guys walking up and down, I say, 'Man, this is just another gig,' so Duke said, 'Press the button and bring the boys a drink, make them doubles!' So now this woman is out there singing, and in the middle of the woman's song, the goddam pit orchestra goes into the national anthem, 'God Save the King' or something, and every son-of-a-bitch stood up. Them people around the curtain, I said, 'What happened, man?' 'In walked the Prince of Wales.' Now, I say, 'Man, I never heard shit like this, this don't make no sense.' He wasn't no bigger than this! So after he sit down, she resumed her act. Now at about fifteen minutes intermission before the second part of the show go on, they opened with us. Now we had been back there tasting, everybody feeling fine, fine. No pain. We had our own lights, pinpoint lights, and Duke say, I want the stage completely dark, one pinpoint on Sonny because we open with 'Ring Dem Bells'. The curtain broke, and the spot's on me and all you can see is my face and hands, hitting anything. I don't know whether it was right or wrong. Just making some noise. Man, about the eighth bar, they stood up, standing ovation. They hadn't seen the whole band yet. Stood up, cheers. No exaggeration.[16]

THE PEOPLE: The house was wildly enthusiastic. It shows you the advance that has been made in jazz during the last few years, that a Negro can come to the largest music-hall in the kingdom, with a modern orchestra, cut out melody and excite a huge gathering, not with tune but with rhythm. When for instance they play 'Some of These Days' it is almost impossible to hear any tune. Where there was a melody you hear discordance. Where there was tenderness, there is now blare. Yet it is so exciting that while some people compare it with hashish, others liken it to falling off a train ... I could hear new ideas being born. I was amazed at the technical perfection of the instrumentation. I looked on a scene gay with colour, modern in style, for the coloured band play surrounded by enormous figures showing Negroes wearing ducal coronets ... Now all this will give you a very scant idea of the show. It must be seen and heard to be believed. You get proof that the much despised Negro is working out a culture all his own. You know you are in the presence of something that will go right across the world.[17]

IRVING MILLS: When Jack Hylton made his definite proposition to me to bring Duke Ellington and his band to Great Britain ... I cancelled several important engagements in the United States and brought the band and its supporting acts across the Atlantic. When Jack Hylton greeted us on the *Olympic* at Southampton, he was able to relieve our anxiety as to what fate awaited us at the hands of the British public. When the curtain rang down after our first performance at the London Palladium, the last shreds of doubt gave way to complete achievement. We had more than realized those wild hopes of success which had sustained us during our voyage from New York.[18]

DUKE ELLINGTON: [Hylton] had seven secretaries for me. They were guys who were to 'divide' the people. Because, you see, over there you always kept a bar set up in your dressing room in the Palladium. If some of the royalty comes back, then you don't let anyone else in. Another class down, you let them in, you don't let anyone else in. They had these seven guys who recognized each section and they would recognize them and keep them divided. It was well understood if you wanted to play in one direction or the other, if you are going to play upstairs, play upstairs and don't go downstairs, and if you're going to play downstairs, play downstairs and don't go upstairs in society. There was a chick there, I was living at the Dorchester, she would come every day and say tonight you're invited to such and such a house. I knew I was invited various parties every night, you know, and she'd say now at this house, so-and-so's house, they're going to be nice people. Now this place there's going to be a lot of freaks there, you mustn't be seen there. I'm going but don't you go! You go to so-and-so's house, he's going to have Members of Parliament there, that's where you must be seen![19]

THE PEOPLE: Well, I wish the wild enthusiasts who cheered his hot jazz would have sat beside me, a few mornings after when, alone on the Palladium stage, Duke Ellington and I discussed his dreams of the future. He has something to say which he is putting into music. So he is writing a suite in which he will tell in polyphonic form the history of his people. He played the themes, with me as his only audience. Now, Duke Ellington's great-grandfather was a slave. That is all he knows. He could not tell you whether his ancestors came from the Gold Coast. He only knows that we white people took Negroes from their homes and made slaves of them and that, now, they are emerging. So this suite, now only in his mind, traces five movements, two of these for chorus, Negro music from its source in the jungle to its present form in Harlem. The episodes are a savage war dance, the captive's voyage over the Atlantic in a slave ship, the old slave days on a Southern plantation, the evolution of ragtime in 'Hot Harlem' and the final recapitulation, an apotheosis aiming to 'Exalt the Negro at least to a point of fuller recognition, and a more comfortable place among people of the world'. All this Duke explained with occasional chords on the piano.[20]

GRAMOPHONE: During their visit Ellington and his band will have been seen and heard by over 100,000 people, which of course excludes the thousands, perhaps millions who were only able to listen to their broadcast. Their two weeks at the London Palladium were insufficient, and a special concert had to be arranged for the intermediate Sunday. Although announced but a few days before it took place, it was, like most other perform-ances, a case of 'House Full'. Over 4,500 attended the *Melody Maker* concert at the Trocadero Cinema, Elephant and Castle, last Sunday and many who applied for tickets had to be disappointed.[21]

The band broadcast on BBC Radio for forty-five minutes on 14 June 1933.

DUKE ELLINGTON: On Sunday we had a concert. On Sunday you don't work in a theatre in England. The concert was at the Elephant and Castle. Sunday I started for the theatre in a cab – saying today Ellington will throw away his showmanship and give us the real, the true Ellington – no commercial endings on numbers at all. I started the concert that way and kept it up all the way down the first half of it. The hot numbers got a terrific reaction, but on the slow numbers they sat back and said when do we get started? So for the second half of the concert I went back and gave a vaudeville show with the B&K endings thrown in. That afternoon we had an audience of more than 6,000 people. Afterwards we headed up to the balcony circle and all my friends were sitting around a table waiting for me, all the heavy men and all the heavy critics. These gentle-men introduced me to Lady somebody and told me she was really the McCoy and she raved about my band and I felt really set up. She went on for about half an hour about the wonder-ful cello player I had, and so after she left they started giving her the rib – to this day they still kid me about that, ain't you got a swell cello player, they say. They really put me on the pan about that concert. Jack Hylton and his wife were on my side – I said these people wanted something and I was going

A CONCERT
OF THE MUSIC OF

D U K E
E L L I N G T O N

PRESENTED BY

THE MELODY MAKER

BY KIND PERMISSION OF
JACK HYLTON
BY ARRANGEMENT WITH
IRVING MILLS

to give it to them – if they weren't going to go for what you considered your high powered jive, why you might as well lay on a little street for them. So they told me I was never going to amount to anything because I didn't have the Spirit of Independence, so the next concert Spike [Hughes] prepared the audience, instructions were laid down how people should act at concerts: when Tricky Sam played a number people shouldn't laugh it wasn't funny, it was a beautiful work of art, they shouldn't clap in the middle of a number and so forth. The second concert was less commercial than the first, but with instructions to the audience by hot dictator Spike. That must have marked the beginning of Spike's breaking up because he didn't come with us when we went away. That argument went on for years.[22]

At the 25 June concert sponsored by Melody Maker *magazine, Ellington performed Spike Hughes' composition 'Sirocco'.*

DUKE ELLINGTON: I'll never forget one day backstage when I happened to walk out of the dressing room and I looked down at the stage door, and there was this *gorgeous* chick, man, she was really too much, you know. Looked real good, and Spike, and I think he was one of the dividers, and he sent her away and I says, 'Who the hell was that, who did she want to see?' He said, 'She wanted to see you.' I said, 'Why didn't you let her in?' 'Oh Duke! She was a whore!' I said, 'Godamn pretty as she is, you should have let her in!!'[23]

IRVING MILLS: One day I get a call from the head of the Palladium, Val Parnell, who said there's a big party that Lord Beaverbrook gives every year of the Economic Conference, and that Jack Hylton was playing up to twelve o'clock and he thought that Duke Ellington, because the younger set of society of the royalty were coming after twelve o'clock and they all wanted Duke Ellington, and would we play it? It would be a pleasure to do that. We finished at the Palladium and the bus met us. I didn't have a dress suit at the time, I wore a tuxedo and Val Parnell got me fixed up to look proper at this party where all of the people were in their full regalia, with all the gold braids and women with diamonds up to here, I never saw such a layout. And all of the help [was in] britches that you see in the old days in the motion pictures. And I was awed by the whole thing. And Duke Ellington took over after Hylton got through. They played waltzes and nice soft music, what they were dancing to. When Duke got up it was an entirely different sound of music, and I found that the people were gathering in front of the Duke Ellington band like they did, the kids at the Paramount Theatre [in New York]. And there was this man standing alongside me who was awed at everything that's going on with this band, the sound of this music compared to the sound of Jack Hylton at the time. He was talking to me and I couldn't understand him. He was talking very, very English and his little mouth closed, you know. Mumbling. And my hearing not being what it should be I didn't pay much attention to him, only to find out later it was Lord Beaverbrook. Well, Duke was a sensation that night. First of all the crowd that was up till twelve o'clock was all the heads of the different colonies, all of the royalty. And then the young crowd came in, and there was different dancing, all the society kids![24]

DUKE ELLINGTON: We went to a party at Lord Beaverbrook's home; a party given for the Prince, and the Prince was there. It was very dicty. We were way up, feeling mellow. It was a beautiful party. They were serving nothing but wine all night long, and good nectar too. Every time they served the guests a drink they served the band a drink and the band was doing fine, I had a rich feeling, playing the piano and posin'. A man came up to me and asked for 'Swampy River', so I gave him that light fluff and I said, you know I never do solos – then the man came back to ask for it and I gave him that drrrrrrrrp! and said how I never do solos, the solos are for the boys in the band – then somebody came up and told me that was Prince George! After which I had to go and take a big deep breath of wine. So we had an interval and then Windsor was standing out in the middle of the floor there and giving me this big long eulogy. And after that, that's when he comes over and says, 'Won't you have a drink with me at the bar?' He said: 'What are you drinking?' So I said gin. So he said he would have the same. Up to that time I always thought gin was sort of a low drink, but since that time I always feel rather grand when I drink gin. The party lasted a long time, and about forty or fifty people were there for breakfast. Prince George plays the piano well. He and I played together several times. Windsor can play good drums – good, hot drums. At this party you played about twenty minutes and you rested forty. They had a gypsy band there for atmosphere – we give them the blossom and the gypsies give them the root! The Prince wanted to show Sonny how to beat those drums – we expected some Little Lord Fauntleroy stuff but he really gave out with some low Charleston.[25]

The two brothers, Prince Edward, then Prince of Wales, and Prince George, were the sons of King George V.

SONNY GREER: We play this party, Jack Hylton played till we got there. So we go in this party, this is God's honest truth, this is no illusion, we come into this party and the place is crowded. At that time Jeanette MacDonald was there as a guest. Anna May Wong, remember her, some movie star and a gang of American movie stars, I will never forget it. We were all dressed in white because it was the summer, we had on white uniforms and special-made, white special-made shoes, all sharp, and before we started playing there's this big magnum of champagne in front of everybody and a bottle of scotch and a bottle of brandy. I look at this fellow, I said little taste, everything fine now, so this cat sitting down on the floor he had one of them brandy snifters, he's going with it. I still don't know who he is. So that goes on, so now me and him are buddies. He heard the guys say, 'Hey, Sonny!' so right away he pick up on my name, Sonny, so after a while he say, 'I can play the drum.' I say, 'Yeah? Come on man!' me and him tight now. He say, 'I play the Charleston.' I say, 'Yeah, man. That's great.' Now the people, the women start drifting by and I see these women bow to this son of a bitch, curtsy. The waiter came up and say, 'Your Highness, some people want to see you.' You know who he was, The Prince of Wales! I never called him His Highness, he called me Sonny, and I'd say yeah, man. Wally Simpson from Baltimore, he finally married her, she hated my guts, hated Duke's guts. We were taking up too much attention, so he say, 'I'm leaving now. I got to say hello to some friends, Sonny, I'll be right back, don't you go anywhere.' 'I ain't going nowhere Wale.' Call him Wale, he thought that was the cutest thing. He never forgot it, I called him the Wale. He followed us to Scotland, he says, 'Sonny, what's my nickname?' I say, 'You're the Wale, man, something else.' He thought it was the greatest thing in the world.[26]

DUKE ELLINGTON: After two weeks in London we went to Liverpool and then to Glasgow. And in Liverpool we played of course for the Prince of Wales, he came and sat in the front row and requested numbers and of course we played like mad and played two or three encores. We didn't know when to stop when the Prince was there. Then we played the King [the national anthem] very majestically. I am very sincere about it when I play the King. We gave a concert also in Blackpool (between London and Glasgow), then back to London and played the Holborn Empire and the Finsbury Park Empire.[27]

DUKE ELLINGTON: The Jiggs Club – that is the *lowest* place. I don't know of any place in America that is down to that level. We (Spike Hughes, Charlotte somebody and others) would go to my place and I would decide we were all jigged up and we should go to the Jiggs Club. I took the whole mob down one night. They never had more than one bottle of anything, so we would go from scotch to brandy to gin – and I'm not forgetting the black-eyed peas. The joint was owned by Alex, an English Jew, and an African guy. They used to serve rice and peas, a real West Indian dish. When you got filled up on gin and brandy that dish tasted awful good. They really didn't have two of *anything* alike down there – two chairs, two tables, two drinks, anything. It was down on Wardour Street.[28]

DUKE ELLINGTON: Prince George wanted to be in on a record date, so we decided to go down and make some records for British Decca ['Harlem Speaks', 'Ain't Misbehavin'', 'Hyde Park' and 'Chicago']. At the last minute they said that Scotland Yard said too many people knew about his coming and so they wouldn't let him come. We had the date anyway. Six Bells, the pub, was next door to the record studio. So by the time we got to 'Chicago' we didn't know whether we were in Chicago or Egypt. These records weren't made for American release, but finally they did release them in America.[29]

The recording session was on 13 July 1933.

DUKE ELLINGTON: And then Prince George gives a party for ten of us. I was playing and drinking, lots of fine people present. I gets up nerve to ask him to play for me, for he sure knows piano. But he says, 'No Duke, I can't come behind you in your piano music.' Did I get it? He just didn't want to cut in.[30]

Prince George enjoyed an unconventional lifestyle for a member of the British Royal Family. He lost his virginity to Noël Coward in the dressing room of London's Duke of York Theatre when Coward was playing 'London Calling'. In 1926 he had a brief affair with the American entertainer Florence Mills (to whom Ellington had dedicated his 1926 composition 'Black Beauty'), followed by affairs with Prince Louis Ferdinand of Prussia and the

Argentinian Jorge Ferara. With Ferara, George formed a menage
à trois *with Kiki Whitney Preston, the American heiress known as
'the girl with the silver syringe', who introduced him to cocaine
and morphine.*[31]

DUKE ELLINGTON: We went to France after London and played
the Salle Pleyel. We played one concert on Thursday and one
on Saturday and they were both so successful they had us do
another on the following Saturday which was also capacity.[32]

DAILY MAIL: Last Thursday evening in the Salle Pleyel, Duke
Ellington and his band treated a sweltering but satisfied audience
to some choice selections of the hottest thing in jazz music,
straight from the heights of Harlem ... This season he was quite
the rage in London. And now his latest conquest is Paris. Like
Alexander the Great, he is looking for new worlds to conquer
... I should like to say in precise, but not pedantic language,
that Duke Ellington 'went over big' ... To cap the climax, the
boys from Harlem gave a second concert, on Saturday evening,
and as there still remain many admirers to be satisfied they are
giving a farewell concert there tomorrow evening.[33]

DUKE ELLINGTON: In between we went to Deauville. I did the
Casino in my usual fashion. Then we came back to Paris and
went around there about a week just blowing our top –
sightseeing. We only worked one day that week, Saturday.[34]

DICK DE PAUW: A tour of six weeks with Duke Ellington and
his boys has provided me with an experience that would make
the most hard baked tour manager point to a crop of new grey
hairs and say 'The Ellington bunch did that!' But even so it is
with many regrets that I have just left them after their triumphs
in Paris. Duke never shows the slightest sign of life before five
o'clock in the evening. Indeed, this business of rousing him and
getting him dressed in time for the first house was the most
bewildering task of the tour.[35]

DUKE ELLINGTON: Paris was wonderful ... You can't imagine anyone going to [a whorehouse] with tails and evening dresses in a party of ten. Real class people, you go there, you are sitting with your party at the table and you have a few drinks and suddenly the wall opens up and there's fifty naked broads standing up on the stage, and this is the show, they just stand there, they just stand there for an hour and everybody who's sitting down at the tables go into conversation and the subject matter is these chicks standing up there with no clothes on! ... At the end of show all these beautiful chicks come on to the floor with their evening gowns on, and they stand out there and they take their bows, and the Madame comes out and she says, 'All these lovely girls are here to entertain you, you can't buy a girl in this house since you have paid your cover charge, and you are cordially invited to have one of our young ladies.' The party I was in, all swell people, some society woman, one of those dowagers from America and Irving Mills with his interpreter. Nobody answers [the Madame] and they all look at me, says, 'Hey Duke, here's your chance, why don't you get a girl?' I said, 'I don't want anybody.' I'd been wailing, they kept on talking to me and I was feeling my champagne and I finally stood up, I got tired of them hollerin' 'Come on Duke!' So finally I got up and waved to the Madame, I says, 'Madame? I'll take the three on the end!!'[36]

DICK DE PAUW: I discovered that Duke suffered from a kind of nervous complex in the matter of time, because, no matter how early he happened to be, he would never commence to dress until the last possible second, and then when everybody around was all worked up and yelling, 'The show's on!' he would scramble on his coat while running down the corridor and, with that bland smile of his, stride onto the stage and commence playing – all in one breath as it were. He simply could not face the ordeal of being dressed-up and waiting back-stage all ready for the curtain to rise – he had to run on in a whirl of excitement in order to get the right mood for that opening number. Do you remember that electrical movement of his right hand off beat in 'Ring Dem Bells'? Whenever I heard it I used to sigh, 'Thank God he's started!' I timed the applause at every first night and the average highest was for 'Mood Indigo', Derby and Bailey's dance, 'Some of These Days' (aided and abetted, of course, by Posey Jenkins's rapturous bows of thanks) and 'Sophisticated Lady', with items by Ivie Anderson and Bessie Dudley in close running. Strangely enough, the results in Paris were almost the same.[37]

DUKE ELLINGTON: Then we sailed from France and came back on the *Majestic*. On the ship I again stayed loaded on champagne and brandy – that is the most glorious glow – and good for seasickness. You must go on board, right, with no worries, no weight on your mind. Then take it slow, and it goes easy, it goes on in pastels. We were away about twelve weeks. Came back about the last of August.[38]

DICK DE PAUW: The Duke has developed an intense regard for the works of Delius and has taken back to America a whole bundle of scores to study. If ever he gets time to absorb them it will be intensely interesting to hear the reaction of one of the world's most refined musicians.[39]

MERCER ELLINGTON: There was one English composer – and that's about the only time I've ever heard him absolutely point out something he liked. And in fact I heard him say this twice: if it was painting it was Monet and most of the artists around the Renaissance period. And Delius was the one person he liked so much in music.[40]

SPIKE HUGHES: I have had several talks with Duke and was glad to notice that his trip to London has had a most stimulating effect. The interest taken in his music by so many different kinds of people has given him something to think about ... I know he appreciated the visit of the sculptor Epstein to his dressing room and the discussion with Constant Lambert.[41]

DUKE ELLINGTON: I want to write a rude song; this was accidentally suggested by Mrs Constant Lambert who referred to our little melancholy tune as 'Rude Indigo'. All I need for the number now is the balance of the title to go with 'Rude'.[42]

On 26 September 1933 Ellington recorded 'Rude Interlude'.

DUKE ELLINGTON: The main thing I got in Europe was *spirit*, it lifted me out of the groove. That kind of thing gives you courage to go on with a lot of things you want to do yourself.[43]

FRANKIE CARLE: [I] was hired to play for the reception welcoming [Duke] home from [his] first European trip [with the] Mal Hallett band in Boston. I was the pianist, Gene Krupa on drums, Jack Teagarden and Jack Jenny on trombones and Toots Mondello on alto. We played for [Ellington] and I'll never forget it.[44]

Ellington played the Metropolitan Theatre, Boston, 18–24 August 1933.

SONNY GREER: We stayed in the biggest hotels. Irving Mills had our accommodation in front, the biggest hotels in the country. They fly – like they fly for the dignitary, the American flag was flown, on the hotel. In honour of us. Just like they fly a flag if a diplomat come and stay in the hotel, they flew the American flag for us. We carried the flag and the prestige of my people. I am an American Negro. You hear the cats say, black this, I'm an American Negro, pal. We carried the flag for the American Negro all over the United States, we carried the flag everywhere. We carried the flag for the dignity of the American all over the world. We were treated with the utmost respect.[45]

OTTO HARDWICK: What was amazing about our trip to Europe was anybody could tell you where the band was staying because on top of that hotel they had their national flag and they had our American flag. And you can imagine how nice it made you feel. It was a wonderful feeling.[46]

SONNY GREER: Irving Mills. He was blue/white diamond. He was the guy. He was *the* guy. He travelled with us. Everything first class, every time you look around, he said, 'I better get you guys another set of uniforms.' Every time we opened up he had boutonniere flowers. He was there to see everything is perfect. In fact, every show we had a different uniform, top to bottom.[47]

IRVING MILLS: I dressed up the band and they didn't have to have one suit, they had to have two, three suits, you know for changes, they sweat on stage. And Duke used to go in privately and order a lot more suits than I tell to the tailor, and all of a sudden I get a bill, and he laughed and I said, 'What did you do here?' So he says, 'Well, you know!' Well, he had such a good personality, and he was such a nice man, that I said OK. But they all had a good wardrobe, I bought the best trunks, I wanted the boys to feel they were tops, over the whole black set, and wherever we went, wherever we were booked, I made sure they get respect and everything, from the theatre manager down to everybody.[48]

CAB CALLOWAY: [Irving Mills] broke down so many darned barriers for Negro musicians you couldn't count them ... white clubs that had never had a black band before, and some of them were reluctant to let one in. But Irving Mills pounded their doors and paved the way.[49]

IRVING MILLS: They knew they were working, they knew they looked good in their costumes. They knew they had a lot of publicity, respect. 'Cause I was a hound on publicity, you know I had six people at one time on publicity.[50]

*

*In September 1933, after dissolving Mills-Rockwell Inc., with Tom
Rockwell, Irving Mills formed Mills Artists Inc., and had what he
called 'An Advertising Manual' prepared, presenting his major
artist Duke Ellington for distribution to promoters, ballroom oper-
ators, theatre owners and just about anyone who might be in a
position to put work Ellington's way. It reveals that Mills and his
assistant Ned Williams had in place a remarkably sophisticated
marketing strategy for Ellington that would not look out of place in
today's music business. It is no exaggeration to say that practically
all the marketing techniques outlined in the Mills manual are still
being successfully employed today. Mills realized that to build
Ellington into a national attraction, it was not enough to release
recordings or secure bookings and leave the rest to fate. Mills set
about creating the right 'image' for Ellington – he was 'a Duke',
'an aristocrat', 'a genius', and not just another bandleader. His
orchestra was 'Famous', it played 'new harmonies' and 'weird
rhythms'. When it came to the music, Mills was careful to define
the evaluative grounds himself, hoping the press would pick up and
elaborate his themes and so present Ellington and his music within
what Mills hoped would be the right discursive framework: that
Ellington was not simply another 'hot band' but a class attraction,
that his music had been praised by classical authorities, that he had
devised a 'new brand of contemporary music', that his genius had
been recognized 'all over the world', and that he had been celebrated
by royalty. Today, with Ellington's place in history assured, it is
easy to forget that in 1933 Ellington was just one bandleader among
many riding out the Depression. To keep his band together he
needed to capitalize on his successful coast-to-coast radio broadcasts and secure bookings wherever he could. Around him were
competitors who were happy, grateful even, just to turn up for a
gig and play. Mills could well have settled for that kind of status
quo, but it is to his credit he recognized Ellington's great genius,
and strove not only to maximize the potential of every engagement
with suitable publicity but also to create an image of someone above*

the competitive milieu of the music business, a creative artist whose aspirations were motivated by aesthetic rather than commercial considerations: in short, an artist who was in a category of his own.

Irving Mills Presents Duke Ellington
by Irving Mills
Advertising Manual[51]

This manual of publicity stories, tips on exploitation and advertising suggestions has been prepared to assist managers of theatres and ballrooms to more intelligently sell this attraction. An effective selling campaign operates to our mutual benefit and we want every manager to feel that every facility of the New York office is at his disposal.

Wire or write to:
Ned. E. Williams
c/o Mills Artists, Inc.
799 Seventh Avenue, New York, N.Y.

Billing
Following is the correct billing for this attraction. Please adhere to this wording and these proportions:

MILLS ARTISTS, INC.
Irving Mills, President

PRESENTS

DUKE
ELLINGTON
And His
Famous Orchestra

Exploitation

In your campaign do not treat Duke Ellington as just another jazz bandleader and do not try to sell the orchestra merely with such phrases as 'the hottest band on earth'. Ellington's genius as a composer, arranger and musician has won him the respect and admiration of such authorities as Percy Grainger, head of the department of music at the New York University; Basil Cameron, conductor of the Seattle Symphony Orchestra; Leopold Stokowski, famed conductor of the celebrated Philadelphia Orchestra; Paul Whiteman, whose name is synonymous with jazz, and many others.

Sell Ellington as a great artist, a musical genius whose unique style and individual theories of harmony have created a new music. Sell his orchestra as a class attraction, a group of stellar artists whose performance has stimulated international interest in the type of music which they have introduced. Do not hesitate to approach music editors and music critics on the subject of Ellington. He has been accepted seriously by many of the greatest minds in the world of music, who have regarded it a privilege to study his art and to discuss his theories with him.

Interviews

Do not hesitate to invite columnists, music editors, radio editors or other newspaper writers to interview Ellington. He is genial as he is intelligent, always creates a good impression upon newspaper people with whom he comes in contact and invariably supplies them with good copy for their stories. His position as a successful composer and creator of a new style in music makes him an excellent subject for such interviews.

Radio

Duke Ellington and his Famous Orchestra are one of the outstanding radio attractions of the present day. This not only opens the radio pages of newspapers to you legitimately for stories and photographs, but local radio stations usually are willing and anxious to effect a tie-up with you for this attraction, if you do not have such a tie-up already in operation for your theatre or ballroom. Be sure to supply small stations with Ellington's latest phonograph records in advance of playdate.

Victor Records

The Ellington orchestra is an ace recording unit for Victor and dealers everywhere will be found willing to co-operate with you upon counter and window displays, or will make their mailing lists available to you for mutual Ellington exploitation.

Autograph Stunts

Duke Ellington is a celebrity and his autograph is eagerly sought by dance devotees, music lovers and radio fans. He rarely plays a ballroom engagement without spending the recess period responding to requests for autographs. Postcard photos of him are available for autograph give-aways in tie-ups with stores or stunts at the theatre or ballroom. It provides a basis for a variety of exploitation ideas.

Sheet Music

Sheet music of Ellington's compositions, such as 'Mood Indigo', 'Creole Love Call', 'Sophisticated Lady', 'Black and Tan Fantasy' and others is available in any quantity for stunts and tie-ups similar to or in connection with the autograph gag. These numbers have been so popularized over the air by his and other orchestras that his fans are clamouring for them. And don't forget the sheet music counters in music stores for special displays. Ellington will visit counters and autograph copies in return for advertising space in daily newspapers.

Newspaper Tie-ups

Ellington lends himself willingly to any tie-ups with newspapers whereby you help them in the collection of a charitable fund in return for publicity space. Alone or with his band he will appear anywhere in behalf of a milk-and-ice fund, shoe fund, boys camp fund or any similar activity, or for the entertainment of war veterans, crippled children, aged persons or other hospital shut-ins.

Instruments

Local dealers handling instruments especially Conn, will co-operate with you on window tie-ups. In addition, sell the city editor or feature editor of your local newspaper the idea of using a story about the effect which the new trend in music has had upon the instrumentation of the modern dance orchestra. The craze for Cuban or Rhumba rhythms and the popularity of Negro or spiritual strains has brought out dozens of new gourds, mutes and other strange instruments. Have your paper send a photographer to picture Ellington with some of these queer instruments; or, if you want advance publicity, borrow the instruments from your local dealer and pose a pretty girl with them. Make sure Ellington is credited with this feature, however, and quoted liberally throughout. Use the special story on the subject from this manual, if necessary.

PRESS STORIES

ELLINGTON HAILED AS A CREATOR OF A NEW DANCE MUSIC VOGUE

Duke Ellington, Harlem's aristocrat of jazz, who will be featured with his famous orchestra at _____ on _____, is hailed as the creator of a new and distinctly original type of dance music interpretation.

When Duke bends over the piano and his masters of melody begin fondling their instruments, one hears the very quintessence of physical Africa moving in sinuous and suggestive rhythms.

No other band is like Ellington's and it is doubtful if any other band will be like it. Whatever number goes into the Ellington music mill must come out Ellington music. No such weird combinations, such unique and effective cross rhythms and counter melodies with strange and broken tempos are attempted by any other organization.

A ballad becomes a plaintive jungle beat, its melody cradled in queer and unrecognizable harmonies. A woodwind arpeggio is imbued with a distinctive and wild fury as it fits into the pattern of an Ellington interpretation.

ELLINGTON COMPOSER AND ARRANGER AS WELL AS MUSICIAN

It's no secret to radio enthusiasts that Duke Ellington, who will appear with his famous orchestra at _____ on _____, is pre-eminent in the field of jazz, and that even to jazz he has contributed something which is distinctly Ellington, making the harmonies and rhythms of his orchestra instantly recognizable when a twist of the dial brings his music out of the night.

But his fellow musicians, white as well as coloured, and students of contemporary music and music critics everywhere quickly realized when Ellington first came into prominence during his first long engagement at the Cotton Club in New York and his frequent N.B.C. broadcasts, that here was a musician who was to leave his mark on American music.

The demand for Ellington phonograph records bears this out, for during a period when radio has made terrific in roads upon record sales generally, Ellington's popularity among serious collectors of discs has mounted steadily, not only in this country, but abroad, where Ellington is highly regarded as a composer and is recognized as the originator of an entirely new type of contemporary music.

ELLINGTON CALLED JAZZ ARISTOCRAT FROM HARLEM

Duke Ellington, whose playing at the famous Cotton Club in New York won him the title of 'Harlem's Aristocrat of Jazz', will be featured at _____ on _____, with his orchestra.

Made popular by radio, Duke and his musicians have created a sensation in theatres and ballrooms from coast to coast, as well as in Europe. They have been featured in a Ziegfeld show, in several motion pictures, and of course, on phonograph records.

Duke and his boys have an instinctive feeling for jazz rhythms and broken tempos and they have the reputation of doing the most inconceivable things to the most trivial of melodies. They can play 'sweet' and discreet jazz in the manner of Mr Whiteman, then turn about and twist their music into weird and primitive strains with all the barbaric rhythms of the jungle.

Ellington's unique arrangements have created a definite new style in dance melody, and his musicians are masters of the intricacies of hot jazz and syncopation. His distinctive brand of music is familiar to almost every radio owner.

A further seven specimen press stories of varying length were also included. Among them UNIVERSITY DIRECTOR CLAIMS JAZZ IS MOST CLASSICAL OF MUSIC, ELLINGTON COMPARED WITH DELIUS, STRAUSS AND RIMSKY-KORSAKOV, RUDY VALLEE LAUDS DUKE ELLINGTON ... COMPOSER, *and* ELLINGTON'S ABILITY AS COMPOSER GIVEN SERIOUS APPROVAL. *They all sought to establish the legitimacy of jazz and Ellington's role as its foremost composer/arranger. Typical is the following extract from a suggested feature.*

ELLINGTON'S MUSIC AND MICKEY MOUSE ONLY
ORIGINAL ART

Constant Lambert, music critic of the *London Referee*, writes: 'Duke Ellington is a real composer, the first jazz composer of note and the first Negro composer of note. There are few contemporary composers who display the invention and sense of style to be found in those two admirably constructed pieces, "Mood Indigo" and "Hot and Bothered" – the final summing-up of the depression and the exhilaration of the mechanical age. Ellington is no mere bandleader and arranger, but a composer of uncommon merit, probably the first composer of real character to come out of America.'

In England, Duke Ellington's orchestra not only played twice for the Prince of Wales who owns the finest collection of Ellington records in Europe, but for Prince George and other notables as well. Theatres were packed where ever he went, and his orchestra gave eight concerts in Great Britain, one in Holland and four in France, at which thousands of people sat for two hours listening to the orchestra play its pianist-arranger-conductor's compositions.

That the European estimate of Duke Ellington's genius as a composer is rapidly spreading to his native country is indicated in several ways. Prophets are notoriously without honour in their own countries. Ellington fortunately has amassed profit if not honour. In one issue of *Fortune* in an article devoted to jazz in general and Ellington in particular, his earnings are estimated at $250,000 a year, so popular is his orchestra with the public.

Probably the first person identified with serious music in America to enthuse over Duke Ellington as composer was an Englishman, Percy Grainger, the noted pianist-composer-conductor who now directs the School of Music of Fine Arts, New York. Grainger played Ellington records for his students and then invited Ellington and his orchestra to play at the university for the class in music appreciation. Present at this concert, and also an Ellington enthusiast, was Basil Cameron, British conductor of the Seattle Symphony orchestra. Another symphony conductor, world renowned, who never misses an opportunity to hear Duke Ellington and his orchestra is Leopold Stokowski, conductor of the Philadelphia orchestra.

So, while English newspapers all assign their first-string music critics to Duke Ellington openings he remains within the province of dramatic, motion picture and radio editors in the United States. But in one year, or five years, it may be common practice to employ the *New Yorker*'s recent ranking of 'Gershwin, Ellington, Grofe', when writing of contemporary American composers.

PUNCH LINES

Harlem's aristocrat of jazz!
Creator of a new vogue in dance music!
The Duke Steps Out!
Primitive rhythms! Weird melodies! Amazing syncopations!
Music no other band can play!
Sensation of two continents!

TRAILER

There is an excellent sound-on-film trailer available on Duke Ellington, animated with colourful effects and packed with good selling copy. Prints may be obtained for use a week in advance of playdate by writing or wiring to:

National Screen Service
Vaudeville Department
630 Ninth Avenue, New York, N. Y.

The text of the trailer follows:

. . . Introducing a moment of melody by Harlem's Aristocrat of jazz!

Listen to this harmony

There is only one band in the world that plays like this! And that band is . . .

DUKE ELLINGTON and His Famous Orchestra

He'll be here next week to give you the greatest syncopation thrill of your lives!

Duke plays jazz as it should be played, with a primitive rhythm that thrills to the finger tips!

And with him will be the California songbird, **IVIE ANDERSON** singing her happy songs!

Get set for an amazing musical thrill with **DUKE ELLINGTON** next week!

IRVING MILLS: They copied our style, including all our manuals that had my advertising.[52]

FREDDY GUY: [Mills] wanted Duke to be the star, not the band. The men were just the rank and file. But I could see through him, man, and [Mills] hated me for it.[53]

IRVING MILLS: [Duke] was a perfect gentleman. He was always very kind, very considerate, and very appreciative of everything that was done for him. He enjoyed the publicity he was getting which was very good publicity by a big staff of people that I had from every angle, from the record angle, from the music publishing, from his writing becoming more and more known around the country, and there was a lot of requests for more of Ellington tunes and we created a slogan around all of the Ellington themes which was called 'From the Pen of Duke Ellington'. And anything that came out of Ellington's [on sheet music] was 'From the Pen of Duke Ellington'.[54]

LAWRENCE BROWN: At first Duke was very much together with the boys, but later on he got confidence in himself and he didn't need them any more. So he went by himself. Also the management encouraged him to go by himself.[55]

IRVING MILLS: I educated Duke, first of all, never to fire anybody; that the band belonged to me and not to him. Until I formed a corporation, I owned the band, you know, he worked for me, I guaranteed everything with my recordings.[56]

RUTH ELLINGTON: [Duke] cleared everybody, a new manager, a new this, a new that, a new girl friend! He cleared everything [with Irving].[57]

DUKE ELLINGTON: We then went to Texas. We stayed there a long time, doing theatres and about six dances a week ... then out west, then back to Chicago then back east and in between times we got to Washington.[58]
    Ellington began his tour of Southern theatres at the Majestic in Dallas, on 30 September 1933, where he broke the house record for that year.

JUAN TIZOL: In Dallas, Texas, we were getting ready to play, and there was a lot of people there, and people started looking at

me, especially this fellow on the right of the bandstand, and I thought to myself, 'I know he's going to be asking me some questions soon.' He said: 'You don't mind giving me an autograph?' and I said, 'You don't want no autograph, you want to ask a question about me.' He said, 'What are you doing playing with these niggers?' I said, 'Let me tell you something; you see that man over there on piano, he got more respect than a lot of white people put together, you know? He got more recognition, you couldn't come to a dance dressed in overalls.' So I didn't give him no autograph or nothing.[59]

IRVING MILLS: We went through Texas that never played a black band, and when Bob O'Donnell booked me in there I said, 'Look, I want to be assured of protection.' And we were booked into a hotel, the Muleback I think it was, and never had a black band up there, and it was for a Prom, you know? So they guaranteed me. I go up to the Muleback, and I've got my fingers crossed, you know, because some guys had, southerners, a couple of drinks and made some remark. So right after the first set, all the girls, everybody, ran up to get an autograph of Duke! And everything was terrific. We had no trouble at all, we went to all the other places in Texas, Austin and other places, never had any trouble, but I always had protection.[60]

SONNY GREER: They never seen nobody like us. Down South, you know, confliction, segregation. They had heard different coloured aggregations that come through on a little ragged-ass bus or something like that, but we had our own Pullman car, had our own baggage car, we had full possession of the diner, nobody could come in our Pullman car because the door stayed locked, because people autographing annoy you, you know. We had our own Pullman car with our name on it, our own baggage car, because we travelled heavy. We had our own lighting equipment, own stage, one of the first bands to use a roll-down stage and roll-back, one of the first bands with all them overhead pinpoint lights, electrician. They never seen that. That's the way Irving Mills made us travel. We pull up, baggage car in the yard and pay extra to park it. We didn't have to go through that junk – coloured over this side, white over this. Our guys in the morning, we didn't have to dress. We'd keep our pyjamas and robes and stay in the car, relax all day until the time to work. And if we wanted something in the morning, we would put an order in and have the guy deliver it to us. When we went to the gig, we have a fleet of cabs wait to take us, bring us back.[61]

DUKE ELLINGTON: The manager would go out and say we want ten taxi cabs. And they would come, and they would talk to us. I'll never forget this Southern cat was driving, he's talkin' and he's hummin', ask him a question, he would answer, he said, 'I guess we all sound pretty funny to ya all down here.' 'Don't worry,' I said, Oh man![62]

SONNY GREER: The average one of them crackers down south, they never been inside a Pullman car, never saw it, and them porters used to put on the dog, them cats would put on them beautiful starched uniforms and the step to come down they would lay it. They were actors too. They would act down. They never seen that. They would come down out of curiosity. Ofays and everybody would come down, we were travelling like kings. That's how Irving Mills had us travel.[63]

LAWRENCE BROWN: It was a very good set-up. They had a manager by the name of Sam Fliashnik, and of course, Irving Mills was the impresario. And our car would be attached to the very front of the car section or the very back so the general public didn't go through our cars . . . and I've seen this manager, Sam Fliashnik, stop the whole train and wouldn't let it move until they put our car in the proper position.[64]

DUKE ELLINGTON: We lived on [the train]. We didn't have to get off, we just stayed on there, and when the train was running we'd go to the diner, if we could stop playing cards long enough! We used to play poker all day and all night, you'd play poker all night long and all day long until it was time to go to work, and get up and shave and go. And race back with a sandwich or something and deal the cards, you know! And Ivie, she loved gambling![65]

BARNEY BIGARD: We was on a train once and we were gambling and Ivie Anderson was in the game. She was always lucky. She'd win. But she did something to Cootie – remember those old things they used to raise the windows up? They had to put it under something to jack it up, like raise it up? So Cootie took one of them things and just looked at her, bam, hit her right on the head. And she had a big gash. So now she's going to kill Cootie. So the train stopped in El Paso, Texas, and it stays there for a while and she went off and bought a gun somewhere. She came back, and I told Cootie, 'Cool it.' I said, 'I think she's got something in her bag.' He said, 'Don't worry, I'll fix it.' Then Duke was talking to Ivie. He said, 'Let him alone and don't bother him because he might kill you.' So I don't know how they cooled it off some kind of way and the first thing you know Ivie and Cootie was going together. I said, 'Oh my God!'[66]

SONNY GREER: Duke thrived [on ideas]. We'd be sitting up playing cards and he'd get an idea, he'd write it down on paper and start writing it, between engagements. The first thing you know, he's sprung it on you. That's why I say Duke always writes his dreams. I don't think Duke ever realized, really realized how great he was. He didn't. Even when the newspapers raved, he never took that serious, you know? Duke was very religious and he believed the Man was looking out for him. He didn't like all that glamour to go to his head.[67]

FREDDIE JENKINS: We had a lot of fun with Duke. He is warm and vibrant, sometimes a little serious but he never loses his sense of humour. Sometimes you can like certain traits in a man and dislike other traits. But you love Duke all the way.[68]

JUAN TIZOL: In some place in Henderson, Texas – that was a tough town. We were playing a dance for a lot of them cowboys and so on, and one of the ladies in there came by and tried to sit down in the same seat as Duke Ellington, you know? Oh, he was scared to death cause there was people in the front there too and this fellow that was dancing with her was out there in front of the bandstand and said, 'I wonder what my girlfriend is doing sitting down talking with a nigger?' So Duke was scared, and called out for Jack Boyd [the road manager], 'Jack, take this lady out of here, take her out!' So by the end of the dance, somebody picked up Tricky's trombone, they picked it up and took it with them. We was getting ready to go on the bus and it was right behind – I mean, Tricky's trombone! So they said, 'You know, I'm gonna take this trombone with me and I don't care if you tell the police.' He was a big man, he said, 'I don't give a damn about the police coming.' Duke said, 'Well, if that's the way you feel about it – there's the trombone. If you want it, go ahead and take it.' That killed him when he said that, he said, 'No, it's all right. I don't want the trombone, all I wanted to see was how you was gonna act about it.' That's about the worst one we had.[69]

DUKE ELLINGTON: It all boils down to the skin disease. This is a period when people are thrown out of places for [being] a Negro . . . they were thrown out of this place and that place.[70]

DUKE ELLINGTON: We used to encounter little things now and again but the Pullman car train was a thing that gave prestige and commanded a certain amount of respect, because we had a minimum of trouble down there. In those days the charter

165

things were very reasonable, it was cheaper than room rent. What would happen it cost the guys $5 a day apiece. We paid our normal transportation contribution, and we would take about $5 from each guy, and the idea of chartering two Pullman cars was – we used to order two drawing rooms and nineteen lowers, and the only way to get them was to get two cars, but with two drawing rooms you had a lot of sitting space, it was clearly good living. And the baggage car – we had a whole lot of trunks and scenery and platforms. And [bassist] Billy Taylor was the cook in the band and he would set up a stove, you want some soul food – you couldn't get [it] on the train, if you really wanted something cooked home style, do it yourself. A lot of fun, a great experience. Private [rail] cars were a priority then, because it would come from the top, the headquarters of the railroad. You get to a town, and they switch you over on a siding the last track on the station and connect you up with steam, water, ice, sanitation, all that service.[71]

DUKE ELLINGTON: Arthur Whetsol made that title ['Solitude']. We recorded it in Chicago – I wrote it standing up. So it really didn't have any emotional foundation. Somebody else was late coming out of the studio, about twenty minutes and I said, 'Oh gee, I can use this time, I need another number.' So I wrote the orchestration standing up for twenty minutes, and Tizol was very fast and he extracted it and we recorded it and as we recorded it the first take, the engineer had tears running down his eyes and Whetsol says, 'That's Solitude.' I never gave it any more thought. It just stayed that.[72]

'Solitude' was first recorded on 10 January 1934.

DUKE ELLINGTON: Then when I got ready to go make a picture, I told my old man – he had arthritis in his knee, he'd be in work a couple of days and have to lay off a couple – I said put the job down, he wouldn't give up his job unless I had another job for him, so I said, 'I have a job for you, you're travelling

with me.' He came up and he joined me in Columbus, Ohio, I gave him a fountain pen and told him he was my social secretary at $100 a week.[73]

SONNY GREER: Uncle Ed. That's what we called him. He used to say, 'Will you ladies join me?' Boy, he was loved ... He came up and he used to make a lot of trips with us too. He never did continuous travel with us. He liked big cities. He'd come and stay with us and go back, just on a visit. He never travelled all them different places. He was beautiful, he was something else.[74]

MERCER ELLINGTON: Uncle Ed would have loved to have been a great disciplinarian, but his relationship with my father became one of disdain because his mother, while visiting Washington unexpectedly, found he had this woman living in the house with him and Ellington didn't like the idea at all that Uncle Ed would be disparaging of his mother, and from that point on they never got a divorce or anything like that but they slept apart. But for the most part, even though he would take [Uncle Ed] from time to time on the road with him, I think basically [Ellington] did not like his father because J.E. had embarrassed his mother.[75]

RUTH ELLINGTON: My father got so desperate, sometimes, looking for people to bring home to feed and so forth, that one day he walked in with all the interns of Harlem Hospital, and he didn't even know them. Just walked in, all these people in white coats came floating into the apartment.[76]

IRVING MILLS: The next time we did a picture for Paramount it was *Murder at the Vanities*, an Earl Carroll picture. And while I was there, Mae West was doing a picture at the Paramount Studio. And I went in to see Mae West who I used to handle before she became a motion picture star – I formed a vaudeville act with her and Harry Richmond. And I told her that I had brought Duke to do [a picture] and I said, just kiddingly, it would be nice to put them in your picture so long as we're here.

She picked up the telephone and called up Bill LeBaron, the head of the studio, she said, 'I want Duke Ellington in my picture.' She was that big that any demand she made, they filled. So we did two pictures at Paramount.[77]

Murder at the Vanities was made at Paramount Studios, Hollywood, between 5 February and late March 1934 and released on 23 May that year. The Mae West film Belle of the Nineties *was made at Paramount Studios between 12 March and 5 June 1934 and premiered at the Paramount Theatre in New York on 21 September 1934.*

DUKE ELLINGTON: We played 'Ebony Rhapsody' for the Mae West picture. The music was written by Arthur Johnson and Sam Coslow and was one of the 28 hits they had that year. We were booked at Frank Sebastian's Cotton Club. Frank Sebastian is always written very large, Cotton Club next and the band gets third billing ... we weren't very successful on the coast. Wingy Manone said about us there: 'Swing hadn't come over the mountains yet.'[78]

Ellington played Frank Sebastian's Cotton Club in Culver City, California, 5–18 April 1934, on an engagement that was scheduled to run until 27 April. The Ellington band 'didn't take nearly as well as expected,' said the Los Angeles Daily News.[79]

BOB UDKOFF: I was working for my father in Los Angeles who had a [clothes] cleaning store and one day I saw a truck marked 'Duke Ellington Orchestra'. I went into this building and I met one particular fellow, Jonesy, who was Duke's valet, bandboy – he was a former waiter from the Cotton Club. I said, 'I'm from the cleaners, do you have anything to clean?' He said, 'Do we?!' They started bringing out these clothes, it was a tremendous amount, and when they were finished I delivered them and over a period of a week or so I got fairly friendly with Jonesy. They were there to make some movies for Paramount – *Murder at the Vanities* with Mae West, and then they did some work in

Duke Ellington. The dapper young bandleader in his early thirties.
(Stuart Nicholson Collection)

Duke Ellington and his Washingtonians photographed around 1925. This version of the band had (l to r) Sonny Greer, Charlie Irvis, Bubber Miley (seated), Elmer Snowden, Otto Hardwick and Ellington. (Ken Whitten Collection)

Duke Ellington and his Famous Orchestra on the set of the film *Black and Tan* in 1929. (l to r) Freddie Jenkins, Joe 'Tricky Sam' Nanton, Cootie Williams, Juan Tizol, Arthur Whetsol, Duke Ellington, Sonny Greer, Freddie Guy, Harry Carney, Wellman Braud, Johnny Hodges, Barney Bigard. (Ken Whitten Collection)

Duke Ellington Meets Hoover

Duke Ellington on the steps of the White House, 1st October 1931, with members of the Welcome Home Committee. But contemporary evidence suggests his meeting with President Hoover never took place. Front row: (l to r) Mrs E. F. Carroll, Duke Ellington, Elrita Skinner and Mrs Eloise Skinner. Back row: Rev. J. C. Olden, J. A. G. Lavelle and James Mills. (Stuart Nicholson Collection)

Duke Ellington and his Famous Orchestra. Photographed prior to visiting the United Kingdom and France in the summer of 1933. (rear) Sonny Greer; (first row) Joe 'Tricky Sam' Nanton, Juan Tizol, Lawrence Brown, Cootie Williams, Arthur Whetsol, Freddie Jenkins; (second row) Otto Harwick, Harry Carney, Johnny Hodges, Barney Bigard, Freddie Guy; (front) Wellman Braud, Duke Ellington. (Stuart Nicholson Collection)

The Ellington Saxophone Section. Photographed in the Cotton Club, Harlem in 1933. (l to r) Otto Hardwick, Harry Carney, Barney Bigard, Johnny Hodges. (Stuart Nicholson Collection)

The Ellington Brass Section. Photographed in the Cotton Club, Harlem in 1933. (l to r) Joe 'Tricky Sam' Nanton, Juan Tizol, Lawrence Brown (trombones); Freddie Jenkins, Cootie Williams, Arthur Whetsol (trumpets). (Stuart Nicholson Collection)

Above: **The Ellington Rhythm Section.**
Photographed in the Cotton Club, Harlem in
1933. (l to r) Freddie Guy, William 'Sonny'
Greer (note microphone since Greer was billed
as 'The Singing Drummer'), Wellman Braud.
(Stuart Nicholson Collection)

Left: **Irving Mills.** Ellington's
personal manager from 1927 to 1939.
(Stuart Nicholson Collection)

local theatres and a place called Frank Sebastian's Cotton Club. One day, Jonesy said, 'Would you mind Mr Ellington's [suit], would you mind taking it to the studio?' I said, 'Of course not.' So we drove up to the gate, Paramount Studios, and Duke introduced me around. As things went on I became closer, they were there for I think two months. They finally got ready to leave, and school had already started and I think it was Johnny Hodges, 'Hey, Bobby, won't you come with us?' 'OK.' I got on the train, they had a private car, and we went up to San Francisco, they were at the Golden Gate Theatre doing five shows a day which was very hectic, and from then we went up to Portland, Seattle, and we got to Salt Lake City and Duke looked up and said, 'Why aren't you in school?' And I said, 'I'm through with school!' He said, 'The hell you are, grow up to be a bum, no education.' He called Jonesy, he said, 'Send this kid home, we could get into trouble, a minor. Should be in school.' As time went on I began to build a friendship with Duke, I think because of the fact that I was not in any way affiliated with him in business, in booking him or in any of the business relationships he had.[80]

BILLY STRAYHORN: *Murder at the Vanities*, [Duke] played 'The Rape of the Rhapsody', that was the name of the number. Oh, it was wonderful, that's what started – that's what really got me. He had a chord which I have never discovered, I haven't heard it since, I couldn't figure this chord out. I went home after going to see his show at the Penn Theatre in Pittsburgh, and I couldn't figure out what was in that chord, it was just wonderful.[81]

BARNEY BIGARD: They put a toothpick under the keys on my clarinet and when I started to blow, nothing came out. And we did it to Hodges, did it to everybody! And we played a theatre in Philadelphia, it's a small stage and in those days they were using klieg lights and Tizol was up on the ramp above the klieg lights and on the opposite side I was next to a klieg light, burning up like mad. Well, that's when 'Mood Indigo' was getting real popular. So Arthur Whetsol and Tricky Sam and myself, we were the trio. We had to go to the front and play 'Mood Indigo'. Tizol was full of pranks. He bought some stink bombs, but he didn't tell nobody nothing. So when we went out to play 'Mood Indigo' he burst one. So while we're playing we started getting this scent, you know? So I'm looking at Tricky, Tricky is looking at me. And Arthur Whetsol, he's so proper, you know, and he's looking at both of us. So when I had to wait for my turn to solo I walked to Duke, I said, 'You ought to be ashamed!' He said, 'Ashamed of what?' I said, 'You did that.' He said, 'I didn't do anything.' So I said, 'Well, there's nobody but Hodges.' So I walked over to Hodges and said, 'Rab, why did you do that for?' 'Do what?' I said, 'You know what you did.' And he got angry with me. Then the scent grew stronger. It got to the first row of people, everybody stirring. So Tricky and I, we're laughing. We were laughing so much we left Whetsol out there by himself, and boy, you never saw somebody so embarrassed![82]

JUAN TIZOL: While we were at the Apollo Theatre, I got that itching powder and I went to Duke, the curtain was getting ready to go up for the start of the show, I said, 'What time is it Duke?' and at that time he had a watch, I was rubbing powder around his wrist. So he started playing and all of a sudden, he started playing with his left hand and rubbing his hand, and he was wondering what the devil that was and he found out sooner or later it was itching powder. I used to play tricks on a lot of people, like the Step brothers, the dancers. I put in some itching powder. I came in early that morning, I was in Boston, I went in their dressing room, in one of their pants, so when they went upstairs to dance, oh my Lord, the red fellow, the one they called 'Red' had lighter tone; oh, he was dancing and squawking,

I said I didn't know anything but they figured it was Tizol doing it. The next day I came to the theatre I went to put on my tuxedo shirt, I notice something's wrong and instead of shaking it off or changing the shirt it was almost time to go on stage, and oh, I was on stage itching like mad![83]

On 7 December 1934, Ellington opened at the Apollo, in New York.

DUKE ELLINGTON: Rex Stewart took Freddie Jenkins' chair.[84]

Jenkins was forced to leave in late November 1934, having contracted T.B. His replacement was cornettist Rex Stewart.

REX STEWART: There I sat for the very first time in the brass section of the great Duke Ellington orchestra, completely bewildered ... I was trying to figure out what was supposed to happen when all of a sudden Cootie nudged me with his elbow and said I was on! Duke stood at the piano giving me his well-known 'show-me' smile. The tempo was way up as I edged to the microphone, tentatively trying to find what out what key they were playing ... after what seemed hours of this, I hit an altissimo A, the band for once hit the same chord, and I was home and free, covered with sweat that poured from everywhere. That was my initiation into Duke Ellington's band, and if I expected any praise for getting myself off the spot, I was certainly mistaken. Nobody said a word.[85]

Rex Stewart joined Ellington on 15 December 1934 at the Ritz Theatre, Woodbridge, New York.

DUKE ELLINGTON: In one of my forthcoming movie shorts I have an episode which concerns the death of a baby. This is the high and should have come last, but that would not have been commercial, as the managers say. However, I put into the dirge all the misery, sorrow and undertones of the conditions that went with the baby's death. It was true to and of the life of the people it depicted.[86]

'Hymn of Sorrow', depicting the death of a young child, was Part Three of the four part Symphony in Black, a film that acquired an almost mystic aura, heightened by its symphonic title, arty set lighting, elaborate presentations by Ellington compositions and a cameo appearance by the singer Billie Holiday. Filmed and recorded in December 1934 and early 1935, it was built around Ellington the composer and what was described in the opening shots as a 'Premier of a New Symphony of Negro Moods'. With an enlarged orchestra playing to an audience of white concert-goers, Ellington was consciously elevating the perception of black music with his Rhapsody of Negro Life. Combining material written specially for the film with adaptations of three previous Ellington numbers, 'Ducky Wucky', 'Saddest Tale' and 'Merry-Go-Round', it was presented as a programmatic suite, building on the concept of an extended composition for jazz orchestra initially advanced on the 1931 recording of 'Creole Rhapsody' and the subsequent 'Ebony Rhapsody' from early 1934, performed as part of the revue scene in the film Murder at the Vanities. Ellington had often voiced his ambitions for writing a major extended work in press interviews throughout the 1930s, and certainly as early as 1933, during his tour of England, he spoke about composing a 'History of the American Negro' in five suites, from Africa to 'Hot Harlem'. Within a year of Symphony in Black, the four-part recording 'Reminiscing in Tempo' would follow, but it was not until 1943 and the Carnegie Hall premiere of 'Black, Brown and Beige' that his ambition was fully realized. Thus these film appearances and recordings, of which 'Diminuendo in Blue' and 'Crescendo in Blue' (both 1937) must be seen as a part, represent clear stepping stones on the way to this major work.

NEW YORK AMSTERDAM NEWS: Duke Ellington's Paramount short Symphony in Black is scoring everywhere it is shown.[87]

RUTH ELLINGTON: Then my mother became ill and she went to Washington for treatment, in September [1934] and finally in March [1935] she was very ill and . . . she went to a sanatorium in Detroit and died there on 25 May 1935. During that time Duke was so, so stricken that the doctors were more worried about him at the very end than they were about her, because they knew she would not make it, but they kept saying there he was sitting up on a chair, straight up on a straight chair, and her pillow was here and he was leaning over on her pillow day and night, day and night for about two or three days and nights without leaving and they said he couldn't continue like that, they were very worried, but he stayed there and never left the room until she died.[88]

DUKE ELLINGTON: When my mother died the bottom dropped out. Before that I'd compete with anybody. I'd say, 'You wanna fight? O.K., because I'm fighting for my mother and the money I get will go to her.'[89]

RUTH ELLINGTON: And then we had that long train ride from Detroit to Washington bringing her back, and then we buried her in Washington – there was Edward, my father and Mercer, because I remember looking back as we came into the train station – it does seem incredible she had gone out a passenger and came back on the freight car – I can remember getting off the train in Washington and looking back and seeing these three men behind me and thinking, there's no other woman now but me.[90]

Daisy Ellington was buried on 27 May 1935 in Washington D.C. Ellington was devastated.

MERCER ELLINGTON: His world had been built around his mother and the days after her death were the saddest and most morbid of his life. He cut down his activity and had been with her frequently during the month before she died, and afterward he just sat around the house and wept for days. Then you could be sure he was drinking. He would be on a drunk for two or three weeks and then come off it.[91]

New York Amsterdam News: It would seem the impression was given out that Duke Ellington had cancelled all future engagements on account of the death of his mother. Mr Ned Williams [of Mills Artists Inc.] has stated that Duke has returned to his band.[92]

Mercer Ellington: His great loss affected his musical output more than anything else that happened in his career. He brooded a long time and the first sign that he was coming out of his despair was 'Reminiscing in Tempo'.[93]

Duke Ellington: I wrote 'Reminiscing in Tempo' that year. It was one of my first ambitious things. It was written in a soliloquizing mood. My mother's death was the greatest shock. I didn't do anything but brood. The music is representative of that. It begins with pleasant thoughts. Then something awful gets you down. Then you snap out of it, and it ends affirmatively.[94]

Variety: The four sides on the two 10-inch platters are replete with all the Ellington orchestral niceties on scoring, arrangement and interpretation.[95]

American Music-Lover: No one who is even remotely interested in Ellington and his artistic development can afford not to give these records a painstaking hearing ... a work of incalculable importance and one not to be judged after one or two hearings.[96]

Esquire: A very ambitious effort ... I won't go into the various effects produced but most of them are beautifully done ... Here it is Ellington collectors, get it![97]

New Yorker: Unusual and interesting.[98]

Washington Post: Picture the Duke sitting down at the keyboard to improvise and instead of evoking tunes and melodic

variations, letting his rhythmic sense – and who has one if Ellington hasn't – run fancy free.[99]

DUKE ELLINGTON: There were a couple more changes in the band around that time. Braud left when Rex [Stewart] joined and Billy Taylor and Hayes Alvis took his place.[100]

In fact, Billy Taylor on bass joined in November 1934. Braud left in March 1935, and bassist Hayes Alvis came in May 1935.

HAYES ALVIS: From 1935 to 1938 I played with Duke Ellington. Rex Stewart and Harry Carney and I were particularly close buddies – we were also the band's vocal trio. Dig us on 'I've Got to be a Rug-cutter'. I also got a kick with working with Billy Taylor, making this the first jazz orchestra featuring two string-bass men. Not everything was fun in Duke's band, however, and I was never what you would call a 'Real Ellingtonian'. You have to follow the band's career real closely and be in the know of what happens inside to see that in Duke's band there are the 'Real Ellingtonians' on the one hand, and the others who 'Just happen to play with Duke' on the other. I cannot explain it but there is a big difference.[101]

DUKE ELLINGTON: The Congress was in early spring 1936. The Urban Room engagement there was a very successful one and I made friends with the chef out there who was a wizard. His speciality was hamburgers, believe it or not, and I believe in giving credit where credit is due. He was terrific![102]

The Congress Hotel engagement in Chicago was from 8 May to 5 June.

REX STEWART: For the very important Congress Hotel debut in Chicago, the Governor outdid himself, outfitting us in crimson trousers, special made crimson shoes, which set off the white mess jackets, boiled white shirts with winged collars and white ties. Duke was overheard saying, 'They may not like our music, but we sure look pretty.' We received an ovation before we played a note. One newspaper critic devoted two-thirds of his column to our appearance.[103]

DUKE ELLINGTON: 'Solitude' was our biggest song following the European tour, but we'd had it on wax a whole year before it became popular. Then there were more theatres and one-nighters.[104]

ADAM CLAYTON POWELL JR: We all know what sharecropping is. It's the feudal system of the South. A family is allocated a plot of ground, a ramshackle cabin, a mule and a plough. All year long they work till harvest time. Then the reckoning comes. Against the bale of cotton is tallied up the rent for ground, cabin, mule, plough, sack of hominy, fat back, sorghum and chewing tobacco. And the tenant farmer always owes, thus being forced to work with all his family another year. Here in Harlem, this condition holds forth, not among our labourers and domestics, but among our top-notch Negro bands. Duke Ellington is just a musical sharecropper. He has a drawing account which has been stated to run around $300 per week. At the end of the year when Massa Mills' cotton has been laid by, Duke is told he owes them several hundred or thousand dollars. He owns the moniker of vice-president of Mills Inc., and is entitled to a percentage of the profits. However, his lawyer and accountant happen to be Mills employees. When they finish totalling there ain't no profits left. The Boys in the band are just hired hands who haven't netted $3,000 in years, despite the fact that it is rumoured Mills pocketed $90,000 in 1934 alone. Now, how is this done? First, nobody is paid unless they are working, and yet their expenses keep on piling up. When they work, Mills gets $4,000–$6,000 per week for the Ellington unit. He pays, let us say, thirteen boys at $100 each, Sonnie [sic] Greer gets $150, Ivie Anderson $75, and Duke $300. That's less than $2,000! In other words, the Broadway boys, without swinging the swivel chair, pocket 50 to 65 per cent of the take. How about one night stands? Here again the hired hands get $20 or a total of about $400, yet the band sharecrops around $1,000 average for one-nighters. For the past few years the band has been laid off as much as it has worked. Oft-times they are shipped hundreds of miles to do a one-night $20 engagement. If they are laid over, out comes both meals and cleaning and pressing uniforms. They could probably make more shaking a tin cup on Times Square.[105]

This article, edited down from its original length for inclusion here, had a dateline of 1936. Whether or not the figures Adam Clayton Powell Jr bandies about are accurate is perhaps less important than the clear suggestion of financial problems between Ellington and the Mills office, flagging up a problem for the future.

LAWRENCE BROWN: I remember one time we left New York to play a New Year's Eve dance and we stayed out there not working for about a month and a half. They didn't return you home. They would carry you to that job, then sit you there till the next job. Because you paid your own expenses, you paid your own room, food, lodging, laundry and those kind of expenses. It was out in Northeast, between New York and Chicago.[106]

OTTO HARDWICK: We just accepted it. But it was a lot of fun, I don't think the money had too much to do with it. All right, you made a living, that was it. The work was a pleasure.[107]

IRVING MILLS: [Duke] gave away a lot of money. Whatever town he went to, there were people on his back for donations, and he helped everybody. He gave away a lot of money. And I used to get the bills, and people'd say, 'The Duke signed so and so,' and I didn't know anything about it. He spent more money than he was making. He gave donations for different charities for the black people. He did a whole lot of things there, because he was in a spot to do it, you know.[108]

RUTH ELLINGTON: Then I found out he had bought a racehorse and he named the racehorse 'Smooth Sailing Love', which we never saw! He never saw it either, because a friend of his whose name was Mexico, who was quite a character around New York, had said, 'Duke, I've got just the horse for you, he's out in California.' So Edward bought the horse, 'Smooth Sailing Love', nobody else saw him and we don't know whether the horse ran or what! But by the time I got out to California he was out to pasture, and I never saw him![109]

MERCER ELLINGTON: Jonsey, Richard Bowden Jones, was the band boy in those days and I had got to the stage where I was allowed to stay out quite late with him ... [he] used to tell me a lot of humorous anecdotes and things about my father I hadn't really known before. For example, how he could sleep, how difficult it was to get him out of bed. How he had a tremendous appetite. How at that time he was a really great, two fisted drinker ... through Jonsey, who lived around him from day to day, I began to know Pop a little more as a person.[110]

THE AFRO-AMERICAN: DUKE ELLINGTON AND SON MERCER ARE GREAT PALS – There's nothing that Duke Ellington, famous bandleader, would like to do more than engage his son in hot debate and Mercer, 16, feels the same way about his father ... The youth is quite a scholar. And Duke admits it, but not to his son. Duke would argue on any subject as long as his son is holding up the other end.[111]

MERCER ELLINGTON: One of the few things that Ellington knew about me, my own activities, was the fact that I was great at maths.[112]

REX STEWART: It wasn't too long after I joined Duke that we embarked on a southern tour. Among the tobacco barns, skating rinks, cotton warehouses and fields were some theatres. Our reception was tremendous and we were compelled to do many extra shows. It almost seemed like a continuous performance.[113]

BARNEY BIGARD: I think it was in Alabama somewhere and we played in this theatre and it was strictly white, you know. So they decided, the manager decided to give one night to the Negroes. But the funny part about it, we'd play a number or whatever, you could see their feet patting on the floor. No applause. They wouldn't – they were afraid to applaud.[114]

REX STEWART: Once it took a full-fledged band mutiny in St Louis to force Ellington to arrange for food for the men, when additional shows prevented us going out to the ghetto area for dinner. Yet . . . our appearance on stage was of primary import- ance. Thousands of dollars on tailor's fees were spent for uniforms. One memorable time, when we were to play the Roxy Theatre in New York and dress rehearsal revealed that none of our five sets of uniform fitted the colour scheme of this particular presentation, a rush order provided us with our sixth outfit – at double prices.[115]

DUKE ELLINGTON: We've never let ourselves be put into a position of being treated with disrespect. From 1934 to 1936 we went touring into the South, without the benefit of Federal judges, and we commanded respect. We didn't travel by bus. Instead we had two Pullman cars and a seventy-foot baggage car. We parked them in each station and lived in them. We had our own water, food, electricity and sanitary facilities. The natives would come by and say, 'What's that?' 'Well,' we'd say, 'that's the way the President travels.' We made our point.[116]

DUKE ELLINGTON: For my part, I've tried to make the best contribution I could to native [American] music – and I'm still trying. Nothing else has mattered to me. Naturally my own race is closest to my heart and it is in the musical idiom of that race that I can find my most natural expression. Just now we're calling it swing ... but it all adds up to a lot of satisfaction at sharing in the achievement of the Negro race.[117]

CHAPTER SIX
STEPPIN' INTO SWING SOCIETY

In 1936, Ellington looked out on a drastically changed musical landscape. On 21 August 1935, Benny Goodman and his Orchestra had opened at the Palomar Ballroom in Los Angeles. The crowd response to his music was so overwhelming it sent reverberations through the music business. With Prohibition a thing of the past, Goodman had hit the right note of optimism to chime with Roosevelt's 'New Deal'. As the Depression eased there was hope in the air for a better future, and this was reflected in Goodman's immaculately rehearsed ensemble that was in essence a fusion between jazz and the American popular song through brilliant arrangements by Fletcher Henderson, Spud Murphy, Benny Carter, Deane Kincaide, Jimmy Mundy and Edgar Sampson. Goodman was swept to centre stage on a surge of popular acclaim – the 'Swing Era' had begun.

Goodman's popularity paved the way for countless new bands to make a national breakthrough to a dance-crazy, jitterbugging American youth. Suddenly there were swing bands, sweet bands and Mickey Mouse bands all vying for their share of an enormous youth market that quickly opened up during the latter half of the '30s. Swing was King and the Ellington band was suddenly one among a very crowded field. Yet despite this huge upswing of interest in big band music, Ellington was not best placed to take advantage of the changing circumstances around him.

Following his mother's death, Ellington's creativity had taken

a nose dive, Variety *noting that his 'discords have grown stale'.*[1]
*His morale sapped, this temporary lack of interest in music came
at precisely the time when Ned Williams, who since 1931 had
imaginatively spearheaded successful publicity campaigns to support Ellington's musical endeavours, left Mills Artists in August
1935. To make matters worse, Irving Mills was now dividing his
energies among the other bands he represented, including Cab
Calloway, Ina Ray Hutton, the Hudson-DeLange orchestra, Wingy
Manone and the Mills Blue Rhythm Band, all being groomed to
make a killing in the big band craze. Yet swing was as much a
social phenomenon as a musical one. The big ballrooms where the
bands played had provided an opportunity for America's youth to
meet, interact and to make new dates since the 1920s.*

*With the swing craze came more and more ballrooms and a
huge rise in their popularity, places where young people had a
chance to meet partners who didn't live on the same block or go
to the same school. For most of these fans it was not the jazz
improvisation that attracted them, it was because the big bands
played music for dancing. And what they danced to were pop
tunes of the day, something for which Ellington showed scant
regard, featuring instead his own compositions with their dazzling
tone colours, highly original writing and the unique solo voices
within his ensemble. In contrast, Fletcher Henderson's writing
for the Goodman band appealed as much to the feet as the heart.
Goodman, a great dancer himself, more than once said he considered his music was made primarily for dancing. His band,
the most popular in America, became widely imitated, creating
a kind of uniformity that was often only personalized by a
bandleader's instrumental prowess. The dichotomy of the Swing
Era was that the music was functional, played for dancing, and
the more the big bands succumbed to musical exploitation, the
more equivocal became the position of jazz musicians in their
ranks.*

For a while Ellington seemed a little out of place in this new market place, as his appearance in the 1937 film The Hit Parade *revealed. Among the numbers he performed was 'I've Got To Be A Rug Cutter' with its answering line, '(So I Can) Swing Out In The Groove'. The fact was that Ellington, to a certain extent, was forced to 'swing out in the groove' to compete with dance bands. Although he had always played music that could be danced to, his was always much more than simply a 'dance band'. His music was richer, explored a wider range of emotions and presented a more varied sound palette than the swing bands whose style took much inspiration from gospel song antiphony between brass and sax sections. Even though Ellington's music looked forward from jazz towards art music, whether he liked it or not box office receipts and record sales were now the arbiters of success and he was forced to position his music within this new, highly competitive milieu. He did this gradually by balancing the opposing poles of commercial necessity and artistic integrity, the out-choruses of 'Dinah's In A Jam', for example, giving the dancers the sort of rocking riffs popular at the time. But the fact remained he was much more at home in the environment of the Cotton Club than he was catering for jitterbugs. On 24 September 1936, the Cotton Club re-opened its doors at a new location on 48th Street and Broadway in the heart of New York's Great White Way with a lavish revue featuring Cab Calloway. On 17 March 1937, Ellington took over, opening the second new Cotton Club Parade, with Ethel Waters and the Nicholas Brothers.*

DUKE ELLINGTON: As far back as 1932 – several years before anybody heard of jitterbugs and jam sessions – I composed, published and played a piece called 'It Don't Mean a Thing If it Ain't Got That Swing'.[2]

DUKE ELLINGTON: Eighty per cent of the so-called 'swing' music is of Negro creation, even though we can see all types of music combined into the integrated unit we call swing or jazz. If the Negro got due credit for his musical contributions to America it would be conceded that the negro has done more to create a distinctively American music than any other race.[3]

DUKE ELLINGTON: In 1937 we made *The Hit Parade* for Republic Pictures. We went back to the Cotton Club that year but the show had been written by the office.[4]

The movie The Hit Parade *was made at the Biograph Studios, New York, and in the Republic Studios, North Hollywood, during January–February 1937. It was released in April that year.*

METRONOME: Duke Ellington and His Orchestra. Cotton Club, New York. MBS Wire ... The Cotton Club draws many ickies who pester Ellington to play pop tunes that were hardly intended for him to attack. He plays them ... [and] he plays them well enough to satisfy those ickies, and even draw their applause ... Of course from a hepper musical point of view, Duke's forte is the kind of stuff that he likes to play and that has made him famous. For sheer originality, interest, and structure his orchestrations ... have yet to be equalled in the field of dancebandom.[5]

DUKE ELLINGTON: Our only hit [in 1937] was 'Caravan' which had first been made by one of the small bands [Barney Bigard's], for the Variety label. That year was the first year we began featuring our several small 'bands within the band'.[6]

HELEN DANCE: The long series of records by small units from the Duke Ellington orchestra, launched in early 1937 on the Variety label, basically owed its being to the fact that Irving Mills was open to suggestions which favoured the fortunes of people contracted to him in his Artists Bureau ... By the time I joined him in 1936, Irving had considerable experience in the recording field and ultimately favoured my proposal for small groups under the nominal leadership of musicians in Duke's band.[7]

JUAN TIZOL: The first composition I wrote for Duke was 'Caravan'. You know how much he gave me? Twenty-five dollars. Until later on, I guess his heart got so – later in the years, he decided to give me a percentage of the composition. Because I sold it outright to Irving Mills, and later on he decided to give me a percentage, and thank God! Everything I did, Duke arranged. All my tunes, I did quite a few tunes. I don't get too much [in royalties], a dollar, three dollars, four dollars, ten dollars, but I get some all the time. And on every one of those tunes, I was always playing a little solo.[8]

In July 1937, sheet music sales of 'Caravan' placed it among the nation's top fifteen best sellers.

HELEN DANCE: The version of 'Caravan' [with Barney Bigard and his Jazzopaters] was very important in ensuring the continuation of my small band programme [for Variety]. I was not particularly enamoured of its exotic motif, but I was delighted when it became a hit ... outselling that recorded by the big band the following May![9]

DUKE ELLINGTON: 'Caravan' – that's one of those things Tizol came up with. See, it wasn't in tempo, he stood [and played it] sort of ad lib. He played it, [the] first ten bars, we took it and worked out the rest of it.[10]

DUKE ELLINGTON: Of course there was the Savoy, the 'Land of Happy Feet', where many great bands played, many great jitterbugs danced, it was a sparkling place ... The Savoy Ballroom was the scene of many battles of music, band battles, most of the battles were between Chick Webb and the visiting bands and of course [Charlie] Buchanan, the manager of the joint, would bet anybody that Chick would cut anybody's band that came there, because he knew exactly when to put him on at the psychological right moment of the evening, and he was usually right – in spite of the fact that Chick did have a wonderful band, not only that, his music was tailored to the people who danced there.[11]

HARRY CARNEY: Chick Webb was always the real challenge to all bands. And there were a lot of times when we, at least I was, apprehensive about going on the bandstand after Chick Webb had played so well.[12]

SONNY GREER: It was a band battle at the Savoy Ballroom in the late thirties. We were pitted against Chick Webb's band. You know the way Ellington rambles at the piano until he sets up the right tension and decides just when to play? Well, that night he went into one of his long intros. The guys seemed to be a little down; some of them had been drinking whisky. Chick must have thought he had us. All of a sudden Duke hit the key notes. The tune was 'St Louis Blues'. I turned to the rest of the band, letting them know what was happening. They all stood up and waited a little longer; I shouted, 'Rollin',' and the whole band exploded. We blew the hell out of that tune. We were gone, man. Mean! Chick came by the stand at the intermission; he was really sad. 'What the hell you cats trying to do to me?' he said.[13]

In a battle of bands at the Savoy Ballroom, Harlem, on 7 March 1937, Ellington and Chick Webb attracted a record crowd of 3,100.

METRONOME: Barney Bigard (2nd sax and featured clarinet[in Duke's band]) – hates playing tenor but dotes on playing clarinet . . . wants Duke to get a straight tenorman . . . a Noo Ohlins Creole who used to play with King Oliver and who's blessed with thousands of relatives who drag him off all trains to kiss him . . . unlimited hot, cold, sweet or bitter coffee drinker . . . a bridge fanatic who's devoted to his wife and three kids . . . described as a yard wide and a yard and one inch tall in stature.[14]

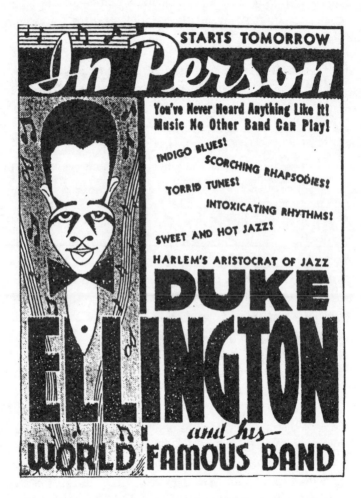

RUTH ELLINGTON: [Then] my father died. He died in the Presbyterian Hospital here in New York. I remember when my father was ill in the hospital there, Duke had said to me, 'If my old man gets well, I'll give him anything. I'll buy him anything he wants.' We were coming out of the hospital. But he did not get well, and within two years we had lost mother and father and I was like a displaced person and I'm sure he was too. I think it hit him very badly.[15]

Ellington Snr died at 11 p.m. on Thursday 28 October 1937. The funeral service was in New York on Saturday 30 October and the body was transferred to Washington D.C., accompanied by Duke Ellington and other members of the family. The body was laid to rest on Tuesday 2 November.

RICHARD O. BOYER: When his father died, in 1937, Ellington suffered an emotional relapse and lost whatever ground he gained [after the death of his mother]. For a time he did almost no composing.[16]

Ellington was the first black entertainer to appear at the Orpheum Theatre, Memphis, Tenn., when he appeared there 2–6 December 1937.

JUAN TIZOL: [In the South] I went over and sat down in the restaurant, at the regular chair and asked for what I wanted, and they wouldn't serve the rest of the band and so I said, 'Well, if you don't serve them, you don't serve me either because I'm with them.' They said we could go back in the kitchen and get it in the kitchen. Or I'd get the food and take it to them [in the bus]. I used to do that all the time in the South.[17]

BARNEY BIGARD: Just Sam [Fliashnik] and I went to get some sandwiches for the boys in the band, so Freddy Guy says, 'Hell, if they can go in there I can go in there too.' So Freddy Guy walks in there. The guy says, 'You'll have to go in the back.'

Freddy Guy says, 'What do you mean, I have to go in the back?' 'Just what I said, if you want something to eat you got to go in the back.' He said, 'Don't you know what I am?' The guy says, 'You still got to go in the back.' He says, 'Man, I'm a Creole.' The guy looked at him, he says, 'I don't care how old you is. You got to go in the back anyhow.'[18]

FBI FILE 100–434443: EDWARD KENNEDY (DUKE) ELLINGTON: The May 12, 1938, issue of the *Daily Worker*, an east coast Communist newspaper, contained an article captioned 'Harlem Youth Parley Rallies for Jobs, Peace'. This article listed Duke Ellington among the prominent endorsers of the All-Harlem Youth Conference which was going to convene on May 13, 1938, in New York City. The All-Harlem Youth Conference has been described as 'among the more conspicuous Communist-front groups in the Racial subclassification' by the California Committee on Un-American Activities. (61–7563–60X6)[19]

In contrast to the widely held belief that Ellington did not involve himself personally in matters of social justice, leaving his music as his commentary on the plight of the Negro in an America divided by racial inequality, Ellington's FBI file reveals otherwise. As will be seen, his activities, especially through the 1940s, were closely monitored and reveal him to be more active in social protest than was hitherto imagined, often lending his name to several prominent and not so prominent causes, and he was informed upon several times. As the increasingly paranoid politics of the Cold War gained momentum, the FBI revelled in the increasingly tense atmosphere (every organization, it seems, was a 'communist front'), their shortcomings eventually being shown up for what they were.

METRONOME: Arthur Whetsol was on the job even when not well.[20]

JUAN TIZOL: We find out that Whetsol was getting bad because he used to go and play whatever he had to play and he was shaking and everything and could hardly make any sense. We started finding out, when it was getting awful bad, he'd get very nervous.[21]

Whetsol left during an engagement at the Stanley Theatre in Pittsburgh in February 1938. He was replaced by Wallace Jones.

DUKE ELLINGTON: Year after year we had a different tune. 'Mood Indigo' had a 1931 copyright, in 1932 it was 'Don't Mean a Thing If It Ain't Got That Swing', 1935 was 'In My Solitude', 'In Sentimental Mood' was 1934, 1936 we got 'Azure', 1937 'Caravan' and 'Prelude to a Kiss', 'I Let a Song Go Out of My Heart', that was 1938.[22]

DUKE ELLINGTON: Usually I gather the boys around me after a concert, say about three in the morning when the world is quiet. I have a central idea which I bring out on the piano. At one stage, Cootie Williams, the trumpeter, will suggest an interpolation, perhaps a riff or obbligato for that spot. A little later on Juan Tizol, the trombonist, will interrupt with another idea. We try that and maybe adopt it. It generally depends on the majority's opinion. Thus after three or four sessions, I will evolve an entirely new composition. But it will not be written out, put on a score, until we've been playing it in public quite a while.[23]

REX STEWART: One way and another, Johnny [Hodges] was involved in several songs which were later attributed to Duke, such as 'I Let a Song Go Out of My Heart'. Actually, we all brought bits and pieces of songs to the boss, maybe sixteen bars, maybe only four and then Duke changed or embellished so really the finished product bore his stamp.[24]

DUKE ELLINGTON: There are many instances where guys have come in with four bars or eight bars and said, 'Hey, this is a good lick!' And I'd say, 'Yeah, it is a good lick, let's make something out of it.' Then you take it home, arrange it up, add what needs to be added to it and it comes up a number.[25]

LAWRENCE BROWN: 'Let a Song Go Out of My Heart', that's an obbligato of Johnny Hodges against the melody of 'Once in a While'.[26]

BOB UDKOFF: Mitchell Parish was a court reporter and part-time lyricist, he wrote the lyrics to so many great things, he wrote the lyrics for 'Sophisticated Lady', 'Mood Indigo'. Irving had him on a salary, a flat rate, and later he insisted upon getting credit so he got his ASCAP. Prior to that, Irving on a lot of the things would put his own name on, although Mitchell Parish wrote the lyrics. Irving had no problem taking the credit![27]

HELEN DANCE: [Mills, whose] reputation was sometimes impugned because of the frequency with which his name was featured on compositions Ellington recorded, maintained that ideas contributed by him to a number of Duke's finished products entitled him to these credits. Duke often defended his views and was not among his detractors. Neither was he maligned by those of us who worked for him ... [we] were awed by an energy which was legendary and found some of us, as a result, up most of the night.[28]

BARNEY BIGARD: [Ellington] said he wrote 'Mood Indigo' at his breakfast while his mother was making breakfast or dinner ... I had given him the last half of the tune already and he just added the first part ... Oh, I got about thirteen tunes I never did credit for, 'Saturday Night Function', 'Rockin' in Rhythm' – he put Harry [Carney's] name on there. Harry couldn't compose nothing if he tried, God bless his soul ... But [Duke] was quite a – he was a fantastic man. I mean, believe me. Course he did a lot of things I didn't approve and a few other guys in the band didn't approve, but nobody would say anything.[29]

FREDDIE JENKINS: All of us were well educated and well trained musically and quite capable of composing. Naturally we improvised most of our own solos and whenever we came up with something like a complete composition that was good enough for the band, the Duke paid us liberally. Where the piece didn't require too much work to fit the band, the guy might share in the ASCAP credit, like Whetsol's 'Misty Morning' or Miley's 'Goin' to Town', or Hardwick's 'Down in Our Alley Blues', or my 'Swing Low'.[30]

BARNEY BIGARD: Duke studied all his men. He studied what their style, how they manoeuvre with their music, with their playing and everything and he keeps that in his mind so if he wrote anything for you, it fit you like a glove, you know, and you're really at home playing it. It's not something that he was just taking from his head and making – trying to see how difficult he could make it or anything.[31]

DUKE ELLINGTON: [In 1938] we wrote the Cotton Club show ourselves, and we were lucky with several hits, 'I Let a Song Go Out of My Heart', 'If You Were In My Place', 'Carnival in Caroline', 'Swingtime in Honolulu', 'Slapping Seventh Avenue' and a few more.[32]

DUKE ELLINGTON: I'll never forget when I wrote 'I Let a Song Go Out of My Heart', [lyricist Henry] Nemo and I. It was the year we wrote the show for the Cotton Club, it was a part of the score and this was a number they threw out of the show. [They put in] 'Swingtime in Honolulu' or something. Nobody has ever heard of 'Swingtime in Honolulu'![33]

Ellington played the Fourth Cotton Club Parade on Broadway 10 March–9 June 1938. It was the first to have a score written entirely by him. The band's major feature piece was one of his finest achievements of the period, 'Braggin' in Brass'.

In the spring of 1938 while playing the New Cotton Club on Broadway Ellington was attracted to a chorus girl called Beatrice

Ellis. In early 1939 Ellington broke off his relationship with Mildred Dixon and moved into an apartment with Ellis, most commonly known as Evie (a contraction of 'evil'), at 935 St Nicholas Ave. Nicknamed 'Thunderbird' by Mercer Ellington, Ellis would remain Duke's companion until the end of his life. He never divorced Edna.

ED ANDERSON: We were at the Cotton Club and Mildred had been quite unhappy about the fact Duke was seeing someone else, and all of a sudden the chorus came out, showgirls, and Mildred pointed to this very lovely-looking girl, very young, lovely-looking girl, marvellous figure and said, 'There she is.' That was just about the time that romance started.[34]

BARNEY BIGARD: When the Cotton Club moved down to Broadway, that's when [Ellington] took up with Bea. And Bea used to be with Willie Bryant. He used to beat the beJesus out of her. And he didn't have any prize there, you know, because she went with Joe Louis at one time and he caught her in St Louis with Joe Louis.[35]

IRVING TOWNSEND: Evie, a dark haired, handsome woman, a former dancer with a dancer's long legs and grace of movement not only remained in an almost impenetrable background, but was completely separated from the rest of Duke's family. When he was in New York she drove him to his appointments in a black Cadillac he had given her, her prized possession ... [Duke] often introduced her in my presence as Mrs Ellington. She shared his only permanent address in New York City and while never married to him, Evie performed many of the duties of a wife even though she was never seen in public.[36]

DON GEORGE: When their Cotton Club days were over, Duke and Evie moved down to an apartment on Central Park West.

Evie became a homebody. She had dinner parties for people close to Duke ... graciously prepared and served with love. She found pleasure in bringing life and warmth to their home.[37]

ED ANDERSON: I don't think it's any secret that Duke left her alone a great deal, travelled all over the world and knew a lot of other ladies.[38]

DON GEORGE: Evie made a personal island of the apartment for Duke; a haven, a port in the storm. She handled everything like nobody else could, sent vitamins to St Louis on such and such a date, called the hospital to get a prescription, called John Popkin at the Hickory House to send the steaks ... on the surface she seemed unaware of Duke's peccadilloes.[39]

FREDDIE JENKINS: Well, the pace caught up with me. Some people call it the 'Too-sies' – too much money, too much drinking, too many women while TOO young. I wasn't the kind of musician who could put his trumpet back in the case and go home when the show was over. I was still keyed up from the excitement and had to have a cooling off period – at least, I thought so. Besides I was never married when I was with Duke so I had no home to go to. So I'd drop in somewhere for a few drinks. When we were at the Cotton Club, Cliff Jackson was at The Lenox next door, and some of us would drop in there. Well, a jam session or cutting contest would start and we'd still be at it in daylight. And it was the same on the road. Everywhere we went some guy in the band knew some place to go. Like in Chicago we'd go out on the South Side to Joe Hughes' or somewhere. That's where we all got acquainted with Ray Nance about five years before he joined Duke.[40]

Jenkins had earlier left the band in December 1935 to recuperate, rejoining the band in March 1937. He finally left the band at the end of May 1938.

DUKE ELLINGTON: 'I Let a Song Go Out of My Heart' got very big, we played it on the radio every night, so we went out of town and we were coming back to the Apollo. We said, 'Oh, man, we got to really – this is the fourth or fifth number, we're going to the Apollo, we're really going to make it really swing, we're going to make a real dressed-up arrangement of it.' So I made a real dressed-up arrangement of it and nobody recognized it! So we had to go back to the record and then everybody understood. And do you know what the arrangement was? The counter melody was 'Don't Get Around Much Anymore'.[41]

Ellington played the Apollo on 10 June.

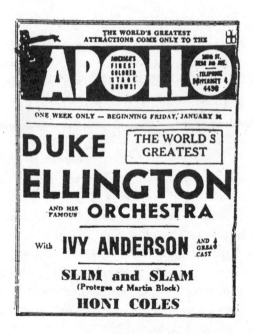

COOTIE WILLIAMS: If Johnny or Barney or any of them were in an argument, wasn't playing the music right, I'd holler at them.

Because Duke would never say nothing to them. I'd be the one that had taken over that spot.[42]

RUTH ELLINGTON: Duke definitely wasn't direct. He wasn't direct with anybody about anything.[43]

DUKE ELLINGTON: I enjoy solving problems. Take 'Boy Meets Horn'. There's one note with a cocked valve [on Rex Stewart's cornet] that has that sound we wanted – E natural. No other note has that sound. The big problem was to employ that note. It was something to play with, to have fun with. It has nothing to do with conquering the world. You write it tonight and play it tomorrow night. That's it.[44]

'Boy Meets Horn', featuring Rex Stewart, was recorded on 28 December 1938.

BOB UDKOFF: I think one of the things that always stood out in my mind was that he never accepted the obvious, just because that was the way that was done; precedent meant nothing to him. As an example there, at one time we were at his tailor's in Chicago, and he was looking at some materials and said, 'This looks nice,' and the tailor said, 'You're looking at the wrong side, the other side is the right side, that's the back of it,' he said, 'Who says? Why? I like this side.' That was his nature, just because that was the way it was done, or just because it was accepted, that way did not make it right, and I think that was a great contributing factor in his music: he didn't follow a leader, he followed what he thought was right.[45]

DUKE ELLINGTON: Don't let them kid you about [Paul] Whiteman. He has been a big man in our music. He's done a lot for it, especially with his concerts where he gave composers a chance to write new, extended works.[46]

On 24 December 1938, Paul Whiteman staged 'An Experiment in Modern Music' concert at Carnegie Hall. Six composers, Bert Shefter, Fred Van Epps, Morton Gould, Walter Gross, Roy Bargy and Duke Ellington, were invited to contribute a composition to form part of a forty-minute musical anthology entitled Those Bells. *Ellington's contribution was a piano feature called 'The Blue Belles of Harlem', which he himself would perform at Carnegie Hall with his orchestra on 23 January 1943.*

DUKE ELLINGTON: On January 3rd 1939, we gave our first serious concert on this side of the water. It was held in City College, N.Y., and we were greatly encouraged by its enthusiastic reception. Following that we were scheduled to give a performance at Carnegie Hall, but at the last moment bookings were set for our second European tour, and the date had to be cancelled.[47]

DUKE ELLINGTON: The nephew of a friend of mine, Gus Greenlee in Pittsburgh, had a nephew, came to me one day and says, 'I've got a young kid, he writes good music, I'd like you to hear some of his stuff, see what you think of it.' I said, 'Sure, come on down some time.' And I used to go to this club there, in Pittsburgh, every night and play bridge, I was supposed to be a great bridge player then and play bridge until noon, and when you're playing a picture house you're due on stage about one o'clock, after the first picture, so this day I came in, played my first show, went up to the dressing room, lay down to go to sleep, and so this guy came in with this little kid. They had a piano, I said tell him to sit down and play something, so this little boy sat down and started playing and he sang a couple of lyrics and, man, I was up on my feet, it was a great marriage of words and music, that Cole Porter type thing, you know? And I said, 'Oh, young man, I'm going to have to bring you to New York, you're going to have to come' – this is Billy Strayhorn – 'you're going to have to come write lyrics for me.' And he said, 'OK, let me know when.'[48]

BILLY STRAYHORN: I was more or less forced by my friends to go and see [Duke], in Pittsburgh. I was a soda jerk and a delivery boy in a drug store. [I had written some things] but they were unheard, they were just heard by the customers of the drug store and they got after me to have someone else hear them. So he was the one. I went to the Pittsburgh Musical Institute for about two months, and the man with whom I was studying, Charles Boyd was his name, was a very wonderful man and he died. And I left.[49]

DUKE ELLINGTON: So [Strayhorn] waited and I didn't send for him, so the next time I see him was in Newark, we were playing the Adams [recte Paramount] Theatre, and he showed up backstage, so I said, 'I'm not going to let you go this time,' so I took him home with me, to New York, parked him in the house with my son and my sister.[50]

Strayhorn joined the Ellington entourage during the band's engagement at the Paramount Theatre, N.J., during the week 20–27 January 1939.

RUTH ELLINGTON: I walked into my living room at 381 [Edgecombe Avenue] and here was this little thing sitting on a chair and I think Edward said, 'This is Billy Strayhorn, he's going to live with us.' And he said, 'Ruth has just come back from Europe,' and at that point Billy was speaking French like a native, and I don't think he had ever been out of Pittsburgh! Billy established instantaneous communication with the family, it was as if he had always been there, and I can remember Billy and I over the breakfast table having long intellectual conversations about life and this, that and the other and we had not seen each other before! He's always been like a member of the family since he stepped in.[51]

BILLY STRAYHORN: In 1934, in Pittsburgh, I heard and saw the Ellington band perform for my first time. Nothing before or since has affected my life so much. In 1939 I became his protégé, enabling me to be closer and see more.[52]

SONNY GREER: Billy [Strayhorn] – Sweetpea, that's his nick-name. He was a guy that everybody loved. All the ladies idolized him because he was tiny and all the ladies wanted to mother him. I never saw a man like that, could cabaret all night long and walk the chalk line. He was amazing. He got me so I hated to look at him. I used to say, 'Man, how you do that?' And he would laugh. And Duke loved this guy.[53]

JUAN TIZOL: He was a good musician, very good. He got everything that Duke had and more. Strayhorn learned. He already knew about it, by looking at the scores he learned a lot and started writing just like Ellington – I'm talking about his chords and so forth. Strayhorn's writing was a little more sweeter, more sweet music than Duke's. You could tell in a way he uses his phrases in music, you could tell it was Strayhorn.[54]

LAWRENCE BROWN: Billy Strayhorn was one of the most under-rated musicians that I've ever known. He was a real, real musician. If you've ever heard a tune that he wrote called 'Lush Life', which is a tune that he brought into the organization in the later '30s, now he was writing, composing, playing that type of music way back then. He really was a terrific musician. Now, take another tune called 'Chelsea Bridge'. If you stretch your imagination a little bit you can almost see Chelsea Bridge in his music the same way you can see the Grand Canyon when you hear the 'Grand Canyon Suite'. All of his tunes have a deep feeling behind them; the one I particularly like was 'I Want Something to Live For'. All of these he writes the music and the words and everything himself and you hear him in his music, which to me is the mark of a real musician. He was a very meticulous little fellow, and he was right in most everything he did. Many, many times Ellington would call him up from out on the road, 'Sweetpea, I want an arrangement on so and so and so and so.' 'Well, when do you need it?' 'In a couple of days.' And Sweetpea, 'All right.' And in a couple of days the most gorgeous arrangement on that particular piece. And that was Strayhorn and he never got the credit.[55]

BOB UDKOFF: In those days being homosexual was in the closet. Now Billy never made a secret of it, when I say never made a secret, there was no discussion about it. That's the way it was, whatever he did, he did it very discreetly. I [once] roomed with Strayhorn and at no time did he ever do anything that would indicate he was anything other than a heterosexual. He was a warm, considerate, very intelligent human being. Very talented.[56]

BILLY STRAYHORN: The first thing he did was to hand me two pieces and tell me to arrange them. They were both for [a] Johnny Hodges [small-group session]: 'Like a Ship in the Night' and 'Savoy Strut', I think. I couldn't really arrange, but that didn't really make any difference to him. He inspires you with confidence. That's the only way I can explain how I managed to do those arrangements. They both turned out quite well.[57]

'Like a Ship in the Night' was recorded on 27 February 1939, 'Savoy Strut' on 21 March 1939, and both were performed by Ellington small groups.

RUTH ELLINGTON: Just before he went to Sweden, at that point I met Evie, just as he was about to sail for Sweden.[58]

DUKE ELLINGTON: We went on the French ship, the *Ile de France*. We went the end of March, and I think as soon as she got out of that New York harbour, boy, she danced all the way to France. Every step. The front end would go up and come down, whooop! Then the ass end would go up and come down, boom! boom! What would happen was the bar closes at two o'clock in the morning, and of course card game was going on as usual, all night and all day, the card game was going on! Play poker all day and all night. Rex and I were the only brave ones in the band, we said, because the rest of them would always put on this big face and say I'm going downstairs to go to bed, while we stayed up the top and ordered – we were drinking champagne and brandy. Every night Rex and I would be ready, those little tables they have in the saloon, they would be lined all the way around with brandy and then we would have this bucket full of champagne, we would sit up there and watch the sun-up, we would never go to bed until daylight. I think Sonny Greer said he was up one night and said there was nobody in the pilot's house, they have about two or three wheels on these big ships, and he went up there and looked in one of those rooms and there wasn't anybody standing there at that wheel! He said, 'Man, they ain't guiding this ship!' Rex and I, we were brave, we stayed up all night long *watching*! We wrote a couple of nice things on that trip, the thing 'Robbins Nest' was taken from.[59]

Ellington sailed from New York on 23 March 1939, arriving at Le Havre on the 30th, opening their 34-day, 28-concert tour of Europe in Paris on 1 April. Despite a request from Irving Mills to the British Ministry of Labour, the band were not allowed to perform in the UK.

DUKE ELLINGTON: We also gave concerts in a bomb-proof underground theatre in Paris which was magnificently received. This time labour regulations prevented us from playing any engagements in England.[60]

SONNY GREER: So we left Belgium and we went to Hamburg, Germany. We got in there at eleven o'clock in the morning. We were supposed to take a Pullman to Sweden, to Stockholm, so we were in this big station like Grand Central Station, only in Hamburg, and all we seen is soldiers, uniforms, soldiers. We were the only civilians there, but they treat us nice. We went up to the diner and an old Jewish couple went up there and they shoved them like dogs, didn't let them go nowhere. Hitler was in power then, all them German soldiers, they took our Pullmans, the man had paid for them, we stayed in the station from eleven o'clock in the morning until twelve o'clock at night, because they took the transportation for the soldiers.[61]

REX STEWART: We were screened by ... those infamous lethal appearing SS guards. They were frightening to see in their jet black regalia embellished with silver death heads on their caps. Even their attitude, their steely glinted, non-smiling frozen glances said, 'Here's death à la carte.'[62]

BARNEY BIGARD: The SS border guards looked like Satan himself, like they would eat you up.[63]

DUKE ELLINGTON: Candidly, we were scared to death.[64]

SONNY GREER: Well, we got out of there and went to Sweden, Irving Mills bribed some guys who had a boat, he took us by boat over there. So we're coming through the line and had to show the passports. We showed our passports, my passport said William Greer, Sonny's a nickname. So the guy with a major's uniform, one of the German officers, he says, 'Hello, Sonny, how you doing?' I said, 'My name's William.' He said, 'Go ahead, your name's Sonny, I saw you in Chicago at the Oriental Theatre!'[65]

DUKE ELLINGTON: We had a highly successful tour playing concerts all over Sweden, Denmark and Holland. I celebrated my birthday in Stockholm, or perhaps I might say Stockholm celebrated my birthday for me. Never was I accorded such an overwhelming reception as I experienced that day. I awoke in my hotel to the strains of the Swedish equivalent of 'Happy Birthday to You'. I was being serenaded by a band which paraded throughout the hotel, broadcasting the happy event. It was a day of celebration and wound up in a tremendously swanky nighterie where they had prepared for us at the head of the room a table for me with a birthday cake for me and everybody stood up while the band played and everybody sang a song of celebration. I went to bed very high, and very happy.[66]

SONNY GREER: In Sweden on Duke's birthday, we were playing up there and 300 little girls, young teenagers sang 'Happy Birthday' in Swedish and walked down with flowers. During the intermission another band played 'Happy Birthday' and they all sang it in Swedish and all of them had a bouquet of flowers, right there to the stage. You can imagine 300 bouquets of flowers and everybody singing 'Happy Birthday'. Yeah.[67]

REX STEWART: I've witnessed many celebrations, but I doubt that I'll ever again capture such a rare moment as Duke's birthday, April 29th, in Stockholm ... what a soul-shaking demonstration of the love Sweden bore for Ellington! [68]

On 6 June 1939, Ellington returned the favour and recorded 'Serenade to Sweden', composed in honour of his triumphant reception.

DUKE ELLINGTON: We played there for thirty-one days, concert tour, all over Sweden, wonderful tour, did a lot of writing while I was riding around in that bus. 'Jack the Bear', 'Serenade to Sweden', and others . . .[69]

DUKE ELLINGTON: We were in London a few hours. I remember that because one or two of the boys had to be poured onto the train, and Sonny locked himself in the you-know-what, and nobody could get in because he went sound asleep![70]

MELODY MAKER: Yesterday ... Duke Ellington and his band passed through London on their way home to New York. Off the SS *Britannia* they arrived early in the morning at Tilbury and left Waterloo at 4.30 in the afternoon to board the *Ile de France* at Southampton, thereby concluding a European barnstorming tour which has taken in towns never before visited by a first class band. Excluding expenses, the band received £1,500 a week from the Scandinavian bookers who brought them over. It has now become known that Ellington and Irving Mills have severed their long business association, which has resulted in the famous Negro bandleader and composer becoming a world-wide attraction. From the time Ellington reaches New York he will be one of the attractions of the William Morris office, said to be out to compete, through a new band department, with the terrific Music Corporation of America.[71]

The band returned to America on 10 May aboard the Ile de France. *It was the last engagement under the auspices of Irving Mills. On their return they were represented by the William Morris Agency, whose band-booking department had been formed only six months earlier.*

JOHN HAMMOND: Duke had a great feeling of loyalty to Irving Mills, who made him into a national figure in music and whose publishing company made him the best paid ASCAP Negro composer in America ... It was not until Bill Morris of the William Morris Agency came along to give Duke Ellington a new sense of personal dignity and to back up his advice with superior bookings that Ellington left Mills.[72]

BOB UDKOFF: What happened as I understand it, is at the time of [his mother's death] he was very distraught. And he said to Irving, his manager, 'I want you to get the most expensive casket made for my mother.' Irving said, 'Oh my God. That will cost $5,000.' Now in 1935, $5,000 was a small fortune. Ellington: 'I don't care, I want the very best.' One day Ellington happened to drop by the office of Duke Ellington Incorporated and he looked at the books, which was an unusual thing for him to do, because, as he always said, he never really cared about money, and as he was looking through the books he saw where Mills had paid $3,500 for this casket. Now, I'm not sure if Mills charged him $5,000, but the very fact that he didn't accede to his wishes made him feel that he didn't have any control, he had asked Mills to do this and he hadn't. And I guess there were other things too, Irving was a very controlling person. Irving – to talk to Irving he invented the wheel, he created the industry, but Ellington always said, 'I don't know without Irving Mills if I would have ever attained what I did,' because he did start him off, and Irving always went first class, he made the band look good, everything was top-drawer. At that particular point, I think, Duke felt that he had had it with Irving, he couldn't control his destiny, so to speak. So Duke traded him his stock in Duke Ellington Incorporated for Ellington's interest in Cab Calloway, because Ellington owned a piece of Cab Calloway and at that time Calloway was very hot, so Irving felt he had a good deal. And of course Irving had his name on so many Ellington compositions, for his royalties from ASCAP, that was another thing that bugged Duke, that Irving had put his name on his songs.[73]

DUKE ELLINGTON: Irving Mills decided in '38 that we should split up, because he wanted to gamble more with his money and so forth, and he knew I didn't want to do it.[74]

IRVING MILLS: I never tried to persuade Duke to sacrifice his integrity as Duke Ellington, the musician, for the sake of trying to find a short cut to commercial success.[75]

REX STEWART: After our very successful European jaunt, the band started hitting on all cylinders like a wondrous musical juggernaut. Virtually everything we did turned out to be something of value, especially on records.[76]

BILLY STRAYHORN: I stayed at home and wrote a few things like 'Day Dream'. When he came back, the band went to the Ritz Carlton Roof in Boston. Ivie Anderson . . . asked me to do some new material for her.[77]

After a series of one-nighters, the band's two-week residency in Boston opened on 24 July 1939.

DUKE ELLINGTON: [While] I was away Billy and Mercer, my son, had been going through the scores, you know, and [Billy] had a good musical education but he had never had any writing experience – orchestration. So he looked at my things and decided, I suppose, that it all looked very simple, so when I came back he said, 'I've been looking at your things and I think I could do some of that.' I said, 'Yeah, all right, have a shot.'[78]

BILLY STRAYHORN: I did all the vocals for Ivie. I did all her things, 'I'm Checking Out, Goom Bye,' 'Lonely Co-Ed' and all those things.[79]

Both these titles were recorded by Ellington in August 1939.

DUKE ELLINGTON: In 1939 there was 'Never No Lament', which eventually turned into 'Don't Get Around Much Any More', after Bob Russell put the lyric to it.[80]

LAWRENCE BROWN: 'Don't Get Around Much Any More' – Johnny Hodges. The saxophone players sat back on the stand and would create these melodic extravaganzas on tunes that were being played, and, of course, they became tunes. Then somebody would put words to it, the lyricist came out of the office's connections.[81]

DUKE ELLINGTON: [Bob Russell also] put the lyrics to ... 'Do Nothing Till You Hear From Me', which was 'Concerto for Cootie', of course. And a thing called 'Sentimental Lady' which we turned into 'I Didn't Know About You'. And 'Warm Valley', but nothing ever happened to that, one of the big request numbers.[82]

BILLY STRAYHORN: 'Warm Valley' ... was less than three minutes long. But we wrote reams and reams of music on that, and he threw it all out except what you hear [on the record]. He didn't use any of mine. Now, that's arranging. The tune was written, but we had to find a way to present it.[83]

'Warm Valley' was subsequently recorded 17 October 1940.

HERB JEFFRIES: I went to the Graystone Ballroom in Detroit. Ellington was playing there. He had played the Apollo Theatre with one of my pictures which was called *The Bronze Buckaroo*, and he called me up on the stage, introduced me. I did some songs with him, it was early 1940 and he said, 'What are your plans?' And I said, 'Well, I guess I'll be going back to California, do some more cowboy pictures.' He said, 'Oh, what a shame, I was gonna ask you to join the band.' I said, 'Well, I think we can put those pictures in the background for a while.[84]

Jeffries, who had achieved some fame in the movies as The Bronze Buckaroo, *a singing cowboy, joined Ellington in November 1939.*

DUKE ELLINGTON: [Herb's] style was more falsetto but very well accepted ... and we agreed that he would come with us for the fun of it plus expenses plus a little plus. While he was with us we played quite a few theatres, picture houses and between shows while everybody else was playing poker, Herb would be ad libbing all over the place and doing imitations – he did the singers of the time – NAMES – Amos 'n' Andy and one day he was doing his interpretation of Bing Crosby and Strayhorn and I both said in unison – 'That's it, don't go any further, just stay on Bing,' and so he did and Herb's imitation of Bing was the foundation until gradually Herb's own singing self took over.[85]

VARIETY: ELLINGTON TO VICTOR – Duke Ellington orchestra switches from Columbia to Victor records under a long term contract that comes effective after the expiration of his Columbia pact tomorrow [22 February 1940]. Change means a hop back to 75c platter as Columbia recently became a 50c label.[86]

CHAPTER SEVEN
IN A MELLOTONE

Once again, a European trip proved crucial in stimulating Elling-
ton's flagging spirits, despite the clouds of war gathering on the
continent. The torment and introspection that was apparent in
compositions such as 'Reminiscing in Tempo' (1935) and 'Dimin-
uendo in Blue' and 'Crescendo in Blue' (1937) gave way to a more
heterogeneous vision that on occasion could be quite outgoing, such
as 'Serenade to Sweden', 'The Sergeant Was Shy', 'Braggin' in
Brass', 'Tootin' Through the Roof' and 'Steppin' In To Swing
Society', the latter setting the tone for the ensuing two years
and pointing the way to the masterpieces about to come. But with
his return to form came the realization of his parlous financial
position. The hospital bills for his mother and father's illnesses
were considerable and added to this he had assumed responsibil-
ity for the hospital care of Arthur Whetsol (whose battle for life
would end on 5 January 1940) and Freddie Jenkins. The harsh
truth was that Ellington had been guilty of letting business matters
drift following the deaths of his parents and was all but broke.
As the reality of his situation came home to him, he began look-
ing more and more to Irving Mills to improve his lot. But Mills
had diversified and Ellington was no longer central to his plans.
It was something Ellington, to whom loyalty was everything,
found difficult to accept. Things seem to have come to a head over
the matter of his mother's coffin and although he subsequently
severed his connection with Mills, it is interesting to note that it

was Mills who negotiated Ellington's deal with the new agency of William Morris, who promptly booked him into such prestige spots as the Ritz Carlton Roof in Boston and the Hotel Sherman in Chicago.

Ellington was not the only band from the Mills stable to make the move to Morris; Eddie DeLange (formerly of Hudson-DeLange) and Ina Ray Hutton were among those who transferred their allegiance. With the addition of Billy Strayhorn to Ellington's entourage, Ellington had on hand an enormously gifted musician who would become his musical confidant, capable of producing original compositions and arrangements the equal of Ellington's own. Their first collaboration together, 'Something to Live For', had been recorded on 21 March 1939, and there is no doubt that a friendly rivalry quickly grew between Ellington and his protégé to see who could outdo the other, resulting in a heightened degree of creativity that began to be felt within the band as 1939 gave way to 1940.

But from the public's point of view, the band lacked the added box-office draw of the 'hot' tenor-sax man like Benny Goodman's Vido Musso or Bud Freeman, Artie Shaw's Georgie Auld, Cab Calloway's Chu Berry or Count Basie's Lester Young and Herschel Evans. But in January 1940 Ellington added Ben Webster, an acknowledged saxophone master willing and able to take on all comers. Also, there had been problems in the rhythm section since Wellman Braud left in mid-March 1935. The two-bass configuration, more a tribute to Ellington's reluctance to fire anyone than for any specific musical purpose, was rhythmically lumpy and lacked the svelte propulsion of, say, Walter Page with the Basie band. But at the end of 1939 Ellington discovered a magnificent young bass player called Jimmy Blanton who quickly made the two-bass line-up redundant. Suddenly there was a spring in the Ellington band's step, and the scene was set for what many consider to be his greatest musical triumphs.

DUKE ELLINGTON: We've made two exciting new additions to the band in the persons of Benny Webster and Jimmy Blanton and we're all of us steamed up about how fine they sound on our new Victor records.[1]

SONNY GREER: The first time I heard Jimmy Blanton was in St Louis. We were in St Louis to play the Chase Hotel, the first time they had a coloured band there. And the night before, we had two days off, so the night before I went out on the town ... We sat down, just relaxing a little taste. So all right, I see this guy, a nice-looking boy. And he played – two or three bass players played before him. He come up there and all my life I'd never heard nobody like this guy. Never heard nobody play bass like him. There were some good bass players, but like him, never. So I rushed back to the hotel and got Duke. I said, 'Man, come and hear this kid play.' So Duke went up and Duke was amazed like I was because he could see further, what he could do. And Duke say, 'I'm going to get him.' So we had Billy Taylor, was our bass player then. So Duke went up to Jimmy and say, 'How would you like to open at the hotel with us?' He said, 'All right.' And sure enough he opened at the Chase Hotel with us. And it's too much. Too much, Duke just turned him loose. And he fitted the band like a glove. All the guys loved him, he was that type of guy, you know? Duke gave him a featured spot all the way through the band, individual solos. He turned him loose and the house caved in. He's something else![2]

Blanton joined Ellington while the band was playing the Club Caprice, Coronado Hotel, St Louis, from 20 October to 2 November 1939.

DUKE ELLINGTON: We already had a bass-man, Billy Taylor, a good bass-man. We added [Blanton] on and we had two basses. And he stayed with the band and we got up to Boston and we were playing the Southland, and one night Billy Taylor was standing up there playing beside him and he just reached down, got disgusted, packed up his bass and walked out, he said, 'I'm not going to stay playing up here with this young boy playing all that bass!' He just walked out![3]

The Southland engagement was from 8 to 20 January 1940.

LAWRENCE BROWN: Oh, Jimmy was terrific. He was around twenty-four, I think, twenty-three or twenty-four, the nicest kid you ever saw. It's too bad, I've always regretted that they never got the true tone with Blanton because in those days they didn't put the mike down near the soundpost in the bass fiddle. The mikes were all up in the air on the fingerboard. Well, if you know the fingerboard is very tinny upside, the real true tone down near the soundpost. A very mellow sound.[4]

BILLY STRAYHORN: 'Jack the Bear' was originally called 'Take It Away'. Duke originally wrote the thing as an experiment. He had big chords working against a melodic thing. It didn't work out and the piece was just dropped. Then Jimmy Blanton came into the band and Duke wanted to feature him as a solo man. We needed some material quickly, so I reworked 'Take It Away' as a showpiece for Blanton's bass.[5]

'Jack the Bear', a feature piece that announced Blanton's stunning playing, was recorded 6 March 1940.

BARNEY BIGARD: When we'd play theatres, they'd be looking for Jimmy and he'd be down in the basement practising. He'd play that bass anywhere, any time of night, wouldn't care how cold.[6]

DUKE ELLINGTON: Ben Webster recorded with us three or four years before he came to the band.[7]

BEN WEBSTER: We made 'Truckin', Johnny made 'Accent on Youth'. I stayed for about three weeks, I begged Duke to stay, it wasn't too feasible at the time. That's where I really wanted to be because I wanted to sit next to Johnny, Carney, I wanted to play with Barney.[8]

This early session was on 19 August 1935.

MILT HINTON: [Ben] always wanted to play with Duke. But there was no way. He would make his desires known that he wanted to play with Duke, and Duke being the very clever man he was told Ben, 'I would love to have you in the band, but Cab's my brother band and I can't take anybody out of his band. *But* if you didn't have a job I'd have to give you one.' This started the chemistry in Ben and he started saving up his money. It was six months after we hit Cleveland, Ohio ... Ben put his notice with Cab ... He went on the corners and told Duke, 'Well, I'm unemployed.' And Duke hired him.[9]

Hinton played bass for Cab Calloway's band in which Ellington and Irving Mills each had a 25 per cent stake, hence the reluctance to appear to 'poach' Webster from a band in which Duke had a financial interest. Webster finally joined Ellington on a permanent basis during the band's run at the Southland Café in Boston from 8 January to 20 January 1940.

BEN WEBSTER: When I joined [Duke] I didn't have any music. He hadn't written any parts for me. I guess I'd been in the band about three months and still no music. I was added to the saxophones, you see, and I was trying to find that fifth part. Barney Bigard used to give me his parts sometimes – he hated tenor – and I'd try to look at Johnny Hodges' music and transpose to tenor.[10]

MERCER ELLINGTON: When Ben first came to the band, Ellington told him to have a seat, never gave him any music and told him to play. So the guys would get mad at him because in finding a note that was a good harmony he would take a note from someone else's part and they told him to get off it! So finally Ben decided he would find a note that nobody had, and that led to the sensuous sound of the saxophone section.[11]

BEN WEBSTER: So after a while I asked the Duke, 'When are you going to write me some parts?' And he said, 'You're doing all right.' He was having fun at me trying to work out the fifth part. So finally, when he started to get me some parts, Tizol – who sat right behind me – noticed that certain notes I played struck him as soft. He asked why I didn't blow those notes out, and I told him some of those notes didn't sound right to me. That's why I blew them softer. He told me, 'Blow them out, that's the way he wants them.' So I did then. You talk about sound . . . Carney was at one end of that saxophone team and I was at the other. And I tried to blend with him. We used to run Duke mad, me and Harry Carney. Duke would say, 'Cut it out fellers, I can't hear anybody else.' I say Pops made me tone conscious and that section did the rest.[12]

DUKE ELLINGTON: You have great people in the same line, you have a section of Johnny Hodges, Harry Carney, Barney Bigard. Ben Webster comes in and sits down and they are all enthusiastic about him being there, got to be right.[13]

MERCER ELLINGTON: When Ben came into the band, Ben got the job because he was sanctioned by Johnny and Harry Carney. Had either one of them given him a no-no, Ben would never have been in the orchestra.[14]

LAWRENCE BROWN: Ben was a disciple of Coleman Hawkins, as most every tenor player was, and Ben loved Coleman and he attempted Coleman's lush, deep tone. Ben was very good, very good. He was one of the giants.[15]

REX STEWART: Ben Webster is not only one of the greatest exponents of the tenor saxophone, but he is also a talented arranger, composer, billiard player and photographer . . . an intriguing character that at times is almost Jekyll and Hyde . . . The person Ben was most devoted to outside of his mother and grandmother was the late Jimmy Blanton.[16]

SONNY GREER: [Jimmy] loved everybody in the band, especially Ben Webster. He loved Ben Webster. Ben would take him everywhere and show him off to people. Benny always had somewhere to go, different clubs, and he'd lay Jimmy on them.[17]

BARNEY BIGARD: If there was a blizzard and there was a jam session, [Jimmy'd] be there, he and Ben Webster.[18]

MERCER ELLINGTON: After the gig was over, they'd go in their different directions and nobody particularly hung with anybody else. When Ben came, he wouldn't accept the fact these people stayed apart and stayed aloof and would say nothing to one another. He drew them out. I think if anything he sort of established a camaraderie, making the band more sociable to themselves.[19]

BARNEY BIGARD: One time when we played Birmingham, Alabama, this white boy was bugging Ben [Webster] all night, offering him drinks out of his bottle, he and his girl were drinking with him, all chummy. After the dance was over, when Ben went next door for a sandwich, this boy was in there too and insulted Ben. It just shows he didn't want anybody on the outside to know he knew Ben.[20]

HERB JEFFRIES: We couldn't stay in hotels, we couldn't eat in restaurants, so they had to pull the Pullman up on the sidetrack and we lived aboard the Pullman. Yet the residents of that town, which of course were basically white, would come backstage and stand, outside in the cold weather, waiting for these men who could not eat or sleep there in the hotels, to get their autographs.[21]

MERCER ELLINGTON: [Ellington] would find Ben, and all of a sudden, the night before a session, he would call him up and see how he was doing. And Ben would be taking care of business, very safe, and everything else, and he'd immediately go to work on Ben, and it was because of creativity. He'd say, 'How do you expect to do a session sober, let's get you some whisky,' and then they'd hang, he'd get Ben blind, and then the next day he was totally uninhibited on what he was going to play because he was just – this was because of Ben's great love for Ellington. He wanted to do such a beautiful job, or wonderful job, he would be just not flexible.[22]

REX STEWART: As a composer and arranger, Ben's most significant contribution was 'Cotton Tail', for which he also wrote the now-famous saxophone section chorus.[23]

'Cotton Tail', one of the classics of the Swing Era, was recorded 4 May 1940. It is one of the key recordings of Ellington's 'Victor period', from 6 March 1940, Ellington's first recording session since leaving Columbia, to 28 July 1942, three days before the American Federation of Musicians imposed a recording ban. Of his total output during this period, which inevitably includes commercial numbers and lesser items, it is stunning to realize that almost half comprise masterpieces not only of jazz, but of twentieth-century music. Several factors make these recordings great, not least the 78 rpm format which restricted playing to something around three minutes. The amount of detailed orchestration and integration of written and improvised themes is remarkable – a lot happens in a very short time span.

    Ellington's organizational methods within the popular song form were both ingenious and resourceful. Often there are several themes in one arrangement, different figures emerge and recede and surprisingly, in view of the time constraints imposed by the 78 record, he introduces transitional and developmental passages. The way Ellington marshals these resources gives a feeling of spontaneous evolution as his arrangements unfurl, even when he is dealing with tightly ordered structures and intricate part writing. There is a feeling of freshness to his compositions that still readily communicates today. Ultimately, however, it was the sound of Ellington's Famous Orchestra that set it apart in contemporary music, with different permutations of instruments com-

bining to create what Billy Strayhorn once called 'the Ellington Effect'.

The use of highly individual, sometimes idiosyncratic soloists in combination created a richness of tonal colour that was quite unique and distinctive. Throughout 1940 Ellington was producing two, sometimes three masterpieces every time he went into the recording studio. Subsequently, many distinguished writers have referred to these as works of genius, such as André Hodeir in his analysis of 'Concerto for Cootie', while 'Ko Ko' has been described as one of the 'monumental events in jazz music'. But in truth, this period is replete with classics which no record collection that pretends an interest in contemporary music – jazz or classical – should be without, including 'Jack the Bear', 'Ko Ko', 'Conga Brava', 'Cotton Tail', 'Bojangles (A Portrait of Bill Robinson)', 'A Portrait of Bert Williams', 'Blue Goose', 'Harlem Airshaft', 'Rumpus in Richmond', 'Sepia Panorama', 'In a Mellotone', 'Warm Valley', 'The Flaming Sword', 'Across the Track Blues', 'Chloe', 'The Sidewalks of New York', 'Flamingo', 'Bakiff', 'Chelsea Bridge', 'Raincheck' and more.

BARNEY BIGARD: We come out of St Louis from a gig and there wasn't a restaurant available to get something to eat. There was some, you know, but we couldn't go in there, see. So we saw this restaurant, there was nobody in it, the lights were on. So [Sam] Fliashnik said, 'Watch, I'll fix that.' He said, 'Stop the bus back here and I'll go in front there.' So he and Herb Jeffries and myself, we went into this restaurant and there's this guy coming out. It seemed as though he was so glad to see somebody in his place, see. So Sam said, 'Can you serve twenty-six people right away?' So the guy says, 'Depends on what they want.' He said, 'Well, ham and eggs, bacon and eggs.' He says, 'Oh, sure.' He said, 'I can fix it up as fast as you want it.' He said, 'Well, just fix up twenty-six right quick and I'll bring the people in because they're sitting out there.' The guy says, 'Sure.' Sam says, 'Now, when you're ready, holler.' So the guy fixed up those twenty-six plates, came to total his costs, and says, 'OK, fella, bring them on in there. The stuff is ready.' When they all walked in there and this guy saw it was nothing but coloons he could have fainted. So Sam says, 'What's the matter?' He said, 'Uh, nothing, nothing.' He wasn't going to throw those twenty-six plates away![24]

Ellington played the Municipal Auditorium, St Louis, Mo., on 27 August 1940.

COOTIE WILLIAMS: The first time I was contacted by Benny Goodman, I told Duke about it. And we used to go out and talk, talk about it, so he would tell me what to say next time he called. And he set the deal up for me. And he said, 'Well, go ahead on. You've got a chance to make some money. And make a name for yourself.' Irving, Benny's brother, approached me, but I liked the band, that was the main thing, it had a terrific beat ... One of the main reasons I wanted to leave [was Duke's rhythm section]. [Sonny Greer]'d get drunk and fall off the drums and things like that. That was no good for me ... Duke would tell me what to tell [Benny], 'No, that's not enough.' Duke told me, only for the sextet, he said, 'You'll get lost sitting back there in the band, so rig up the thing so you'll only be featured with the sextet.' So he drew up a contract where I was only to be featured with the sextet. Duke thought of that. Well, to tell the truth, that was the most relaxed thing that I ever had in my life in music. Any job or anything I ever had my life in music. That year. I enjoyed playing. Everybody in the sextet was great. And each man you had to follow to play behind, you had to play. And that sextet used to romp. And there wasn't no slack there. You got a cheque every week, and I had never been used to that. Sometimes when he felt, he kept the band off. He'd start with the band and then crowded nights and things, he'd keep the sextet on, sometimes that sextet would stay on an

SOUVENIR PROGRAM

OF THE

KENTUCKY STATE COLLEGE ALUMNI ASSOCIATION

(*CHICAGO CHAPTER*)

IN THE 14th ANNUAL SCHOLARSHIP DANCE

PRESENTS

Coming!
HARLEM'S
Aristocrat
OF JAZZ!

DUKE **ELLINGTON**

AND HIS | IN HIS

Famous | *Only*

ORCHESTRA | 1940 SOUTHSIDE APPEARANCE

"The Duke"
IN THE BEAUTIFUL

Parkway Ballroom

South Parkway at 45th Street

MONDAY EVENING, OCT. 28, 1940
CHICAGO, ILLINOIS

hour and a half. Then sometimes, if the trumpet player wasn't there, the snag used to come in. He wanted me to sit in the band and play, and sometimes I'd do it. I enjoyed it, I enjoyed playing with the band, because he had all good men in the band and he rehearsed the band. And man, that band played. They were two entirely two different men, Duke and Benny, I learnt a lot from both men. Charlie Christian was a good buddy, we used to hang out together and Georgie Auld . . . The last session I made [with Duke] was 'Concerto for Cootie' . . . Ray took my place.[25]

Williams left the band on 2 November 1940 to join Benny Goodman after handing in his notice two weeks earlier.

RAY NANCE: I joined at a good time, Jimmy Blanton and Ben Webster were in the band and so was Tricky – the master . . . I always remember him with his zipper bag full of mutes, medicines and whisky. He was an original every way.[26]

LAWRENCE BROWN: Well, Ray Nance was a triple threat, or would you call him a quadruple threat. He was a good trumpet player, he had such terrific ideas, he was a terrific violinist, he could dance, he could sing – he was just an all-round musician's musician.[27]

Nance joined Ellington in time for a dance date at the Crystal Ballroom, Fargo, N.D., on 7 November 1940.

BEN WEBSTER: It was so cold there that night we played in our overcoats, and some of the guys kept their gloves on. Sometimes, when you've travelled all day in the bus, and had no sleep and are just dead tired – that's when you get some of the best playing out of a band. And sometimes the opposite.[28]

The live recording of the Fargo date is one of the highlights of the big band era.

DANIEL HALPERIN: The emptiness of the dance-hall made us feel ill at ease and silly. We stood to the right of the vacant bandstand watching a tardy sweeper run a polishing mop over the floor. Harry Carney was the first musician on the stand and began to finger the big baritone saxophone set before him on a small stand of its own. Jimmy Blanton appeared on the other end of the stand and took up his bass just as a few couples came in and sauntered across the floor to the bandstand. Slowly they drifted in. Wallace Jones smiling, Lawrence Brown sophisticated and bored, Ben Webster looking dangerous and mean, Rex Stewart blowing strange noises on his shining cornet as he walked toward his seat, Otto Hardwick adjusting the support strap round his neck, Fred Guy disdainful in a shy way. Just then Carney stood up, looked around him, began to tap his foot and suddenly, without any warning whatsoever, the orchestra burst into full cry. It was an unexpected explosion of sound; startling, thrilling. While coloured lights glittered on their polished instruments and Hardwick's bald pate and they tapped their feet in rhythm to the music, the glorious power of it rolled out from the musicians engulfing us. And the bored precision with which it was all done! At one moment while brass chopped through a passage Johnny Hodges was talking animatedly with Hardwick. Then, as if he had received some secret signal, he put his instrument to his mouth and dashed into an intricate run with other saxophones. The timing of it, from talking to playing, was perfect. At the same time I felt cheated by the records to which we had been listening for so many months. They were nothing like this.[29]

TOM WHALEY: Juan Tizol, he did the copying before I come in there. In 1940 I was hanging around, I don't know how, but I got in touch with Duke or Duke got in touch with me and sure I says. I thought I was going to arrange, see, but he said he wanted a copier, so I said I'll go ahead and copy. I got along with all of them. Ben Webster, he would say, don't wake me up Tom. Ben would have his beer and have a bottle and he'd sit there and drink all the time and he would get high but you wouldn't know it, see, he would get them sleepy eyes and go to sleep. Ben would rehearse and rehearse and then get on stage and play something altogether different! Otto Hardwick, now he was a great musician, he and Harry Carney. On alto and baritone sax they were great, they would control the music, if it's soft and, oh, it was great.[30]

Whaley remained a copyist with Ellington (a task that Tizol also continued to do on a less demanding basis), until 1950, when he left 'for more money'. He rejoined after a trip to South America, and remained a copyist until Ellington's Sacred Concerts began, at which point he also took on the responsibility of rehearsing the choral music on Ellington's behalf.

DUKE ELLINGTON: [Strayhorn] was with us for a while, then he went out with us on one-nighters, and we'd played this dance and then we were supposed to catch a train early in the morning, the train was there because we had a sleeper laying out there, but of course nobody had sense enough to get on the sleeper and go to sleep! They had to raise the street until all the juice joints had been closed, and Strayhorn had been a very well behaved young man, very nice, and we had great respect for him. But the musicians do this sort of thing after hours and they took Strayhorn out, and I was down in the station and here comes Strayhorn, this nice little schoolboy whom we had all looked down upon to look up at, and here he was, running drunk, and he's got my hat on. So here comes Strayhorn juiced with my hat on, and Sonny Greer has been priming him for his entrance now because he's got him juiced, and he comes over and he looks at me, Strayhorn looks at me, and he points his finger, and he says, 'Hey, man, I don't dig you!'[31]

BILLY STRAYHORN: Ivie Anderson looked after me when I joined the band – they all looked after me when I joined the band on account of I was a mascot or something or other. Ivie would take me, if I wanted to go out, I would run with Ivie. Ivie, Lawrence, go cabareting but they would take me with them, see to it I got back home and everything. She was a wonderful, wonderful woman.[32]

HERB JEFFRIES: We were playing in [New] Jersey, this Frenchman by the name of Ted Grouya came backstage to speak with Ellington. Duke was busy in a meeting at that time and he said, 'Go downstairs and take a listen to a song – they're ballads, and see if there's anything this guy's got you might like.' So I went down to the rehearsal hall and I heard several of his tunes and the 'Flamingo' tune sort of appealed to me. When I went back up and spoke to him he said, 'Did you like anything?' I said, 'Yeah, the guy left me a copy of it.' And he said, 'Give it to Strayhorn, and let's see if Strayhorn likes it and you go over it and if it's any good maybe we'll do it on stage and give it a test.' He was a very clever man. He would take songs and he would test them on the stage performances. If the audience reaction was really high, it was sort of his testing ground as to whether it was worth recording or not. And we got such a tremendous reaction from our stage performances that he called me in and said, 'We're gonna record this number.'[33]

'Flamingo' was recorded on 28 December 1940. It was a hit.

DUKE ELLINGTON: In 1940 [Strayhorn] did an orchestration of 'Flamingo', which was our first record with Herb Jeffries. This I think was the renaissance of vocal orchestration, because then it began to blossom. Before then an orchestration for a singer was usually pretty tepid, it was just background and that's about all. But now this had real ornamentation fittingly done, supporting the singer and also embellishing the entire performance of the singer and the band.[34]

HERB JEFFRIES: I had a million seller [with Duke], 'Flamingo', which Tony Martin covered about six months after I had the hit. He came to see the show one night. I heard he was in the audience, and I peeked through the curtain and saw him sitting there. After the show, I'm driving up Wilshire Boulevard and who should pull up next to me at a light but Tony Martin. He yells out, 'Hey, Jeffries, I caught the show, you were terrific.' I said, 'Yeah, I saw you sitting in the audience.' We were rapping back and forth like that and he says, 'Incidentally, I recorded "Flamingo".' I said, 'I know. You copied my record.' He said, 'How do you know that?' I said, 'Because you made the same mistake in the lyrics that I did.' He said, 'Pull over, you son of a gun.' And we pulled over on Wilshire Boulevard and I told him the story of how, when I went in to record that song, I didn't have any music with me. Once in the studio, I got so excited that I couldn't think of two words in the song. So I made up the words in their place. Tony recorded the song never knowing that some of the words I sang were made up.[35]

For most of the 1930s, the radio networks had been at loggerheads with the main performing rights organization, the American Society of Composers, Authors and Publishers. By 1937, network radio broadcasting was enjoying an annual turnover of $55 million, generated by some 722 broadcast licensees. Continuing arguments with ASCAP *were compounded by demands from the firebrand president of the American Federation of Musicians Chicago Chapter, James Caesar Petrillo, who wanted more stringent warnings directed at radio stations on recordings intended 'for home use', on the basis that recordings played on air put union musicians hired by the radio stations out of work. The seeds were being set for a power struggle within the music industry. In 1935, when NBC and CBS were considering the renewal of an* ASCAP *contact, CBS lawyer Sydney Kaye proposed an alternative to* ASCAP's *autocratic demands, a corporation that subsequently became known as Broadcast Music Incorporated. A start date of 1 April 1940 was set for the new organization and in February that* year they opened an office with a temporary staff of four. New ASCAP terms unexpectedly gave momentum to the fledgling company amid accusations that ASCAP was attempting to 'split our industry in hostile camps' with a sliding scale of royalty fees based on the turnover of radio stations. Variety calculated that using this new scale of charges ASCAP would collect $7.1 million instead of $4.3 million, based on 1939 turnover figures.[36]

The task of selling the fledgling BMI as an alternative to ASCAP to radio stations was given to Carl Haverlin, who promptly brought in more than 85 per cent of the industry's time-sales income fee. By September 1940, BMI's office staff had increased to 220 full-time employees, who were now insisting on a reduction of ASCAP registered music on the airwaves in favour of BMI tunes. While not all radio stations had moved to BMI, the portents were clear. An ASCAP–BMI radio war was beginning in earnest. BMI required a gradual reduction of ASCAP material and threatened to cut off radio broadcasts of bands that did not comply. During Ellington's residency at the Hotel Sherman in Chicago during September and early October 1940, Downbeat claimed he was playing 'four BMI tunes nightly'[37] in rotation during his broadcasts. Yet during a broadcast from the Crystal Ballroom, Fargo in North Dakota, on 7 November, he was unaffected by the ban, performing numbers across his entire repertoire. It was, however, clear which way the wind was blowing, and that money could be made by all the big bands by plugging their own original music on the airwaves and opening their own publishing companies, licensed through BMI, to collect performance royalties. Ellington was finally forced to react to the situation when he opened an extended engagement at the Casa Mañana night club – formerly Frank Sebastian's Cotton Club – in Culver City, California, on 3 January 1941. There, with regular broadcasts over the local radio station KHJ, an MBS affiliate that relayed several programmes to the national network, he finally acknowledged he had to create a new library of BMI registered tunes for his band to continue broadcasting.

BILLY STRAYHORN: At the end of 1940, there was a fight between ASCAP [American Society of Composers, Authors and Publishers] and the radio and at the beginning of 1941 all ASCAP music was off the air. When we opened at the Casa Mañana, the third of January 1941, we had air time every night but could not play our library. We had to play non-ASCAP material. Duke was in ASCAP but I wasn't. So we had to write a new library.[38]

DUKE ELLINGTON: I was in a bit of a pickle because we were playing a ballroom out there [on the West Coast] and we're broadcasting and I can't broadcast any of my material because the broadcasters won't allow anything by ASCAP on the air. So I've got all these yearlings around me, Strayhorn and Mercer.[39]

MERCER ELLINGTON: Strayhorn and I got this break at the same time. Overnight, literally, we got a chance to write a whole new book for the band. It could have taken us twenty years to get the old man to make room for that much of our music, but all of a sudden we had this freak opportunity. He needed us to write music, and it had to be in our names [because we signed with BMI]. We were sharing the same room and we had all this work to do. When I was up during the day, Strayhorn would use the bed, and while he was up at night, I would sleep in it ... At one point he was having some sort of trouble and I pulled a piece out of the garbage. I said, 'What's wrong with this?' And he said, 'That's an old thing I was trying to do something with, but it's too much like Fletcher Henderson' ... It was 'A Train' ... I flattened it out anyway and put it in the pile with the rest of the stuff.[40]

BILLY STRAYHORN: 'Take the A Train', the little version that was on the Victor 78, that was exactly as I wrote it. It just happened to come out to three minutes.[41]

'Take the A Train' was subsequently recorded on 15 February 1941. When it was released it stayed on the record charts for seven

weeks, becoming an Ellington bestseller, and was quickly adopted as the band's signature tune.

DUKE ELLINGTON: Rex Stewart got temperamental or something, he was originally supposed to play the solo, then it was given Ray Nance and he blew this chorus which was one of the great choruses of all time, one of the great trumpet solos of all time – Ray Nance's solo on 'Take the A Train'.[42]

HARRY CARNEY: When Ray Nance first joined the band and we recorded 'A Train', Ray Nance was criticized for what has become the classic solo in 'A Train'![43]

LAWRENCE BROWN: And they still listen to [Nance's] original chorus on the original rendition of 'A Train'. They still try to pattern it after that chorus. He *played*. He was too much, as we say, too much.[44]

RUTH ELLINGTON: Duke said, 'We'll have our own music publishing company so we can own the rights for broadcast.' When I graduated from Columbia [University] in 1941, he said, 'We're going to have a music publishing company and you're going to be the President, Ruthie!' Which was a shock, since I was studying to be a biology teacher![45]

In 1941, Ellington struck a blow for control over his own creative and financial affairs and formed his own music publishing company, Tempo Music. When, in 1942, his contract with his existing publishers, Robbins Music, expired, it enabled him to take over the rights of his own songs and collect in full a royalty from the sale of sheet music and recordings of his compositions.

DUKE ELLINGTON: We were very social conscious, and many things had to be said, and I was out in the neighbourhood of California, about a year around Hollywood, a lot of those intellectuals – some of them were labelled communists.[46]

FBI FILE 100–434443: EDWARD KENNEDY (DUKE) ELLINGTON: A confidential source who has furnished reliable information in the past advised that the name of Duke Ellington appeared on a list of the Committee of Sponsors for a dinner given at Ciro's Restaurant, Hollywood, California on November 10, 1941. The dinner was given under the auspices of the American Committee to Save Refugees, the Exiled Writers' Committee, and the United American-Spanish Aid Committee. The American Committee to Save Refugees has been cited as a Communist front by the Special Committee on Un-American Activities. (100–7061–115)[47]

DUKE ELLINGTON: Fifteen Hollywood writers and I did *Jump for Joy*.[48]

Ellington's musical Jump for Joy, *with his band in the pit, opened at 9.10 p.m. on 10 July 1941 at the Mayan Theatre, Los Angeles.*

BOB UDKOFF: I saw *Jump for Joy* I think seventeen times, and it changed every night. *Jump for Joy* was so ahead of its time . . . a lot of good material in there, a good deal of it was written by Sid Kuller.[49]

SID KULLER: These weekend jam sessions at my home became a ritual. It was the talk of Hollywood, people were begging to be invited. This went on and then one weekend I didn't get in until one in the morning. The place was swinging. Duke was at the piano, Sonny Greer was at the drums, Mannie Klein was blowing trumpet, Lawrence Brown was there, Barney Bigard, Harry Carney, and I walked in, 'The joint sure is jumpin'.' Duke turned and said, 'Jumpin' for joy.' I said: 'That's it, why don't we do a show with Ellington, *Jump for Joy*?' Bill Burnett, the writer from Warners, said, 'Count me in!' Tony Garfield said, 'Count me in too!' And before you know it, everybody's pledging money.[50]

The Playgoer

THE MAGAZINE IN THE THEATRE

OFFICIAL PUBLICATION OF THE

Mayan Theatre

Hill Street at Olympic Blvd.
PRospect 0526
PRospect 9593

PUBLISHED BY

JOHN F. HUBER

1633 South Los Angeles Street
Los Angeles • PRospect 8131

Eastern
Representative
S. M. GOLDBERG
420 Madison Avenue
New York City

Official
Publication
of the leading
reserved seat
theatres of Los
Angeles & Hollywood

FIRE NOTICE—Look around now, choose the nearest exit to your seat, and in case of disturbance of any kind, to avoid the dangers of panic, WALK (do not run) to that exit.

» PROGRAMME «

Premiere—Thursday, July 10, 1941

AMERICAN REVUE THEATRE

(Walter Jurmann, chairman)

Presents

DUKE ELLINGTON

in

A Sun-Tanned Revue-sical

"JUMP FOR JOY"

with

DOROTHY DANDRIDGE · IVY ANDERSON
HERB JEFFRIES

Music by DUKE ELLINGTON and HAL BORNE
Lyrics by PAUL WEBSTER
Sketches by SID KULLER and HAL FIMBERG
Staged by NICK CASTLE
Costumes, Scenery, Lighting by RENE HUBERT
Sketches Directed by SID KULLER and EVERETT WILE

•

Additional Sketches, Lyrics and Music

SID KULLER, OTIS RENE, LANGSTON HUGHES, CHARLES LEONARD,
MICKEY ROONEY, SIDNEY MILLER, RAY GOLDEN,
RICHARD WEIL, MERCER ELLINGTON

VOCAL ARRANGEMENTS

HAL BORNE, Assisted by EDDIE JONES
"Jump for Joy" Number by EDDIE JONES

MUSIC ARRANGEMENTS

DUKE ELLINGTON, WILLIAM STRAYHORN, HAL BORNE

Entire Production Supervised by HENRY BLANKFORT

DUKE ELLINGTON: These picture writers wanted to do this show, *Jump for Joy*, an all-Negro show with a social significance theme. The idea was to banish Uncle Tom from the theatre, and there was all very clever material contributed by these people and from the show we got some good tunes like 'Jump for Joy', 'I Got it Bad and That Ain't Good', 'Brownskin Gal in the Calico Gown'. We had Ivie Anderson, we had Herb Jeffries, who were members of our band, put them in the show, and we also sent for Joe Turner, that his first time out of Kansas City – the blues singer – and put him in the show. Ivie was doing 'I Got it Bad', and she also did 'Rocks in My Bed'. Herb Jeffries did 'Jump for Joy'.[51]

BOB UDKOFF: The backers for *Jump for Joy* were the leftist Hollywood crowd, people like John Garfield, a group of Holly-wood people who put the money for it. It had great talent in there, acts like Marie Bryant, Pot, Pan and Skillet, a guy named Wonderful Smith who had a dummy telephone talking to President Roosevelt, and they would come up with new ideas after each show, they'd have a meeting and discuss new thoughts, some of the gag writers, 'Why don't we try this, why don't we try that.' And there was a threat made by some hate group because one particular number, I forget the name, it was like the advent of Civil Rights demands, and they had to take it out of the show, a lot of fear in those days.[52]

MERCER ELLINGTON: We had things in there that were sort of deriding the South, and as a result we had a couple of bomb threats and things of that sort and there was one song there called 'Passport from Georgia' – and 'Jump for Joy' is not what you would call complimentary to the South – so that these people really wanted to get rid of the show ... ['Passport for Georgia' was taken out of the show] because of the threats.[53]

DUKE ELLINGTON: We had twelve weeks of discussions after the show [finished each night] concerning the Negro, the race, what constituted Uncle Tom, what constituted chauvinism, what constituted everything. We had to change a sketch practically every night because fifteen cats would sit up and *prove* in their discussions *why* this thing, where it appeared was very, very funny and appeared to be legitimate, but *actually* it was a form of Uncle Tom because there was a compromise there. It was done on a very high level, pinpoint fine, and you get to see these things from all the different angles.[54]

METRONOME: Down to catch Duke Ellington's *Jump for Joy* show and then to see Duke backstage. He's very intent on making this thing go over in a big way. Eventually he wants to bring it east, but not for quite a while.[55]

DUKE ELLINGTON: It was well done because we included everything we wanted to say without saying it. Which is the way I think these social significance things should be handled, if it's going to be done on stage. Just to come out on the stage and take a soap box and stand in the spotlight and say ugly things is not entertainment.[56]

DUKE ELLINGTON: The theme had to do with burying Uncle Tom in the theatre. We buried Uncle Tom in the opening scene. We had children running around singing, 'He enjoyed himself, let him go!' We had Broadway producers and Hollywood producers trying to keep him alive with a hypodermic needle.[57]

HERB JEFFRIES: We had too many chefs. I think at that time we had maybe seven different people who were financing the show and when you get that many chefs it becomes highly complex and there was trouble and arguments. Unfortunately, because of financial problems it didn't survive.[58]

Jump for Joy *closed on 27 September 1941. The show cost approx. $7,000 a week and was never profitable enough for its backers to consider mounting it on Broadway.*

SID KULLER: The most gratifying thing about the show was that the black newspapers came out and said: 'For the first time since we have been going to the theatres to see black performers and black shows we could walk out of the theatre and hold our heads up high.'[59]

DUKE ELLINGTON: One of the greatest lights of my life was one night in 1941 when Orson Welles came to see our show *Jump for Joy*.[60]

DUKE ELLINGTON: He was in the front row with Dolores Del Rio and after the show he says, 'Have Duke Ellington come out to my office at RKO tomorrow and I'll have something for him.' So there I was at 9 a.m. but Mr Welles was not there so I waited around. Finally he came in with a big burst and said, 'Hello, Duke! How are you. I'm Orson I know you and you don't know me and Yap, yap.' He went on and on and never stopped talking. Then he says, 'I have an idea. I saw your show last night and it's a great show, but if I was doing it I would do this and that and move this from the opening to the finale.' He went through every move of the show, 'But enough of that,' he says. 'If you want to re-do it I'll be glad to come in with you, but what I want you for now is for you to do a film. It will be called *It's All True* and it's going to be the history of jazz.' He went on to name the positions I would have. I would be the co-producer. Produced by Duke Ellington and Orson Welles, story by Duke Ellington and Orson Welles, directed by Duke Ellington and Orson Welles. Music by Duke Ellington. Arrangements by Duke Ellington. 'Now,' he says, 'You'll get those credits and further-more, certain royalties. You can start work today! You get $1,500 a week. Now there it is and if you don't take it you're a fool.' And I looked at him and said, 'Where's the paper?' And with that I got the $1,500 a week and a whole lot of assistance. People who were looking up stuff, historic stuff, and so forth. I think I wrote 28 bars, a trumpet solo by Buddy Bolden which, of course, was to be a symbol of the jazz. It was very good, but Orson never heard it, and I can't find it. I don't know where it is. It was the only thing I ever wrote for the $12,500 I got. The film came to nothing; Welles had a difference with RKO and went off to South America or someplace.[61]

Welles was in Brazil in February 1942, shooting carnival scenes intended as a backdrop for part of the film. But RKO terminated its stormy association with him in June 1942 and the project was cancelled. Nevertheless, the concept of a history of jazz enacted against an exotic backdrop remained in Ellington's mind, and later provided the basis for his A Drum is a Woman, *televised in May 1957.*

MERCER ELLINGTON: Ben [Webster] was demonstrating the feeling 'Bakiff' should have, the guys kept playing it in a certain fashion and he said, 'No, that's not the way it goes, it goes like this (hums).' And he would hum that to them. The old man listened to him, he said, 'Wait a minute!' He called a break, brought back and gave the music to them again. This time Ben was playing the lead, Johnny Hodges and the rest of them were playing the parts under him and that was the first time he came up with the idea of a tenor playing the lead above the rest of the section, rather than double it underneath, he came up with what is recognized as a 'tenor lead'.[62]

'Bakiff' was recorded in Hollywood on 5 June 1941.

MILT HINTON: Blanton was a weak kid. He might get on a bus soaking wet after a gig and drive two or three hundred miles like that while his clothes dried on him. Eventually he got tuberculosis and of course we had no penicillin or sulpha drugs then. The only treatment was to go to bed and rest. So he got sick in California. The reason I know this is Duke was closing there and we [the Cab Calloway Orchestra] were the next band to come into the ballroom where he'd been. Ben said to me, 'Bear's pretty sick. We gotta leave him in a rest home here.

Please go out and see him.' I said, 'Don't worry, I'll be there.' It was way out of town, but I went every other day. Had to hire a car to get me there. He had a lovely room, but he was twenty-two years old, at the peak of his career, and his band was going off and leaving him. He's from Tennessee and he don't have a friend in California, and his poor heart was broken. You could see the loneliness of it took his strength and will to live.[63]

When Ellington left the Bay area of Los Angeles in November 1941, Blanton was hospitalized.

DOWNBEAT: Hollywood – Dr Leonard Stovall, head of L.A.'s Stovall Clinic and attending physician to the late Jimmy Blanton, the brilliant young bass player who played with Duke Ellington here in 1941 and died near here in August 1942. 'The disease was just too far advanced when he came to us,' said the doctor, 'but he remained cheerful and seemingly hopeful to the very end.'[64]

Jimmy Blanton died on 30 July 1942.

REX STEWART: Junior Raglin [was] the bass player who was hired after Jimmy Blanton became too ill to continue. I couldn't say if his feet hurt, if he didn't know any better or was a bit zany. Whenever he could get away with it he played perform-ances in his ordinary felt bedroom slippers. Now, remember, this band had Duke in the vanguard wearing his hand-made, square-toed shoes, and most of the fellows followed his lead with very classy footwear. Junior also differed from the norm . . . the fellows would be scattered all over our Pullman, some in a poker game but Junior left all these activities to us as he sat quietly in a seat by himself, enthralled by stacks of comic books.[65]

TOM WHALEY: I'll tell you about Junior. Junior would never put on a clean shirt. Always a dirty shirt. I said, 'Do you see Duke out there immaculate, and look at you!'[66]

BILLY STRAYHORN: We were going to play the University of Pennsylvania, on the way there we had to go on the train and we had to get off at Lewiston, I think it was, we had to get off the train and get a bus, and about halfway to where we had to get off [the train] we were in the diner, and Edward says, 'Oh, yes. They've asked us to write a little something or other.' It turns out they had a little contest and everybody had to turn in a title to which he was going to write a melody. So he didn't think about it until we were almost there, he wrote it and orchestrated it, as we were in the bus. We got there and he met the committee and they gave him a list of titles to select the title from, so he handed it to me, so I chose it and wrote the lyrics and we extracted the arrangement and taught it to Ivie, we did it about the third set didn't we! Fun . . .[67]

REX STEWART: The war had not broken out yet but there was an almost imperceptible tightening of the nation's economic belt ... I couldn't help notice our theatre and dance dates began to show a slow but certain decline in attendance. And our jumps grew longer (we made one such trek in unheard of fashion – Indianapolis to New York in a day in a coach). Everybody started bitching, 'What happened to our Pullmans?' We were told that there were none available. So, as our activities slowed down a lot, we were also laid off more than ever before.[68]

HERB JEFFRIES: ['I Don't Know What Kind of Blues I Got'] really wasn't supposed to have had a vocal on it at all. It was sort of an instrumental and overnight Ellington could get an idea and the next day he might come in and change the whole formula and say, 'Well OK, I want you to sing this.' And if you remember the record, it was instrumental for a long time and then all of a sudden, for some unknown reason, a vocalist [me] came in and started singing something – 'Snake Mary'. 'Snake Mary' was the star in this thirty-two bar opera.[69]

'I Don't Know What Kind of Blues I Got' was recorded on 2 December 1941.

JUAN TIZOL: 'Perdido' was written on the train, a coach train. I wrote 'Perdido' and Herb Jeffries was next to me in the seat in the coach, and I started singing this thing, and he started singing it too, and I gave it to Duke. And he took it right there and made some kind of arrangement, a small thing, on the trip where we were going to play a dance. I extracted it, so we wrote it, he arranged it, and we played it that same night, because there was nothing to that first arrangement of 'Perdido'.[70]

'Perdido' was recorded on 21 January 1942.

It's TEMPOTIME as well as wartime!

It's The Duke And His Son, with | And It's Latin America in Jitterbug Time, with

MOON MIST | PERDIDO

BOTH RECORDED BY

DUKE ELLINGTON

TEMPO MUSIC, INC., 1775 BROADWAY, NEW YORK

REX STEWART: Then things got really tough; the phonograph ban started and there was no recording . . . this cut down our income. Then the record companies weren't even pressing the hits because shellac was hard to come by. Food rationing meant the fare was even worse in the greasy spoons that catered for us. Going on the road was tough. Trains were commandeered; the armed forces, of course, took precedence, while we scrambled to get to our gigs however possible.[71]

BARNEY BIGARD: Well, the war, you know, we used to have the Pullman and all and they couldn't get that any more and the last job we had to get a seat anywhere on the train and I was sitting in the baggage car. I left in the West Coast to settle.[72]

Bigard ended his thirteen-year association with Ellington on the band's return from the Pacific Northwest coast in the first week of July 1942.

LAWRENCE BROWN: I think [Ivie Anderson's] husband requested that she get more money and that was unheard of. So I think he had her pull out. She had some property here in L.A., and she really didn't need to struggle along like that. But when she pulled out she sort of went as a single doing a stint in the cabarets.[73]

At the end of August 1942, Ivie Anderson left the band 'due to poor health'.

JUMP FOR JOY RIGHT AFTER THE SHOW
AT
IVIE'S CHICKEN SHACK
1105½ East Vernon Avenue   ADams 0446
IVIE ANDERSON, Proprietor • Open Nightly 7:30 P.M. to 7:30 A.M. • MARQUE NEAL, Manager

DUKE ELLINGTON: 1942 we were at the Sherman House in Chicago, that's when Joya's mother brought her down from Detroit and she sang with us there, because Ivie had decided to go out on her own, and Joya [Sherrill] was with us for a while. Joya was very young and immature as a professional artist, she only stayed with us for a short while, I don't think she made any one-nighters. And then she went home to Detroit with her mother.[74]

Ellington was at the Panther Room of the Hotel Sherman from 17 July–13 August 1942. A more experienced Joya Sherrill would rejoin Ellington later in the 1940s.

DANIEL HALPERIN: Hardwick and I watched Hodges change the lights in his room. He had drawn the curtains and the room was in darkness while he made the solemn business of removing the hotel's bulbs from their sockets, replacing them with small, dark, coloured bulbs of yellow, red and blue and sprinkling these with eau de cologne so that when lit they made a sizzling sound and, after a moment or two, clogged the room with a thick scent. 'They're Rabbit's love lamps,' Toby told me. 'He brings his own *ambience* with him.' And I looked back as we left the darkened room to see Hodges lying contentedly on his bed.[75]

LAWRENCE BROWN: Shorty Baker was one of the best of the best. He worked with us for quite a while. His lush tone, and his beautiful way of making his passages and the things he picked out to make in his passages were really something. He was with Andy Kirk and then he came with us, finally.[76]

Harold 'Shorty' Baker joined the band on 15 September 1942, expanding the Ellington trumpet section to four.

SHORTY BAKER: When I first joined that band, they let me sit there playing wrong notes for a week without telling me the parts had been changed! Nobody ever marked changes. The trumpet parts were full of traps. I wasn't used to that sort of thing. In St Louis, where I came from, musicians were family. If your ass was out some kind of way, somebody would pull your coat and let you know.[77]

MERCER ELLINGTON: We did *Cabin in the Sky*, a motion picture. It had both Ethel Waters and Lena Horne in it, and they chose my song for the [band] scene, which is 'Things Ain't What They Used to Be'.[78]

Cabin in the Sky *was filmed at MGM Studios, Culver City, California, between September and November 1942 and released in February 1943.*

NEW YORK TIMES: Bountiful entertainment.[79]

DOWNBEAT: One of the truly fine entertainment pictures to come out of Hollywood, the extraordinary talent and sincerity of the performers outshining any white cast ever assembled for a film musical.[80]

DUKE ELLINGTON: After *Jump for Joy* we came back East, we were out there a couple of years in California, we played the territory [there] all up and down, ballrooms and shows, theatre, and we got back East and we didn't have much promotion when we went back there, and we had a hard time getting proper money going into the Apollo [Theatre, in Harlem], so I didn't take it, so William Morris says to me, 'What you need is a Carnegie Hall Concert.'[81]

FBI FILE 100–434443: EDWARD KENNEDY (DUKE) ELLINGTON: The Artists' Front to Win the War made its debut as a mass meeting at Carnegie Hall, New York, on October 16, 1942. Exhibit Number 1, which appears to be a programme of the above described mass meeting, reflected Duke Ellington as one of its sponsors. The Artists' Front to Win the War was cited as a communist front by the Special Committee on Un-American Activities in a report dated March 29, 1944. (61–7582–1298)[82]

DUKE ELLINGTON: So I started whipping up material for a Carnegie Hall concert. And we planned it for – there was a big Russian War Relief, and we played it on 23 January 1943. I think I started writing 'Black, Brown and Beige' on the 19 December. We were playing the theatre in Hartford [Conn.], and Frank Sinatra was the extra added attraction, he was that weekend, when I started and I wrote it was writing all the way down from Hartford down to Bridgeport, Detroit and all these other places, I was always writing in the hotel, backstage at the theatre, Columbus, Ohio, and we got back to New York and introduced 'Black, Brown and Beige'.[83]

The Hartford engagement with Sinatra, who had just left the Tommy Dorsey Orchestra, was in fact on 11–13 December 1942.

VARIETY: ELLINGTON'S CARNEGIE CONCERT ALREADY SRO: MARKS 20TH ANNI AS MAESTRO. Carnegie Hall N.Y. is virtually sold out for Duke Ellington's concert there this Saturday (23). Russian War Relief, for whose benefit the programme is being conducted, claims that the only sale at the b.o. that evening will be standing room only in the balconies and possibly seats on-stage, which has been done before.[84]

Ellington's Carnegie Hall debut on 23 January 1943 was completely sold out days before the event. Even though the 3,000 house seats were sold, the demand for tickets remained so intense that a further 200 people were seated on stage. The proceeds of $5,000 were donated for the benefit of Russian War Relief.

ED ANDERSON: On the afternoon of the concert I didn't even have tickets and it was a complete sell-out. I called Duke: 'Come over to rehearsal this afternoon and we'll see what we can do,' he said. Over at the rehearsal hall Duke was rehearsing and still writing parts of 'Black, Brown and Beige', the fifty-seven minute tone poem to be premiered that night. He presented me with a couple of tickets for the front row centre. What a thrill it was hearing Johnny Hodges playing 'Come Sunday' that afternoon at rehearsal for the first time, practically before the ink on the music sheets was dry.[85]

Anderson had booked Ellington for his Carnegie Hall debut in October 1942, but the date was cancelled because of Ellington's participation in the filming of Cabin in the Sky.

SONNY GREER: ['Black, Brown and Beige'], we laid that on Carnegie Hall. And every year after that, the man say, you oughta come back, every year we'd come back. Come back with a different programme. We would play – Benny Goodman played, well any time he can play he's gonna play the same

Saturday Evening, January 23, at 8:45

Twentieth Anniversary Concert
Proceeds to Russian War Relief

DUKE ELLINGTON
AND HIS ORCHESTRA

Personnel: Duke Ellington, pianist-leader; Johnny Hodges, alto-saxophone; Otto Hardwicke, alto saxophone; Chauncey Haughton, tenor saxophone & clarinet; Ben Webster, tenor saxophone; Harry Carney, baritone saxophone; Rex Stewart, cornet & trumpet; Ray Nance, trumpet & violin; Harold Baker, trumpet; Wallace Jones, trumpet; Joe Nanton, trombone; Juan Tizol, trombone; Lawrence Brown, trombone; Sonny Greer, drums; Fred Guy, guitar; Alvin Raglin, bass; Billy Strayhorn, ass't. arranger; Betty Roche, Jimmy Britton—vocalists.

PROGRAM
I.

ELLINGTON-MILEY	Black and Tan Fantasy
ELLINGTON-CARNEY	Rockin' in Rhythm
MERCER ELLINGTON	Blue Serge
	Jumpin' Punkins

PROGRAM CONTINUED
. . . —

II.

ELLINGTON	Portrait of Bert Williams
	Portrait of Bojangles
	Portrait of Florence Mills

III.

ELLINGTON	Black, Brown and Beige

(A Tone Parallel to the History of the Negro in America.)

Intermission

IV.

ELLINGTON	The Flaming Sword
BILLY STRAYHORN	Dirge
	Nocturne
	Stomp

Program Continued on Second Page Following

PROGRAM CONCLUDED
•

V.

ELLINGTON	Are You Stickin'?
	(Chauncey Haughton, clarinet)
TIZOL	Bakiff
	(Juan Tizol, valve trombone; Ray Nance, violin)
ELLINGTON	Jack the Bear
	(Alvin Raglin, string bass)
ELLINGTON	Blue Belles of Harlem
	(Duke Ellington, piano)
ELLINGTON	Cotton Tail
	(Ben Webster, tenor saxophone)
ELLINGTON-STRAYHORN	Day Dream
	(Johnny Hodges, alto saxophone)
WARREN-GORMAN-LESLIE	Rose of the Rio Grande
	(Lawrence Brown, trombone)
ELLINGTON	Trumpet in Spades
	(Rex Stewart, cornet)

VI.

ELLINGTON	Don't Get Around Much Any More
	Goin' Up
	Mood Indigo

(Duke Ellington and his orchestra are under the exclusive management of the William Morris Agency, Inc.)

DUKE ELLINGTON AND HIS ORCHESTRA

Twentieth Anniversary Concert.

CARNEGIE HALL
New York

Saturday Evening, January 23, 1948
at 8:45 o'clock

Proceeds for Russian War Relief

PROGRAM

I.

Black and Tan Fantasy...*Ellington-Miley*
Rockin' in Rhythm ....*Ellington-Carney*
Blue Serge ....*Mercer Ellington*
Jumpin' Punkins ....*Mercer Ellington*

II.

Portrait of Bert Williams ....*Ellington*
Portrait of Bojangles
Portrait of Florence Mills

III.

Black, Brown and Beige...*Ellington*
(A Tone Parallel to the History of the Negro in America.)

—— *Intermission* ——

IV.

The Flaming Sword ....*Ellington*
Dirge ....*Billy Strayhorn*
Nocturne
Stomp

V.

Are You Stickin'? ....*Ellington*
(Chauncey Haughton, clarinet)
Bakiff .... *Tizol*
(Juan Tizol, valve trombone; Ray Nance, violin)
Jack the Bear...*Ellington*
(Alvin Raglin, string bass)
Blue Belles of Harlem...*Ellington*
(Duke Ellington, piano)
Cotton Tail ....*Ellington*
(Ben Webster, tenor saxophone)
Day Dream ....*Ellington-Strayhorn*
(Johnny Hodges, alto saxophone)
Rose of the Rio Grande...*Warren-Gorman-Leslie*
(Lawrence Brown, trombone)
Trumpet in Spades...*Ellington*
(Rex Stewart, cornet)

VI.

Don't Get Around Much Any More..*Ellington*
Goin' Up
Mood Indigo

tunes. We had a complete programme, new. It wasn't something people heard before, and they knew that. They looked for that. Never disappointed. Packed and jammed, hanging on the ceiling, chandeliers, you know. We was packed. Because when the concert – the blizzard didn't start until after the concert started. Nobody thought – like that was one of the big blizzards in New York because my wife and daughter was down. Couldn't get no cabs to run. They just kept the hall open all night long because people couldn't get home.[86]

LAWRENCE BROWN: And I remember one of [Shorty Baker's] terrific things he did was on a transitional phrase, I think it was, 'Black, Brown and Beige'. Which he played all by himself, in no time, just played and it was so terrific that at the concert in Carnegie Hall the audience gave him applause, really applauded, very definitely for this passage.[87]

DUKE ELLINGTON: The reason why that number was titled 'Black, Brown and Beige' – I started off with the entrance of the Negro into America in 1619 off the slave ships. It has to do with the state of mind, not the colour of the skin, because when they arrived everything looked real black, the Negro thought when he was being brought here from Africa that he was being brought as food, because he was a very delicious thing, and he expected to be eaten, but when they got here they saw all they had to do was work, it lightened, it got to be brown. First thing they did was work and that was 'Work Song'. The next thing was spiritual, singing counter melodies to the hymns being sung in the church, they were on the outside. So gradually it got lighter, and of course in 'Black, Brown and Beige' we went on to cream, and so forth, various other degrees, but it never got quite white. There was still a little jazz in there! Then we got the blues. In the Spanish American wars, Negroes would come home decorated and would attract attention and attract someone else's woman and then you get the triangle. And another hero would come back and someone else had his woman, that's another triangle, and the blues was born after the Spanish American war as a result of these triangles. There was always a guy on the corner who had the blues.[88]

THE NEW YORK HERALD TRIBUNE: The whole attempt to fuse jazz as a form with art music should be discouraged.[89]

WORLD TELEGRAM: It is far from being an en toto symphonic creation.[90]

NEW YORK SUN: One can only conclude that the work would be much better if scored for full orchestra.[91]

DOWNBEAT: Duke fuses classical and jazz![92]

DUKE ELLINGTON: We stopped using the word jazz in 1943, that was the point when we didn't believe in categories.[93]

Given the extent to which Ellington had consistently revealed his ambition to write a major extended composition for at least ten years prior to 'Black, Brown and Beige', today the critical reaction seems as puzzling as it was ill-informed, the Downbeat *review of the concert noting, 'None of these gentry [knew] much about jazz and even less about Ellington.'[94] No review, for example, attempted to situate 'Black, Brown and Beige' in the context of his earlier extended compositions so as to create the right discursive framework in which to consider a work of such importance. Now widely recognized as a landmark in jazz composition, it perplexed audiences as much as critics more used to the standard fare offered by the popular dance bands of the day. Ellington's reaction to this uncomprehending criticism was such that he never played the piece in its entirety in public again and became reluctant to use the word jazz to describe his music since he felt the term limited how his music was perceived. Categories in music are, after all, only an after-the-fact rationalization, to define music in its market, used by the music industry to organize the sales process. The sad fact is that as much as Ellington wanted to move beyond such arbitrary category – jazz – his accomplishments remained forever tied to his audience's received notion of what the term meant, so increasingly defining him in terms of his past accomplishments rather than his current aspirations. He knew categories excluded as much they included, hence his desire, in the main only posthumously realized, for his music to be considered 'beyond category' in order that it be dealt with on its own merits and not artificially pigeonholed into this genre or that where inappropriate evaluative criteria might be brought to bear.*

With jazz remaining located within an urban popular entertainment context, Ellington remained troubled by its vernacular origins in the New Orleans whorehouses, saying, 'It's the equivalent to saying jazz was born in a house of ill repute.'⁹⁵ He saw this as an obstacle to a democratization of white cultural connoisseurship that had, in the main, failed to recognize the great contribution Afro-Americans had made to American culture through jazz. This perceived stigmatization of jazz within cultural circles had been eroded in the 1920s by the flamboyant white bandleader Paul Whiteman, through his concert-style presentation of jazz-influenced numbers arranged for an enlarged dance-band ensemble augmented by strings. What seems clear is that Ellington was attracted to the manner in which Whiteman presented his music, rather than his music per se. He respected Whiteman's attempts to elevate the status of jazz through concert-style presentations of extended works, most notably George Gershwin's Rhapsody in Blue, *premiered at the Aeolian Hall on 12 February 1924, but also in subsequent commissions that included George Antheil's* Jazz Symphony *(1925), Ferde Grofé's* Metropolis *(c. 1928) and Ellington's* The Blue Belles of Harlem *(1938). It is interesting to note that Ellington himself signifies on* Rhapsody in Blue *in the coda of 'St Louis Blues' during a live broadcast in 1940.*

As Ellington noted in his autobiography, Music Is My Mistress, *in 1973, 'Whiteman dressed [jazz] in woodwinds and strings and made a lady out of [her],'⁹⁶ and there is no shortage of examples of*

Ellington expressing his admiration of this in print during the 1930s. Indeed, in the late 1920s and early 1930s Ellington often billed himself as 'The Paul Whiteman of Harlem', and it was in this role, with studied concert-style presentations of his music in Murder at the Vanities *and in* Symphony in Black *that we see Ellington also making a 'lady out of jazz'. His immaculate appearance in bow-tie and tails with baton in hand running counter to Hollywood's racial stereotyping and a source of black pride in Depression hit America. With his presentation of 'Black, Brown and Beige' in the nation's foremost concert hall, not only was he making a lady of jazz, but he was also correcting the Aeolian Hall ledger. This time the lady was black, something he would proclaim even more vividly with* A Drum is a Woman *in 1956.*

DUKE ELLINGTON: I wanted to do 'Black, Brown and Beige' to tell all the things about the Negro in America. The Negro's contribution.[97]

MERCER ELLINGTON: Basically, 'Black, Brown and Beige' was his criticism of his own race. And their prejudices within itself. There were these different castes: the black, the brown or tan ones and the ones light enough to pass for white. And yet they wanted, as a whole, the race wanted recognition and equal rights and yet within themselves they restricted each other.[98]

SONNY GREER: All through the years, Duke has been deeply concerned about his race and its problems. The feelings of the Negro, as interpreted by him, are there in the music. But the man never makes it a great point of his interest; he's too subtle for that. He just composes works like 'Black, Brown and Beige', *Deep South Suite, Harlem* – leaving it to the people to find and interpret his thoughts for themselves.[99]

DUKE ELLINGTON: We started doing a series of Carnegie Hall concerts every year starting with 'Black, Brown and Beige' – in its original performance it was forty-seven minutes long – 1944

'New World A-Comin'' another extended piece which was between twelve and thirteen minutes long; in 1945 was *The Deep South Suite* and then came 'The Perfume Suite', and *The Deep South Suite* was 1946, 1947 was 'The Liberian Suite', celebrating the 200th anniversary of the Republic of Liberia, and in 1948 was 'The Tattooed Bride.'[100]

DUKE ELLINGTON: We attracted so much attention then that the guy – Dave Wolper at the Hurricane Club on Broadway – sent for us. As a matter of fact Courtney, Cress Courtney got us over and we stayed there for six months, on the radio every night.[101]

Ellington's first New York location job in five years opened on 1 April 1943 and closed on 23 September 1943.

DUKE ELLINGTON: We broke the colour barrier at the Hurricane by threatening to walk out; this was a six-month engagement. I did have the boss's backing, though; the head waiter had to be threatened to be fired, he really didn't want us.[102]

DUKE ELLINGTON: Dave Wolper was the owner of the place and I found that I had to go to him one day and say, 'Dave, you know some of my friends have been coming here and the head waiter has told them that the place is sold out and there's no reservations, and if this continues I can't stay here, because I'm embarrassed before my neighbours.' And so with that, Dave went to the door and raised hell with the head waiter, and the head waiter says, 'Oh, I certainly did not,' and he swore what had happened two or three times [had not] until we actually caught him doing it, and this was the beginning of the Broadway opening up as far as night clubs on Broadway was concerned, this was the absolute beginning of it.[103]

DUKE ELLINGTON: Jimmy Hamilton came along in 1943, he was playing a more advanced style of clarinet, he was playing bop and all that, on clarinet and there was really no-one else playing like that. He was unique.[104]

Hamilton joined Ellington during the Hurricane engagement in April 1943.

JIMMY HAMILTON: He had a very warm way of trying to confidence you to come, he call, 'Hey, baby! How you doing?' 'Fine.' 'How do like to come with the band?' It really didn't mean anything, I was working, and the main thing at that time was for a musician to have a job. And I didn't want to travel, and I was really kind of negative. But I told him I didn't like travel, he said, 'Well, we're coming into New York in about two weeks,' they were up in Boston, 'and we'd like you to come down and see me, we're going to be there about six months in New York.' So, you know, fine. I thought about it, but I really didn't want to go out on the road. He came, so I went by the Hurricane, and sat in, played a couple of things for him. He liked what I did. I joined him . . . I had started out around $30 a week with Eddie Heywood, and then I went to about $87 a week, so I felt pretty good. Then when I joined Duke I was making about $125 a week. What! I heard musicians made this kind of money, but I'd never made any.[105]

DUKE ELLINGTON: Al Hibbler I met first in L. Rock Ark. I knew was a singer but had never heard him sing. Our paths crossed from time to time until '43 we were playing the Hurricane Club, 49 & B'way, and Mary Lou Williams and Shorty Baker came up and told me that Al was downstairs in the Turf Club and that it was possible to maybe get him to sing for us. So I sent for him. They brought him up and he sang something. I naturally liked it – but the thought of adding to the payroll was of quite some concern and a smart business mind would not have considered it. But me – well, my ear makes my decision. So I said great – I like it – you just started work. It was much easier than I thought it would be because he has ears that see, he learned song after song and soon he was our major asset, truly a great investment both $ wise and the luxury of my ear was kept in deep fat – He had so many sounds he told of fantasy beyond fantasy.[106]

Hibbler joined Ellington during the Hurricane engagement in May 1943.

AL HIBBLER: He wouldn't let anybody touch me, he had a way of bringing me on stage, he called me, just do this, 'Walk towards me,' and I'd walk towards him, I'm the straightest walker you've ever seen in your life, and I'd walk to him, walk me out on stage and he'd take his shoulder and put it against mine and when we get to the mike, he just turn his shoulder like that and a lot of people actually believed I could see for a long time.[107]

Hibbler would remain with the band until September 1951.

JIMMY HAMILTON: I was a different type player to what he had, I wasn't a New Orleans type player, I was a modern kind of musician that come along with more techniques towards playing music, a better foundation for playing music. I think by us becoming acquainted with one another he got ideas how to write for me.[108]

AL HIBBLER: Ben Webster told me a lot about singing, Ben always wanted me to sing the low notes. I would sit by him and he would take that horn and blow the low notes right in my ear, 'Get *down* there, way *down*.' Ben Webster was a favourite of mine.[109]

BEN WEBSTER: I had a chance to make a little more bread. I didn't want to do that, but I had the chance to make a little more bread and I didn't know how to even say to Duke I was going to leave, I didn't know how to say that to this man.[110]

Webster departed on 13 August 1943 to pursue a solo career, opening at the Three Deuces on 52nd Street. He was succeeded by Elbert 'Skippy' Williams.

DUKE ELLINGTON: While we were playing the Hurricane I lost money every week, and I needed a little cash one day and I decided to go up to the William Morris office and negotiate a small loan. I wanted about $500 or something like that to 'tide me over', I was up there, 'Hello so and so,' and this office boy came along and said, 'Oh, Mr Ellington, I have some here mail for you.' A couple of letters, I looked at one of them, because I had to make an approach for this loan because I just couldn't walk in and need money, I had to have my dignity and all that too. It was a matter of whether I could afford to borrow $500. Maybe I should ask for $2,500. So I'm getting my perspective adjusted for this thing, and I opened the letter and there's a cheque in there from RCA Victor. And I looked at it because the cheque was supposed to go to William Morris, and I slipped it back in and said damn. That's $2,500! That's what I need. I said I better check again, it's liable to be $22.50. It was $22,500. And I put that thing back in the envelope and ran out there like a stick-up man! What had happened, this was after the recording strike, after the recording strike we hadn't recorded anything, so we had no records, but a record we had recorded instrumentally in 1939, 'Never No Lament', Bob Russell had now put a lyric to it and it was now doing very well by the Ink Spots and also another band. And this is what the cheque was for, the accumulated royalties, their re-release of our instrumental under the new title. We had been banging it on the radio every night, and our record had gone on top of everyone else's. And here I was in possession of $22,500! Man.[111]

DUKE ELLINGTON: We stayed six months. We deliberately did it and used to lose about $500 a week to do that, but when we came out after being on the radio practically every night we were so hot we could go out and demand a tremendous amount of money. In a very short while we wiped out our deficit.[112]

DUKE ELLINGTON*

SHATTERS
BAND POLICY
RECORD
AT CAPITOL, NEW YORK

$85,000 [BIGGEST GROSS IN 12 YEARS!]
FIRST WEEK—WITH RAIN AND NO HOLIDAY!!

VARIETY: Neither the illness of two key performers nor the sanctified atmosphere of Carnegie Hall put the brakes on Duke Ellington Saturday night when he and his coterie of standout jazz musicians played a return engagement at the 57th Street N.Y., lair of longhairs ... The Duke premiered 'New World A-Coming', his own brainchild suggested by the closing passages of Roi Otterley's bestseller, which proved to be an unpretentious but pleasant and generous slice of Ellington ... Deliberately, as explained by the Duke – always a gracious, modest and winning master of ceremonies, by the way – it's an attempt to explain the mood of his race's (facing) future in America.[113]

'New World A-Comin'' was premiered at Carnegie Hall, 11 December 1943.

VARIETY: CAB AND DUKE INSIST THEY ENTERTAIN NEGRO SAIL-ORS – Chicago [December 1944]: Cab Calloway and Duke Ellington, both playing engagements here, have taken the stand with Amusement & Recreation Division and USO Camp Shows that they will not play any dates at Great Lakes Training Station this year unless they are allowed to play before the 8,000 coloured trainees at the station. Both leaders are willing to play two shows on their day off but are determined that one of the performances will be for the benefit of their own race. Neither bandleader has ever refused to play a date for servicemen.[114]

DUKE ELLINGTON: 'New World A-Coming,' 'New World A-Coming,' and I mean it.[115]

CHAPTER EIGHT

THINGS AIN'T WHAT THEY USED TO BE

Although Ellington had gradually lost key sidemen since 1942, the war years proved to be his most financially successful yet. The August 1943 edition of Metronome *magazine, for example, awarded the band the only A-plus rating in the magazine's history, and with his run of hits continuing, including 'Don't Get Around Much Any More' and 'Do Nothing Till You Hear From Me' from 1943 and 'I'm Beginning to See the Light' in 1944, Ellington was able to command between $1,000 and $2,600 for a one-night stand, putting him into the top earnings bracket among bandleaders. Artistically, too, he was continuing to expand his horizons with ambitious, extended performances for his Carnegie Hall recitals following the success of 'Black, Brown and Beige' in 1943.*

But as the war drew to a close, the music business was once again in flux. Although no one quite realized it at the time, the curtains were slowly closing on the big band era. The sombre realism of a country at war had meant that the romanticism of a singer was more in keeping with the times than the powerful, driving big bands; lovers were being parted, the mood was sentimental. Billie Holiday's 'All of Me' became a favourite of homesick GIs and a re-release of Harry James's 1939 'All or Nothing At All' became one of the first big hits for Frank Sinatra, who as 'The Voice' would shortly exceed the popularity of any big band.

Within jazz, bebop was gradually becoming the predominant form of expression, while mainstream black audiences had begun dancing to the sounds of rhythm and blues, with Louis Jourdan at the forefront of the craze scoring hit after hit. The writing was on the wall when, in December 1946, eight major big bands broke up, including those led by Benny Goodman and Harry James.

As the '40s wore on, more personnel changes within Ellington's band – sometimes one position changed as many as three times in a year – combined with Ellington's relaxed attitude to band discipline sometimes meant below par performances. Yet his recordings between 1944 and 1946 for RCA Victor and his 1946 Musicraft sessions in the main fail to suggest any slackening of creative resolve. For Victor, 'Black, Brown and Beige', then the most adventurous long-form composition in jazz, made it onto record in highlight form in December 1944, and in July 1945 another extended piece, 'The Perfume Suite' was recorded. Other highlights included the wonderfully ironic 'I'm Just a Lucky So-and-So', a haunting 'Transbluency', and imaginative recastings of 'Memphis Blues' and 'Royal Garden Blues' that do not look out of place alongside his 1940–2 recordings. Of the thirteen titles he cut for the Musicraft label, 'Happy-Go-Lucky Local Parts 1 & 2' and 'The Beautiful Indians Parts 1 & 2' offer two absorbing longer studies.

In August 1947 Ellington signed with Columbia Records, and while he would subsequently record important pieces such as 'Liberian Suite' and 'A Tone Parallel to Harlem', he also recorded some dogs such as 'Singing In the Rain'. Even so, he managed to balance the ledger with his recording of 'Clothed Woman' from December 1947, the first wholly atonal composition in jazz.

On 13 November 1948 his seventh, and final, concert in the Carnegie Hall series premiered the extended composition 'The Tattooed Bride', but even today his extended compositions from this period still rank among his least understood works, often with a grittiness and awkwardness that flew in the face of jazz convention. By 1949, bandleader Woody Herman wound up his famous Second Herd and, heavily in debt, fronted a sextet in Las Vegas, while in 1950 Count Basie was finally forced to reduce his big *band to a six-piece – or an eight-piece when finances permitted. Times were hard for the big bands, but Ellington would soldier on, often forced to subsidize loss-making engagements from the royalties he earned from his compositions. Yet as he entered 1944, he had no inkling that his most difficult period as a bandleader lay just around the corner.*

DUKE ELLINGTON: We went back to the Hurricane [in 1944], and while we were there, in addition to the other things like 'Don't Get Around Much Any More', and 'Do Nothing Till You Here From Me', and those things, I had 'Just A Lucky So and So' and 'Don't You Know I Care (Or Don't You Care To Know?)' which turned out to be big numbers, I had three numbers on the Hit Parade at the same time.[1]

Ellington returned to the Hurricane on 30 March 1944 and remained there until 7 June.

FBI FILE 100–434443: EDWARD KENNEDY (DUKE) ELLINGTON: Information was received from a confidential source who has furnished reliable information in the past that in January 1944, Duke Ellington mailed out approximately 1,500 letters on behalf of the National Committee to Abolish the Poll Tax and that the committee had been receiving money from the people Ellington contacted. The National Committee to Abolish the Poll Tax has been cited by the California Committee on Un-American Activities in their 1947 report as 'among the Communist-front organizations for racial agitation' which also serve as 'money-collecting media'. (100–11507–204)[2]

FBI FILE 100–434443: EDWARD KENNEDY (DUKE) ELLINGTON: According to a source who has furnished reliable information in the past, in a 'report of the National Board' presented by one Herb Singer at the American Youth for Democracy National Convention, June 13–16, 1946, held in New York, New York, the following was presented. 'The New York "Tribute to Fats

Waller" at Carnegie Hall in April 1944, sponsored by American Youth for Democracy, turned into a tremendous, spontaneous demonstration of inter-racial unity. Among those who joined with American Youth for Democracy in this event were Duke Ellington and others too numerous to mention.' American Youth for Democracy has been cited by the Attorney General of the United States as Communist within the purview of Executive Order 10450. (61–777–642, p. 41)[3]

Among the other 'subversives' engaged in this 'tremendous, spontaneous demonstration of inter-racial unity' in honour of Waller (d. 15 December 1943) held at Carnegie Hall on 2 April 1944 were Eddie Condon, Pee Wee Russell, Mezz Mezzrow, Jack Butler, Erskine Hawkins, 'Hot Lips' Page, Mary Lou Williams, Art Hodes, Willie 'The Lion' Smith, Pops Foster, Slick Jones, Sidney Catlett, the bands of Count Basie and Teddy Wilson, the Mills Brothers, the Al Casey Trio, Josh White, and a host of dancers. Ellington played a solo piano tribute and Adam Clayton Powell Jr delivered a speech.

FBI FILE 100–434443: EDWARD KENNEDY (DUKE) ELLINGTON: On May 14, 1944, according to a confidential source who has furnished reliable information in the past, a concert was held at Carnegie Hall, New York City, under the sponsorship of the Joint Anti-Fascist Refugee Committee. Duke Ellington was said to have volunteered his professional services for this concert which was reportedly attended by 2,000 persons. The Joint Anti-Fascist Refugee Committee has been cited by the Attorney General of the United States as Communist within the purview of Executive Order 10450. (100–7061–631, p. 20)[4]

The concert included performances by Jimmy Savo, Paul Draper and the dancers Rosario and Antonio. Ellington appeared near the end of the concert to perform several of his compositions.

JUAN TIZOL: I left Duke [on 21 April] 1944. Harry James's base was right here [on the West Coast], Duke's was New York.

Harry James called me up at [The Hurricane] and they wanted to know if I could come in their band. I said, 'Well, I guess so' – especially I wanted to come to California, I wanted to go home. I didn't want to keep on the road any more.[5]

LAWRENCE BROWN: For many years we had buses that didn't even have a rest room on them and they'd have to pick their stops and everything like that. Very bad. Would you believe it? One time I rode a bus all the way from Seattle to Washington to New York City straight through. We had a driver that could stay up looked like forever ... imagine, a man sitting at the wheel twelve, fifteen hours. When I was on the road with the band we would play the date and then get on the bus and the band would sleep. In fact, I left my car on blocks the whole time I was on the road for about twenty years. I didn't care anything about the road, you know.[6]

AL SEARS: It's like nothing else! Really you've got no idea what it's like till you've actually tried playing in the band. You start at the letter 'A' and go to 'B' and suddenly, for no reason at all, when you go to 'C' the rest of the band is playing something else which you find out later on isn't what is written at 'C' but what's written at 'J' instead. And then the next number, instead of starting at the top, the entire band starts at 'H' – that is everybody except me. See I'm the newest man in the band and I haven't caught on to the system yet![7]

Sears joined Ellington in June 1944, replacing Elbert 'Skippy' Williams who in turn had replaced Ben Webster on 13 August 1943.

MERCER ELLINGTON: Al only knew when he saw certain things on the paper, what keys he had to push down! But he couldn't sing the melody or tell you what the name of that note was![8]

FBI FILE 100–434443: EDWARD KENNEDY (DUKE) ELLINGTON: On August 7, 1944, the *Daily Worker* contained an article captioned 'Stars Lead Coast Dem. Committee,' which reflected that bandmaster-composer Duke Ellington was a member of the executive board of the Hollywood Democratic Committee. The report of the California Committee on Un-American Activities in 1948 described the Hollywood Democratic Committee as a communist front organized in 1942. (100–138754-A)[9]

DUKE ELLINGTON: Here's the recipe for 'Duke's Special'. Start with a foundation of three slices of cake – all different. Top each slice with a generous helping of ice cream – chocolate, vanilla and strawberry – a different flavour for each piece of cake. The chocolate ice cream should then be topped with chocolate sauce and nuts; the strawberry gets cherry sauce, chunks of pineapple and marshmallow; while the vanilla ice cream should be completely hidden under a variety of fruit cocktail.[10]

JOE 'TRICKY SAM' NANTON: He's a genius all right, but Jesus, how he eats![11]

DUKE ELLINGTON: In 1944 was when we had the three girl singers . . . in 1942 Joya Sherrill who was just a young girl, who brought her mother to work with her, we playing the Sherman house in Chicago and Joya was there and her mother was chaperoning her, after that we got Betty Roché, and then we had three girl singers, Joya Sherrill, Kay Davis and Marie Ellington, who [became] Marie Nat 'King' Cole! She was married to an aviator who was a very distant relative of ours down in North Carolina, and he was a hero overseas and he came back and chartered a plane to North Carolina and crashed en route.[12]

Marie Ellington joined the band in October 1944. She claims she was fired by Duke when he discovered 'I was planning to leave anyway'[13] at the end of Ellington's three-month stay at the Club Zanzibar at 49th Street and Broadway in December 1945. It was while she was working there as a single in 1946, touted as 'The

next Lena Horne', that the Nat 'King' Cole Trio were added to the roster of artists that included The Mills Brothers, Eddie 'Rochester' Anderson and the Claude Hopkins band. She married Nat 'King' Cole on Easter Sunday, 1948.

SONNY GREER: Ciro's in Hollywood. So I recall the opening night. That was *the* cabaret. They never had no coloured band, we were the first one. We played out there on a month's engagement, that's where the Hollywood stars hung out. So the first night different people come from New York, New York actors and big stars, so they come over and so Duke went down and sit at the table because he's a star, so this cat, this Greek or whoever he was, he say, 'Listen, Mr Ellington, we don't allow the help to socialize with the guests.' So the next night George Raft was big then, star, big party, sixteen ringside. They come in and he was a pal of mine. Because before he went to Hollywood, he drove for my boss [at the Cotton Club]. They sponsored his trip out there and he made good, so anyway, I was, 'I'll be right down, as soon as I'm off.' So his favourite number was 'Sweet Georgia Brown'. We tore it up for him. So, all right, we're finished, we go down, me and Duke. Here comes the maitre-d. 'I'm sorry Mr Ellington, but the help don't sit at the table with the guests.' George Raft had sixteen people, 'These are my friends, they can't sit down?' He said, 'I tell you what to do, pal. Let's take the whole table and put it in the alley there and sit everything up there and we won't disturb your guests and Sonny and Duke are going to have a sip.' They brought the whole table out in the alley. We sit down and cabareted up a storm. And Georgie told this character, 'Listen here, fellow, any time I come in this place, and somebody's a personal friend of mine, don't you ever try and insult them, because I'll see that nobody comes in here. You will have to wait on other waiters.'[14]

Ellington played Ciro's in Los Angeles 16–28 February 1945. It was the first time a high-priced, big-name black band was booked into this famous night-spot.

JIMMY JONES: Duke had Junior Raglin and he would get drunk, so Duke said, 'I'd better hire another bass player so I can be sure to have one.' So he added Al Lucas – he had two bass players. But Al and Raglin started going out and getting drunk together. Duke said, 'Gee, I'm paying two bass players and neither one of them are here!'[15]

In mid-June 1945 Al Lucas was added on bass. On 13 October Raglin left to join trumpeter Ray Nance, who had left the previous month. Raglin's replacement was Lloyd Trotman.

LAWRENCE BROWN: Pettiford patterned after Blanton in his soloing, see, a bass didn't solo too much before Blanton. [After Blanton] they had to look for other bass players and they fooled around with this one and that one until finally they landed on Pettiford, who was very good. And Pettiford went a step further, he did on a cello what Blanton had done on a bass, made a sort of solo thump instrument or plucking instrument out of the cello.[16]

Oscar Pettiford replaced Trotman on 19 November 1945.

DUKE ELLINGTON: Russell Procope came in 1945. He had been with Fletcher [Henderson] when he was a young kid, he had been with John Kirby's group, and he opened up on a Treasury Broadcast, we used to do, a Saturday afternoon 4 o'clock Treasury broadcast [*Your Saturday Date With Duke* on the ABC Blue Network].[17]

While playing the Howard Theatre, Washington D.C., 19–25 April 1946, Otto Hardwick walked off the stand and left the music business for good. His replacement was Russell Procope.

RUSSELL PROCOPE: Duke asked me to come with him. Otto Hardwick had wandered off and got lost and Duke didn't know where he would find him. When I joined it was just on a temporary basis for a broadcast he had to make in Worcester, Massachusetts. He asked me to take a train up and I had no idea I would be with him one week or even a month later. After the broadcast he said, 'You might as well stay for a dance we have tonight in Providence.'[18]

DUKE ELLINGTON: Otto! He used to get twisted so many different ways it wasn't funny![19]

RUSSELL PROCOPE: One night led to a week, a week led to a month, a month led to a year and I wound up staying twenty-eight years![20]

LAWRENCE BROWN: Russell was terrific. I don't think he ever became greater in his capabilities than with the John Kirby Sextet. That was really one of the famous groups of its day. Now Russell's tone was a bit hard and to match it against Johnny Hodges' lush tone, and the band leaned more towards the lush type of work. So he soon switched over to clarinet.[21]

DUKE ELLINGTON: Russell was a good combination, he's a good first man and he played that good New Orleans clarinet which was a complete contrast to Jimmy Hamilton, who was strictly Boehm, and Russell, who was Albert.[22]

FBI FILE 100–434443: EDWARD KENNEDY (DUKE) ELLINGTON: On March 11, 1946, *The Washington Daily News* contained an article captioned 'Politician Eye Ickes New Role of Prophet for 10 Million Voters'. The article reflected former Secretary of the Interior Harold L. Ickes had become executive chairman of the Independent Citizens Committee of the Arts, Sciences and Professions. The article reflected 'some notable Negro artists and authors are on his committee's national board of directors or are vice-chairman. Among them are Duke Ellington, band leader . . .' The Independent Citizens Committee of Arts, Sciences, and Professions was cited as a communist front by the

Congressional Committee on Un-American Activities, House Report 1954. (100–338892–41)[23]

DUKE ELLINGTON: *Jump for Joy* ... there was just music in a scene I was playing on the stage, 'Subtle Slough', which turned out to be 'Just Squeeze Me, But Please Don't Tease Me'.[24]

'Just Squeeze Me (But Don't Tease Me)' was recorded on 9 July 1946.

TOM WHALEY: One of those roads coming in from San Francisco, we had been out all night, see, and I said to Tricky, I'm going to bed, so he said all right. I got up and I called him [in the morning] and he didn't answer, so it's time to go to the show and still he didn't answer and when they come in there and found – he had a haemorrhage. He was dead.[25]

On the morning of 21 July 1946, forty-two-year-old Nanton was found to have died in his bed at the Scraggs Hotel, San Francisco.

JUAN TIZOL: Tricky was a hell of a nice fellow. Only he liked his whisky. When he got full of whisky, you didn't know what he was going to play![26]

DUKE ELLINGTON: Django, you know what Django used to do? We brought Django to America, we decided, after all our concerts were all booked and advertised, as Django was available, and I said bring him! So we added him to the concert programme, for kicks, this is it. He's a great man, he's available, what the hell, I want to hear him myself, I don't care if anybody else wants to hear him! So we had this luxury sitting before us every night. I shall never forget, I think the first concert was in Indianapolis, and we used to have a wonderful audience there. I forget what spot I had him in, somewhere in the first part of the second half, something like that, first we'd put up something like 'Honeysuckle Rose', and people would say, 'I think it *is* Django!' But nobody had said he was going to be there or anything! And then I would say, 'We're going to play, Django is going to state a theme and follow through.' And so we would just hit him with a pin spot and he'd be sitting there, black out the whole stage, he'd state some theme, every night it was a different theme, and none of this stuff was recorded, what a horrible thing. He'd play these wonderful things and just sit there in that one soft spot, and just play and play. So much happening there. It was a gas. But you had to stay with him every minute because if a chick went by, he'd be behind her, if somebody was coming down the elevator and he sees a sharp chick, oh man! He'd get in the cab with her, Django was too much man![27]

On 30 October 1946, the French guitarist Django Reinhardt arrived in New York 'to become part of the Duke Ellington' concert troupe. The Indianapolis date was 9 November, which Billboard *claimed was, 'The first American appearance' of Reinhardt.*

LAWRENCE BROWN: Ah, Django. That was the first time we ran into a real terrific guitar player. Django didn't have but three fingers. Yeah, he had three fingers and he would do impossible things with those three fingers on guitar. He didn't stay over here very long, just made a tour or two, Ellington brought him over here and oh, yes, he really registered with the American audience.[28]

SONNY GREER: Something else. He was something else, man. Django Reinhardt – yeah. We brought him from Europe. First time ever in America, played at Carnegie Hall. The gypsy from the French Hot Five. I tell you, man, that cat could take a guitar and make it talk. Nobody played like him – only had three fingers on one of his hands. Little guy, tiny. I bodyguarded him. I remember one time we played a concert in Pittsburgh. So he, a French boy living here, so he say, 'Come on Sonny, we go have a drink.' I say all right. So we go in this high-class joint, we stand at the bar, cat don't pay him no mind. So you know, French hot, so he knock on the bar, 'Service!' And the guy says,

'I can serve you Mister,' but he wouldn't serve me. 'What'd he say that for?' Had to drag the guy out of the bar. He wanted to create a scene. I said, 'Man, it's nothing. Forget it.' He says, oh, a lot of French. I don't know what he was saying but I know it was hot![29]

Reinhardt used to play with the Quintet of the Hot Club of Paris – Greer's 'French Hot Five'. The Carnegie Hall concert featuring Reinhardt with the Ellington band on 23 and 24 November 1946.

CHARLES DELAUNAY: I went along to see him on the evening of his first concert [at Carnegie Hall] and he was really pleased to see someone from Paris whom he knew . . . The concert finally began at 8.30. The hall was packed out. I can safely say that by far the greater part of the audience was made of admirers who had waited for this moment for ten years. Duke played as wonderfully as ever and announced Django at 10.30. He had no arrangement to play but was backed by Duke . . . Django received a great ovation and took six curtain calls. The next night he arrived at Carnegie Hall at 11.00 after Duke had regretfully announced he would not appear; but he brought the concert to a close all the same, amidst thunderous applause. When the concert was over Django was asked to explain his appalling behaviour. He did so with good grace. It seems he met the French boxer Marcel Cerdan. He was happy to find a Frenchman . . . and time passed quickly, Django paying little heed; and when he finally realized how late he was he was already overdue. He leapt into a cab and asked to be driven to Carnegie Hall![30]

SONNY GREER: We were playing a concert, I think it was in Boston. At the auditorium in Boston. So we had about an hour before – we always got to the place about an hour or so, the band would be relaxed. So me and him, he was sitting backstage playing one of the things he used to play with Hot Five, a fast thing, you know. So I had some brushes and a newspaper. So just me and him were playing. He said, 'I like that.' Duke come in and said, 'I like that.' So as a surprise encore, we did it. Me and him and Duke was playing a little piano in the back, and the bass. We done it, it was a big thing. Duke said, keep it. I don't know what it was called, he had some fancy French name for it, he used to play it with the French Hot Five.[31]

The Boston concert with Reinhardt was on 1 December 1946.

CHARLES DELAUNAY: [Django] shared a two berth compartment with Duke, the sidemen occupied the sleeping car proper. Before lying down Django had to go through the carriage to get to the toilet and was flabbergasted to see that all the musicians were wearing [under] pants with flowers on them. He could not resist taunting them in English, 'You're crazy!' he told them, so astonishing did it seem to him. Returning to his own compartment, he was on the point of telling Duke all about it but the first thing he noticed on sliding back the door was Duke's underwear, which was even more gaudy than his musicians![32]

DUKE ELLINGTON: [In December 1946 we did] *Beggar's Holiday* with John Latouche, one of the great writers of all time. He did the broken lyrics, but the show was not a success financially. It was a tremendous artistic success because so many things have been taken out and used since, and just about all the cast have become tremendous stars since that time. I'll run them off, Alfred Drake, Zero Mostel, Marge Champion, Libby Holman. Oliver Smith did the designs ... The thing that was wrong with the show was that it was about twenty years ahead of its time. To begin with we had a mixed cast. The Polish chief was a Negro, Drake was McHeath and Peachum was Zero. Libby Holman was Polly and then the chief's daughter fell in love with Mr McHeath and in those days people couldn't understand why you put white people and black people on the stage when

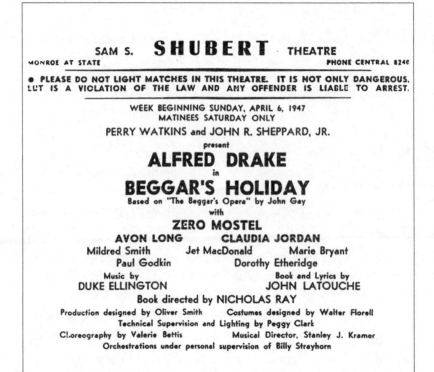

SAM S. **SHUBERT** · THEATRE

MONROE AT STATE   PHONE CENTRAL 8240

● PLEASE DO NOT LIGHT MATCHES IN THIS THEATRE. IT IS NOT ONLY DANGEROUS,
BUT IS A VIOLATION OF THE LAW AND ANY OFFENDER IS LIABLE TO ARREST.

WEEK BEGINNING SUNDAY, APRIL 6, 1947
MATINEES SATURDAY ONLY

PERRY WATKINS and JOHN R. SHEPPARD, JR.

present

ALFRED DRAKE

in

BEGGAR'S HOLIDAY

Based on "The Beggar's Opera" by John Gay

with

ZERO MOSTEL

AVON LONG   CLAUDIA JORDAN

Mildred Smith   Jet MacDonald   Marie Bryant

Paul Godkin   Dorothy Etheridge

Music by   Book and Lyrics by
DUKE ELLINGTON   JOHN LATOUCHE

Book directed by NICHOLAS RAY

Production designed by Oliver Smith   Costumes designed by Walter Florell
Technical Supervision and Lighting by Peggy Clark
Choreography by Valerie Bettis   Musical Director, Stanley J. Kramer
Orchestrations under personal supervision of Billy Strayhorn

they're not calling each other bad names. So down it went, but it was very wonderful.[33]

Beggar's Holiday *opened 26 December 1946 for a preview performance at The Broadway Theatre on Broadway at 53rd Street with 'orchestrations under the personal supervision of Billy Strayhorn'.*

GEORGE ABBOT: I was brought on board [as director], and it was evident to me that a great many changes had to be made, including some new songs and other changes in music. I never saw Duke Ellington, never worked with him. Billy [Strayhorn] took care of whatever I asked for. He sat down and wrote it right there, whatever was needed.[34]

DOWNBEAT: *Beggar's Holiday* is the first Broadway stage production to use blacks and whites with complete indifference to their colour, merely cast according to their capacities and treated on-stage as characters of their parts.[35]

VARIETY: After halting out of town [*Beggar's Holiday*] came to Broadway, then exited way in the red, a Chicago date followed, but that ended after slightly more than a week.[36]

The Broadway run lasted only 108 performances, from 30 December to the last week of March 1947.

DUKE ELLINGTON: It was just ahead of its time. Because in 1947, the audience, the critics, nobody could understand why anybody would have an integrated show. It just didn't fit their idea.[37]

FBI FILE 100–434443: EDWARD KENNEDY (DUKE) ELLINGTON: On May 5, 1947, the *Brooklyn Eagle*, a daily newspaper published in Brooklyn, New York, reflected that a bazaar sponsored by the National Council of American–Soviet Friendship had opened with a variety concert on May 4, 1947, at City Centre Casino Ballroom, New York, New York. The article reflected that Duke Ellington was one of the persons starring in the concert. The

National Council of American–Soviet Friendship has been designated pursuant to Executive Order 10450. (100–146964–1301, p. 17)[38]

LAWRENCE BROWN: 'On a Turquoise Cloud' I have co-composer credit. This young lady that was vocalist with us, Kay Davis, was a graduate of Northwestern University in the field of music, and her voice was very, very beautiful, very, very piercing. And this number we recorded, she was part of an instrumental trio and her voice pierced through everything so strong we had to find a way to shade her voice down without destroying her delivery. So I finally rigged up the outfit of taking a metal derby, which we use in orchestral work, and putting a cloth towel inside the metal derby and letting her sing with this in front – right directly in front of her mouth, so that when you hear this record it sounds like she is open like the rest of the horns, but actually she is singing into a metal derby with a towel inside it! That's the only way we could get her voice toned down so that it would fit with the rest of the instruments.[39]

'On a Turquoise Cloud' was recorded on 22 December 1947.

DUKE ELLINGTON: I wrote the 'Liberian Suite' in a hotel in Salt Lake City, Fletcher [Henderson] was there at the time with his band, he and Horace his brother, they had a band, and they had a night-spot out of town. I used to go out there, hang out at night after hours.[40]

Ellington played the Rainbow Rendezvous, Salt Lake City, Utah, 12–19 July 1947.

DUKE ELLINGTON: The President of the Republic of Liberia came to the premiere [of the 'Liberian Suite'] at Carnegie Hall. I'll never forget, he was supposed to show up that day at a cocktail party at the Warwick Hotel, it started snowing and he didn't show and we said what the hell could have happened, because he had left his hotel and we went running down Fifth

Avenue looking for him, and there he was standing in a store window, and he said he'd never seen anything so pretty in his life as snow – Mr E. V. King, he excited me by saying I had Africa in my soul.[41]

'The Liberian Suite' was premiered at Carnegie Hall on 26 and 27 December 1947. Audience turnout at the first concert was severely affected by one of the worst snowstorms to hit New York.

DUKE ELLINGTON: When I wrote 'On a Turquoise Cloud' I had the tone of Kay Davis's voice in mind. She's a great musician as well as having a great voice and she could read at sight. The first time we did 'Turquoise Cloud' was at Carnegie Hall and we had a very short rehearsal that afternoon just to run through it once. At the concert that night she put the music on the stand with the other musicians and read it right on down like we did.[42]

Kay Davis earned one of the biggest rounds of applause of the concert for her performance of 'On a Turquoise Cloud'.

DUKE ELLINGTON: 1948 I had an operation, that's when I had this big scare. They took a benign cyst off my left kidney. In '38 I had an operation – hernia and in 1918 I had an operation – hernia. So I have [three] designs by [three] different masters of surgery![43]

En route from Washington to New York, after playing the Howard Theatre on 26 March 1948, Ellington collapsed and was rushed to the Harkness Pavilion of the Columbia Presbyterian Medical Center for an emergency operation.

MELODY MAKER: ELLINGTON IS HERE! The big excitement of the week in musical circles is the arrival in this country of the U.S. genius of jazz, Duke Ellington. Making his first working visit to England since 1933, he arrived last Saturday at Liverpool in the S.S. *Media* and opened at the London Palladium on Monday for a fortnight's season.[44]

Ellington arrived in England on 19 June 1948, opening at the

London Palladium for two weeks on 21 June. Because of the
Musicians' Union ban he performed as a 'cabaret' artist with
vocalist Kay Davis and trumpeter/violinist/vocalist Ray Nance
backed by the Skyrockets band. He then played nine U.K. dates
and several Continental dates with a British rhythm section
comprising Malcolm Mitchell guitar, Jack Fallon bass and Tony
Crombie drums.

JACK FALLON: Somewhat nervously we watched the Duke sit
before us as we played and, to our immense relief and joy, he
showed his approval. Suddenly we were members of an Ellington unit![45]

TONY CROMBIE: We travelled in a band bus with about forty
other people, including barbers, dentists, hairdressers, gangsters,
funny men, a huge entourage. Kermit Golder, Jack Robbins was
on the coach who was extremely funny with a dead pan face, it
was quite riotous and of course Ray, who killed me.[46]

MALCOLM MITCHELL: The one thing that sticks out in my mind
was the first time Kay sang, I was just amazed to hear this voice,
I didn't know where it came from because she wasn't on the
stage. She used to start off-stage, and that magic voice filled the
auditorium from nowhere.[47]

TONY CROMBIE: I didn't get to speak to Duke very much. In
fact, he seemed rather shy of white people generally. Although
he was world famous and idolized everywhere he went, the fact
he had been a second class citizen in his own country maybe
affected his demeanour with us whiteys.[48]

JACK FALLON: When we were in Manchester, I went up to my
room and I was getting comfortable, and who should be on the
phone but Duke, he says, 'Where are you, you better come
down, there's a party happening here!' And I came down, there

was seven or eight girls around a grand piano, and he's sitting there![49]

TONY CROMBIE: One night in Edinburgh when a local big shot threw a party for Duke a super grand piano was laid on and although Duke was asked to play, he kept saying, 'Later on, later on.' After a while, Jack and Malcolm started to play and I sat at the piano – just comping. We played only a few bars when the Duke edged me off the piano. To this day I don't know if this was because he couldn't stand my piano playing or I was stealing some of his thunder![50]

MELODY MAKER: The Jack Fallon trio have come up to the highest expectations with its [sic] unobtrusively modern interpretations and smooth accompaniment. Duke himself, *MM* learns, is well satisfied with the work of his supporting rhythm trio, the members of which he introduces personally from the stage. He is enthusiastic about his concert tour, gratified at the keen interest the fans are showing in his more ambitious compositions.[51]

JOHNNY HODGES: When Duke came over to England in 1948 by himself with Ray Nance and Kay Davis, I got a little group for about seven weeks, while he was away. It was nice, Strayhorn on piano and we had Tyree Glenn, Jimmy Hamilton, Junior Raglin, Sonny Greer – and Al Hibbler was with us too. That was just a little preview, and it turned out all right.[52]

JIMMY HAMILTON: We weren't working so we formed a little, small band and we opened a club and we were doing good business, man. Jammed every night, up on 125th Street, and word got to Duke, and when he come back off the boat, he didn't even go home. He came straight to the club where we worked.[53]

DOWNBEAT: NEW YORK – Duke Ellington picked up where he left off prior to his European junket, and set out on a tour of one-nighters beginning in Canada and circling through New England to New York City.[54]

DUKE ELLINGTON: You just grow and grow and grow and it gets more expensive. Getting rid of the guitar was a useful economy.[55]

Fred Guy, with Ellington since 1925, left at the end of the band's engagement at Chicago's Civic Opera House in January 1949. He was never replaced.

LAWRENCE BROWN: After a while it just seemed no reason to have a rhythm instrument like that. Duke sort of figured that it was an excess carriage and he'd rather him stay at home. So [Guy] had a job there in Chicago and so he went into that.[56]

DOWNBEAT: DUKE SHOULD DISBAND – The Ellington band, while better than many now playing, is a disgrace to the man who heads it and the men who play in it.[57]

DUKE ELLINGTON: The other bands are more concerned with the styles of the times and we've hit a period now when everything becomes confused. We've had bop and progressive and wilder types of things and we've also had a tremendous drive on Dixie. Our band, though, is sandwiched in between. You see, we're more concerned with *who's* playing it. I'm more of a primitive artist in that I only employ materials at hand. I always write for the men in the band. That has sustained us throughout.[58]

MERCER ELLINGTON: Ruth did not allow Evie in her home. This was one of my perennial arguments which always kept me spitting against the wind because I never wound up being on anybody's side, but I simply told him, if your woman is not accepted someplace, then you no longer confined to go there.

He didn't agree with that too much, he loved his sister very much and I believe he loved Evie very much.[59]

MERCER ELLINGTON: So when Easter, Christmas came around, or whatever, instead of him taking a grip on it, he ran! So he couldn't demand everyone would be in one room. The only way he could compensate for it was to see each one, one at a time, there were many times when he got tired of this, so as a result of this he planned as best as possible to be working on holidays. Christmas, Thanksgiving, whatever. If there was anyplace he could go to work he would do it, and his main source of escape was the Blue Note in Chicago, so that, come what may, holidays you'd find him playing Chicago. This was for a while, over a period of twenty-five years.[60]

Ellington first played the Blue Note in Chicago 14–27 March 1949. In all, he played the club seventeen times, forty-five weeks in total, until the club closed in 1960.

DUKE ELLINGTON: The Blue Note in Chicago. This was a wonderful place. This was where you could play what you – you could play yourself. The man who ran it, Frank Holzfeind, was the equivalent to the impresario of an opera house or something. He only hired who he liked, and our thing there with him was we used to go in there for four weeks in December, and we'd go four weeks in the summer, that was our location.[61]

DUKE ELLINGTON: That concert with the Robin Hood Dell Orchestra with Russ Case in Philadelphia, when we did 'Non Violent Integration' before 125,000 people. I did this thing called 'Monologue' which is a very quiet little thing with the accompaniment of three clarinets. So Juan Tizol says, 'Man, you can't do that thing here! You gotta blow loud!' So I says all right, so we'll change it. But Walter Pidgeon, who was the M.C., he got up and announced 'Monologue'. So I had to get up and do it. Now, 'Monologue' is a thing which doesn't get belly laughs, it just gets giggles. So I heard these 125,000 people giggle. And I thought it was a tremendous bang![62]

On 25 July 1949, in an attempt to attract a large crowd to the ailing series of outdoor classical presentations at Robin Hood Dell, Philadelphia, the Ellington orchestra, Sarah Vaughan and the Philadelphia Symphony Orchestra drew a crowd of 13,000 (according to Downbeat *magazine). 'Monologue' – also known as 'Pretty and the Wolf' – was later recorded on 24 May 1951.*

DUKE ELLINGTON: The Hurricane – we played it as The Hurricane for two years, '43 and '44, and then we played it as the Zanzibar in '45 and in '46 [*recte* '49] we played it as Bop City – it took on all those names. In the interim we had played a place over on Fifth Avenue called the 400 Club. All this time, from the time the William Morris Agency gave up their band department, Courtney was handling me, Cress Courtney was handling me himself and he did some wonderful things, the whole time he was with me.[63]

Cress Courtney was head of the William Morris Agency's band division, and handled Ellington's bookings through the agency. In September 1949 Ellington secured his release from the agency, at which point Courtney formed his own agency handling Ellington until Duke signed with Joe Glaser's Associated Booking Corporation in 1951.

DUKE ELLINGTON: In 1950 we went back to Europe again, we were all set up to play all the stuff we had been writing for the last ten years in the concerts and all that and they didn't know anything about it and they screamed bloody murder! They said, 'This is not Ellington! Not Ellington!' And we had to cut out all the stuff we had done in the last ten years and go back to 'Black and Tan Fantasy'.[64] *Ellington's first post-war European tour with a full band opened on 5 April 1950 at Le Havre, France, and ended seventy-four concerts later in Hamburg, Germany, on 10 June.*

DUKE ELLINGTON: For our concert tour Sonny [Greer] was not too stable. He had been having little attacks so I took along another drummer [George 'Butch' Ballard] as a sort of insurance against being with no drummer. When Greer got to Europe he was a man who was very close to the grape, and so I'll never forget, I looked up and there was neither one of the drummers, and finally they both came stumbling in, with their arms around one another blind drunk. This is what happens when you take out insurance![65]

LAWRENCE BROWN: Something happened and Ben Webster couldn't go to Europe in '50 or '51, I think it was. So we contacted Don Byas and took him on the concert tour in Europe and, truthfully, Don Byas was second attraction to that whole band. He played so much tenor that it was a shame, we should've left him home! Yeah, he really took over. Terrific.[66]

Don Byas joined the band in Paris on 12 April for the duration of the tour.

FBI FILE 100–434443: EDWARD KENNEDY (DUKE) ELLINGTON: On September 30, 1950, *The Leader*, a weekly magazine, contained an article captioned 'No Red Songs For Me' by Duke Ellington. A foreword by the editors indicated that *The Daily Worker*, on May 27, 1950, had first reported that Ellington had signed the Stockholm Peace Petition and that on August 25 and 27, 1950, additional stories had been published repeating the false claim. It was also stated that Ellington, upon his return from a European tour, had repudiated the allegations. In Ellington's article he stated that during a stay in Stockholm, Sweden, in the course of a European tour, he had been approached by an individual who requested that he, Ellington, sign a paper indicating opposition to the atom bomb. Ellington denied signing the paper and stated that the individual had departed. He continues by stating that when he arrived back in the United States people began telling him about the *Daily Worker* had written a story about his having signed a communist petition whereupon he immediately sent a wire demanding his name be removed from the petition and threatening a legal suit if this was not done. He stated that apparently his telegram hadn't had much effect and he was taking this opportunity in *The Leader* to state that unless his name was removed from the so-called 'Stockholm Petitions' within 48 hours after publication of the statement, he, Ellington, would authorize his attorney to begin legal proceedings against those who were 'trying to defame my name and reputation'. In this article Ellington further stated 'I've never been interested in politics in my whole life and don't pretend to know anything about international affairs. The only "Communism" I know is that of Jesus Christ. I don't know of any other.' He further stated that during the last war he had helped sell bonds for the purpose of defeating Germany, Japan and Italy and in the event of another war he would help sell bonds to defeat whoever is then America's enemy. (62–60527–33549)[67]

This sad reflection on the politics of the Cold War appears to have had an effect on Ellington, who thereafter protested he was non-political and exercised great caution in overtly supporting social or political issues. After 1950, very little he did seemed to have interested the FBI. After citing some fourteen innocuous events they deemed worthy of their attention between 1938 and 1950, nothing attracted them between 1950 and 1960. However, this did not stop them continuing to circulate his file in response to 'enquiries' up to 1970 with thirty-two-year-old information on it, saying 'The foregoing information is furnished to you as a result of your request for an FBI file check and is not to be construed as clearance or non-clearance of the individual involved.'

MERCER ELLINGTON: That's when the business of him not wanting to be involved in various conversations about race began, because sooner or later someone's going to take it and turn on him.[68]

PAUL GONSALVES: I never dreamed I'd be fortunate enough to have worked in both the Ellington and the Basie bands. The few years experience in Basie's band were a wonderful experience – the freedom and the way it swung. But you got the feeling with everything that you knew what range it would be in musically. For about a year, I was in the Dizzy Gillespie band. That made me realize the pace at which things were changing. I hate to use the term bebop or modern music, because I think Basie and Ellington are modern bands too. It was just that a new era started with Gillespie, Parker and Monk. So many strides have been made that a musician, if he is going to be active, must have an open mind and make some effort to keep up with all those things. As for putting them to use with the organization that you're with – that's something else.[69]

Gonsalves joined Ellington in September 1950. He had spent three years in Count Basie's orchestra from 1946 before joining Dizzy Gillespie's big band for a year in 1949.

LAWRENCE BROWN: I never knew too much about Paul. But he was very good, he fit perfectly, he had a beautiful personality. Beautiful personality. Getting a little heavy on the stand once in a while, but a beautiful personality.[70]

PAUL GONSALVES: After being in Ellington's band I realize there is a difference in musicianship between [Ellington and Basie's bands]. This isn't meant in a derogatory way, but this band [Ellington's] is able to do a lot more than Basie's. The scope is broader. Basie realizes himself that he isn't the musician that Duke is. With the writing of Ellington and his protégé, Stray-horn, you've got the greatest in the field of jazz. There's so much music coming in – and it's not just the blues. You never know what you're going to be playing.[71]

LAWRENCE BROWN: When Cat joined the band he became the executor of the high notes. Well, Cat was the, well, I think, the greatest of the high-note men. Originally, I think, Cat came with Lionel Hampton's band, into the East, then he came over to Ellington. He had a little band in and out, they all try to advance themselves by getting a band, but usually there's too much pressure, too much hard work and they're not used to it, and they usually tire out and go back to the band. Killian was first, not quite as high or as strong as Cat. No, Cat was very strong. Killian was nice, very nice trumpet player. But we'd say Cat was the bull. He was very, very strong.[72]

Al Killian left Ellington in August 1950 having joined Ellington as high-note trumpeter in December 1947. He was shot dead in Los Angeles on 5 September 1950. His replacement was Cat Anderson, who joined the band in December 1950. He had previously played with Ellington from 1944 to 1947, leaving to form his own band for two years before playing in the Boston area for Sabby Lewis and Jimmy Tyler.

CAT ANDERSON: The band used to play Mary Lou Williams's arrangement of 'Blue Skies'. It wasn't just a trumpet feature then. There was a chorus of tenor by Al Sears, a release by [trombonist] Claude Jones and Rex Stewart used to play the ending. We were in the theatre at Canton, Ohio, when Rex didn't show. After listening to it all week – and I'm a great listener to anything good, especially on trumpet – I knew his solo. So when Duke asked if anybody wanted to play it, and nobody volunteered, he said, 'What about the new trumpet player?' I told him I'd try, and after the other solos I came down front and played it an octave higher. When I ended on double C, and the people were applauding, Duke said, 'Good, we'll keep it just like that.' As luck would have it, Rex came in the stage door as I was blasting away. He didn't speak to me for fifteen years.[73]

MERCER ELLINGTON: One of the worst times I know of was when we played Boston, Mass., a theatre on a Saturday morning, to an audience of twenty-five people. Well, Duke Ellington paid guaranteed salaries to the men whether the audience came or not, and the only thing that maintained the band under those conditions was the fact he got royalties from his songs, so he re-invested his royalties and sweated his way through the '40s and into the '50s.[74]

Ellington played Scollay Square, Boston from 22 to 28 November 1950. The theatre had formerly kept to a strict picture-only policy for ten years but with such poor business, it quickly returned to its former policy after Ellington's engagement.

DON GEORGE: It was intermission. The first half of the show had been played without a drummer because Sonny Greer was missing. Duke didn't know whether to feel concerned or angry when Sonny came staggering in, blind drunk, weaving from side to side. Duke started eating him out, cussing him, using some words I'd never heard before. Sonny gazed at him sorrowfully through his stupor and said, 'Duke, if you knew where I'd been today, you wouldn't raise your voice to me, and you wouldn't swear at me and you wouldn't say those terrible things to me.' It stopped Duke, and I wondered what Sonny was going to come up with. Duke asked, still steaming, 'Well, where were you today?' Sonny looked at him forgivingly through his alcoholic haze and said, 'Duke, today is Rosh Hashanah, and I was at shul davening all day.' We just broke up.[75]

BARNEY BIGARD: I think he actually fired Sonny [Greer] because, well, Sonny wasn't doing the job. I mean, he stayed stoned all the time and he had to eventually fire him because he wouldn't straighten out.[76]

SONNY GREER: My wife was ill, you know? So it was a toss-up between I stay with my wife or go with the band. Naturally, I stayed with my wife. We were good friends [with Duke] until he died. You know, Duke – I didn't have to ask for no money. Duke was never – there's one word I say for Duke, the word 'no', he didn't use that. The guys will verify if you ever was to ask someone, no matter the amount of money, he didn't know how to say no, because they were his family, the band. That was his first love. And the guy, he never was a man that valued money above everything else. You understand? And the guys could go to Duke and any amount of money that was necessary, they could get it.[77]

Greer remained on the payroll until Ellington's death in 1974.

DUKE ELLINGTON: Sonny Greer was the nearest thing to a brother I ever had. Greer always knows where to come when he wants something. He's very close, just like a relative.[78]

SONNY GREER: It took years before I got used to being away from the guys, and most of all Duke. The man's family; he's been like a brother to me.[79]

BRITT WOODMAN: I turned to Lawrence Brown and said, 'Thank God I've got a fortnight to learn the book.' 'To hell with that,' he said, 'I'm taking off in the morning.' I felt lonely and insignificant. A kind word from someone would have made all the difference. But the old guard of the band were tough on newcomers. Until a musician had earned their respect he was made to feel an outsider. I realized also that if I failed in my first solo with the band it would be hard afterwards to gain that respect. Fortunately though the show went well for me. I had no difficulty in sight reading the scraps of parts, for which I had to thank my years of study. And I found the tempos Duke set both stimulated and relaxed me, a rare event in jazz. By the end of the show I'd caught on to some of the subtle and unwritten voicings in the orchestration. When it was over Duke sent for me and thanked me.[80]

Woodman joined the band during an engagement at the Thunderbird in Las Vegas that opened on 15 February 1951. It was intended he understudy Lawrence Brown for two weeks. Brown left the following day.

LAWRENCE BROWN: Johnny and I left the band and were joined by Al Sears in New York. And we had the nucleus of a very nice little group. Seven of us at first. Seven of us. Four horns and three rhythm. Did a lot of recording and played a lot of different places. Went to Europe. Played a tour with our great, great friend Norman Granz. And Norman really liked the band. And he did everything he could to help us.[81]

Hodges' group consisted of Emmett Berry on trumpet, Al Sears on tenor, Lawrence Brown on trombone, Leroy Lovett on piano, Joe Benjamin on bass and Sonny Greer on drums.

JOHNNY HODGES: We decided to try [bandleading] again. It's all right for once in a while. Too much headache. *Entirely* too much headache.[82]

CUE HODGES: Johnny knew Duke was hurt. That wasn't what he wanted. He wanted something good for himself. He didn't want anything bad for Duke.[83]

DUKE ELLINGTON: So when I got Bellson, Willie Smith, Tizol, the band had a new drive. A personality change – three new guys made for a personality change because Hodges, Greer and Lawrence Brown left the band.[84]

Drummer Louie Bellson, alto saxophonist Willie Smith and valve trombonist Juan Tizol joined Ellington in the middle of his engagement at the Orpheum Theatre, Omaha, Nebr., during the week of 23–29 March 1951.

JUAN TIZOL: I was with Harry James in one club and Duke was in another club [in Las Vegas], so I used to go there between intermissions and he asked me if I could get Louie [Bellson].

He asked about me, to get me, and I said, 'Well, how about Willie Smith too?' So the three of us, we went to Duke Ellington. Oh, Harry was mad at me. Oh, the band were crazy about Louie. I can remember when he first came in, how the band used to look so bored during a drum solo – or just bored most of the time – and then when Louie came in they all turned around and watched and applauded, and stood up.[85]

LOUIE BELLSON: Ellington's arrangements never had drum parts. But not once did he say, 'This is how Sonny Greer did it.' He said, 'Do it in your own way.' He made you create. I was interested in arranging. I had studied as a kid, and I had written arrangements for Harry James and Tommy Dorsey. Tizol persuaded me to bring them in – 'Skin Deep' and 'The Hawk Talks' – and Duke recorded them.[86]

Ellington recorded 'The Hawk Talks' on 10 May 1951 and 'Skin Deep' on 12 August 1952.

BARNEY BIGARD: Bellson was the one who did a good job. Well, he knew what he was doing, and naturally he was looking out for himself, he and Pearlie May [Pearl Bailey, Bellson's wife], so I knew that wasn't going to last long, which it didn't. But every now and then he'd go help out with the Duke. He helped Duke out when he had a chance.[87]

BRITT WOODMAN: When the band reached New York it seemed like everyone had turned out to hear the new men. Birdland was packed for the opening night and we suspected some had come along to criticize. Nevertheless the show was a tremendous success. At the end people were coming up and saying, 'What a lot of fire there is in the band's playing!' Count Basie was one who came up.[88]

Ellington opened in New York at Birdland on 3 May 1951.

MELODY MAKER: DRUMMER BELLSON MAKES THE NEW ELLINGTON BAND ROCK – The eagerly awaited debut of the 'new' Duke

Ellington orchestra took place last week when Duke opened at Birdland. It was the band's first night-club appearance in this town since the days of the late lamented Bop City, and a big proportion of the opening night crowd consisted of musicians and friends of Duke, who were anxious to find out how the personnel changes of recent months had affected the band. It didn't take long to find out. After the first set everyone was commenting that Duke finally had a swinging, rocking band that should bring him out of the doldrums into which he had fallen in recent months ... the most important thing of all is Louis Bellson. It is amazing how much difference one man can make to an entire band.[89]

DUKE ELLINGTON: For the first time we took the big band into Birdland, it was the first big band to go in there, then all the other big bands went in there.[90]

LOUIE BELLSON: Duke and Strayhorn were full of superstitions. Nobody was supposed to wear anything with yellow on it. Nobody was supposed to button a shirt all the way down the front. Nobody was supposed to whistle in the dressing room.[91]

LAWRENCE BROWN: Oh, very superstitious. Very superstitious. Don't put any buttons on the piano keys. Like if you had a button, don't put it on the piano keys, he wouldn't sit down there.[92]

MERCER ELLINGTON: He never wore brown suits from the time his mother passed away because the day she died he had on a brown suit. He practically got to a place where there were really only two colours that didn't represent something unpleasant because he associated these things – the only things he associated with good times and things that were right were the colour blue and the colour white.[93]

DUKE ELLINGTON: Clark Terry just does everything! He blows great lead, plays fine modern jazz et cetera.[94]

Terry joined Ellington on 11 November 1951.

CLARK TERRY: When I first joined Ellington, the band was not really too cordial to any newcomer. Many times Duke wouldn't call a tune. He would suggest what he had in mind through an introduction which all the guys who had been there for some time would know. They were nice guys, I can't say they wanted to freeze you out, but it was just customary for the band members to be that way to new people. So I'd look over to see what they're playing. Then all of a sudden I found a friend in the next row [trombonist] Quentin Jackson. 'Hey Butter,' I'd say through the side of my mouth. 'What are they playing?' 'Oh, 156,' he'd say. Then I'd flip, flip through the book. There's 155 and 157 but no 156. So I'd growl to Butter, 'It's not here!' 'Fake it, baby!' he says.[95]

DUKE ELLINGTON: I just call 'em [the tunes] and watch them look for them – *all* the way through the number![96]

CLARK TERRY: I went in and I asked him for a salary I felt was fairly decent and he didn't have any qualms about it so he gave it to me, but I found out later there were guys two or three times what I was getting![97]

COOTIE WILLIAMS: Clark Terry's a wonderful trumpet player. Oh, he's terrific. He has a great sound, and he produces. That's what I like about him, you know, he has a great, real great sound on his horn. And he's a very fine musician too. But I don't think he had a good chance there in the band. I maybe figure – Duke figured that if he left, he'd leave a big hole, so he didn't give him his full rein.[98]

CLARK TERRY: I was lucky to get a piece to play like 'Perdido'. I'm just one of the few people who soloed in the band that Duke only wrote one piece for. I think 'Juniflip' for the flugel was the only thing he wrote for me from start to finish.[99]

DUKE ELLINGTON: Willie Cook has great taste. He plays good melodic licks with a slight bop touch.[100]

Cook joined Ellington on 15 November 1951.

WILLIE COOK: Clark and I joined Duke about four days apart; they had a show going, *The Big Show of '51*. Duke was such an influence over people. You could learn just by sitting in there and listening to his arrangements. You could see how jazz had evolved from the very beginning up to the point where we were at the time, and you could also surmise how it might be in the future.[101]

From 21 September 1951 until 29 November 1951, the Ellington band toured as part of a package in the 'Biggest Show of 1951'. Also in the show were Sarah Vaughan, Nat 'King' Cole, Marie Bryant and dancers Stump & Stumpy, Patterson & Jackson, Peg Leg Bates and Timmie Rogers. It represented Ellington's first bookings through the Moe Gale Agency, with whom he signed in July at the instigation of Cress Courtney. The tour was not without controversy.

THE AFRO-AMERICAN: ELLINGTON PLAYS AS ATLANTANS ENTER BACK DOOR – Atlanta: More than 1,000 indignant Atlantans tore up their $2.50 tickets refusing to enter the Municipal Auditorium here Friday after rudely being informed the front door was for white only. While this number angered over the disgusting Jim Crow arrangements refused to enter the small back entrance, more than 4,000 crowded in to see and hear Duke Ellington, Sarah Vaughan and Nat (King) Cole. There were 1,500 white record fans with a great big section all to themselves ... Approached backstage by the *Afro*, Duke Ellington, a greasy stocking on his head, snapped, 'I don't want to discuss it.' It was the same attitude he took in Richmond during the fight over segregation at the Mosque. While patrons were forced to undergo segregation, the white members with the Ellington and Cole aggregations were allowed to perform. This was in contrast to Birmingham, where Police Commissioner Eugene Bull Conner informed the white musicians they could not play on a stage with coloured musicians.[102]

The controversy at the Municipal Auditorium, Atlanta, was on 10 November 1951. Earlier in the year, on 28 January 1951, Ellington had played the Mosque Auditorium, Richmond, Va. The local members of the NAACP picketed the theatre in protest at segregation. Ellington pulled out of the engagement, complaining it prevented the members of his band earning their living.

DUKE ELLINGTON: All this fighting that's going on now about race is for the Negro at the bottom. It isn't doing the Negro who's got something any good.[103]

THE AFRO-AMERICAN: DUKE CALLS FIGHT FOR [CIVIL] RIGHTS SILLY – St Louis, Mo: Declaring with pointed emphasis 'We ain't ready yet,' Duke Ellington, world famed swing orchestra leader, said in an interview here that fighting being carried on in an effort to gain integration is 'a silly thing', at the matinee performance of the *Biggest Show of '51* ... According to the Duke, the fighting being carried on by some people is getting us nowhere. He could see no particular progress over the last few years and questioned 'the good it's doing us' to get one or two people in a few white schools or certain jobs. Several times during the conversation he referred to 'those people' but would call no names. He did mention the Richmond incident when the Richmond NAACP picketed the Mosque Theatre where he played to a segregated audience. Ellington maintained that there are so many arguments against us that our efforts are futile. As he prepared to return to the stage he said, 'No, we ain't ready yet. Get together $100,000,000 and then we can do something.'[104]

DUKE ELLINGTON: You own $100,000,000, you go and demand something, you're somebody, you're somebody of substance.

You don't walk in and say I represent 20,000,000 people, you say I represent $100,000,000. It has a different image.[105]

MERCER ELLINGTON: [They] took a statement of Ellington's out of context, from the article and says, 'Duke Says We Ain't Ready!' One reason for the statement was that we ain't ready because we didn't have the money to go to court to litigate and to keep on appealing and do what was necessary. But [the paper] implied 'Not ready for education' and 'Not educated well enough to accept freedom' and so forth. We had a hard time going around trying to explain that and trying to straighten out the whole thing . . . The point was which way do you want it? Do you want to go ahead and start fighting with no money? Or do you want to get money from the sources which it is available . . . His philosophy towards race was the achievement of financial support in order to go about these things legally . . . the answer, as is being proved, is money, he felt the solution was economic.[106]

THE AFRO-AMERICAN: DUKE ELLINGTON'S VIEWS ON JIM CROW SHOCK NATION – Maestro Says 'We Ain't Ready Yet.' He intimates that coloured people who live in the South know the law – that calls for the practise of jim crowism – and they might as well make themselves satisfied with their lot and stay in their 'places'. Says the Duke: 'This thing about sitting anywhere they (coloured people) want is so much bunk. If you go South don't you have to sit in the rear of the streetcar?' With the NAACP his obvious target, the Duke questioned the progress that has been made in the past few years . . . Early in February the Duke showed evidence that the civil rights battle was getting 'under his skin' when he was quoted in the daily press as saying: 'Why do they do this to me? Why only the other Sunday I gave a concert in New York that netted them (the NAACP) about $10,000.'[107]

THE AFRO-AMERICAN: DUKE BENEFIT FOR NAACP NETTED $1500, NOT 13GS. The record shows that Duke at times has tried to win more support from coloured people by attempting to prove he is a great race man who has contributed heavily to their cause through organizations such as the NAACP. A closer look at the record will show this to be false ... A case in point is the benefit performance which Duke staged last Jan. 20 at the Metropolitan Opera for the benefit of the NAACP ... From the box-office standpoint the performance was a great success with about $14,000 being collected from the sale of tickets ... In selling $7,500 worth of tickets, the NAACP ran up expenses of approximately $1,900 ... Duke's organization also came up with approximately $7,500 in ticket sales ... [but] Duke's organization reported that their expenses with the promotion were approximately $6,000 ... The net result was that when the two operations were dovetailed, the expenses shared and the profits accounted for, the NAACP 'benefited' about $1,500 from a $14,000 promotion ... The inescapable fact in the whole thing ... is that Duke, like so many great bandleaders of today is faced with economic ruin in this day of small combos, television and cocktail rooms.[108]

Clearly the black press were not about to forgive easily the 'We Ain't Ready Yet' incident. The fact of the matter was that Ellington was damaged by his statement and it took some time to weather the storm. Nevertheless, despite something of a feud that developed between him and the NAACP, he continued to make contributions to the organization but thereafter was far more circumspect in his handling of racially motivated questions from the press, his replies always graciously avoiding any contentious issues. Eventually the differences between Ellington and the NAACP were patched up and on 11 September 1959 he was presented with the Spingarn Medal for 'the highest or noblest achievement by an American Negro during the preceding year or years'.

MERCER ELLINGTON: When he was quoted as saying: 'Blacks are not ready for independence and equality because it costs too much to take cases to court' they cut the last half of that and he was branded a traitor to his own, it was pure character assassination.[109]

MERCER ELLINGTON: [Cress Courtney] wanted my father to invest, or go for the percentage deal, of a show called *The Big Show [of 1951]* that had Nat Cole, Three Tons of Fun, Patterson and Jackson, tremendous number of acts, really great acts, tap dancers, they were all on the show. For some reason Ellington decided no, he'd rather take the cash guarantee. Courtney, in spite of what Ellington told him, took the deal himself, and paid Ellington the guarantee and because of that particular run, Courtney became a millionaire.[110]

LOUIE BELLSON: Duke's discipline was very much different to anybody else. Duke, his idea, he told me many times, he said: 'Look, if I had to worry about my band, I'd be six feet under ground. All my guys are over twenty-one years old. If this guy acts up for two or three days, all I can do is go to him and say, "Are you OK, are you all right?" I can't worry about them, they're men. They should know how to handle themselves.' So as a result, sometimes the discipline would fall apart at times.[111]

MERCER ELLINGTON: He never cared about time[keeping], because he didn't care about time himself. If a man was late or didn't show up for the job, he understood that. He accepted that as artistry, which it might well have been. But when it came to the things that would irritate him was to mess with his art. If you were in the band and played great solos, fine, but if you, after playing your solos, didn't play the parts – in other words, if you could run with the ball fine, but when the time came to block, and you didn't, you were gone. He would never fire you. He would never fire a man, he would let him know where he was at, where his tolerance point cut off and he would irritate that man to the point where sooner or later he would quit.[112]

DUKE ELLINGTON: Irving Mills made an approach, he came back with a brilliant idea that he wanted to get back into action, and I started going to him, but decided against it.[113] *In the 28 February 1951 edition of* Variety *a story was floated of a possible Ellington–Irving Mills reunion. Clearly Ellington was circumspect about renewing their association and nothing tangible seemed to develop during the rest of that year. However, at the end of 1952 Mills organized a series of events intended as a celebration of Ellington's 25th year as a bandleader, counted from the first major Ellington–Mills collaboration, the Cotton Club opening on 4 December 1927. Events included two weeks at New York's Paramount Theatre that grossed $122,000, during which time he guested on the radio shows of Steve Allen and Art Ford, a two-day Carnegie Hall spectacular on 14 and 15 November celebrating Ellington with a host of jazz stars and a week of of 'Silver Jubilee' programmes from Ellington's week-long stint at Birdland broadcast by NBC. Mills even talked* Downbeat *magazine into a massive Silver Jubilee feature on Ellington in their 4 November issue, in which Mills contributed the feature 'I Split With Duke When Music Began Sidetracking'. Clearly Mills had not lost his touch after his heavy involvement with the motion picture industry and seemed poised to rejuvenate Ellington's flagging career after passing through the hands of several booking agents but Ellington, after expressing initial enthusiasm, pulled out of the deal.*

SONNY GREER: [Charles Mingus] was a hard character to get along with. Temperament. He wasn't good for a bunch of guys' organizations because he would create lots of little disturbances. The thing about Duke's band, we had a band of individual stars. They could stand on their own two feet and as a team.[114]

At the Bandbox in New York between 30 January and 2 February 1953, bassist Charles Mingus deputized for bassist Wendell Marshall, who was on leave of absence to get married. On 2 February Mingus was unceremoniously fired by Ellington.

CHARLES MINGUS: Tizol wants you to play a solo he's written where bowing is required. You raise the solo an octave, where the bass isn't too muddy. He doesn't like that and he comes to the room under the stage where you're practising and comments you're like the rest of the niggers in the band, you can't read. You ask Juan how he's different from the other niggers in the band and he states that one of the ways he's different is that HE IS WHITE. So you run his ass upstairs. You leave the rehearsal room, proceed toward the stage ... and [as] the curtain of the Apollo Theatre goes up a yelling, whooping Tizol rushes out and lunges at you with a bolo knife. The rest you remember mostly from Duke's own words in his dressing room as he changes after the show.[115]

Note that Mingus places the event at the Apollo, where the band played for the week commencing 20 February 1953 which was also Louie Bellson's final week with the band. Bellson was replaced by Butch Ballard, who was in turn replaced by Dave Black in June that year. Black remained for two years.

JUAN TIZOL: What really happened, this little piece of music I wrote for him. So I ask him about it, and he took his bass down, and I went down there and I showed him and said, 'Try to play this to see what it sounds like on bass,' and he tried and so forth, and he wanted to raise it an octave higher. I said, 'I don't want that. If I wanted to write that for a cello, I would have wrote it for a cello! I want to hear this on bass.' So apparently, he got insulted or something. I said, 'Well, go ahead and do what you want. I'm going upstairs to my dressing room.' So he followed me upstairs to tell me, what's this that and the other and so forth; I don't know; he raised a lot of hell, so by this time it came for the show. I went downstairs and he was still hot and said he was going to kick me in the behind, you know? 'I should kick your behind.' I said, 'You gonna do what?' and he repeated it. So I said, 'I tell you what I'm gonna do; I'm going upstairs and when

I come back I would like you to kick me right in the behind.' And I went upstairs and when I came down, he thought I had a knife. And he grabbed one of those big pieces of iron that holds curtains and he got it in his hand and I remember, Carney said, 'Watch out, Juan, he's got a piece of iron!' But he was still thinking I had a knife. Well I used to carry a knife with me. Because you can never tell, especially around Harlem or somewhere like that. But not this time. After the show he went upstairs and in my dressing room, and I was so nervous, I was crying. And he came up there and the manager was there at the door of my dressing room, he still wanted to keep saying something; I don't know what it was, but he wanted to keep on arguing with me. And I didn't respond or anything. I stayed right like that in my dressing room, and Celley was there trying to hold him back. So Duke came over, I don't know how, but he told Celley [the road manager] to throw him out, to give him his two weeks notice and pay him off and let him go.[116]

Tizol left the band to return to Harry James in November 1953. He was replaced by John Sanders three months later.

DUKE ELLINGTON: I say sex is no sin. The sooner more people find that out, the better off we'll all be. We need to start discussing sex so much and need to start enjoying it some more ... I want to tell you what I think the sex act is. I think it is like a lovely piece of music, conceived quietly in the background of mutual affection and understanding, made possible by instincts which lean toward each other as naturally as the sunflower slowly turning its lovely face to the sun. I think it is an aria of the sex symphony, an aria which begins beautifully certain in its rightness, moves with that certainty to a distinct tempo of feeling, sings itself happily, steadily, working, working, to a screaming, bursting climax of indescribable beauty and rapture then throbs, spent and grateful in a rededication for the next movement of its perfection.[117]

at the JAZZ CORNER of the World

BIRDLAND

B'WAY
at 52nd
NEW YORK
JU 6-1368

proudly presents

FOR TWO BIG WEEKS

DECEMBER 10th thru DECEMBER 23rd, 1953

DUKE ELLINGTON

AND HIS 16 PIECE ORCHESTRA

Featuring

CAT ANDERSON — DAVE BLACK — HARRY CARNEY
WILLIE COOK — PAUL GONSALVES — JIMMY GRISSOM
JIMMY HAMILTON — RICK HENDERSON — QUENTIN JACKSON
WENDELL MARSHALL — RAY NANCE — RUSSELL PROCOPE
BRITT WOODMAN — CLARK TERRY — ALBERT COBBS

PLUS

"The Amazing"

BUD POWELL TRIO

CURLY RUSSELL — Bass   **ART TAYLOR — Drums**

WHEN IN FLORIDA VISIT OUR OTHER

BIRDLAND

2200 Park Avenue, Miami Beach

DON'T FORGET OUR
MONDAY NITE JAM SESSIONS

DWIGHT D. EISENHOWER: Once again I want to tell you how much I enjoyed your contribution to the entertainment at the dinner given by the White House Correspondents last Saturday Night.[118]

Letter to Duke Ellington from the President of the United States, The White House, Washington, dated 12 March 1955.

JIMMY WOODE: I remember very distinctly we were in Savannah, Georgia, and I don't know why we were rehearsing because the band seldom rehearsed, and the police came in and said, 'You, you, you and you, out!' That was probably about '55, '56. Off the bandstand. They were white or light – Dave Black was the drummer. A very plush, beautiful club, in fact it was called the Savannah. And Dave was the only white, but there were three blacks that were very light. What can you do?[119]

The incident occurred between March and June 1955. Woode had joined the band in early January that year, Black would leave in July.

DUKE ELLINGTON: You play down South, you play segregated audiences. Everybody who plays down there plays 'em. There's no other way. I mean, there, unless you, er, change the legislature. That's a job to be done, it calls for organization and a lot of money.[120]

DUKE ELLINGTON: Don't let anything or anybody bug you. More and more people everyday are becoming 'bug' pushers. If what somebody says bugs you and they know, they are certain to repeat it. Crackers found out that Negroes hate being called 'Boy' so they made 'Boy' their platform. So as my Doctor, Arthur Logan says, Bug Disease is the worst. Don't let anybody bug you.[121]

MARIAN LOGAN: Edward knew he was a hypochondriac, lots of people are. Big deal. That doesn't mean anything. Edward liked the idea of having his doctor at his beck and call, anywhere, anytime, and Arthur was complicit in it too. Arthur went along for the ride. You know why? He loved it too![122]

CLARK TERRY: Up early every morning, get in that bus, travel hundreds of miles, play a dance or a concert, but mostly dances in those days.[123]

DUKE ELLINGTON: Dance audiences are different. People want to hear something, they might want to hear a waltz, some old couple might want to hear – why not play it for them? Not that we have the music in the book, but I'll go around the band and say who knows this, who knows 'Roses of Picardy'. I'll start and play the first chorus on the piano, [we] just play it and the people are happy, so what![124]

DUKE ELLINGTON: It's getting to be more a business than an art, isn't it? 'Dance music' is now little more than what we have always called the 'business man's bounce'. We're getting instructions on how to play for dances from heads of college prom committees. They like medium dance tempos ... not too loud. At least it's a change for us and that's fine. Sometimes though, our followers want to hear some of the things with which we have been associated. I refer them back to the committee. Usually some compromise is effected.[125]

MERCER ELLINGTON: The fifties was a very rough and terrible period.[126]

DANIEL HALPERIN: The conditions in which the musicians worked and lived were often distressing. I have one vivid memory of Duke, naked and wet with sweat, struggling into a fresh pair of trousers in a makeshift dressing room rigged up under the bandstand ... his torso gleaming in the glare of an unshaded overhead light bulb, the gold cross round his neck swinging to and fro, an expression of complete disgust on his face.[127]

DUKE ELLINGTON: In 1955 we went out to the Aqua Show, out in Flushing Meadows, we played there that summer. While I was playing the Aqua Show, I wrote *A Man With Four Sides*, I'd come home every night and work on my play, and that year after I'd finished it out there, I had readings. I read the play, had my singers, pianists come in and demonstrate, invited a lot of nice fat millionaires, they drank up my liquor and I never got around to asking them how much they wanted to invest in the show.[128]

The engagement at Eliot Murphy's 'Aquacade' at Flushing Meadows, Long Island, New York, lasted from 22 June to 2 August 1955. It is generally recognized as the nadir of Ellington's career, where he was second on the bill to the Dancing Waters, a water fountain display. The band was augmented by a string section and a harp and accompanied ice skaters, dancing exhibitions and comedians. Ellington himself was only required to perform a medley of his hits. Many fans thought he had reached the end of the road.

CLARK TERRY: It just seemed like a stupid, senseless gig, but it was regular employment.[129]

DUKE ELLINGTON: The fun of writing and participating in the music is the motivating force that keeps us going on and on. It has nothing to do with money.[130]

MERCER ELLINGTON: As wonderful as Duke Ellington was, as creative an artist as he was, he had come upon hard times ... He wanted the band to stay together and as a result when the jobs became few he kept the band organized so he didn't care where he had to get the money from, whether it was royalties or whatever, he used this to keep the orchestra organized.[131]

DUKE ELLINGTON: When we finished the Aqua Show and we started out, it began to appear as though I was at my peak or somethin'. That's when Johnny Hodges came in – his wife called

up and asked if I wanted an alto player, I said, 'Oh yeah!' Sam
Woodyard came in the band then and we had a real good drive,
Jimmy Woode was playing bass, it was a good solid foundation,
we were playing some nice sounding things.[132]

*Drummer Sam Woodyard joined Ellington in July 1955 while
the following month Hodges returned to the fold after an absence
of four and a half years.*

SAM WOODYARD: The first time I went into Columbia [record-
ing studios] with this band, a guy came out of control with a
blanket before we ever started playing. I broke him out of that.
'Put it over your bass drum,' he said. 'For what?' 'We do it for
all the drummers who come in here. If you don't cover the bass
drum the needle starts jumping.' 'That's your business. Don't
tell me how to play my drums. You just move the microphone
back, because I'm going to play the way I usually play for the
band.'[133]

JOHNNY HODGES: Nobody tells me how to play anything. He
says: 'You play this,' and I play it *my* way. That's all. That's the
way it's been – and that's the way he's been, over the years. But
he knows how to back you up. He's always built arrangements
around different fellows in the band. He knows what would fit
me better than anybody. In fact, he knows what's best for me,
I'll put it that way.[134]

DUKE ELLINGTON: [The term jazz] drives people away, I don't
see the necessity for using it.[135]

CHAPTER NINE

NEWPORT UP

In 1950 Ellington had entered the world of long-playing recordings with Masterpieces by Ellington *for Columbia Records, and with what were described on the record sleeve as 'uncut concert arrangements' of 'Mood Indigo', 'Sophisticated Lady', 'The Tattooed Bride' and 'Solitude' he went well beyond the time constraints imposed by the 78 rpm recording. Clearly the new medium offered Ellington great potential, but despite a vivid version of 'A Tone Parallel to Harlem (The Harlem Suite)' that lasted 13 minutes 45 seconds on* Ellington Uptown *(recorded in 1951 and 1952), in general his time with the company appeared to lack focus. Certainly the band was rejuvenated when Louie Bellson and Willie Smith joined its ranks and contemporaneous reviews acknowledge this.*

In 1953, Ellington signed with Capitol Records. Again his output was variable, overtly courting the mambo craze on the one hand, while retreating into past triumphs on the other, either in a trio setting or with his big band. In short, Ellington seemed to be struggling to find a role for himself and his band within the ever-changing musical environment around him. But on 6 April 1953 he recorded a new instrumental, 'Satin Doll'. While it didn't speed to the top of the bestselling charts, it became an enduring contemporary standard, one of those Ellington tunes that every jazz musician has, at some time in his or her life, played.

But the reality of the early '50s was the struggle to find work to keep his band together. Ballrooms were closing all over the country and people were increasingly turning to a novel new device called 'television' for their entertainment. Regular prestige bookings at the nation's top night-spots had become a thing of the past, replaced by a relentless grind of one-night stands, criss-crossing America, appearing in school gymnasiums, Elks Clubs and in second-rate hotels.

There were highs, his Silver Jubilee as a bandleader celebrated in New York the fall of 1952, and there were lows, the intolerable racial situation he had to confront when, to keep his band together, he had no option but to accept bookings south of the Mason–Dixon line with the attendant problems of playing to segregated audiences. Such bookings attracted adverse comment in the black press, who felt that, with the steadily rising momentum generated by the Civil Rights movement, Ellington should be declining such bookings. But if Ellington agreed with their ends, he did not agree with their means – quite simply, he could not afford to turn down work. So the local chapters of the NAACP turned out in protest wherever he played a segregated gig, annoying Ellington who, despite his difference of opinion with them, was continuing to make regular donations to the national organization and felt the local protesters were trying to put him and his musicians out of work.

In late 1955 he terminated his association with Capitol, and went to the independent label Bethlehem where he recorded two albums, one of which, Historically Speaking – The Duke, was one of his most satisfying records since Ellington Uptown in Hi-Fi from 1951–2, a highlight of his early '50s period with Columbia.

In the summer of 1955 the band was energized by the return of Johnny Hodges and the arrival of drummer Sam Woodyard. In 1956 Time magazine decided to mount a cover feature on Ellington, the sixteenth American-born musician to be so honoured. In June, as Ellington sat for artist Peter Hurd's cover portrait, things seemed to be on the up. The previous month, in discussions with

Carter Harman, Time magazine's music editor, Ellington suggested the magazine focus on an upcoming date featuring his band and the New Haven Symphony Orchestra on 12 July 1956 where he would be performing 'Night Creature', a piece for jazz band and symphony orchestra that he was having difficulty getting recorded.[1] *Before that, however, he was due to appear at the third annual Newport Jazz Festival organized by George Wein at Freebody Park, Newport, Rhode Island, on 7 July 1956. Although he had been booked to appear in 1955, prior commitments had prevented him from attending. While Wein's previous two festivals had proved hugely successful, no-one could have predicted what was about to follow.*

GEORGE WEIN: The Newport Jazz Festival was very hot, the whole world was talking about it. We were in vogue. It was *the thing*. It was after the opening concert and I get a call, it was Duke. 'George, what do you want me to do Saturday when I get in?' I says: 'What do you mean, "What do you want me to do?"' He says, 'Well, anything special?' I says: 'Have you prepared any special material?' He says: 'No. Nothing special. I figured we'd go up there and do our thing.' I says: 'Do your *thing*? You mean do the medley [of hits] or something like that?' He says: 'Yeah. I thought maybe we'd do that.' I says: 'You better come in here with something new and swinging or the critics are going to kill you. You better do something.'[2]

IRVING TOWNSEND: Ellington . . . had not been drawing large audiences. Even George Wein was not sure enough of Ellington's drawing power to make him the star attraction. Ellington the composer was in limbo. His best writing was, according to the ever present critics, fifteen years behind him and he was reminded of it everywhere he went. All anybody wanted to hear was 'Sophisticated Lady' and 'Mood Indigo'. Jazz writers reminisced about the old band . . . His years of hits during the big band days were gone. His last Columbia contract had produced neither sales nor distinguished albums ... but there was hope for better things. Ellington at fifty-seven had survived the collapse of the rest of the bands by being willing to accept low prices, by accepting all one-nighters ... but there had been too many weeks when Duke had met the payroll of the highest paid band anywhere out of the money he made as a writer and publisher of his own music.[3]

DUKE ELLINGTON: The thing that I remember about Newport is that we opened with the national anthem, played a number and then didn't come back until last. I said to George Wein, 'What are we – the animal act, the acrobats? By the time we get [back] on, we'd be playing just exit music, because a lot of people have to get over that bridge by a certain time, or make a curfew, or catch a suburban train because they have to go to church tomorrow morning, and any number of things!' I really griped, but I went along and we did the best we could.[4]

GEORGE AVAKIAN: Shortly before the band went on-stage, Duke Ellington got them together. It was the only time I ever heard him do this. He said something like: 'Well, you know, guys, I know we've worked on this new piece for the Festival, and George is sticking his neck way out making this recording. I know we're going to give a good performance. I want you to know it means quite a bit to everybody, George, us ... and I'm going to try something a little bit different and just see if it works. Let's play "Diminuendo and Crescendo in Blue".' I didn't realize it at the time, but the band just looked at each other, and Paul Gonsalves said, 'That's the one where I blow?' The Duke said, 'Yes ... and keep on blowing. We'll tell you when to stop. That's all you've got to do.'[5]

DUKE ELLINGTON: As far as the time was concerned, it was over. It was after twelve o'clock and it was illegal for the park to be opened. It was raining and the police were threatening to come and lock everybody up, and George Wein the impresario, he was walking up and down with his raincoat on making motions like he wanted us to stop and the crowd were yelling, 'Go, go, go!' And Paul Gonsalves stood up and blew twenty-seven choruses and it was a riot. It was a sensation.[6]

Ellington's appearance at the Newport Jazz Festival on 7 July 1956 earned one of the biggest ovations ever earned by any artist in the festival's history. It also rejuvenated his flagging career, largely through Paul Gonsalves' long solo linking two pieces Ellington had originally recorded in 1937, 'Diminuendo in Blue' and 'Crescendo in Blue'.

GEORGE AVAKIAN: The audience started to really feel the electricity the band was creating, Duke kept shouting encouragement to the sections of the band. The audience started to ease out of their seats to get a better view. Jo Jones, the drummer, was in a cubby-hole beside me, I was crouching down near him, being careful not to get in the way of that rolled-up *Christian Science Monitor* he kept swatting the stage with, beating out the rhythm. Jo kept swatting the stage, yelling out encouraging words. The sax section were the only ones able to see Jo. They started to shout back at him. The rhythm section, Sam Woodyard on drums and the bass, started to play to Jo as much as anybody else. More people began to dance in the aisles. Paul played a fantastic twenty-seven choruses, Duke himself was swinging pretty hard on piano. The clarinets came in when Paul finished his last chorus. There was supposed to be a four bar break after they finished. It was extended to seven, heightening the tension even more. It was excruciating. The final choruses finished with Cat Anderson on trumpet, wailing out those screaming high notes. Pandemonium broke out after that.[7]

CLARK TERRY: [The audience] gave vent to their feelings, and expressed themselves, they were dancing, they were jumping up down and leaping around. And when Duke saw that, he injected a little more fire, and of course it brought a little more fire out of the band, and it was a good night![8]

PAUL GONSALVES: On the subject of those twenty-six choruses of mine on 'Diminuendo and Crescendo In Blue', we hadn't played that number for about four or five years. He just happened to call it one night in Birdland in 1951, when Louie Bellson was in the band. The way the tenor solo came in – I had the feeling during the piano modulation that I'd like to take a solo. I took quite a number of choruses on it. Ellington decided on the spur of the moment that we would open with that when we did our spot at Newport. I guess everything seemed to gel, so he let me play as long as I wanted to. It wasn't planned. It was a thing that just happened by chance. I never guessed it would get that much attention.[9]

DUKE ELLINGTON: Actually, it was a re-birth. Paul Gonsalves blowing twenty-seven choruses with Sam Woodyard and Jimmy Woode behind him and the newspaper, Basie's man, the drummer Jo Jones, he was beating the newspaper, it was a great thing.[10]

The recording of the concert, Ellington at Newport, *became Ellington's bestselling LP.*

GEORGE AVAKIAN: Gonsalves really meant it when he said, 'Is that the one I blow on?' Duke had read correctly that there might be a tremendously electric performance if he pulled a surprise like that. It was the infectious rhythm of the band plus Paul that made it great . . . it just goes on and builds. It's simply something that could not ever be duplicated.[11]

JIMMY HAMILTON: It was of those moments, you strike something and you drive, we didn't know this was going to happen, but it happened! It was the right time.[12]

DUKE ELLINGTON: We made the cover of *Time* magazine on the strength of that.[13]

TIME: The event last month marked not only the turning point in one concert: it confirmed a turning point in a career. The big news was something that the whole jazz world had long hoped to hear: the Ellington band was once again the most exciting thing in the business. Ellington himself had emerged from a long period of quiescence and was once again bursting with ideas and inspiration.[14]

DUKE ELLINGTON: I always say I was born in 1956 at the Newport Jazz Festival.[15]

PAUL GONSALVES: Since that time, we've more or less played ['Diminuendo and Crescendo In Blue'] every night and it's become something of a frustration. People request it and expect me to do the same thing every time – even to the point of having them ask to see how *long* I'm going to play, rather than *what* I'm going to play. After a few years of that you don't want to play it at all. Also, it's gotten to be a thing now that if I've got a tenor solo on any number it has to be a *long* one. I don't think that's right, or fair, either. Maybe some nights you're right mentally, but not physically.[16]

JIMMY MAXWELL: I was very friendly with Clark Terry and it was he who arranged for me to join the orchestra. They were not a demonstrative band, a bit tired and old to be truthful. Johnny Hodges kept calling me 'young man' – I was forty-four years old at the time. I substituted off and on with the band from time to time – on the Newport Jazz record, that one with 'Diminuendo and Crescendo in Blue', I played a part of that as Willie Cook didn't get on the bandstand in time and was standing in the wings.[17]

DUKE ELLINGTON: I was doing a concert with the New Haven Symphony the next night after the Newport Jazz Festival, so I wasn't really aware of all that happened at Newport till after I got through my concert in New Haven. That's the night when the doctor had told me four months before that I was a little heavy, I should take off twenty pounds, and he gave me a diet list – which I tore up and went on my own diet. The diet was steak, grapefruit and black coffee, that's all. Four times a day and I'd probably eat a double steak each time and when Arthur came up to New Haven for the concert, he took one look at me and said, 'Go get yourself a banana split.' I had lost thirty pounds! I was standing up conducting the orchestra, and conducting and getting to the last part of 'Night Creature' and then my pants were falling off and I could feel them, and I was reaching down to pull them up and they wouldn't come up! And the fiddlers in the front were laughing their asses off because I was standing on them, and that's the reason why I couldn't pull them up, and I was in a helluva fix with tails on and conducting and going on and I reached the screeching end, so I had to stop and pull up my pants and then turn around and take a bow. Oh boy! That was somethin', that was![18]

The concert with the New Haven Symphony at Yale Bowl, New Haven, Conn., was on 12 July 1956.

IRVING TOWNSEND: The recording and editing of Ellington's *A Drum is a Woman* took up most of three months, a period which established my relationship with Duke. *A Drum is a Woman* is one of Ellington's most complicated fantasies. It is also one of his most revealing works. It is an allegory paralleling the history of jazz, as he described it, in which an elaborately fabricated drum is turned into a very sophisticated lady who travels from Africa to the Caribbean to New Orleans to New York and finally the moon, meeting in each place a simple man always named Joe, and touching him with her spell before leaving for the next Joe. The idea was first suggested by Duke to

Orson Welles in 1941, set aside, but never forgotten. *A Drum is a Woman* [was] written, composed, narrated and performed by a man who saw himself as the one 'Joe' Madam Zajj could not leave behind. To the end of his life he thought of *Drum is a Woman* as one of his supreme achievements.[19]

The recording of A Drum is a Woman *took place between 17 September and 6 December 1956.*

DUKE ELLINGTON: Billy Strayhorn and I did *A Drum is a Woman* which is actually the history of jazz, only we don't use the word jazz, we use Madame Zajj, which is jazz backwards, and of course she does exactly what jazz did, and she picks up her influences here and there and so forth and continues and with great anticipation, because we had her doing 'Ballet of the Flying Saucers' – and that was in 1957.[20]

BILLY STRAYHORN: I suppose the largest hunk of collaboration was *A Drum is a Woman*, in which we just kind of did everything. He wrote lyrics, I wrote lyrics, he wrote music, I wrote music, he arranged and I arranged.[21]

CLARK TERRY: He said to me once, when we were making a record called *A Drum is a Woman* and it was about New Orleans, Mardi Gras and all of that. He said to me, 'Sweetie, you're going to portray the role of Buddy Bolden.' I said, 'Maestro, I don't know anything about Buddy Bolden. Not too many people around know much about Buddy Bolden.' He says, 'Oh, sure. Buddy Bolden was suave, he was debonair, and he was just a marvellous person, he loved beautiful ladies around him, had a big sound, he tuned up in New Orleans and across the river in Algiers he would break glasses he was so powerful. He loved diminishes. You know all these things.' He says: 'You *are* Buddy Bolden! Play me some diminishes and bent notes!' So I started playing and he said, 'That's it, that's it!' And that's exactly what came off on the record of *A Drum is a Woman*. So he could masterfully psych you into doing exactly what he wanted you to do![22]

DOWNBEAT: Music history and television history were made on the night of 8 May [1957] when, thanks chiefly to the superhuman efforts of Columbia Records' Irving Townsend, who brought Duke Ellington and U.S. Steel together, the first television jazz spectacular was performed. Here at last was an answer to the complaints that jazz and television are incompatible, for the show was a sumptuous wedding of visual and aural delights.[23]

A Drum is a Woman *was first shown on* CBS-TV's The US Steel Hour *on 8 May 1957.*

JOHNNY HODGES: I like *A Drum is a Woman.*[24]

DUKE ELLINGTON: Jazz has lived a funny sort of life. First of all it was 'disgraceful'; then Paul Whiteman made a lady out of it, and now it's grown up to where it's accepted all over the world. Now, when someone says to me, 'Look, there's a jazz musician,' I take it as a form of flattery. But I don't know where jazz itself starts or where it stops, where Tin Pan Alley starts or where jazz ends, or even where the more serious music and jazz divide. There is no specific boundary line. I see no place for a boundary line. You know what it is about music? When it sounds good, it is good.[25]

REX STEWART: Long after I left the band, [Harry Carney] acted as Ellington's chauffeur. The rest of the band went by bus or train or whatever, but Harry drove Duke from gig to gig in his perfectly kept-up car and was an easy and relaxed companion for his boss.[26]

DUKE ELLINGTON: Harry and I are driving into a new state, and one of us will say, 'I wonder if so-and-so and his wife will drive that hundred miles to see us this time.' You get to the date, look up, and they're there. And in between towns there's also a marvellous freedom in the car from telephone calls and business. Harry and I don't talk much, so I can just dream and write.[27]

JIMMY HAMILTON: When I first joined the band, Duke did a lot of travelling with us in buses, trains, and then it went to planes. But then it got more so that he didn't travel all the time with us, if it was a bus he didn't travel with us, he might take a plane and get there in a hour, while we had to pay the dues to get there. The guy was older than us and we wanted to preserve the guy, without him we weren't nobody, so we liked to see him taken care of, but we wanted to be taken care of too.[28]

DANIEL HALPERIN: [Ellington] was the great man who lived in another hotel and another world altogether, the sphere of important people, big-time agents and impresarios. The musicians were a colourful, exciting crowd. The two circles overlapped only on the bandstand.[29]

CLARK TERRY: One night having slept in the bus, it was discovered that the food bought at our last stop had been left behind. Everyone was dragged. No breakfast and no chance of a stop – no time. 'Never mind,' smiled Shorty Baker, 'now's the time to open that parcel my mother sent me. That lovely fried chicken and devilled eggs, plenty for all!' It was a gag of course, but Shorty was able to make everyone feel just that little bit better.[30]

In July 1957 Harold 'Shorty' Baker returned to the band.

CLARK TERRY: [Play] until the early hours and then drop into bed – which was often enough your seat on the bus. Musicians are apt to get a bit salty under these conditions – lack of sleep, lack of food and lack of everything else that makes life worth living.[31]

DUKE ELLINGTON: It's a funny thing about it, sometimes you say, well, I know these guys are going to be dead making this 500-mile ride, and they come up and they've got a dark look on their face and growl and they blow right up to the ceiling![32]

On 25–26 June 1957, Ellington and Ella Fitzgerald collaborated on The Duke Ellington Songbook, *produced by Norman Granz.*

NORMAN GRANZ: It was done under the worst conditions. He was under contract to Columbia but I had Johnny Hodges. When Hodges rejoined the band in 1956, I managed to force a few concessions. I would have Duke for one LP, two if I used Ella. We planned far in advance, but in the end Duke failed to do a single arrangement.[33]

ELLA FITZGERALD: It was a panic scene with Duke almost making up arrangements as we went along. Duke is a genius – I admire him as much as anyone in the world – but doing it that way, even though it was fun at times, was kind of nerve-racking.[34]

NORMAN GRANZ: Well, we came into the session and did the whole thing in two days. There was nothing written. Duke would ask Ella what key she was in and he would have to transpose and there would be a lot of furious writing to change the key. Then Ella would try and fit in and the band would get swept along by its own memories of just how it ought to play, and so Ella, as you can hear on some songs, was fighting for her very life with Cat Anderson hitting those top notes or even fighting Johnny on something else. Really, at one point she became so nervous, almost hysterical, that she began to cry. Duke went over to her and said, 'Now, baby,' in his most gentle tones. 'Don't worry, it'll all turn out fine.'[35]

JIMMY WOODE: Ella and Billy [Strayhorn] had a rough time. That wasn't the way either of them liked to work. They were perfectionists. They were accustomed to planning and having the work fine-tuned to perfection. The idea of faking your way through 'Chelsea Bridge' by humming along was terribly difficult for them to accept.[36]

DUKE ELLINGTON: Billy Strayhorn is my writing and arranging companion. There are no assigned duties, he has no programme to write, or anything like that. We have something to do and I say, 'We have to do this.' And it just happens, you know.[37]

BILLY STRAYHORN: He's not demanding at all, that's what makes him so monstrous![38]

MERCER ELLINGTON: The competition and the challenge of outdoing each other caused greatness in both.[39]

BILLY STRAYHORN: There are no restrictions on my writing. There are no restrictions either on material or length. That's why I like working with Duke. I've always written what I wanted for Duke. Sometimes I turn in things, other times we have a conference. We carp at each other all the time, sometimes he wins out, sometimes I do. I'm certain Duke has influenced me. He says I've influenced him, but I don't know. I'm not even sure he knows. That's inevitable. We've been together so long. We discuss things, but I find that if I'm going to do the arrangement, it's about the same as if he would have done it.[40]

DUKE ELLINGTON: I may be somewhere, I'm in Los Angeles and he's in New York, and I get to the seventeenth bar of a number and I decide, 'Well, I think I'll call Strays.' I'll call, and say, 'I'm in E-flat or someplace, and the mood is this, and this guy is walking up the road and meets a certain intersection and I can't decide whether he should turn left, right or go straight ahead or make a U-turn.' And he says, 'Oh yes, I know what you mean. I think you can do that much better than I could.' That's his first response, and all the time he's thinking how he can outdo me and very often without any more than that we come up with practically the same thing.[41]

BILLY STRAYHORN: I do remember the Great South Bay Festival. We were supposed to write a piece to be premiered there, and I was in New York, [Ellington] was – I don't know where – but not out of telephonic communication, of course. He called me and said we have to have this thing ready for such and such a day, which of course is only two days ahead of us at that time. He said write so and so, and I said OK. I go into these things blindly, just go ahead! So when he got to New York there was not time to rehearse this thing . . . a long piece – about twenty minutes – and . . . we were going to play this at the performance for the first time, the band hadn't seen it! Which all of this he explained to the audience, he told them he didn't know what was going to happen, so they played it down and I was sitting in the back of the audience listening to it, so the section I had written was in the middle of this thing. It was just amazing because I discovered what I had written had been more or less a development of what he had written and I hadn't even known what he had written![42]

The Great South Bay Jazz Festival at East Islip, Long Island, New York, took place on 3 August 1958.

On 3 October 1958, the Ellington band arrived in Plymouth aboard the S.S. Ile de France for a nineteen-date tour of the U.K. before moving on to the Continent, opening in Paris on 28 October and closing the tour twenty-one dates later in the same city. The band appeared in Leeds on 13 October.

DUKE ELLINGTON: The thing I remember most is being presented to Her Majesty, Queen Elizabeth. We were playing at the festival at Leeds and they had a ball with about 200 or 300 people, of which seven were going to be presented to Her Majesty, and I was one of the seven. And I was so thrilled by the whole thing. I was so impressed by Her Majesty because I noticed that she spoke differently to every person who was presented to her. She spoke French to the French, German to the German and when she spoke to me she spoke American-English. And this was the most amazing thing I had ever seen. And she was very casual about it and we talked quite a lot. As a matter of fact I was the last one in the line and she was sort of relaxed when she got to me and we talked about her family, her father King George, her uncle Prince Edward and the Duke of Kent whom I had an occasion to meet. The Duke of Kent and I used to play four-hand at the piano at night, and Prince Edward was at several parties at which we played when we were there in 1933. Then one night, we had to hold the show for him at Liverpool. At another party he sat in on drums. So of course, most of these things I had to tell Her Majesty. Then she told me about all the records of mine her father had. The she asked me, when was your first time in England? Oh, I said, oh, my first time in England was in 1933, way before you were born. She gave me a real American look; very cool, man, which I thought was too much.[43]

DUKE ELLINGTON: Shortly after meeting Her Majesty I wrote a suite of numbers which I called 'The Queen's Suite', we recorded it, but only allowed one record to be pressed – it is of course in Her Majesty's possession.[44]

REX STEWART: When I attended a few concerts by the band recently, I was amazed he didn't change shoes [between sets, like he usually does]. Later I found out the reason. These were the pumps he had worn when he was presented to the Queen of England and despite their shabby appearance, they were now his favourites.[45]

On 19 February 1959, Ellington recorded the album Jazz Party *at the Columbia Studios in New York.*

DUKE ELLINGTON: We had Moe Goldenberg playing the melody on tymps in our record of 'Tymperturbably Blue'. We had nine tymps on that and he was running around from one to the other playing melody. That was an album called *Jazz Party* – a good album, I thought. But I guess there were too many different types of things in it.[46]

JIMMY JONES: The record *Jazz Party* that I was on with the band, it was a double date, you know. One date, then we had dinner, then we came back and did the second one; when we came back, Duke had told Bobby Boyd, the road manager, to get Dizzy Gillespie because he wanted some discipline. And he got it. When Dizzy walked in the studio, everybody was sitting up like tin soldiers. But now Clark Terry didn't have to worry about it, because Clark could handle himself. Everybody had to play and pay attention! There were a whole lot of people there, it was like a party, people were having drinks, Ellington had a lot of tympani and things. In the beginning he just happened to look around the room and there his doctor and I, we were having drinks together, Duke just pointed at me to come over and sit down. Now, I didn't know the red light was on, Irving Townsend was the producer in the booth at that point, Duke counted off and started 'Hello Little Girl', Jimmy Rushing sang it. And Dizzy Gillespie was playing on it too, that was just one take. None of us were supposed to be there. The band were there of course, the tympani players and all that, but we weren't. I doubt if I could do that again! He called them virgin takes. See, if you think about it, you get too intellectual, and he's got a point there. You know, if you go back and try and outdo yourself.[47]

DIZZY GILLESPIE: I just happened along one day and we blew and they taped it and they put it out. And when I got no money, I mentioned it, very gently to Duke, and he smiled and says, 'Well, Diz, I can't pay you what you're really worth.' Whee, was that a cunning, elegant man! So I smile and I says, 'Don't give it no mind Duke. Just so long as you *pay* me!' And maybe a year later, he did![48]

DUKE ELLINGTON: *Anatomy of a Murder* was my first movie score as such. I never thought it would earn an academy award because it really hadn't an outstanding melody to hang on to, yet, it was a thing that was handled properly and with respect to the music – no, that's not a good way of saying it. What I mean is it wasn't done with the intention of trying to get a tune out of it, or a movie theme that would get an award. I was trying to do background music fittingly. And that, of course, I think is important![49]

Ellington recorded the music for the Otto Preminger film Anatomy of a Murder *on 29 May and 1–2 June 1959.*

DUKE ELLINGTON: When we did the Preminger picture, we get to Hollywood and the guy gives me a beautiful seven-room apartment with a patio bigger than the apartment, and what I used to do for three weeks was to walk around the patio and, 'Hey look at the beautiful mountains over there,' and, 'Hey, there's Sunset Boulevard down there,' and people would come out and we'd have drinks and I'd show them all over the place, and so one day he calls up and says, 'Hey Duke, you know we're recording the day after tomorrow!' and so you have to get things together, quick![50]

CLARK TERRY: [Ellington] was a compiler of deeds and ideas, with a great facility to make something out of what would possibly have been nothing.[51]

JIMMY HAMILTON: He would try anything. There were many things that people would run from and not try, because they were afraid it wouldn't work. He tried, and it worked. That's good, that's what helps you to stay healthy and keeping up with the times, and keeping the musicians interested in playing. I don't think there was anyone who could interest musicians more than he.[52]

DUKE ELLINGTON: Lawrence Brown, the guy plays so much gut-bucket and he's so respectable it's not funny![53]

Lawrence Brown returned to the Ellington fold on 26 May 1959.

BOB UDKOFF: I don't know if it's generally known but he and Lawrence Brown didn't have a conversation for some twenty years, never spoke. When I say never spoke, if they were doing a recording, Duke would say, Lawrence do this, but there was never any personal contact.[54]

KENNY CLARE: The night I played with Duke Ellington on 11 July 1959, at Lambertville, New Jersey, was a unique experience I will never forget. After a couple of numbers I really started to become aware of the band. But the most exhilarating feeling of all was Duke's own playing. He must surely be the best big band piano player ever. When he plays those end-of-the-piano chords he makes it sound like another section has arrived. It really makes you jump and he doesn't ever do it where you'd expect. But surely one of the best musical moments of my life was when Duke announced, 'Ladies and Gentlemen – Kenny Clare wants you to know he loves you madly!'[55]

The British drummer Kenny Clare, who was playing opposite Ellington in the Johnny Dankworth band for the duration of the engagement at Lambertville Music Circus from 7–12 July 1959, later went on to join the Kenny Clarke–Francy Boland Big Band.

On 22 February 1960, after an 8.30 p.m. concert at Shriver Hall, Johns Hopkins University, Baltimore, Md., before an audience of 1,000, Ellington went to the Blue Jay, a nearby restaurant where he had been informed black students had been refused service. Ellington too was denied service, but the outrage at least made the national news.

IRVING TOWNSEND: While we were recording a new version of his 'Happy-Go-Lucky-Local' in a Hollywood studio, he mentioned the piece had been stolen, retitled and turned into a well-known hit by another musician. 'You can sue for every cent of royalties,' I reminded him. He turned to me and said, 'We must be flattered and just go write something better.'[56]

Piano in the Background, produced by Townsend, and recorded in late May-early June 1960, included the version of 'Happy-Go-Lucky-Local' to which he refers. Jimmy Forrest, who had played briefly in Ellington's saxophone section in August 1946, earned a certain degree of notoriety with his version of 'Night Train'.

MERCER ELLINGTON: In one instance a suit was instigated for [Ellington] which never came to the courts and was settled out of the courts, and that was involved in a song called 'Night Train', written by Jimmy Forrest. Jimmy Forrest had been in the orchestra and it was proven that note for note 'Night Train' was the part Jimmy Forrest read during this record date. And it wasn't the melody, and he took that particular part and used it to create this new song which became a big hit and they justified it in some kind of way, and made a deal with Ellington, so he was satisfied after that. I think what they did was make a cash settlement.[57]

MERCER ELLINGTON: He never said he needed me for anything. I used to always have to, 'Can I go and do this?' or go hang around, or go buy my own ticket and show up where he was. Even when I went to his birthday out in Las Vegas, he was playing the Riviera Hotel, I went there to wish him a Happy Birthday, he kept me there for four weeks copying music. He never said he needed me![58]

Ellington played the Starlight Lounge of the Riviera Hotel, Las Vegas, from 2 March to 24 May 1960.

MERCER ELLINGTON: My contribution was Aaron Bell, to the Ellington band, at a time when the rhythm section was shakier than it had ever been. The one thing that bugged him more than anything else was not to have a bass player who could really get it straight.[59]

Bassist Aaron Bell succeeded Jimmy Woode on 12 April 1960.

AARON BELL: My first album with Duke was in Los Angeles, *The Nutcracker Suite*. He also did some Grieg on that album. It was a very loose session and I remember thinking to myself, 'This is strange.' It always seemed to me that they weren't prepared. He and Strayhorn would be in there writing. They'd write a few bars and say, 'Play this, let's hear this.' And then eventually it would get together, but I was always uneasy. I'd say, 'We're not going to get anything down.' He'd get what he wanted because he was constantly, in his manner of things, manipulating. I don't mean in a bad sense. He knew every man in the band and he knew their personalities. When he wrote, he wrote with that individual in mind. He got the best out of them in that way. He was a good psychologist. He knew life, he knew people. I used to ask him, 'Duke, where do you get your ideas for writing music?' He said, 'I just watch people and observe life, and then I write about them.'[60]

The Nutcracker Suite *was recorded on 3 June 1960.*

DUKE ELLINGTON: You have a wide range of personalities, and every night you see this menage, and you're watching and make observations, and I imagine it's what the scientists do in a mental institution.[61]

MERCER ELLINGTON: When he did 'The Nutcracker' I did all the copying for both he and Billy Strayhorn, and never got any assignment to do a part of the work, just to do the copying![62]

AARON BELL: He's found a way to stay young. Watch him some night in the wings. Those bags under his eyes are huge and he looks beat and kind of lonely. But then we begin to play, he strides out on the stand, the audience turn their faces to him and the cat is a new man.[63]

DUKE ELLINGTON: We've been doing jazz waltzes all the way back. There was that waltz with a beat in the *All American* record. One of the first things I wrote when I came to New York was a jazz waltz called 'Come Back To Me', I sold it outright. There was a terrific one in *Jump for Joy*, and there's a jazz waltz in 'Black, Brown and Beige', in the Harlem scene – 'Sugar Hill Penthouse'. There's a jazz waltz in *Paris Blues* too.[64]

And, of course, part of Ellington's long piano introduction to 'Take the A Train' was played in waltz-time. The All American *record to which Ellington refers was cut on 23 January 1962, the waltz number was called 'Back to School'. Once cited by Mercer Ellington as one of his favourite Ellington recordings,* All American in Jazz *was of Ellington arrangements of the Charles Strouse and Lee Adams Broadway musical* All American.

DUKE ELLINGTON: The film *Paris Blues* was something different. I'll tell you what happened with that. We started in Hollywood and we did what they call pre-recording. This film was about musicians, Paul Newman and Sidney Poitier were musicians in a band, Newman a trombonist and Poitier a tenor saxophonist, so we had to have a track for them to use that wouldn't be kidding the musicians and kidding the audience. This had to be done pretty early. So before they left to go to Paris we did this and when they got to Paris and decided to change the script, well! So some of the pre-recording had to be done over again. So they say, you'll have to come to Paris immediately. Well, I had engagements with the band but I went straight over and we did some of the pre-adjusting of the recording. So I stayed there eight weeks with the picture, doing nothing really. Just sitting around and once or twice a week they would call and send the car to take me to the studio. It was a wonderful experience, I loved it. Going to Paris – it's fun anyway. Paris is a great place. It's changed a lot since the war, but it's still wonderful.[65]

FBI File 100–434443: Edward Kennedy (Duke) Ellington:

Date: December 29, 1960

To: – Blanked Out –

From: John Edgar Hoover, Director

Subject: Edward Kennedy Ellington – Security Matter

– Possibly One, Perhaps Two Paragraphs Blanked Out –

This matter is being referred to the Legal Attaché in Paris for his information in the event Ellington's activities while in France come to his attention.

ATTENTION: SAC, NEW YORK, AND LEGAL ATTACHÉ, PARIS

For the information of the Legal Attaché, subject was never the subject of a main case file. However, Bureau files indicate Ellington has some affiliation with numerous communist front groups such as the All Harlem Youth Conference, the Hollywood Chapter of the Veterans of the Abraham Lincoln Brigade, the Artists' Front to Win the War and the National Committee to Abolish the Poll Tax. Furthermore, Ellington reportedly volunteered his professional services for a concert held in 1944 in Carnegie Hall, New York, sponsored by the Joint Anti-Fascist Refugee Committee. He appeared at another concert in 1947 sponsored by the National Council of American-Soviet Friendship. He also, according to an article in the October 10, 1943, issue of 'The Worker,' sponsored the candidacy of Benjamin J. Davis, Jr., Communist Party candidate for city councilman in New York. Ellington was born 4/29/99 at Washington, D.C.

NOTE ON YELLOW: Subject not on S.I. He is a well known Negro musician who is presently travelling abroad, according to information received from the State Department in memorandum received 12/21/60.[66]

DUKE ELLINGTON: Later I had to do all sorts of things for this film [*Paris Blues*]. I had my bookings all set up so that it would be convenient to the whole thing. I was in Las Vegas, which was only half an hour ride from Los Angeles. I thought they were going to do the score there, then suddenly they're going to do it in New York. So I got out to go to New York. And the funny part about it is that when you're *out* on location they pay your expenses – they give you so much a day. Being in L.A. I had settled down and got an apartment and so when they changed their plans, naturally I had to pay for everything. But the funny thing about it was that although they didn't pay expenses for us in Los Angeles (that's what *they* call home), when I came to New York and *was* living home, they paid my expenses![67]

The pre-recording and recordings for the soundtrack of Paris Blues *took place between May and December 1960 and in March 1961.*

BOB UDKOFF: Johnny [Hodges] was not very articulate. I'm being kind, he had little or no personality, friendly, pleasant, but he expressed himself through his horn. Beautiful player, very soulful, but you couldn't have a conversation with him.[68]

DUKE ELLINGTON: Johnny is the type of musician – tuning up is not important to him, he just blows in tune.[69]

BILL BERRY: When I was there, it was the height of all the Civil Rights business and we used to play black theatres in Chicago and New York and the mood was not too friendly towards white people. At the Regal Theatre in Chicago, the black guys in the band were afraid to go there it was so rough. The first day we were there, as always, you had a nine or ten o'clock rehearsal and then Johnny [Hodges] took me, before the show, about noon, around three or four restaurant bars in the vicinity of the theatre and introduced me to the bar tender or the owner. I didn't realize it at the time but that was so I could go in these places all that week we were there, I don't think anybody else white would have gone, and if anybody gave me a hard time, the bartender would say, 'Wait a minute, he's all right.' And that was all Johnny.[70]

DUKE ELLINGTON: We've done more benefits for civil-rights groups than anybody, and I don't think there's been any doubt how we felt concerning prejudice. But still the best way for me to be effective is through music.[71]

NEW YORK POST: Las Vegas – Two members of Duke Ellington's band face preliminary hearings April 19 [1961] on narcotics charges. Saxophonist Paul Gonsalves, 40, and trumpeter William Nance, 41, were arraigned on charges of illegal possession.[72]

At their trial in the autumn of 1961, Gonsalves was let off on probation and Nance was incarcerated for sixty days because of a suspended sentence incurred in 1956.

MERCER ELLINGTON: Because the guys were merely smoking pot, the charge against them was light, but the case helped induce the paranoia Ellington was developing. He felt there were people who wanted to harm him and hold him back.[73]

DUKE ELLINGTON: We've always had critics who would deliberately pick on us because we always had a pretty good and high batting average . . . in other words it was considered expedient to pan Duke mainly to attract attention to themselves who would normally go unnoticed.[74]

CLARK TERRY: Oh, Mex [Gonsalves], he would never stay in touch with his mother, his family. He was delinquent like that. It was kind of pitiful because he was a victim of drugs and alcohol and anybody who wanted to use him could take advantage of him.[75]

DUKE ELLINGTON: Paul Gonsalves is a guy who has not one devious facet in his whole being, you know. Here's a guy who doesn't do anything but tell the truth, he never did anything to anybody but himself. He made a couple of mistakes himself, and that's it.[76]

MERCER ELLINGTON: He felt, I think, personally, that a person in the influence of narcotics was more creative than if they were plain sober – or whatever. Don't forget, Freud advocated drugs for creativity and being able to get things to a point where your mind was freer to develop, and if ever Ellington was prone to the admiration of anything, it was creativity. So he had no qualms about hiring or watching a man – although he never advocated it – but knowing a man was under the influence of narcotics being relative to his music. He felt he was getting the most creative feeling as a result of this.[77]

MERCER ELLINGTON: Duke Ellington – he went through all the stages of anybody else who went through that – whisky, pot and coke. In various areas.[78]

DUKE ELLINGTON: A couple of albums that I enjoyed making were the two albums I did with Louis Armstrong for Roulette. It was a matter of trying to pick things that I thought that Louis did to the best advantage. Then of course there were two or three things he wanted to do himself, too.[79]

Ellington's first date with Armstrong and his All Stars was 2–3 April 1961, replacing Billy Kyle on piano.

STANLEY DANCE: To see Louis at work under these circumstances was, for us, a rare privilege. He never spared himself and he was so quick to grasp the whole conception of an interpretation ... at the piano Duke was full of ideas and a great source of inspiration ... his solos differed from take to take, and on one number he broke everybody up by playing like Ray Charles. Such was their mutual respect there was never any clash of authority between him and Louis; he organized most of the routines, but when Louis required some modification there was no problem.[80]

DUKE ELLINGTON: There's a certain symbol in Armstrong, which everybody in the world – some people speak more loudly about than others. I mean Miles Davis, when he wrote about Louis Armstrong in *Playboy* he just opened right up. He did it very cleverly, he mentioned the Uncle Tom business up in the front part of it and down the bottom, after putting a couple of chapters in between, he said if somebody wants to send some good representative down South, send Uncle, er, er, send Louis down there because he'll make everybody happy! Suppose they enjoy it? It interferes with the race problem, you can't sell your race for your personal gain.[81]

BILLY STRAYHORN: He gets, Louis Armstrong gets, a big contract [based on the Uncle Tom thing] and he [Ellington] gets nothing, because he represents the opposite.[82]

DUKE ELLINGTON: It's a matter of dignity, it's a matter of embarrassing the race.[83]

DUKE ELLINGTON: Louis Armstrong is not alone – what the hell! This whole thing is big. When they got ready to send somebody to represent America in Russia, they sent *Porgy and Bess*, which is the image of the Negro they want in Russia. *Porgy and Bess*, those people in those alleys, waking up, dusting those carpets out of the window and beating their brooms in time and all that bullshit. You want to know about America, we're going to make a cultural exchange, we send you *Porgy and Bess*, this is the complete image of our Negro.[84]

JIMMY JONES: Roulette Records had recorded Louis Armstrong and Duke. Bob Thiele was instrumental, I think, in putting that together. So Duke was with Columbia at that point, so Ellington was the big band Columbia man and Basie was the big Roulette man. So to make it even, the companies got together and had a handshake on it and said instead of recording just Basie on Columbia, let's record both bands, you know?[85]

DUKE ELLINGTON: The Basie thing, I mean it's easy to pat the foot to. If it's one of the things they know well, of course they can go along with it melodically too, he isn't too extravagant melodically, actually. They hardly ever play anything you can't hum.[86]

JIMMY JONES: They did the whole album in one day. They had been on the road, just passing through, and Tom Whaley – Duke's orchestrator – had a table off to the side, you know, and he was writing [like mad]. Duke was so smart, I think it was Teo Macero in the booth, the producer, and they wanted to make it a battle of jazz, but Duke didn't want it that way. When Thad Jones took a solo, Duke would have his reed section play behind him. And when Ray Nance would play a solo, Duke would have Basie's reed section play behind him. So it was like all one complete thing. And I think what Duke was really thinking about was, 'Gee, I've got ten great saxophone players, two great drummers, two fine bass players, you know?' And he just wished he had more time to do it. But when they did it – a couple of guys almost started a fight, but they cooled out, you know. Within Duke's band. That's when the deportment always went haywire. I think it was Tizol and Cat Anderson, something like that. So I told Duke, I said: 'I told you about writing those high tension chords!' He just walked away, like he's saying, 'I don't know what I did.' He was never at a loss for that. He would start something and then walk away from it like a kid standing over gasoline, tank full of gasoline and dropping a match in it! I think he used it to real advantage, you know, real positive advantage. Now this was basically Ellington's date, because it was with his company and Duke used some things out of *Paris Blues*. The thing he used that Louis Armstrong played in the picture [called 'Battle Royal']. And I'll never forget the way the Basie band looked, because they had Marshall Royal, Budd Johnson. They had, you know, two great bands. But Duke had written so many, you know, he had wrote very like clashes, notes rubbing together. And when they finished doing ['Battle Royal'] some of the Basie guys were soaking wet. So Marshall Royal told me, he said: 'The old man is really splitting atoms on that one!'[87]

First Time, combining both the Duke Ellington and Count Basie bands, was recorded in New York on 6 July 1961.

MARSHALL ROYAL: Basie and Ellington were recording side by side, the two bandstands in the studio with a complete roster of musicians. We tried to pick out tunes that were appropriate to be performed by both bands. This was a little bit discouraging for a while but during the two separate recording sessions [morning and afternoon], it was interesting to see how Ellington arranged and put together little scraps of paper to make an arrangement called 'Battle Royal'. It was sort of an exciting tune and a real flag waver.[88]

DUKE ELLINGTON: This guy, he said a thing about, 'Duke Ellington composes by sitting around with a lot of guys in the band and somebody plays something and he says "Oh yes!" and we all get together.' It's a lot of shit, but it's a beautiful romantic story.[89]

On 5 September 1961 Ellington cancelled a concert at Little Rock, Ark., when informed by the NAACP the concert would be segregated. He also ensured the subsequent two concerts, at the Music Hall, Dallas, Texas, on 6 September, and the Music Hall, Houston,

Texas, on 7 September, were unsegregated. It marked the first time either venue allowed an integrated audience.

BILL BERRY: We did the Goodyear film, they were going to make these concerts with various groups and they were going to send them around the world and one of their biggest plants was in South Africa. We did it the way you do a film, you go in one day and record it and you go in the next day and act like you're playing – it's called sidelining. So we recorded one day and went back the next to film it and there was this big long confab going on in the booth, of course we couldn't hear what was going on in the studio. I found out later that the producers when they saw me in the band they said this was going to South Africa, we can't have this. And Duke said, as only he could, he said, 'What a shame, we had so looked forward to working with you on this project.'[90]

The Goodyear Jazz Concert *was filmed and recorded in New York City on 9 January 1962.*

DUKE ELLINGTON: The Twist is bringing people back to dancing, which I think is a very good thing, but I don't know how much it's benefiting jazz groups generally. Some of them might not bend to conform to it. It seems to me with everyone in the world doing The Twist, you're out of step if you don't do it. I do it. I don't like to be odd.[91]

DUKE ELLINGTON: For the album with Coleman Hawkins, we had some music for that date, although I do know the Hawk, very, very well, musically.[92]

Duke Ellington meets Coleman Hawkins *was recorded on 18 August 1962.*

AARON BELL: Coleman was very excited on that date. He said it was the first time he'd ever played with Duke. That was strange to me, I didn't realize it was the first time. It was a very nice loose date. I remember one of the ballads we did, 'Mood

Indigo'. It was one of Duke's ballads. We played it down the
first take and the engineers said, 'What are you going to do?
You want to do it again?' Coleman said yes, but Duke said,
'Don't touch it, don't touch it. Leave it like that, just like it is.' I
can understand why. Coleman probably thought there was
something he missed or wanted to play better, but you listen to
the record and there's nothing you could have done to it and
Duke knew it.[93]

DUKE ELLINGTON: We got into something else in that date we
did with Coleman Hawkins. We recorded some 'Limbo Jazz' for
the benefit of the limboists![94]

AARON BELL: That number, 'Limbo Jazz' on the Coleman
Hawkins album wasn't a mistake. What happened is we were
running the number down. Duke was a great one for going
for a first take. He hated going over and over until the men
lost their spirit. They were recording in the studio. Sam [Wood-
yard] didn't know, so he was just humming away. Duke, I guess,
when he went to edit and everything, he told them to take that
one![95]

DUKE ELLINGTON: *Money Jungle* with Max Roach and Charlie
Mingus was quite an experience. One thing great about it was
that it was done from a very primitive artistic perspective. For
instance, we had one meeting one day in the office. We sat
around, talked a little bit about something and that was it. The
next meeting we had was the recording date. I did go through a
few bars and they fell in, and it was just that. One number in
particular was as close to spontaneity as you can get, I believe. I
explained what we were going to do, with no thought as to what
they were going to do. I said, 'Now we are in the centre of a
jungle, and for two hundred miles in any direction, no man has
ever been. And right in the centre of this jungle, put in the deep
moss, there's a tiny little flower growing, the most fragile thing

that's ever grown. It's God-made and untouched and this is going to be "The Little African Flower" [listed on the recording as "Fleurette Africaine"].' I started to play, and we played to the end and that was it. People like Mingus and Roach, they are so imaginative, and I thought this was the greatest example of it. Everybody gave his own impression of this little number, though it's possibly a little surrealistic.[96]

Money Jungle *was recorded on 17 September 1962.*

DUKE ELLINGTON: A funny thing happened in the middle of the session. Mingus suddenly and without warning started to pack up his bass and when I enquired where he was going and what was the trouble, he said, 'Man I can't play with that drummer.' I said, 'Why? What's wrong?' He said, 'Duke I've always loved you and what you're doing in music but you'll just have to get another bass player.' And I said, 'You mean just like that in the middle of a date – come on man, it can't be that serious.' But he kept packing and went out of the door to the elevator, I followed him to the elevator and after he roll off a few more beefs, I slowly and quietly said, 'Mingus, my man, UA [United Artists, the label for whom they were recording] gave you a full page ad in Xmas *Billboard* – it was beautiful – yeah.' Then I continued, 'You know if Col Rec [Columbia Records] had spent that $ on my promoting I would be with them today.' He paused, thought for a second and said, 'Man, you're right. OK I'll play your session.' Picked up the bass, came back into the studio and we recorded very happily ever after till the album was done.[97]

MAX ROACH: In the studio with Charles Mingus and Mr Ellington, so that was like phew! That was a moment.[98]

MERCER ELLINGTON: He had an argument with Max Roach, and they vowed never to record again, and *didn't*. They both had their interpretations of what they thought should be done at the time. In fact, originally, it was a contract for two albums to be dubbed for United Artists, and they only did the one, and they could never get the three of them back together.[99]

DUKE ELLINGTON: Roach's rhythm embellishments couldn't have been more fitting or sound more authentic. While Mingus with his eyes closed fell into each and every harmonic groove adding counter melodies as though he had been playing it all his life. It was one of those mystic moments when our three muses were one and the same a one take too – I was gassed.[100]

DUKE ELLINGTON: The album on Impulse! with John Coltrane, we used my own drummer and bass and Coltrane's drummer and bass on other tracks. There wasn't really any great difference, for it's something we're more or less accustomed to. I mean, we're accustomed to writing music and adjusting backgrounds to the soloist who's in the foreground ... because whatever the guy's going to play, you have to fit in.[101]

Duke Ellington and John Coltrane *was recorded on 26 September 1962.*

BOB THIELE: As Coltrane's record producer, I had grown very concerned with his escalating self-critical obsession in the studio. Trane had become impossible to be pleased when ever we recorded. He would ask for one take after another, with each subsequent take inevitably less exciting and genuine than the previous attempt. Of course, Ellington knew, from decades of experience making classic records in the studio, if you get it, save it. His style was to capture the musical essence as quickly as possible on records. From the start it worked out beautifully. He and Coltrane got along as two old cronies who had shared a lifetime of enthusiasms. The first tune was Duke's immortal 'In a Sentimental Mood', and after an exquisite first – and I was sure never-to-be-bettered – take, I looked out of the booth into the studio at

John and Ellington, and only Duke was smiling. Coltrane was going to say, 'Let's do it again,' and Duke was going to say, 'That's beautiful.' I felt so good about the take that I ran over to Coltrane and said, 'John, that was it.' And Duke, as if on cue from a prepared script (he was unaware of Trane's super critical compulsions) immediately added, 'Bob, you're absolutely right. Why play it again? You can't duplicate that feeling. This is it. John, don't ever do it again here.' So Coltrane said to use it as a master and we went on with both his and Duke's current rhythm sections alternating on each tune, and in mostly first takes, to record one of the all time classic jazz albums.[102]

RUTH ELLINGTON: The cemetery in Washington was sold, which was a traumatic shock for Duke. We received a letter saying, 'If you want your people, dig 'em up, otherwise if you don't we'll move them to Maryland.' So of course, I could see he was in such a state of shock because that's what an artist is, he's hypersensitive. One of the A&R people at his record company told me Duke phoned him up at three o'clock in the morning. Didn't announce who he was, just went on about the cemetery. And so I said to Duke, 'You stay here and pick out a new plot, I will go to Washington and pick the bodies up.' This was in the early '60s, so they had been buried for a very long time and one didn't know what one would find. Fortunately, he had them buried in glass, cased metal coffins which were in turn kept in steel vaults. The caskets were pretty intact, in fact, so we brought them up. Rev. John Gensel, the jazz pastor, he buried them again. After this situation, because they didn't ask our approval, or the chance to buy the cemetery, he had a completely different way of thinking about Washington. It was like Washington had disinherited him. When he went there he usually stayed quiet in his room, whereas before that incident he would be out visiting friends and so forth.[103]

On 28 November 1962, Frank Sinatra threw a huge press party for Ellington in the Guild Hall of the Ambassador West Hotel in Chicago. It was to celebrate Ellington's new contract with Reprise records, the singer's own record label formed in 1961 and bankrolled by nascent corporation giant Warner Bros. After his long association with Columbia records, Reprise gave Ellington considerable autonomy as an artist. In all, he would record eight albums for the label, beginning the next day when he started work on the album Will the Big Bands Ever Come Back?

DUKE ELLINGTON: I thought it would be a very good idea to be contracted to some company which is controlled by an artist rather than a businessman. It gives the soul a better opportunity, I think, it's turned out very well, so far, nothing has been released so far but what has been recorded we're extremely satisfied with. We'll probably get around to – Frank is great and I'd love to do an album with him and if and when he feels that it will be good for him, that's it. These things are only good when you feel like it. It's just like a beautiful girl, the proper time to have tea with her is when she feels like having tea![104]

MERCER ELLINGTON: There was nothing really stimulating or great taking place, [Ellington] had become a producer for one of the record companies and all that, and although he was writing music like 'Volupté' and a lot of other things like that, it just didn't have any bang to it. So one day – he'd be in the studio and he'd need something or feel he had to add something to what it was ... so he says, 'Some guy is going to be out today' – I've forgotten who it was – he said, 'Give me a trumpet player.' So I called Cootie [Williams], I said, 'Cootie, do you want a record date?' He says, 'Yeah. How much does it pay?' I says, 'Double scale.' So he says, 'Yeah. I'll take it.' So he went through this business. I know he'd take it for anything he could get at that point, so I had to preserve his dignity. So he wanted to know where was the thing and so forth. He's thinking it's my date. So I told him what studio it was, what time to be there, and all that. And when he got there, Duke Ellington was recording, and I pointed to a chair, told him to sit down, and he stayed there from then on! That's how he wound up back in the orchestra. Ellington put the paper down, and then they went back over the thing they had been blowing, and when Cootie came in he just pointed to him. They started recording and at a certain point he pointed to Cootie and Cootie started playing, and that's the way the date went![105]

The recording Will the Big Bands Ever Come Back? *for the Reprise label began on 29 November 1962 in Chicago, when 'Volupté' was recorded (later released on the album* Afro Bossa*). Will the Big Bands Ever Come Back? took a further five dates in New York City during December 1962 to complete. Williams marked his return to the Ellington fold after a twenty-three-year absence on the first New York date on 11 December with a solo on 'Tuxedo Junction'.*

BILL BERRY: When Cootie came back in the band, we were playing some tune and we got to the last note and I played the note I'd been playing for a year, and Cootie looked at me and he says: 'That's my note!' Jeez, he was there before I was born, he was right, it was his note so I found another one![106]

CLARK TERRY: But that's the way Duke likes to live. He wants life and music to be in a state of becoming. He doesn't even like to write definitive endings to a piece.[107]

BOB UDKOFF: You couldn't have a conversation with ... Cootie Williams. Cootie was another one that was pleasant, nice, but all he could talk about was horses. He was a big horse player.[108]

MERCER ELLINGTON: Cat Anderson and Cootie Williams were constantly challenging each other like two mountain goats who was going to be the one who had full command of the trumpet section.[109]

JIMMY JONES: I guess everybody knows how Cat Anderson and Cootie Williams did not get along. But they were rehearsing where there was a stack of empty ashtrays close to Duke and Cootie was – I don't know, he was in one of those moods where he didn't feel like playing what Duke wanted, and Duke started throwing ashtrays and Cat Anderson said, the way he described it, he said – you know he called Duke Piano Red – Cat says he grabbed his horn and ran because Piano Red might miss his mark and hit him. He was really throwing at Cootie, you know. He was very serious. Cootie kept fooling around with some chart he'd written and he'd called the rehearsal because he was serious about it. And Cootie didn't feel like – because Duke, see, they never expected Duke to get showing his temper like that. But he did, because he'd been cool for so many years, you know. Apparently cool. But that night, the first guy in his chair and very orderly, like a Boy Scout, was Cootie Williams (laughter).[110]

BOB UDKOFF: Cat Anderson [was the kleptomaniac in the band]. They would have all their clothes in the bus and Cat would sneak off and steal the money out of their pockets! They knew it was him and asked for it back![111]

JIMMY HAMILTON: Cat Anderson had a personality that nobody liked, nobody liked Cat because he seemed to be like, have double standards and 'course maybe there's a reason for it because [after Cat died] I found out that he had some kind of tumour in his head and the doctors said this had something to do with his personality, but we all didn't know that then, you know. And there was Cootie in the band who was kind of touchy, so we had these two elements in the band at the same time! So they used to call them bookends, bookends. Trumpets, bookends because they put Cootie on this end and Cat on the other because if they didn't do that, they'd be fightin'![112]

DUKE ELLINGTON: In 1963 we went to Europe and on to the Continent.[113]

The first of two European tours in 1963 opened 12 January in London and ended in Paris on 1 March.

HARRY CARNEY: When we make the European tours, they are pretty rugged, due to the fact we have to get up so early in the morning to start travelling. It seems as if all the planes leave bright and early in the morning and there have been a few occasions when you fly from one point to another where you have to change planes and sit around the airport for three and a half hours, this takes its toll.[114]

COOTIE WILLIAMS: You don't have no proper time to go to sleep, proper time to eat. Up early, run to the airport, get on the plane. Sitting around the airport all day, you get into a different country to sit at the airport only to go play the concert, and you play two concerts and you get to bed around twelve, one o'clock and you're up about six the next morning and you grab a hot dog or a hamburger, and try and go to try blow your horn, sometimes you don't have time to get a meal and you don't live right.[115]

HARRY CARNEY: When we finally arrive at our destination, and are able to perform and the people are appreciative, that sort of inspires us, and we forget about the happenings of the day, how strenuous it is and so forth.[116]

DUKE ELLINGTON: Just before we left [Paris] I became an A&R man. I found Dollar Brand, I recorded with a South African girl Bea Benjamin, I recorded 'The Three Fiddlers' – Nance, Grappelli, Sven Amundson – I also recorded Bud Powell and after that I had pneumonia and was confined for a short spell.[117]

The session with Bea Benjamin, produced by Ellington on 23 February 1963, was finally released under Benjamin's name in 1997 as A Morning In Paris.

DUKE ELLINGTON: We recorded just recently and it has been released on the Reprise label, an album called *Symphonic Ellington*. There's 'Night Creature', originally performed in 1955, originally performed with the Symphony of the Air, 'Harlem' which was done with the NBC Symphony in 1950, and then we did a new thing which I did one morning when I found out I could only have the La Scala Orchestra in Milan for two hours, so I had to scratch out a quickie, which is in the album and it's called 'La Scala She Too Pretty To Be Blue'. This was inspired by the magnificent performance of the strings and the horns of the La Scala orchestra.[118]

The Symphonic Ellington *was recorded with several European orchestras during the tour, collectively referred to on the album jacket as 'Duke Ellington and his Orchestra and 500 of Europe's finest musicians'. The centrepiece of the album, 'Night Creature', was a musical impression of a transvestite.*

DUKE ELLINGTON: Jazz covers so many characters of sounds, it parallels the times of the American people all the time ... here we are in the space age and all categories [of music] will be eliminated, it's what I've said all along, the only thing that matters is if it's good or bad.[119]

CHAPTER TEN

SERIOUS SERENADE

Following his Newport Jazz Festival appearance in 1956, Ellington's career, treading water for much of the early '50s, took off. His new recording contract with Columbia yielded a bestselling album in Ellington at Newport *and a series of imaginative albums followed including* A Drum Is A Woman, Jazz Party, Such Sweet Thunder, Piano in the Foreground, Piano in the Background, *and* The Nutcracker and Peer Gynt Suites. *His renaissance was recognized with invitations to work on two major motion picture soundtracks (he would later do two more, in 1966 and 1969) and, in 1958, he was introduced to Her Majesty Queen Elizabeth II at the Leeds Festival during a nineteen-date tour of England, Wales and Scotland.*

With air travel coming into its own, Ellington began venturing more and more on to the international circuit and in 1963 his value as an international ambassador on behalf of his country would be recognized with a tour on behalf of the State Department of America.

In tandem with his growing celebrity came the return of two individual voices from his earlier ensembles, Lawrence Brown, one of the great lyric trombonists in jazz, and Cootie Williams, master of the plunger mute. His band was now one of the great attractions in modern music with strong, distinctive soloists in every department. Ellington had arrived at a new creative peak that many observers found every bit as exciting and stimulating as his

triumphs of the early '40s. It was a remarkable achievement for a
man entering his sixties.

In 1962 he signed with Frank Sinatra's Reprise label, and was
given carte blanche to record whatever he wanted and to act in an
A&R capacity for the label. In practical terms it meant he was able
to fulfil a long-standing ambition by recording his work for jazz
ensemble and symphony orchestra, including 'Night Creature',
which he had premiered as early as 1955 at Carnegie Hall in a
concert entitled 'Excursions into Jazz' with the Symphony of the
Air under the baton of Don Gillis.

Never one to stand still and bask in the glory that was now
coming his way, in 1963 he was invited to write a musical that
would be presented as a part of the Century of Negro Progress
Exhibition to be celebrated at Chicago's McCormick Place exhi-
bition complex.

DUKE ELLINGTON: In 1963, *My People*, in Chicago, it ran at Evi
Theatre for six weeks, 9,000 people a day. Based on the cultural
contribution of the negro, the foundation was built on the
sweat, blood of the negro. We went on for an hour and twenty
minutes and never mentioned the word 'colour'. I did the
words, music and choreographed. On the subject of colour we
had a little girl tell the story of the green people and the purple
people ... who fought and fought till they both won and lived
in a state of monotony since they both felt they had won an
empty victory. So they both fought until they both lost. They
were all dead and there was blood everywhere, no purple blood,
no green blood, it was all red. After the little girl finished telling
her story, we had Joya Sherrill come out and say, 'We finally
got on to the subject and we're sorry. We tried to hold it back
as long as we could so we're going to discuss colour now.' And
then we had her sing, 'What colour is virtue, what colour is
love, give me a hint of what makes me compatible.'[1]

My People *opened at the 5,000-seat Arie Crown Theatre in*

Chicago's McCormick Place on 16 August 1963 as a part of the Century of Negro Progress Exhibition.

TOM WHALEY: I used to copy and run out and listen to the show, copy and listen to the show. *My People*, it was the education of the negro through music. He had the people coming up from the pit, they were in rags, my people, our people in rags coming up and then at the end they were doctors and lawyers and everything. And he developed it and oh, it was beautiful and the last thing was 'What is Colour, What is Virtue?' [2]

DUKE ELLINGTON: You have to hear 'My Mother, My Father', the heritage song from *My People*, that's really a thing of love. [3]

JIMMY JONES: He called me, from Canada, he was doing a Shakespearean play, to conduct *My People*. He can speak in an oblique way, it's never quite direct, you know. So he says, 'Hey, James, this is Eddie Ellington.' I said, 'Hi, Edward, how do you feel?' So he says, 'I've got some singers I want you to take a look at,' and it was Lil Greenwood, Jimmy Grissom, Joya Sherrill. So he says, 'Then there was a choir there that I want you to work with,' and the next thing I knew I was in McCormick Place in Chicago and I was conducting. It was band number two, I played piano too, Strayhorn did some writing, we did some things out of *Paris Blues* and *Black, Brown and Beige* – he just went in the book, and then Duke, the old man, wrote some more things. We had guys like Louie Bellson, Joe Benjamin and Bill Berry and Duke says, 'I'm going to give you Russell Procope and I'll go get Hilton Jefferson for the road band.' Oh, I had a great band, John Saunders, Booty Wood, all these guys in the family. By this time he knew, you know, that I knew and was interested in it, that's the main thing. Some very funny things happened. He would never give me conductor's sheets. I would ask for conductor's sheets and he would walk away, and Stray-

Billy Strayhorn with **Duke Ellington** directing the band at a recording session in 1940

Duke Ellington Orchestra at the Crystal Ballroom, Fargo, ND, 7 November 1940. (l to r) Barney Bigard, Johnny Hodges, Rex Stewart, Otto Hardwick, Ray Nance, Wallace Jones, Ben Webster, Joe 'Tricky Sam' Nanton, Juan Tizol, Lawrence Brown, Harry Carney; (rear) Sonny Greer. (Photograph by Jack Towers, courtesy Ken Whitten Collection)

Duke Ellington and his Famous Orchestra. This 1941 photograph was taken just weeks before Jimmy Blanton was forced to leave the band with tuberculosis in October that year. (trombones, l to r) Juan Tizol, Joe 'Tricky Sam' Nanton, Lawrence Brown. (saxes, l to r) Johnny Hodges, Barney Bigard, Ben Webster, Otto Harwick, Harry Carney. (trumpets, l to r) Wallace Jones, Rex Stewart, Ray Nance. (rear) Sonny Greer. (front, l to r) Freddie Guy, Duke Ellington, Jimmy Blanton. (Ken Whitten Collection)

A break during a recording session at Fine Sound Studios, West 57th Street, New York. (l to r) Johnny Hodges standing behind **Duke Ellington**, Sam Woodyard, Cootie Williams, unknown trumpeter, Mercer Ellington. (Raymond Ross Photography, New York City)

A rare photograph from 1964 taken in Ellington's dressing room at Basin Street East in New York City of **Beatrice 'Evie' Ellis**, Ellington's companion from the spring of 1938 until his death in 1974. Despite Ellington's frequent affairs, 'Evie' remained loyal to Ellington, with whom she shared his New York apartment.
(Raymond Ross Photography)

The Duke Ellington Band in rehearsal in the ballroom of a mid-town New York Hotel in the early sixties. The saxophone section (l to r): Harry Carney, Russell Procope, Johnny Hodges, Jimmy Hamilton, Paul Gonsalves. At rear (l to r): Tom Whaley, Mercer Ellington, unknown, Ed Shaughnessy, Snooky Young, Stanley Dance, Billy Strayhorn. (Raymond Ross Photography, New York)

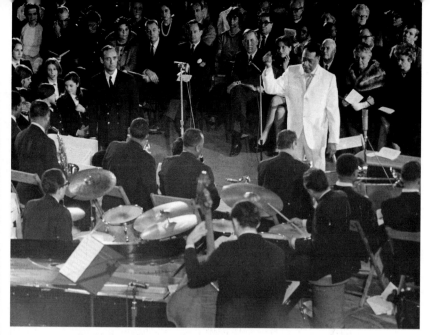

Above: **Duke Ellington** conducts his Second Sacred Concert in the Cathedral of St John the Divine, 112th Street and Amsterdam, New York City on 19 January 1968. The second drummer with Sam Woodyard is Steve Little. Les Jeunes Choir, to the upper left of the photograph, was directed by Roscoe Gill, facing the camera alongside Ellington. (Raymond Ross Photography, New York)

Below: A scene from Duke Ellington's funeral in the Cathedral of St John the Divine in New York City on 27 May 1974. Over 10,000 mourners filled the church, while the service was relayed to 2,500 outside. (Raymond Ross Photography, New York City)

Edward Kennedy Ellington. Quite simply one of the most important figures in twentieth-century music, caught during a break in rehearsals for *A Concert of Sacred Music* in New York, 1966. (Raymond Ross Photography, New York City)

horn was like a little monster, 'Don't let him get away with that!' I'll tell you what [Duke] did. He's never lost for words, no matter what the situation is, so he eventually made a reply. He says: 'Well, James, you know this is not like a recording date where you can go and re-record or patch over. You have to know the score, in case someone is missing. You will have to know what to do next or where to tell the band to go.' And I couldn't argue with that point, you know. And he taught me that, but in such a way. He was a strange type of teacher. Then of course, we had the Alvin Ailey Dancers, Talley Beatty Dancers and the Irving Bunton choir and our principals I mentioned before and Bunny Briggs. It was a fantastic show. Ill advertised, and it just caught on by word of mouth. It ran for three weeks, only booked for three weeks.[4]

DUKE ELLINGTON: Only about a minute of social protest is written into its script, because while this aspect warrants notice, it unfairly tends to overshadow the continuing contribution of the Negro to American life. *My People* is definitely not political. It has social significance, but the accent [is] on entertainment.[5]

VARIETY: The Production didn't jell as a unified whole.[6]

DUKE ELLINGTON: You can do something from purely the entertainment level. You take *My People* or *Jump for Joy*, there were a million laughs in both of them. If you're going to have a show on the stage I think it has got to have the dramatic content and I think if you are clever enough then you can say all you want to say as far as social significance is concerned without getting up on the soap box and actually doing it. You can see a cat on the corner of 125th Street who is screaming the stuff, but it isn't entertainment. If it goes on the stage it should be entertainment, no matter what you say. We send them out of the hall, the theatre, on our closing number 'What Colour is Love? What Colour is Virtue?' which is a big question. If you answer the question, it says everything you want to say.[7]

My People, *with its subtle racial message, was out of tune with the prevailing mood of Black social protest in America as the Civil Rights movement brought issues to a boil with their unequivocal demands for racial equality. With lukewarm press notices, the production had difficulty filling the 5,000 seat Arie Crown Theatre twice a day, but it played its full run until 2 September. But of the anticipated 800,000 visitors to the Century of Negro Progress Exhibition, only 100,000 turned up.*

MERCER ELLINGTON: Ellington, when he did My People, not only constructed the lighting and everything else on stage, he painted the sets. I wish I could get my hands on it – he painted the sets and drew out the whole. Everything was done exactly as he wanted it, which is why he enjoyed that show, plus it was dedicated to his main man, Martin Luther King.[8]

MARIAN LOGAN: I introduced him to Dr Martin Luther King, standing on a windy corner on Michigan Avenue in Chicago.[9]

MERCER ELLINGTON: He adored Martin [Luther King]. He thought he was one of the few real people who were involving in matters that count.[10]

DUKE ELLINGTON: In order for him to say hello to me, he had to have his chauffeur stop this long Cadillac. An aide got out and opened the door, and two motor policemen in front and two more behind had to stop so that he could shake hands with me. This is the way the man lives and travels who is representing that oppressed race.[11]

MARIAN LOGAN: Martin is sitting in his limousine and he looks up and he sees Edward and jumps out of the car, and he runs over to him and they embrace like they were old friends ... [Edward] said let's go over to McCormick Place, where Strayhorn was rehearsing the cast [of *My People*]. He said: 'Strays, put on Bam.' And they come out with 'King Fit the Battle of 'Bam', which was King fought the battle of Birmingham, and that was the song that Edward had written. Martin was very moved.[12]

DUKE ELLINGTON: You got 20,000,000 negroes, every negro give one day's pay. £100,000,000. All this bullshit, they had the biggest parade in the world, ever, all these people – everybody who went to Washington that day [28 August 1963], instead of spending $50 or $100, all they do is just give $5. You'd have $1,000,000. This is very simple, simple arithmetic. Anybody who gets involved in all this high-powered bullshit you know, about these demonstrations and all that, they get their pictures in the paper, and it's great they get on television, but fuck it. The cause stands still. They show 200,000 people marching up and down The Mall in Washington, so you know what the final act is? A cracker standing up there saying, 'If they want to walk with those people, let them go.' He's the star of the fucking show, he closes the bill! Nothing, if you've got no fucking money, how you're going to buy somebody without money? I told them once, I told them helluva long time ago – they told me I didn't know what I was doing and I should go play my music. It's the only way, you've got to have $100,000,000. If they had $100,000,000 when I told them to get it, they would have had it three years later. I told them in 1951. How much would $100,000,000 be worth today? . . . It pays all your expenses and you still got your principal. The only people who did any good out of the goddamn parade was the people who owned businesses in Washington, the hotels, and all that, they had a fucking ball, put all the fucking money in their pockets. To begin with, let's take, for instance, the propaganda. It was helluva demonstration, the biggest demonstration in the world, but anything they do *after* that is anti-climactic, it's too big to follow, what else can they do? How can you do your best number and follow it? This is simple dramatics, this is a kind of thing you think of in a high school play. You don't have to be no master-mind to figure that out.[13]

DON GEORGE: Intellectually he didn't agree with the way the civil rights situation was being handled. He didn't really believe in the marching and the suffering and the killing. He watched it on television sometimes and said, 'Those cats are crazy.' On the other hand he had such admiration for Martin Luther King, Jr.[14]

Ellington had spent a hectic two months with his involvement in My People, *a period made even more frantic by a commission he had received from the Stratford, Ontario, Shakespearean Festival to provide musical accompaniment for their production of* Timon of Athens, *performed at the Festival Theatre in Stratford, Ontario, on 20 July 1963.*

DUKE ELLINGTON: While I was doing *My People* I was also writing the background music for the Stratford, Ontario, production of *Timon of Athens*, a Shakespearean classic directed by Mike Lingham. This show went to England and played the Chichester Festival, February 1964.[15]

VARIETY: [The] music for ballroom ballet is catchy and otherwise unobtrusively appropiate.[16]

During a brief layoff on 3, 4 and 5 September 1963, both Johnny Hodges and Paul Gonsalves took the opportunity of recording albums of their own. On 6 September the band assembled at Idlewild Airport to embark on a tour of the Near and Middle East and India under the auspices of the US State Department.

LAWRENCE BROWN: The State Department tours were sponsored by the State Department, so they were more – oh, I wouldn't say luxurious – you had the best treatment. You had nice hotels. You didn't have to get out and fend for yourself, you know, getting a hotel. And the food and everything, we had just about the best you could get and we did a lot of sight seeing. We very seldom had one a day concert. It was two a day. So you get up in the morning, you made the plane to the next place. You got there, checked into the hotel, had dinner, went to the first concert at six or something and after that little intermission did a second concert. You went home and went to bed and got up the next morning to go again. So it wasn't too enjoyable that way, but on the Middle East tour you didn't work quite that way. It was more leisurely and you got to see quite a few things.[17]

HARRY CARNEY: September 9th 1963. Damascus, Syria. We enjoyed a swell flight with stops in Rome, Istanbul and Ankara arriving in Damascus Saturday 9:45 p.m. Sunday 10:30 a.m. at Ambassador's home, The Honourable Ridgway B. Knight. Brunch at home of Mr and Mrs Amos, Director USIS Library. At 6 p.m. left for home of Mr and Mrs John H. Tobler, Counsellor for Economic affairs for cocktails and cook-out. Very Fabulous! Monday. In the Main Square a banner saying 'Welcome Duke Ellington to Damascus' in English and Arabic – also across hotel front. At 10 a.m. Strayhorn and I were taken on a grand sightseeing tour by Ghassan Ramadan, one of the foremost record and music enthusiasts, who afterwards took us to his home for coffee, and he played some Mingus, Cannonball along with Ellington. Our first concert 4:30 in the very modern theatre at Damascus Fair which started August 27th and runs for twenty-seven days. Duke of course felt out the audience and we wound up with great enthusiasm and chants of 'Duke Ellington'. Off on Tuesday and Wednesday another concert same place. Tuesday: Ambassador's reception – in honour of the band.[18]

DUKE ELLINGTON: I remember we were in Kabul, and we were playing this concert. First of all you figure out, you say well, I wonder if these people have ever heard of us before, I wonder if they've heard of 'Mood Indigo' because they've got their own thing going out there, and it's good too. I used to ride around all night long and listen to the records they were playing in the cafés and things. And along about halfway through the concert you'd see almost the entire audience rise and start walking. This is a little frightening. And you look around and there's nobody to tell you anything, this is outdoors, in a field. And then they come back, later. And then you find out what they did they got up at that point because that was when they had to go face east and pray, but you don't know why – a funny feeling![19]

Ellington's stay in Kabul was from 18 to 20 September 1963.

HARRY CARNEY: September 24th 1963. New Delhi, India. Concert tonight being held at Vigyan Bhavan which, according to the opinion of so many, must be really a fine place to play. Yesterday visited Bharatiya Kala Kendra with Duke, Sweetpea and Procope. The people performed on various instruments, gave solo dances as well as ballet 'Kumar Sambhav'. A fascinating and informative visit. The band played in the evening for students, pros, press and radio. At 6:30 p.m. Triveni Garden. There for lecture, demo of music concerning history of Ellington and changes in forms of jazz. [Drummer] Sam W. [Woodyard] is a big smash hit. They really dig rhythm.[20]

DUKE ELLINGTON: Those Indian press cats, at a press conference, I'm totally aware of the fact that out in that part of the world they're going to throw in a couple of communist boys to upset me, you know, they always get back on that race situation in America.[21]

LAWRENCE BROWN: Mostly you were associated with the USIS representative and Americans that were over there in other capacities, not too many local people because they couldn't talk to you, number one, and so you stayed more or less to yourself, there wasn't time to really get around.[22]

DUKE ELLINGTON: When the guy asked me – he was a great communist and supervisor when we were out on the State Department tour – he said: 'Why, if the United States Government was so great, why didn't they subsidize the artists?' And I says, 'Why? I don't know why they don't, but I know damn well sure I wouldn't want to be subsidized by anybody in the Government of the United States or anybody else.' I said, 'To lose the thrill of the chase and the competition that goes with this free enterprise, you lose a hell of a lot more than money, because if somebody is going to subsidize me they're going to tell me how much to spend, because I can't spend any more than they can give me. And if my drive and so forth is greater than another guy's then I'm entitled to earn more and spend more. If I was subsidized I would lay around, get fat, uninspired, work up to a quota, make a showing and flop the rest of the time off. What are you working for? Work your arse off and have nothing to show for it afterwards? I work, work and work and if I don't there's a guy across the street who will.'[23]

HARRY CARNEY: New Delhi, India. Just left Duke in hospital. Duke has to remain here for at least one week. Very happy to report that otherwise everyone in the band is very co-operative and doing a grand job.[24]

DR ARTHUR LOGAN: I found him there physically in pretty good shape but pretty badly depressed: Edward said he had never seen such poverty.[25]

HARRY CARNEY: October 8th 1963. Madras, India. Good news – Duke is joining us tonight in Bombay. Band has been doing great.[26]

LAWRENCE BROWN: And then we were down in the island of Ceylon. And that was something else, the storms and things, the rainstorms they have down there – sound like it's going to blow everything away. They call them monsoons, we had a couple of those.[27]

The band stayed in Colombo, Ceylon, from 13 to 26 October.

LAWRENCE BROWN: We were in Turkey when the news came. We had gone to bed in this hotel, and our agent, government agent, came around and knocked on the door and said, 'We're leaving, they've assassinated the President.' So tomorrow, next day we got together and left. But one thing, the whole country seemed to close up in commemoration of the President, they really observed that incident.[28]

President John F. Kennedy was shot in Elm Street, Dallas, Texas, outside the Texas School Book Depository Building at 12:30 p.m. on Friday, 22 November 1963. Mortally wounded, he was rushed to Parkland Hospital, Dallas, where he was pronounced dead at 1 p.m.

MARIAN LOGAN: Edward was beside being beside himself. The whole tour was strange and now the President went and died on him. He had a big problem with death – not just his own, but anybody's. He couldn't deal with it.[29]

The tour was cancelled before the scheduled concert on 22 November 1963 in Ankara, Turkey, where the band remained before flying out on the 28th.

DUKE ELLINGTON: In the Far East where there are billions of people, a very, very tiny percentage of them have even heard of the word jazz, or know anything about it, so we can't depend on the word, we can't depend on anything. You just have to go out and you do a performance, and if performance is believable they respond. If it's acrobatic they respond, if it's sensuous they respond, and that's all we can depend on. The name doesn't mean anything.[30]

JOHNNY HODGES: Duke Ellington was impressed [with that tour], he wrote a suite about it, the 'Far East Suite'. Very little escapes him, he gets his ideas from everything he sees and hears.[31]

DUKE ELLINGTON: The tour was a great adventure for us on what is indeed the other side of the world. Sometimes I felt it was *this* world upside down. The look of the natural country is so unlike ours and the very contours of the earth seem to be different ... you let it roll around and undergo a chemical change and then seep out on paper in the form that will suit the musicians who are going to play it.[32]

'Far East Suite' was subsequently recorded in December 1966.

DUKE ELLINGTON: The whole time, that whole twelve weeks tour [of the Far East] I never saw a boy and a girl hold hands![33]

In February 1964, Ellington embarked upon his third tour of Europe in the space of twelve months. He opened at the Royal Festival Hall in London on 15 February, where tenor saxophonist Paul Gonsalves was indisposed.

MELODY MAKER: Tubby Hayes found himself yanked from a comfortable seat in the audience, his tenor – rushed from the Ronnie Scott club by taxi – thrust in his hand, and deposited into the greatest saxophone team in jazz. In a situation typical of the disciplinary nonchalance which surrounds the Ellington orchestra, Britain's top tenorist was deputizing for the unwell Paul Gonsalves, faced with legendary Ducal scores, half myth, half notated. If Tubby felt a bit apprehensive as he scanned the music for 'Perdido' it didn't show. After two storming solo choruses in 'The Opener', everything was swinging. Sam Wood-yard leaned across from behind his drum kit to shake Tubby's hand, Jimmy Hamilton smiled his approval and even impassive Hodges was seen to be moved. Duke added his approval by stomping into the blues for another round of Tubby's tenor and the audience went wild.[34]

PETE KING: [Tubby] was the supreme musician and appearing with the Duke without rehearsal wouldn't phase him one little bit. I had a seat in the front on the opening concert and watched him sail through the arrangements. I was very proud of him, and many of the audience were ecstatic.[35]

TUBBY HAYES: While I waited for my tenor, Billy Strayhorn put the music in order for me. The band went on and started the programme without Paul or me. Then the horn arrived and I crept out on stage feeling pretty terrible ... Duke made his announcement, then he called 'Perdido', which didn't exactly help. And Jimmy Hamilton said, 'Don't worry looking, there's no part for that!' Well, we got through that. There were a few others without parts for me, including 'Rockin' In Rhythm' in which the reeds went down the front for a featured passage. Being an Ellington admirer I had some idea of how most of the things went. As far as 'Rockin'' was concerned, Carney had the lead on clarinet and so I doubled the melody an octave down and it seemed to be all right ... and so it went on. So that was a terrific experience, and when Duke asked me to do the second concert as well I was knocked out. One thing I'll never forget is sitting down at the end of the band and looking back along that line of saxophones: Hamilton, Hodges, Carney, Procope. Man, it was beautiful.[36]

MERCER ELLINGTON: The one who ruled the saxophone section was Johnny Hodges. In fact, Johnny would actually demand that there would only be a certain amount of solos given to any saxophone player because he wanted the lion's share of practically anything that was being done. Harry Carney was not a part of the sax team [for the purposes of this] because Harry Carney was too much a friend of Duke Ellington to allow Johnny to do that to him . . . He was very adamant about what was his, if you were aware of the way the presentations of the band took place, Johnny never played anything the first half, the second half he would play three or four numbers back to back. I swear this is what happened – Johnny had Paul [Gonsalves] relegated to the throwaway part of the concert. Paul's solos always took place at the beginning of a concert. We would open up with 'A Train' or whatever, then it would be Paul for one or two numbers, that was all, and you hardly hear from Paul any more in the concert. The last big thing that was worth anything, that you knew of or heard was Johnny Hodges! There was all kinds of chicanery![37]

DAILY MAIL: BBC-2, which starts tomorrow, may have a pack of experiments lined up for the future, but they're playing it safe – and cool – with the Duke Ellington Orchestra on Tuesday at 9:40.[38]

Ellington's hour-long programme televised on 21 April 1964 (videotaped during his February tour of the UK) was shown at a peak viewing spot to inaugurate BBC TV's new UHF station using the new 625-line format, BBC-2. The programme was the first in the famous 'Jazz 625' series that documented a wide range of jazz musicians in the 1960s. Sadly, the BBC never followed through with this highly acclaimed series, and by the 1990s their coverage of jazz was non-existent, the Corporation obsessed with audience ratings, despite its public service remit.

PERRY WATKINS: I think Billy's illness upset [Ellington]. I know it did, because I was on the road with the band. We did twenty-seven gigs in thirty-one days and we really had no time to think very much, and during that time the news of Billy's illness came.[39]

In early 1964, Dr Arthur Logan diagnosed cancer in Billy Strayhorn's throat.

MARIAN LOGAN: Arthur said, 'Edward is terribly, terribly angry. I think he blames me. "How can you tell me this? Do you know what you're saying? Why didn't you tell me this before?" I said, "I just diagnosed him." '[40]

BILLY STRAYHORN: Edward told me not to worry about a thing.[41]

DUKE ELLINGTON: Strayhorn is a *good* piano player. I'm just a jive piano player. I'm the same thing I was when I started out, in the days of the piano plunkers.[42]

REX STEWART: On stage, Duke projects an image of youthful exuberance which would do credit to a far younger man. While leading some of his bouncier tunes, he does a sort of go-go dance, his rhythmic movements cueing the musicians.[43]

DUKE ELLINGTON: I used to be a pretty good dancer at one time. I think it's very important a musician should dance. Of course, I don't do the Twist very violently myself. I know a few steps in the Latin-American dances too. I'm the type of ham who displays one or two Sunday-punch steps. When you get the audience, then you leave them! 'He's a great dancer,' they think, but what you did was your whole routine, dramatically paced to get favourable audience reaction![44]

AARON BELL: Many times on record dates, in order to get the right feeling, [Duke] would dance. He'd get in front of [drummer] Sam Woodyard and set him to a certain kind of dance to help Sam get whatever he wanted, and how he wanted it. He really was a genius. He knew how to get whatever he wanted and he always knew what he wanted.[45]

JOHNNY HODGES: I was surprised by Japan, everybody was so nice over there, and they went for jazz so much. Japanese musicians they're on the ball too. We had a chance to see the country and it wasn't hard at all.[46]

On 19 June 1964 Ellington began a tour of Japan that took in eighteen concerts, ending in Tokyo's Koseinenkin Kaikan Hall on 11 July.

BOB UDKOFF: Duke worked for Disney on Disneyland and did have dinner with him one night. [Disney] used to have an apartment over the Fire Station, and he commissioned Duke to take the music from *Mary Poppins* and set it into his form – as he put it – he commissioned it, gave him a sum of money and said, 'I don't care if we sell one record, I just want to hear what you're going to do with it!'[47]

JOHNNY HODGES: I like the *Mary Poppins* album too. I was surprised with that. We made 'A Spoonful of Sugar' that I had to play. When we made this sort of thing, we didn't know what we were doin', just figuring we'd run two minutes of this and two minutes of that and when it was released it sounded completely different.[48]

Mary Poppins was recorded on 6–9 September 1964 in Chicago.

At the end of 1964, Ellington's son Mercer, now in his mid-forties, joined the band as its manager. He was also asked to bring his instrument and was soon playing in the trumpet section.

MERCER ELLINGTON: Pop had never asked me to do anything for him before. I would rather have stayed where I was [as a disc jockey at Radio WLIB] but all my life he had taken care of me ... I was glad to do something. In a sense Ellington was very possessive and saw to it I never got too far from his sphere. I'd wander, but not too far. I guess you don't want to go away really, you just don't want to be taken for granted.[49]

MERCER ELLINGTON: If he needed a road manager, work which I detested doing, and I knew I could do it well, the one thing I wanted to do was to have a job that I did, and the deal I made was that I would keep his books and take care of arguing and fighting with the men and arguing with him, provided I made some advance in my own playing, trumpet playing.[50]

MERCER ELLINGTON: It was a very difficult band to handle. The problems of habits of drunkenness and all that were very slight in comparison to one other that I had to face. I had Johnny Hodges, Harry Carney, Cootie Williams and Lawrence Brown. In the thirties these were the people who took me to the beach, hold me by the hand, take me to the movies, buy me lollipops, whatever. And suddenly I was in a position wherein I had to ask them to be on-stage at a certain time, get up when they were sleepy, get on the bus when it was time to leave and so forth. That was the most difficult part of the job, was to go back to these people who you knew loved you and to scream and holler at them and insult them. You know, I could get them to do it, but it called for some very stringent things in order to get them to do it. And I had to sacrifice our relationship in order to get the job done.[51]

MERCER ELLINGTON: One of the things that happened when I came in, I physically had to fight off, throw people in the band – irritate them, do anything I could to get rid of the bunch [who were taking drugs]. Because we had got to a place where the band had become so involved with a lot of them who weren't taking their lives seriously and were causing problems for Ellington, we couldn't get a hotel in Boston. Not one hotel would accept the Duke Ellington Orchestra because they had people who were either outlandish as a result of drugs, or who had broken into different closets and stolen stuff, who had gone out of windows to keep from paying the rent. And so finally we got an orchestra together where we didn't have to worry about it. What I did to keep them from sneaking out of hotels without paying the rent, I started going to the hotel every time and checking everyone out and whatever bills they had left, I charged it to their salary and deducted it from the money they had coming at the end of it. So we finally squelched that.[52]

MERCER ELLINGTON: Ellington wouldn't ever say I'm lonesome or let's talk. That would demonstrate a point of weakness. So sometimes, in the middle of the night, he'd call me up from his hotel room, start an argument and in the middle of it say, 'Well, bring your ledger down here – let me take a look at it.' So I'd go over to his room and in the middle of looking at the numbers, he'd say, 'Do you want some coffee or something?' Having gotten me over there he would transpose the argument into a social situation.[53]

MERCER ELLINGTON: I never became someone with the ability to play Ellington's music until I was a member of the orchestra, because the sound you hear when you're inside the orchestra is completely different to what you hear when you're outside and I got to know the workings of the different sections and so forth.[54]

DUKE ELLINGTON: I wouldn't have thought we would have done as well without Ray Nance as we've done.[55]

Nance left Ellington for good, after what amounted to a 25-year association, in June 1965.

In June 1965, Ellington's nomination for a Pulitzer Prize 'for the vitality and originality of his total productivity' was rejected, resulting in the resignation of two of the three-person committee.

DUKE ELLINGTON: Fate's being kind to me. Fate doesn't want me to be too famous too young.[56]

DUKE ELLINGTON: What else *could* I have said? In the first place, I never do give any thought to prizes. I work and I write, and that's it. My reward is hearing what I've done, and unlike most composers, I can hear it immediately. That's why I keep these expensive gentlemen with me. And secondly, I'm hardly sur-

CHARLES H. LOCKIER
by arrangement with
HAROLD DAVISON
and NORMAN GRANZ
presents

DUKE ELLINGTON

AND HIS FAMOUS ORCHESTRA

COLSTON HALL · BRISTOL
ONE PERFORMANCE ONLY   Manager: F. K. COWLEY   ONE DAY ONLY
FRIDAY, 19th FEBRUARY at 7.30
TICKETS   20/-   17/6   15/-   12/6   10/6   8/6   6/6
From Charles H. Lockier Ltd., 29/31 Queen's Road, Bristol 8 (Tel. 2-3885) & Colston Hall (Tel. 2-1768)

prised that my kind of music is still without, let us say, official honour at home. Most Americans still take it for granted that European music – classical music, if you will – is the only respectable kind. I remember, for example, that when Franklin Roosevelt died, practically no American music was played on the air in tribute to him. We were given a dispensation, I must admit. We did one radio programme dedicated to him. But by and large, then as now, jazz was like the kind of man you wouldn't want your daughter to associate with.[57]

DUKE ELLINGTON: Reverend Canon Yaryan and Dean Bartlett came down to a little place we were playing in Redwood City, and they knew all about me and the religious songs I had done and couple of shows and also in 'Black, Brown and Beige' and of course they had heard Mahalia Jackson sing a couple of them, and that didn't do any harm either, and they said that they would like for me to do a Sacred Concert up at the Grace Cathedral in San Francisco. And this, of course, knocked me completely out and I said, 'Well, look, wait a minute, I have to think. I have to think because this is quite a thing.' You say, well, I'm going to go up in this beautiful cathedral and make my kind of noise and this has to be right, because when you play or say something in a church you can't be acting, you've got to mean what you say because you never know what's going to fall on you if you don't. So anyway I called them back in about a month, and I said, 'OK, I'm ready, let's do it.' So they booked it up.[58]

DUKE ELLINGTON: They were very, very specific about it, saying it should be written totally in my character, the way I wanted to do it, it didn't make any difference – I didn't have to copy any format or anything, to be performed as a big mass and they would like for me to be there and do it, in San Francisco, up on top of the hill, in the big cathedral. There have been two or three 'Jazz Masses', they call them 'Jazz Mass', I heard one that was done in England and it was done by a priest, he wrote it, and it was like a hotel jazz band music with a choir. And they said some of the things from *My People* should be included. And it should be done, take a quotation from the Bible, I'd love to do it! I have a wonderful idea for one of them, the first four words, 'In the Beginning God'. Nothing else. All these other things happen after that.[59]

DUKE ELLINGTON: After [Strayhorn] got sick I was doing the Sacred Concert music, I was up in California, or Vegas or somewhere, and he was in hospital in New York and I called him up because the doctor said keep his mind busy, don't let him sit around and think. So I told him what I was doing, the title of the Sacred Concert is the first four words in the Bible, 'In the Beginning God', six syllables, take it and make it into an introduction, or an interlude or establish a theme, and he did, he did it for male voices, brass section and whatever, the funny thing was the theme. His theme started on the same note as mine, it started on F, and ended a tenth above, on A-flat, and out of the six notes only two of them differed. Nothing like Billy Strayhorn![60]

DUKE ELLINGTON: Once you get involved and you come up with things, and they open their eyes, and they say, 'Where did you get that?' or something like that. You don't know where you got it, it just came, like a line, 'Heaven to be is just the ultimate degree.' Discussing heaven you say well, when you get to heaven, that's the opportunity of employing all the sense you didn't know you had, in the sense of positive sensitivities, the joy.[61]

MERCER ELLINGTON: When we did our first Sacred Concert, we rehearsed most of the music in and around Reno, on the way to San Francisco. He was flying back and forth, and he had a guy who was the choral director directing the choir in Los Angeles.

He had a copyist working in New York, so we never really heard the first episode until we performed it. Throughout his life he was cryptic and he never let the right hand know what the left hand was doin' because he always liked the idea of showing surprise. In his words, 'The mystery of the business must always be preserved.'[62]

A Concert of Sacred Music *was premiered at Grace Cathedral, San Francisco, on 16 September 1965.*

LOUIE BELLSON: [Duke] asked me to sit in at the Grace Cathedral in San Francisco for his first Sacred Concert. He said, 'I want you to play a drum solo in church. You are thunder and lightning.' That's what I thought about when I soloed at the end of 'David Danced Before the Lord', while the band played and a choir chanted and all hell broke loose.[63]

RUTH ELLINGTON: I do know that he had read the Bible through four times by the time he was thirty, he used to, out on the road, put a pillow on the floor and say his prayers all the time.[64]

MERCER ELLINGTON: There was only two things in his life, his music and his ladies. That was it.[65]

JIMMY LYONS: Duke Ellington had his grandma groupies. He attracted them at twelve and eighty-five. Dressed to kill. Made-up, you know, like it was Christmas night. Came back to see their idol. Beehives and blue hair. He would kiss their hands, he would wear you out with all that.[66]

MERCER ELLINGTON: There were women, usually widows whose husbands had been fans of the band, who had become emotionally attached to him and sexually involved. Some ladies divorced their husbands or broke up their marriages because of him.[67]

DUKE ELLINGTON: The girls that impress you are the ones you pursue. The difference between not being grown-up and grown-up is when you're not grown-up you're pursuing a girl that

THE PROTESTANT COUNCIL
OF THE CITY OF NEW YORK
AND

THE FIFTH AVENUE
PRESBYTERIAN CHURCH

PRESENT

a concert of

sacred music

BY

duke ellington

SUNDAY, DECEMBER 26, 1965
NEW YORK CITY
EIGHT O'CLOCK AND MIDNIGHT

doesn't want to do it to you. When you're grown up, you find the girls want to do it more than you do.[68]

RUTH ELLINGTON: I think Edward regarded women as flowers, each one lovely in their own way, and they absolutely adored him, it was shocking! I couldn't believe it, absolutely shocking! The way the women fell on their faces in front of him, you know?[69]

DON GEORGE: As time went on Duke became more careless about his inflagrante delictos, and they came more and more to the attention of Evie, who was a lady of deep passions that were impossible for her to subdue at times.[70]

REX STEWART: Many of the lovely ladies upon whom Duke cast an approving eye, and then heaped exquisite compliments have succumbed. The number of conquests is uncountable.[71]

DUKE ELLINGTON: We entered my place. I always lock the door so if I get lucky I wouldn't have to retrace my steps and possibly allow for a cooling of period and be compelled to rekindle the fire of desire in my prey. She was a fragile bit of femininity as ever I'd seen. Such gentility, such poise. There she was in my pad and I lumbered around like the sophisticate of sophisticates making wise in the eyes like those guys in the cigarette ads, I thought as worldly as worldly. After all I was a musician and had done over half the one-nighters in the USA. How much more worldly can you get and you know what chicks like her who had never been very far from home think of musicians. Experience has taught me that the sort of chick such as she, quiet when drinking, could be a thinking type chick. To all my approaches she countered with gentle diplomacy always allowing me time and space enough to get my foot back out of my mouth. Smiling she waited, apparently not on guard, for me to get myself organized for my next attack. If I speculated she was thinking just what she was thinking about she seemed to be enjoying some security, either from my advances or from the reassurance I would protect her from herself. She and I were alone, very pleasantly, agreeably indulging ourselves in intellectual conversation which always rises to the realms of sex. I, of course, insidiously guided and pursued this line until she was trapped and hooked where she wanted to be. Strong sense of respectability, she was taught from youth that a girl just does not – on her first date with a fellow. Lets her hair down, dropped her [dress], her starched petticoat and suddenly there I was.[72]

MERCER ELLINGTON: Women were his hobby, his leisure-time pursuit – this accounting for his expression 'Music is my Mistress'. Because it was really a cop-out when asked what his interests were, his out, and it became a very prolific expression![73]

While Ellington continued to maintain a joint residence with Evie, his most frequent companion in the latter years of his life was Fernanda de Castro Monte.

DON GEORGE: She was a tall, strikingly handsome, blonde lady who stood bold, with her boots and her suede pants and suede suits with slits at the side. She could be humble or forceful. Duke liked that. She knew people all over the world and was a great ambassador for him ... I have seldom been privileged to meet someone who looked like she did, or spoke so many languages, or was as bejewelled.[74]

DUKE ELLINGTON: I have a story. This guy was hittin' on a girl at this party, and she's a nice little girl and he pursues her, and she's nice and shy and modest and took it for granted he was being extremely flattering about the whole thing, she didn't allow him to touch her and so on, and so he kept on pursuing, pursuing throughout the length of the party, and the time came to go home and he said, 'Well, can I take you home?' and she said, 'Yes, of course.' They get outside and he starts to call a cab, and she says, 'Oh, no, no, don't do that, taxis are expensive, why don't we just take a walk.' He says fine, and so they're walking through the park, so the girl says, 'Isn't that a lovely setting there? That would make a wonderful picture, wouldn't it?' And he says, 'Yes, yes, yes. I've done quite a few things like that myself.' And she says, 'Oh really, are you an artist too?' 'Oh, yes, you bet.' And he says, 'Oh, where are your paintings?' And she says, 'Oh, at home.' He says, 'Why don't you let me come and see your paintings?' And so with that, the damn thing is switching, and she in a very naive sort of way is saying what normally would be expected for him to say, 'Come up and see my etchings!' And so they go, and he's inclined to be a bit of a wolf, and he goes in, makes certain the door is locked and takes the key and hides it, so she can't get out and all that kind of bullshit preparation. And they get in and he fixes a drink and they have a little moment of reflection, and no more is talked about the pictures they're supposed to see, and she takes a drink and sort of slinks into the corner and falls very helplessly, and he's going to pull his shoulders up and go for the real kill. He's going to give her the embrace of all embraces and when he gets there suddenly he realizes she is waiting for his ass, and she grabs this son-of-a-bitch and he realizes suddenly he is in the claws of a tigress! And then he begins to shake and he's terrified and he says, 'How can I get out, oh, oh,' and he forgot where he hid the key and he can't get out! That's it, and he's consumed! (laughs). That's *somebody's* true story! Must be![75]

DAN MORGENSTERN: I had planned to see Duke in concert here in New York, and the night before, I saw a musician friend (who will remain nameless) who had intended to go with me, but a job had come up and so he was unable to come with me. But since his girl friend wanted to see Duke we all agreed that I should escort her. We were sitting in the front row and when

Duke came out he saw me and smiled and waved, and saw my companion, who was a very attractive young lady, and from then on Duke was playing up to her, smiling his gracious smile at her, making announcements specifically to her and so forth. Well after, we went backstage and I introduced the girl to Duke, who immediately engaged her in conversation. I knew several of the guys in the band, Paul Gonsalves was a particular friend, and got talking to them. When it came time to go, she came up to me and said, 'Oh, I'll be going with Duke!' Well, she was over twenty-one, I just smiled, she knew I would be discreet, but I think had she been *my* girl friend, and Duke really didn't know whether she was or not, I think I would have been very cross with his behaviour, but that's what he was like when it came to women.[76]

JIMMY JONES: He called me to come out here to [Los Angeles] to do an album called *Ella at Duke's Place*. I was sitting at home and he was working out here on the West Coast at that point, and he says, 'I would like for you to come out and write some scores with me.' Just like that. The set-up was for me to go with Ellington, because Strayhorn was quite sick at that point and to pick up on Strayhorn's slack, so Duke wouldn't have so much on his back. But Norman Granz stole me away from him, which was financially lucky for me! Anyway, [for the album] he used 'Passion Flower', which was Strayhorn's, it was already there. She sang it. She was able to sing it in the key Johnny Hodges played it in. And then the Duke said 'Azure', and I did 'Calico Gown'. There were four things I did, I didn't do but four. Gerald [Wilson] brought a tune in.[77]

Ella at Duke's Place *was recorded in November 1965.*

DUKE ELLINGTON: Our programme always has some old stuff, some new stuff and, we hope, interesting stuff throughout, and, of course, the major purpose in all of these appearances is showing off the soloists.[78]

JOHNNY HODGES: You know you're going to play 'A Train', you know you're going to play 'Mood Indigo', you know you're going to play 'Sophisticated Lady', you know you're goin' to play 'Things Ain't What They Used To Be', 'I Got It Bad'. You know that's all comin'. I know I'm going to play 'All of Me' and 'Passion Flower', and that Duke will play his albums *Ellington '65* and *Ellington '66*. People want to hear them, and he has to put them in sometime, the first show or the second show, so you get all that up together and put it on your music stand.[79]

BILLY STRAYHORN: He has to play some of the Ellington standards because otherwise the audiences would be disappointed. But he'd much rather play the new things.[80]

MERCER ELLINGTON: He evolved a medley [of his hits] where he bunched them all up, and he got them all over in about ten minutes. 'I'm Beginning to See the Light', 'Mood Indigo' and it served another purpose because when it comes to ASCAP, you get so much for the numbers you perform, he had enough in there for them to be counted as performances, and so in ten minutes he had twenty tunes he had performed that he would get the dough for as far as ASCAP was concerned![81]

DUKE ELLINGTON: I find I have all these other lifetimes to compete with, and this is the hardest, because now I have to compete with an illusion that somebody has in their mental ear of what we played in 1927, someone else has an illusion of something else, and we have to compete with this and an illusion is very difficult to compete with.[82]

JIMMY JONES: There was one time in Basin Street East, you know they have a high bandstand there. Paul didn't come back from Third Avenue where that little bar was where they'd take the intermission. So Duke was playing with four saxophones, and I asked Strayhorn, 'Doesn't it bother Duke?' And Strayhorn says, 'Duke doesn't know that he's not there.'[83]

Ellington played Basin Street East 12 November through to 4 December 1965. The second headliner was Mel Tormé.

MEL TORMÉ: There are probably equal amounts of ego and status in the matter of billing. There is also one other factor: business. If, say, a club owner comes to New York with the idea of buying Mel Tormé for his bistro in Cleveland, shows up at Basin Street and finds that Mel is not genuinely headlining that prestigious musical venue, he is liable to do one of two things: refrain from buying Mel at all or alter his thinking on how much money he is willing to pay Tormé. In fairness to Duke he was fighting for the same thing I was. I commanded top billing everywhere else and had made my acceptance of this date conditional upon that clause in my contract. Duke had no clause – nothing of any kind. I guess when you are as big as Duke Ellington, you take it for granted that your position on the bill is automatically on top. I sat down and told him everything, including my earlier refusals to play New York unless I could come back headlining. My idol was cold and adamant. No sale. I left his dressing room broken-hearted and disillusioned. A columnist named Frank Farrell had written a column about the Ellington–Tormé squabble. My felicitous relationship with Duke Ellington had been badly damaged. I finally, unhappily gave in. Duke had his top billing. Months later in a foreign country, who should I run into in the lobby of a foreign hotel but Duke and his entire band. He beamed, gave me a bear hug, kissed me on the cheek and said, 'Hey, baby. Love you madly.'[84]

On 24 January 1966, Ellington embarked on a tour of Europe and the United Kingdom that ended on 25 February. On several Continental dates the band was joined by Ella Fitzgerald and her trio – Jimmy Jones on piano, Joe Comfort on bass and Gus Johnson on drums.

JIMMY JONES: There was a time when we were in Italy, and this was Ella, Ella Fitzgerald and Duke Ellington. So I'm conducting the band from the piano [while Ella did her set] and I could see Paul to my left. He was – well, he was feeling pretty good that night. And they had a big television show going on. They were televising this thing. And in the middle of our set, we would use the trio – put in some ballads – then go back to band. And I could see this leg coming off Paul's chair. But I'm watching Ella out in front, because I've got to watch her. And I saw Paul begin to lean over and lean over and he was going. And he fell on the floor, and you know what he did when he got up? He looked out into the audience and said, 'Shhhh, don't tell nobody!' And the television cameras were all over the stage and Ella Fitzgerald had to stop singing because the audience broke up laughing! And then, on the intermission between shows, he says, 'Man, did you see where I dropped my horn?' I said, 'You fell on the floor, man, you did more than dropping your horn.' He thought he'd dropped his horn![85]

ED ANDERSON: I saw him get very mad at Paul Gonsalves one night in Europe, boomf! At which point he fired him from the band and he told him to get his ticket and go home and he didn't never want to see him again, and, of course, then next night Paul is on the stand again, playing with the band.[86]

FBI FILE 100–434443: EDWARD KENNEDY (DUKE) ELLINGTON: Information has been received that bandleader Duke Ellington would appear with James Forman, Student Non-Violent Co-ordinating Committee, on a programme sponsored by the United Ministers on Texas Southern University campus in October, 1966. Forman was to speak on the theme, 'Black Power: A New Religion?'[87]

DUKE ELLINGTON: Stop and think of the way Southern congressmen and senators tie up Congress with filibusters and delaying tactics against the passage of civil rights measures to protect minorities from persecution ... when they [the minorities] are at the same time being insulted, policed and spied upon by congressional committees, the FBI, the American Legion, the White Citizens Councils and everybody else.[88]

RUTH ELLINGTON: I remember one instance when he was receiving the press ... and one of the black writers said to him, 'What do you think of the Black is Beautiful Movement?' He said, 'I wrote "Black Beauty" in 1928.' So the reporter said, 'Yessir, Mr Ellington!' And that was the end of that.[89]

DUKE ELLINGTON: Every time you walk out on to the street and you're exposed to a white citizen you're acting on behalf of the race, you are *supposed* to command respect for the race whatever you do. This has not been taught, this has not been organized and seen to. For Chrissake every time somebody does something good, ten arseholes go out and do something bad, so what? So you're fucked.[90]

DUKE ELLINGTON: I never have problems that interfere with me having problems.[91]

DUKE ELLINGTON: You pick up the paper and all these rapes, and all this bullshit, they're people who have come up from down South. They took a Cadillac car from two women, two society women over in New Jersey. They come out of Georgia just thirty days before that, working in a garage. These people should be screened, somebody has to tell these people what the job is to be done and how it should be done. Everybody should play their part, not everybody just going for themselves. A lot of this was promoted by the White Citizens Committee, the people who put out this sheet, you never saw one of those papers? One of those tabloids they put out once a week, they have all sorts of things, all sorts of lies, I saw them when I was down in Albany, Georgia – 'Do you realize that negroes are grabbing white women in Washington right in the street and raping them?' and all that sort of shit. I mean, just fiction. And so the negroes down there think it's happening, they don't know better, so they come up, they feel their obligation to join the race.[92]

Edna Ellington contracted cancer in December 1965. After numerous operations she died in January 1967 at St Barnabus Hospital, New York, where she had been for thirteen months. From Italy, Duke Ellington cabled a tribute to his wife of fifty-two years, 'She loved life. She was a woman of virtue and beauty. She would never lie. God bless her.'

MERCER ELLINGTON: Immediately I made up my mind I would be near [my mother]. Even though she had lost her voice many months ago, we could still communicate. We understood each other and I wanted to be near should she regain consciousness. While she never did, I am glad I was near at the end and to sustain me was her nurse and friend of many years, Edith Junior. Mother was my favourite and I was hers. May she rest in peace.[93]

MERCER ELLINGTON: I don't know if there was some sort of fiendish glee that he got out of getting a man to really mess up, one case he outdid himself and he was the sorriest of everybody who was involved. We had Bobby Durham as a drummer for the band. He used to ride Bobby, I don't know what it was about Bobby, he was determined to really get this man to bend to his will or change his mind or somethin'. That was what was wrong with him. Finally he fired – one of the few people – he fired Bobby Durham. He said, 'Where did you get that drummer from?' I said, 'You make him so mad you haven't heard him yet.' Anyhow, he fired Bobby. Bobby didn't give a damn. He stopped trying to impress Duke Ellington and relaxed and played what he played and that was it. And [Ellington] said,

'How come he never played like that before?' And then he told me to get him back. He hadn't been out that band ten minutes before he was hired by Oscar Peterson!![94]

One of the few musicians other than Charles Mingus to be fired by Ellington, Durham joined the band on 28 March 1967 and left in May or June that year.

BOB UDKOFF: Billy had a great relationship with Lena Horne and when he was sick he stayed with Lena out in Palm Springs. And I went out to visit him one day and she just treated him like a baby, he just couldn't swallow, he had a tube, because his oesophagus had gone, but she was wonderful to him.[95]

LENA HORNE: He couldn't do much anymore. He hadn't mentioned anything about what he wanted to do now – he knew he was dying. We didn't have to talk about it.[96]

MARIAN LOGAN: [Strayhorn] didn't write anymore after 'Blood Count'. That was the last thing he had to say. And it wasn't 'Good-bye', or 'Thank-you' or anything phoney like that.[97]

BOB UDKOFF: It really tore Duke up when Strayhorn died. He called me, talked to my wife, when he heard. It was imminent – Strayhorn had cancer of the oesophagus and there was very little they could do for him, Duke called and said, 'Billy's gone.' And I said, 'Would you like for us to come on up?' He says, 'It's always nice to have people you love near you.' He didn't say, 'Come up' – that's his way. So we got on a plane, he was up in Reno, and when I got there Mercer was on the floor below and Duke was still sleeping, about three, four o'clock in the afternoon. And I contacted Mercer, went up to his room, and Mercer says, 'I heard him walking all night, what happened?' I said, 'Well, Strayhorn died.' He just said, 'Oooh!' He hadn't called Mercer![98]

At 4.45 a.m. on 31 May 1967 Billy Strayhorn died.

DUKE ELLINGTON: Oh, man. I was knocking my head against the wall. My sister called me at the time of death, and I decided that instead of knocking my head against the wall I just started thinking things, I was thinking them, I picked up a pencil and started writing about him, and it turned out to be a very good eulogy. But that was it, boy. It was a knockout. Because who can replace him, nobody like Strayhorn.[99]

MARIAN LOGAN: Arthur said Edward just cried. He said, 'This is too much for me Arthur.' And he just cried. Arthur said, 'Are you going to be all right?' And Edward said, 'Fuck no, I'm not going to be all right. Nothing is all right now.'[100]

DUKE ELLINGTON: [Strayhorn's] greatest virtue, I think, was his honesty – not only to others but to himself.[101]

MERCER ELLINGTON: It was a big blow to the old man. He couldn't accept any kind of misfortune. He couldn't accept that Strayhorn wasn't there anymore.[102]

LAWRENCE BROWN: [Strayhorn] was the genius, the power behind that throne all of those latter years. There were so many things left unfinished that Strayhorn did, many of the things you think were new, were things Strayhorn left unfinished.[103]

MERCER ELLINGTON: When Strayhorn passed, [Ellington] was in the midst of various projects and, realizing he did not have Strayhorn at his side, found that in order to cover the same ground that he had been covering, found he had to work harder. If anything, Strayhorn's passing stimulated Ellington's ability to write and to write more music than he had to do before.[104]

DUKE ELLINGTON: I'm writing more than ever now. I have to. Billy Strayhorn left that big yawning void.[105]

MERCER ELLINGTON: Ellington, when he wrote something, if he thought somebody was going to have a problem with a part, he'd get 'em off on the side before he called a rehearsal and make them familiarized with the music he was about to do.[106]

JIMMY JONES: It was Sinatra's birthday and they had been trying to make an album together for years and could never make their schedules coincide, and so when they finally decided to do it there wasn't time – the only way they could meet was so soon that there wasn't time for Duke to do some arrangements for Frank, so Frank says, 'OK, I'll have Billy May do some things.' So it turned out not to be Ellington music and the only Ellington number on it, Frank wouldn't do it without one Ellington number, the only Ellington number there was, 'I Like the Sunrise'. Jimmy Hamilton called me. He says, 'Man, do you know what we're doing?' We're in town, over here recording.' And I came from way over on Carmona to where the studio was. And the next thing I knew I was playing 'I Like the Sunrise', I did it [arranged it] for Ella and Duke! Because after I left [the *Ella at Duke's Place* session] I gave him the parts, but we didn't talk about who done it [with Sinatra]! It was Sinatra's birthday and he bought some booze or something, and he put it right within Paul Gonsalves' reach. I said, 'That's the wrong place for it!' So after the date was over we started to jamming and playing 'Happy Birthday', and everything else, you know. And Duke sent four bottles of Dom Perignon champagne to Frank with roses. I know because I ordered it, for the birthday celebration. And Frank magnanimously passed the Dom Perignon to the band, and Duke was mad. He said, 'I didn't buy that Dom Perignon for this band' (laughs).[107]

Edward K. and Francis A. *was recorded 11–13 December 1967. Sinatra's birthday was 12 December. Most of the arrangements were by Billy May.*

DUKE ELLINGTON: A good way to operate the business is to operate your budget according to, first, the leader, set aside a chunk of money, he has to have this amount of money every week. Now, how much can we afford to spend for the band, how much can we afford to spend for arrangements, how much can we afford to spend for transportation out of this, then you always figure the agent's commission, and this is sound business practice. But the way we operate is *this* way and does *not* make sense! And a lot of people look at me as if I'm an idiot.[108]

MERCER ELLINGTON: Which is one of the reasons we argued and fought so much. It was almost as if we were the same person and I analysed him so much through the years, I knew exactly where he was, what made him tick and as a result I could anticipate – and one of the things that definitely did not help was going to college and studying two years psychology and philosophy, so when he came up with all the false ways of arguing – hollering loud, extending the argument or arguing in a circle – I used to tell him, 'This is what you've done!' He would get really upset, 'Don't you pull that school shit on me!'[109]

MERCER ELLINGTON: He could be ranting backstage, and the minute he crossed the wings the whole complexion and everything else could change. He was the most highly self disciplined person that I think I've been around.[110]

DUKE ELLINGTON: And we did a *Second Sacred Concert* in '68, and the main thing about that was that I brought Alice Babs from Stockholm to do that, and that was wonderful.[111]

On 19 January 1968 the Second Sacred Concert *was premiered at the Cathedral of St John The Divine, New York.*

ALICE BABS: The things you read about Black Power. I hear this number and I could cry . . . It's hard to believe how such things can be. They want freedom *now*. They can't wait any longer. So much talk . . . When I sing 'Freedom' I feel I have to change also. *We* have to change. We need to free ourselves of the thoughts we harbour about other races. When I heard 'It's

Freedom' I was happy. I told myself this would be performed all over the world. It says something the world has a need to hear. Duke has written, 'Freedom is not just a word, Freedom is something we have to have.'[112]

COOTIE WILLIAMS: That number he wrote for me, 'The Shepherd', it was a funny thing. First he was playing it on the piano. He wasn't playing it, he was just running it over. He called me down and said, 'Hey, Coots, come here.' He said, 'How do you like this number? Do you think you would like to play this number?' I said, 'Yeah.' I said, 'I'll play it.' So he wrote a lead sheet out on it. So I started messing around with it. He said, 'What do you think of it?' I think it was about a week. I said, 'Give me a chance. Give me time to feel the thing, so I can get something out of it.' So I started playing it. He said, 'Yeah, uh-huh, you're right.' And that's how that number came about.[113]

DUKE ELLINGTON: It has been said that what we do is deliver lyrical sermons, fire-and-brimstone sermonettes and reminders of the fact that we live in the promised land of milk and honey, where we have prime beef and 80% butterfat ice cream. I am sure we appreciate the blessings we enjoy in this country, but it wouldn't hurt if everyone expressed his appreciation more often.[114]

DUKE ELLINGTON: My music got me into church and privileged me to do my Sacred Concerts, obviously music is my language and possibly my most eligible form of semantics if I am to speak to GOD.[115]

CHAPTER ELEVEN
HALF THE FUN

The death of Billy Strayhorn was a huge blow to Ellington. It provided him with an unwelcome reminder of his own mortality, something he was at pains to avoid confronting. It brought home in no uncertain terms how much he had to say musically and how little time was left in which to say it. He threw himself into his work. The most immediate result was the album And His Mother Called Him Bill, *a heartfelt tribute to Strayhorn, recorded just three months after his longtime collaborator's death. Along with albums such as* Far East Suite, *recorded the previous year,* Afro Bossa *and* The Symphonic Ellington, *it numbers among the finest of his latter day recordings.*

By now much of his energy was being thrown into his religious works, something which he felt sure posterity would remember him by. His First Sacred Concert was performed around fifty times at churches and cathedrals around the world, and was preserved on Duke Ellington's Concert of Sacred Music *(1965). His Second Sacred Concert, a work he considered 'the most important thing I have ever done', subsequently appeared as* Second Sacred Concert *(1968).*

Celebrated and feted, Ellington was accumulating honours, awards and honorary degrees faster than he could find a place to store them. On one occasion, when friends bound copies of his original scores as a birthday gift, he offered profuse gratitude when presented with them at a party held in his honour, but left without them. His interest, as ever, was in the future rather than his distinguished past.

Despite his age, Ellington's appetite for work remained undiminished, and at the age of seventy-two he did not flinch from an international touring schedule more gruelling than at any time during his long career, with successive tours of Russia, Europe, South America and the Far East. But a lifetime of trials and tribulations in maintaining what he called 'the highest-paid big band in the world' were now beginning to catch up with him.

BOB UDKOFF: Jimmy Hamilton used to sell whisky. He would sell Paul Gonsalves and Willie Cook and all these guys 50c a shot – he'd carry a bottle! And they could never accumulate enough money to buy a bottle; well, they could, but they never thought about it until Mercer, one day he says, 'Why you giving this guy . . .' So Jimmy quit the band, he said, 'Can't make any money here!'[1]

MERCER ELLINGTON: Jimmy Hamilton charged Paul Gonsalves $40 so he could get a drink one night! He wasn't against him drinking, it would be different if he charged him that to make him keep from drinking, but no! What Jimmy was interested in was the $40![2]

After twenty-six years, Jimmy Hamilton left the Ellington band to pursue a freelance career. His last date was 1 July 1968 at Lambertville Music Circus, Lambertville, N.J., and after a three-day lay-off Harold Ashby joined the band. He had deputized in the Ellington band from time to time since 1960.

HAROLD ASHBY: I started working with Duke regularly on 5 July 1968, when Jimmy Hamilton left. You know some people liked the Ellington forties band and some liked the sixties band, but I believe Duke matured with his writing. If you put on some of those old records you'll see that. Duke knew his men, their styles, and what they played best and he wrote for them.[3]

LAWRENCE BROWN: The South American tour was State Department-sponsored. It was nice, very nice, especially Mexico, Mexico City, and it was nice that way. But you finally get tired of seeing so much – so many poor people, you know, so much poor existence in the world. It kind of gets to you after a while, and one thing it's very high, next thing it's very low. So then you don't know where to go on the in-betweens because you don't know whether the food or this is safe, or that's safe, you know.[4]

Ellington's first tour of South America opened in Sao Paulo, Brazil, on 2 September 1968 and finished in Buenos Aires on 15 September. A second 'Mexican' leg began on 23 September in Mexico City, returning to the United States on 30 September.

MERCER ELLINGTON: We were there for a week and a half and finally the State Department got in touch with us, wanted to know if there was anything they could do. We said, 'Yes, send some cigarettes!' They told us what the cost of the cigarettes was going to be and would we send the money for the cigarettes. This is the regard of the State Department versus the approval of the people themselves of South America. They finally had a reception for [Ellington] at the embassy. We all went and we were assigned a man per person so we could make ourselves familiar with the South Americans. We in turn introduced the men who were assigned to us to the people at the party. They had no idea of anybody, no interest in Ellington himself. We wound up getting real popularity, it came as a result of the people themselves.[5]

DUKE ELLINGTON: The generosity and enthusiasm of the audiences were altogether the inspiration of a lifetime – a virtual summit in my career. Everything and everyone has been so completely and warmly attuned that I am completely overwhelmed and at a loss to express my appreciation. Perhaps I can do so at a later date in music.[6]

Latin American Suite *was recorded in New York on 5 November 1968 and Las Vegas 7 January 1970, although the release of the original vinyl album was delayed.*

DUKE ELLINGTON: You can hum a tune from New York to Washington and when you get there forget it: if you go directly into something else, you come back, 'What the hell was that I was humming?'[7]

MERCER ELLINGTON: He always equipped himself with a pad and pencils, plus we would lay a Wurlitzer [electric] piano, take the legs off, lay it on the bed alongside him so if during the night he became so involved with the idea of preserving a thought he wanted to be sure he had the least germ [of an idea] because that was so important. He said he lost too many things by having the things evaporate into air and not being able to recall them, he didn't intend to let that happen again.[8]

JIMMY JONES: Paul Gonsalves was possibly one of the most beautiful human beings I ever met. I remember one time I was in Vegas with Nancy Wilson, Duke was in the Sahara. So we went down to catch Duke's band after we finished our show and Paul was sober as a judge, but he fell down on the stand. He just happened to fall down, off his chair, but the way he stood up. He stood up to let everybody know that he was all right. And Duke walked to the mike and said, 'Isn't that amazing? This man doesn't even drink!' And we broke up![9]

Ellington played the Casbar Lounge of the Sahara Hotel, Las Vegas, 4–29 March 1969.

DUKE ELLINGTON: They much prefer you don't gamble, you know. From the racial viewpoint.[10]

DUKE ELLINGTON: Everything has to do with those tables, the show goes on, the show is supposed to be hour and fifteen minutes, you come off on time. If you don't there's some guy standing there looking at you, 'What's wrong with you, man? Don't tire these people out, they want to stay at the tables.'[11]

DUKE ELLINGTON: Everybody plays segregated audiences, anybody who's anybody at all plays Las Vegas.[12]

RUTH ELLINGTON: On his 70th birthday in 1969, I went with him to the White House. I drew up the guest list and supervised the invitations because he was so busy. And we had to get it organized; we were limited in the number of people we could invite at the White House, but it was a wonderful occasion and a great honour.[13]

Ellington's 70th birthday was hosted by President Nixon at the White House on 29 April 1969 with a large assembly of specially invited friends, colleagues and personalities. He was presented with the Presidential Medal of Freedom, America's highest civilian honour.

BOB UDKOFF: Ellington had this thing about the four kisses, kiss you twice, that's one for each cheek, and when he said that to Nixon, Nixon got red! He drew back and laughed. He was charming. Now I have never been a fan of Nixon's, because my political leanings are not that way, having lived in California and seen some of the things he did to people like Gerry Wise and Helen Hagen-Douglas, I disliked the man. But that evening he was charming. He had just been elected, he was ebullient.[14]

PRESIDENT RICHARD M. NIXON: I've lifted my glass to emperors, kings and prime ministers, but never has a Duke been toasted. I ask you all to join me in raising our glasses to the greatest Duke of all.[15]

BOB UDKOFF: Ellington and his sister went up to the living quarters and when they came down the staircase they came down together, the four of them. Nixon couldn't have been warmer and more charming than he was on that evening – and what an array of musicians![16]

BILL BERRY: I played for Ellington's 70th birthday at the White House and the waiters who work all the functions there said it was totally different from any other party they'd ever had in the White House. The Supreme Court was there, and the President, and the cabinet, all the biggest people plus Dizzy Gillespie and Benny Goodman and all kinds of musical luminaries. Ellington was the kind of guy when he walked in a room the light went on. Armstrong was like that too. Even if somebody didn't know who they were they can feel this magnetism.[17]

DUKE ELLINGTON: There's over-indulgence of this age bit, and it's annoying, and I am tempted to be a little nasty about it, because people usually follow it by saying 'Oh, you're seventy years old, aren't you!'[18]

BOB UDKOFF: Duke used to deduct $100 a day for expenses, which was probably justified. He was a very generous tipper. He had a doctor bag which Strayhorn had given him years back, a porter would take it, he was very aware these guys had to make a living and he felt that he wanted to contribute, a guy carries his bag, he'd give them $10, cab drivers, bell hops. So he deducted $100 for expenses, but he couldn't prove it. He didn't have any receipts.[19]

BOB UDKOFF: There was a problem with Internal Revenue, it was a substantial amount of money, probably well over $1,000,000.[20]

By 1969, tax agents attended Ellington concerts to be sure they got their money.

MERCER ELLINGTON: During those last horrible days financially, last financial horrible days, he had so many problems with taxes, also meeting expenses for rent and the number of people in the family he supported, it kept him to a point where basically he had about three possessions, he had a white overcoat, he had an electric piano he used to sleep with and a steak sandwich in his pocket. He never had anything much of anything that was really material, he had three pairs of pants he used on the road, some cashmere sweaters and a hat. As far as luxury was concerned, he didn't own any building, he didn't have an automobile, he didn't have lavish jewellery, he had some things that people would present [him with] and all that, but [that was it].[21]

BOB UDKOFF: I will say that had Nixon remained in office it was in process of being taken care of. They did that with Joe Louis. Nixon loved Ellington, but the roof was falling in on him. And Mercer [later] sold a lot of copyrights to pay off the IRS.[22]

MERCER ELLINGTON: [I owned the Ellington catalogue and rights when Ellington died] and I passed them on to Famous Music for the most part, and I did it mainly to take care of taxes.[23]

NORRIS TURNEY: In 1969 I replaced Johnny Hodges for about two weeks when he was sick. We were playing at the Rainbow Room when Johnny came back and he said, 'What are you doing sitting up there?' I said, 'Nothing man. Just trying to hold a gig down for you.' When they phoned a month later it was to replace Benny Green in the trombone section. So I went back and started playing in the trombone section for a while [on alto sax].[24]

The Rainbow Room engagement was from 28 July to 30 August 1969. Turney rejoined the band at the Casbar Lounge of the Sahara Hotel in Las Vegas in October.

DUKE ELLINGTON: We play at the Rainbow Grill in New York and the Rainbow Grill is a place on the sixty-fifth floor of the RCA building, and in order to get to the bandstand from the dressing room you've got to go through the whole room and by the time you get to your dressing room it's time to come back because business associates and people say, 'I had to come over and catch you, and I've got a big deal and what are we going to do after you get through, we'll stop at Rubin's and have a cup of coffee.' And everybody has a 'big deal'.[25]

MERCER ELLINGTON: It was as if it was a good way for him to take a vacation. He got his joy from just being in the club, being informal, having his friends around. He never made any money in the Grill, he used the two front row tables, big tables, every night with his own parties. That was another argument we had, because by the time we got through we never made any money on the job. And I'd be left with the problem of how to pay the men off, plus, by the time we got to the end of the week, the money the job was supposed to pay us was used up![26]

NORRIS TURNEY: One day we were playing in Columbus, Ohio, and Duke was in his dressing room, he called me in, said bring your flute. Back in those days I used to practise the flute about eight or nine hours a day – whenever I could, I guess he heard me. So Duke said play on this, playing some chords, I played behind him, it was in B-flat then it went to D-flat. So I guess about two or three weeks later he came up with this chart on 'Fifi'. That was the first time Ellington used a flute in his band.[27]

Ellington played a one-night stand in Ohio on 9 September 1969. 'Fifi' was later recorded on Duke Ellington's 70th Birthday Concert, *made during their tour of England which wound up a European itinerary that had opened on 28 October 1969 in Milan and finished in Bournemouth a month later on 30 November.*

NORRIS TURNEY: I remember we were coming in from West Berlin into East Germany. I didn't have a visa, I was just new in the band then, and we got to the border. And one guy said, 'He can't go in.' So Duke got off the bus and walked very non-chalantly into the office. He had an album, gave the guy an album and they let me in. That was during the Cold War! The power of Duke Ellington.[28]

Ellington crossed the border into East Germany for their Berlin date on 8 November 1969.

JOE BENJAMIN: [I joined the band] in January 1970 officially, but unofficially I go back a long way. I've been in and out of his payroll for years. For about the umpteenth time the phone rang with somebody from the Ellington organization asking if I'd join the band. This time I agreed. It wasn't easy to decide. Can I contribute anything to a man who has been a genius all those years? I thought about the times I'd done copying for the band. We go back to 1947 without second thoughts. And I did the original copying on 'Harlem' in 1949 or '50. After you have decided, and joined the band, then of course you find it rewarding. Ellington alters things when you're doing them, and that's what keeps you interested – if you care, and I do. We'll play the same arrangement at two concerts and it will sound different. The band was on its way to Japan without a bass player. I joined within two or three days for that tour which went to Manila, Taiwan, Burma, Hong Kong, Australia and New Zealand. The first notes I played with the band were in Tokyo. That was an initiation as it were.[29]

The Far East tour opened on 10 January 1970 and wound up in New Zealand on 9 February.

FRED STONE: After about three weeks in the group doing section parts, I asked him if he could give me some solos to play. He looked at me and said, 'What do you want, old Clark Terry charts to play? Wouldn't you rather I wrote something that suits the way you play?' And I thought, well, that'll teach me to open my big mouth; that serves me right. And then he wrote an important part of his *New Orleans Suite* for me.[30]

Fred Stone replaced Willie Cook on 24 March 1970. On 27

**Colston Hall
Golden Jubilee**

BRISTOL CORPORATION CULTURAL COMMITTEE
(Entertainments Manager : F. K. Cowley, M.I.M.Ent.)

Tuesday 25th Nov at 6.45 & 9.00 pm

The Entertainments Department by arrangement with

Robert Paterson presents

DUKE

ELLINGTON

and His ORCHESTRA

TICKETS :   40/-   35/-   30/-   25/-   20/-   15/-   10/-
from **COLSTON HALL** (Tel. 21768), **LEWIS'S TRAVEL BUREAU,**
BLACKBOY RECORDS, and **BRIGHT'S TRAVEL BUREAU**

P&S DEPT. P3861

*The album 'Duke Ellington's 70th Birthday Concert' was recorded at this 1969 date in
Bristol and the following night at Manchester's Free Trade Hall.*

April recording began on New Orleans Suite. *Stone was featured on 'Aristocracy à la Jean Lafitte'.*

DUKE ELLINGTON: At the New Orleans Jazz Festival we premiered another work called *The New Orleans Suite*, and we would like to have Norris Turney come up for the solo spot. He, ladies and gentlemen, will attempt to give a tone parallel to the excruciating ecstasy one finds oneself suspended in when one is in the throes of the tingling, rhythmic jollies of Bourbon Street.[31]

The New Orleans Suite *was premiered at the Municipal Auditorium, New Orleans, La., during the New Orleans Jazz and Heritage Festival on 25 April 1970.*

NORRIS TURNEY: When we were on the road, [Johnny Hodges] would come up about seven or eight in the morning, and wake me up. He couldn't sleep too well. He'd do this every day. Just as soon as you got to sleep, here he comes. 'Come on by and have a taste,' he'd say, or, 'What do you want to eat?' If he'd been out across town some place, he'd bring something. He'd have a few drinks and then go back to bed. The fact that he didn't sleep well or for long didn't help him any and he was always nervous.[32]

NORRIS TURNEY: I really feel bad about Johnny passing and I miss him a lot. His wife phoned and spoke to my wife, 'Marilee, Johnny died, he died in his dentist's office.'[33]
Hodges died on 11 May 1970.

REX STEWART: For whatever reason, Johnny had a strange way of airing his grievances. He was very visible in the front row saxophone chair near the piano from where he directed remarks and questions to Ellington, out of the side of his mouth. It was hard for Duke to ignore him and he always put on that wide, phoney smile and did his best.[34]

COOTIE WILLIAMS: [Johnny Hodges.] That was a very close relationship there, between those two. Johnny was real close to him. They were real tight.[35]

JIMMY JONES: Johnny Hodges was mad at Duke about something, and you know Johnny Hodges was short. He called Duke a name Duke didn't like, and Duke picked him up, like beside a wall, and held him up, and Johnny's feet were dangling off the ground. He said, 'Nobody calls me that.' And Johnny – no, he never said that again.[36]

DUKE ELLINGTON: I shall not attempt an appraisal of my GOD. I have neither the brain nor complete enough measuring rod. My GOD has invested time and unlimited shepherding. I thank my GOD and pray that my GOD, my soul will keep.[37]

FRED STONE: I remember a concert we did with the Cincinnati Symphony at which one of the guys in the band had rather too much to drink beforehand, and tripped going up to his seat on the stage. He fell over and lay there while all the other guys walked around him. Nobody looked at him, nobody said anything. Ellington made a jocular remark to the audience about how rare to find a musician who absolutely refused to take a drink under any circumstances, and the audience thought it was a comedy routine. Later, he picked himself up, went to his seat and played the show, and did his solos with the fellows on either side of him holding him up. He played superbly well – ideas, timing, execution, all perfect – and nothing was said about the incident. The whole thing was like an Abbott and Costello short.[38]

MERCER ELLINGTON: The average bandleader says, 'You're not doing a job for me, keep it up and I'll fire you.' That wasn't Ellington. His thought was you'll feel the rap if you don't straighten out, and he'll do it. An example was Paul Gonsalves. He would come in and he would be drunk or something like that. In order to get Paul to straighten out, he would put Paul on the microphone out front and play four or five songs that were tremendously fast so that by the time he had played them he was sober again.[39]

BOB UDKOFF: I was driving Duke to a performance he was doing with Tony Bennett in Los Angeles, and it was raining and I had my windshield wipers on and I was making a turn and I put the turn signals on, with an audible ping, and he said, 'Hey, I like that!' and he scribbled something on a match cover, the beat of the windshield wipers and the turn signals, and that was it. Several months later he was doing a thing for Alvin Ailey, *The River*, and he was playing the tape, he had a cassette of the music and he said, 'You hear your windshield wipers?' Now this was nearly a year later![40]

MERCER ELLINGTON: The thing I consider his greatest work, it's called *The River*. It was commissioned by the American Ballet Theatre. And we had the good fortune to play it with Alvin Ailey in the State Theatre ... he loved the idea of writing for ballet. In fact, he was very happy to have the commission for *The River* and also for various things that he did for Alvin Ailey from one time to another. And don't forget, he started in the Cotton Club, and that was where he became highly aware of dance.[41]

The River, *commissioned by the American Ballet Theatre, was premiered on 25 June 1970 at New York's State Theatre and recorded privately by Ellington himself later in the year.*

ALVIN AILEY: *The River* is a ballet for which Duke wrote the music and which we had a very close collaboration. It is a ballet that was commissioned by American Theatre Ballet and I actually spent time with him on the road while we were trying to conceive this ballet. He had by then collected all the great Water Music of the world, Handel's *Water Music* and Debussy's

La Mer, he had researched accurately all the Water Music, all the water themes and all of that to prepare for this ballet. Looking through the Ellington canon of music I found this piece called 'Night Creature', a piece which was for a symphony orchestra and the Ellington band, and recorded with Ellington on piano and all his wonderful soloists like Johnny Hodges, and Paul Gonsalves together with the Paris Opera Ballet Orchestra and the Swedish Symphony Orchestra – it was educated music. There is a sensuous second movement based on a piano solo of Ellington's.[42]

FRED STONE: First of all there is the obvious pleasure of playing with a band in which every member is an exceptional musician, in which every member is an accomplished soloist. Then there was the sheer exhaustion of the schedule the band keeps – in Europe we played fifteen countries in four weeks, without a single day off and sometimes as many as four flights in a single day.[43]

On 28 June 1970 Ellington arrived in Europe for a tour of seven countries, winding-up on 1 August in Belgium. On the band's return, Stone, exhausted, returned to his native Canada. His replacement was Harold 'Money' Johnson.

THE NEW YORK TIMES: LENINGRAD GOES WILD OVER DUKE. Leningrad, Sept. 13 – The applause began before the curtain went up on 'C Jam Blues' and kept on after 45 minutes of encores capped by 'Take the A Train' at the opening tonight of Duke Ellington's five week tour of the Soviet Union. When the programme ended, the Russian audience refused to move. Hundreds of enthusiastic young Leningraders jammed the aisles, whistling, cheering and clapping wildly.[44]

On 10 September 1971, Ellington left New York for an extended tour of Russia and Europe, arriving in Leningrad on 11 September and closing the tour in Barcelona, Spain, on 14 November.

BOB UDKOFF: He was greeted there like the Beatles were when they first came to the United States. Throngs of people, it was an exciting experience.[45]

RUTH ELLINGTON: In Russia he said people came from Siberia, 5,000 miles to Leningrad, Moscow and threw their arms around the musicians and wept – Russian people![46]

BOB UDKOFF: He did an interview and a visit to the Moscow Jazz Orchestra, directed by Shostakovitch's son, who since later defected, Maxim Shostakovitch, and he said, 'My father is a great admirer of your music, he's now in hospital, do you think you could possibly come by?' Ellington says, 'I'd be honoured to meet your father.' So I went with him, I didn't go in, but Duke went in, I don't know if the young man interpreted or Shostakovitch could speak English, but Ellington was very, very touched by that.[47]

MERCER ELLINGTON: The Russians used to provide supper for the band every night, but ... Pop began to find the fare too bland. One night he had a craving for caviar, but the chef in charge of us said it could not possibly be obtained at that time. Bob Udkoff bet him that it could, went out and returned with some in twenty minutes! Money had talked again.[48]

DUKE ELLINGTON: We did what, five weeks, and the shortest concert we did, including encores, was three hours and a half. And the longest was four hours and five minutes and at the end of this period, nobody had left the hall. Nobody had left their seats. And then after that, they normally walk down towards the stage and I'd come out and do Billy Strayhorn's 'Lotus Blossom' which is just piano, and they would just float serenely away.[49]

MERCER ELLINGTON: One of the things that really exhibited well in [later] years was the piano solo he does on 'Lotus Blossom'. He always did it at the end of concerts as a sort of memorial to Billy Strayhorn.[50]

BOB UDKOFF: At the American Embassy they had a party and Ellington met Khachaturyan and also Duke did a Sacred Music concert for the employees of the embassy. Just for the employees. The Russian trip was fabulous.[51]

DUKE ELLINGTON: What I appreciated also was that they kept our entire trip completely on the art plateau, no deviation from art. When we arrived, one hour after we arrived, we were at the Bolshoi, the next day it was the Rachmaninov opera, Shostakovitch picture, the Rimsky-Korsakov opera, you were invited to a symphony rehearsal, a radio, TV show, vaudeville show, the circus – the elephants, everything, nothing away from music, ever.[52]

ANDREI VOZNESENSKY: Ellington is our god. His tour in the USSR was a triumph. People stood in the street for days in the hope of getting tickets. We love him . . . like one of our own.[53]

DUKE ELLINGTON: You go to Russia and you hear all this great Russian masters' music; every time you get to these places where the flavour is so strong like when we were in India and the Far East and the Near East, these flavours are so strong when you are there, and immediately after you leave you're afraid to touch them because you're afraid that you'll duplicate. And so I would rather stay away from it for a couple of months like we did with the Far East tour, and let it come out in my own language rather than in the language I heard.[54]

After closing their tour of Russia and Europe in Barcelona on 14 November 1971, the band took a direct flight to Rio de Janeiro for a 24-day State Department tour of South America that opened on 16 November at Rio de Janeiro's Teatro Municipal and closed in Monterrey, Mexico, on 10 December.

MERCER ELLINGTON: The beautiful thing about Rio de Janeiro was that when we arrived there we found ourselves in a summer climate and were able to bask in the sunshine. After five weeks in Russia and 30 days of consecutive concerts in Europe, we really appreciated it. Besides that, Brazil made a big impression on us because all the people seemed to be happy, friendly and smiling, in great contrast to the attitudes we found in Russia and parts of Europe.[55]

MERCER ELLINGTON: In my experience, and that of Harry Carney who has been with the band since 1927, the whole tour through Russia, Europe and Latin America was the most rigorous and demanding we have ever been on.[56]

DOWNBEAT: The Duke Ellington Show, as it was billed at the Rainbow Grill, was exactly that – an entertainment consisting (first and foremost) of the Ellington brand of band, the comic monologue, the sing along, 'story' telling, the sing-alone, and even a little impromptu dancing at the conclusion ... At last one of the elderlies made her way to the Duke and planted a kiss on his revered cheek. He gave her a hug and proclaimed, 'My this is really wonderful.'[57]

After spending Christmas in New York's Rainbow Grill with a slimmed-down band, the Ellington band re-formed to fly out to Tokyo on 5 January 1972, opening their tour of South East Asia the following day at Tokyo's Koseinenkin Kaikan.

Press Conference During January 1972 Tour of Japan (Extract)

Q: President Nixon is going to visit Red China, how about you? If you have an invitation from them are you happy to go there?

Ellington: I cannot tell you the future, I broke my crystal ball, I cannot tell you the future. I can only tell you I have been every place I've ever been invited.

Q: Are you interested in going to Red China?

Ellington: I'm not interested in going anywhere where I'm not invited. You don't understand. I am never touring, I'm not a sightseer. Wherever my music takes me, that's where I go. If I'm invited to play music, anywhere in the world, and I've been almost everywhere, and Red China is just another geographical location on the map. It isn't a point, actually to discuss, I don't think. There is no reason, why would you discuss it. Why? I want to know. Why would you discuss it?

Q: Because Red China is a – people are interested in Red China right now.

Ellington: What people?

Q: President Nixon is going to go.

Ellington: You asked about me . . . I don't do everything the President does.

Q: I'm sorry but . . .

Ellington: But you're asking me a personal question. I'm here playing music.

Q: We want to know about Red China.

Ellington: The idea of it is, I don't know what it is you want to *know*, but I don't want to get mixed up in any, er, diplomatic or political situation because you made a mistake, and you made a mistake when you asked me about Red China.

Ellington walked out of the interview.[58]

MERCER ELLINGTON: We ducked that kind of conversation because it was communist-inspired, which it was.[59]

The band's South East Asia tour wound up with a concert in Honolulu, Hawaii, on 15 February 1972.

PATRICIA WILLARD: He got very paranoid in later years.[60]

DUKE ELLINGTON: There are so many insecure little people who would enjoy the opportunity to vote – to judge – to contribute to the making or breaking of some poor artist who has spent his or her entire life in dedication to his or her art.[61]

BARNEY BIGARD: The time that I was teed off on him was at the concert at Carnegie Hall when he was supposed to introduce some of his past musicians in his band, you know, for the Newport Jazz Festival which was George Wein's idea that he'd like to reminisce, you know, get a few of his men that was in his group. So that night Sonny [Greer] was there, Ray Nance was all dressed up, bless his soul, and he had his fiddle. So when the curtain went up for the concert, Sonny was downstairs. They called me down. I came down and I sat. And Duke was announcing. So all of a sudden he called, 'Here's the great Greer!' And that's all. The boy hadn't gotten off the drums yet. Sonny had to climb up on the stage to get on the drums and Duke said, 'We're going to do a little something we did together for a while.' And Sonny was trying to ask him, 'What are we going to play? What are we going to do?' He said, 'That's all right, just follow.' So Duke started playing anything [it was a portion of 'Soda Fountain Rag'] and Sonny is fooling with the drums and hitting the cymbals. And the first thing, you know, Duke said, 'Oh, that's enough of that.' And then he went back to the mike, left Sonny up there. Sonny had to hop down off that stage to get back out. And that's all he said about Sonny. I said, 'What is this business?' So I sat there and he turned around to look, to see, and he saw me looking at him and all he says then, 'And now I'd like to introduce one of my fine clarinettists I had in the band, Barney Bigard.' Boom, that was it. He got up there so I started – he gave an introduction, playing the tune and he's playing it slow, like a drag. And now it's getting to be sixteen – and I said, 'No, keep your cool. Just go ahead and bear with it.' And I'm getting him to pick it up, but I can't get to him. He doesn't want to see that at all. OK, I go through and the thing was – the people, they liked it and I could have taken an encore, anything. That was it. So I said, 'Well, that was fine.' So Nance is in the wings all dressed up and his fiddle's raring to go. He never did call Nance. Never. I said, 'Well, I'll be darned.' And he had some old funny singers, I don't know whether they were European singers or what. Girls, a couple of girls and it didn't mean a thing, absolutely nothing.[62]

The Carnegie Hall concert, on 1 July 1972, was conceived as an event to feature Ellington's music and alumni. Greer was brought on stage but Ellington did not allow him to play more than a few bars. Ray Nance was not brought on stage at all although Bigard played three numbers.

PATRICIA WILLARD: He got Norris Turney to quit by doubling the tempo behind him on solos. He played so fast as to try to, I guess, make it too fast for Norris to be able to play and I was told by members of the band that Norris, right in the middle of his own number, closed up his instruments in their cases and walked off the stand.[63]

MERCER ELLINGTON: Norris had a thing, he spoke to Ellington and asked him not to do one of the tunes as quickly as he was doing, he said the tempo was too fast. Ellington immediately played it faster and with that Norris quit. This had nothing to do with Norris's creativity, we knew all about that when he joined us.[64]

Norris Turney left the band on 1 February 1973 at the Persian Room, Marco Polo Hotel, Miami Beach, Fla.

COOTIE WILLIAMS: We was playing up at the race track. I went out to play the 'A Train'. I come back to my seat, and they wanted me to take a bow, and I couldn't hardly get up to take a bow. I said, 'Something's wrong, I got to go home. I got to go home, there's definitely something wrong with me.' But during that period of time Duke called me, he says, called me twice, he says, 'Are you ready to come back to work?' I said, 'No, man. I ain't thinking of work no more.' He said, 'I miss you so much.' He said, 'Come on back. You don't have to blow. Just sit up there and hold on.' I said, 'OK. I'll do it for you. Nobody in the world I would do this for but you.' And that's when I went back to work with him. The doctor had given me the OK, I could go back to work . . . I had retired and he called me and told me to come on back. I didn't have to play. Just to sit there. He missed looking at me, seeing me. And that's the main reason why I came back to the band.[65]

Williams left the band in February 1973 with a mystery chest ailment while the band were playing Houston, Texas. The San Jacinto Medical Center suggested the rest of the band be checked to ensure the contagion had not spread. Two men were urged to have follow-up examinations with their own physicians, as the beginnings of something serious were suspected. They were Ellington and Harry Carney. Williams rejoined Ellington in September 1973.

RUTH ELLINGTON: The only thing that was important to him was his music, how it touched people, the pictures it gave them and the fact that he spent the last ten years of his life writing music to the glory of God, from which everything came. That's all that's important.[66]

DUKE ELLINGTON: I think that when a man alone so much over a period of years, he sort of feels he has a direct line of communication to GOD. How right and how wrong can he be considering the fact that sometimes he has had to leave pleasant company in order to get complete isolation.[67]

MERCER ELLINGTON: As is the case with most stars and people of genius, they found themselves leading a very lonely life.[68]

REX STEWART: I have been close enough to and also far enough away from Duke to see the inevitable change in him as a person. His transition from Washington and Room Ten to command performances for royalty was a long and arduous trail, speckled by the various joys and sorrows of life. And even Ellington is not exempt from the immutable law of change. He grows grander but more introspective. He has apparently learnt to give more of himself in public but less in private. The strain of constantly being on stage has taken its toll, the hassles with band personnel, with bookers, with schemers and parasites who attempt to pinch a bit off the top. These have caused the famed bags under his eyes to grow baggier. The hail fellow, well met, who was a buddy to his boys is no longer there – and understandably so. As he sardonically proclaims 'I love you madly' to his admiring followers, I wonder if he has not subconsciously hypnotized himself into believing it.[69]

MERCER ELLINGTON: As the days went on, the smile turned into a grimace, there wasn't any sincerity there at all, it was just like he was on-stage and the people would just more or less have to accept him on those grounds or they would just disappear from the scene. I think he got pretty cynical there towards the end, especially when he knew he had cancer. As much as he would never talk in terms of posterity or of the sort, at this point he knew the game was up; there was no point in going through the finger exercises or trying to preserve his image, by this time he knew he no longer had an image. He didn't want anyone to take his picture.[70]

HAROLD ASHBY: In Westminster Abbey, you know, that was the beginning of the time when he was sick, all the cameras flashing in his eyes – he didn't like that. So Duke hollered at me! When we went to Copenhagen I was up there asleep and Duke called me on the phone, about eleven o'clock, he told me to come down, and he said, 'You know, nobody's perfect.' And I said,

'Well, Duke, I know that,' and he said, 'Because there's only one perfect being.' And in other words, I believe that was his way of apologizing, 'cos that's the type of person Duke was.[71]

On 24 October 1973, Ellington performed the Third Sacred Concert *at Westminster Abbey, London.*

MERCER ELLINGTON: I think that he was aware of his inability to function as usual for the first time when we did the Sacred Concert at Westminster Abbey. He was never satisfied with the performance, consequently never satisfied with the recordings we had done.[72]

RUTH ELLINGTON: I went with him in 1973, when he did the Sacred Concert at Westminster Abbey. On that particular occasion, for instance, after the concert at Westminster Abbey, Prime Minister Heath was there, Princess Margaret. And there was a dinner for him at 10 Downing Street. That's the highest honour you can get.[73]

On Sunday, 25 November 1973, Dr Arthur Logan fell to his death from a pedestrian bridge over the Henry Hudson Parkway in Harlem. To this day nobody really knows what happened.

IRVING TOWNSEND: The sudden death of [Dr] Arthur Logan in a fall from a bridge over New York's West Side Highway in 1973 was one of the great losses Ellington had to sustain ... a distinguished Harlem surgeon and civic leader, [he] was much more than a doctor to Duke. He never missed a recording session and would sit with his attractive wife Marion on the sidelines until all hours of the night, somehow managing to appear at his clinic at eight every morning.[74]

DON GEORGE: Duke was in London when Logan died. They kept the news from him for a few days but when he found out he was completely devastated. Strayhorn was gone, and now Logan. Logan's death broke Duke's heart. For the remainder of his life it disturbed him. He always yearned for some explanation of why and how it happened.[75]

MERCER ELLINGTON: Basically speaking, Arthur killed himself and I think the reason he did was because he was in trouble with the loan sharks.[76]

DUKE ELLINGTON: Every man prays in his own language and there is no language GOD does not understand.[77]

MERCER ELLINGTON: He didn't give a damn about what the public thought of him, he was worried about what God thought of him.[78]

ED ANDERSON: Christmas Eve 1973 and Duke was playing an engagement at the Rainbow Grill in New York. My wife and I dropped by to wish him a merry Christmas. Just before the last show we placed a tiny Christmas tree on the piano nest to the keyboard. When he noticed it he seemed delighted, picked it up, waved it gaily at the band and audience and executed a little dance. We went back to his dressing room and I said, 'We came here instead of going to church tonight.' He replied, 'You're in church when you're here. Don't forget, wherever you are, "Somebody Cares" [the title of one of his songs from the Third Sacred Concert].' Not having seen him since the first performance of the Third Sacred Concert in Westminster Abbey we told him how much we had liked it and spoke of its exceptional spiritual quality. 'I have so much more to do,' he said, 'I have so much more to do.'[79]

GEORGE WEIN: Duke was not well the last few years of his life, but it didn't keep him from performing, but he'd get very tired. But at the pace he worked, it was incredible that he continued to do it.[80]

DUKE ELLINGTON: We go out and people say, 'Don't you get tired of writing? In a different city every day? Oh my!' I did a thing over in Paris, I got on the plane, a beautiful girl was serving me caviar and champagne all the way there. What's tiring about that?[81]

DUKE ELLINGTON: Ever onward and upward to the end where all ends end – just before the beginning.[82]

DUKE ELLINGTON: My opera is just waiting for an impresario, that's all. It's at the point of realization, all I need is a date. You say what day you want me to present it and I'll finish it. I wouldn't finish anything if I didn't know when I was going to play it.[83]

By 31 August 1973, Queenie Pie – An Opera Buffa In Seven Scenes, *words and music by Duke Ellington, was virtually completed. The outline and breakdown of cast even had Lena Horne pencilled in for the lead.*[84]

MERCER ELLINGTON: He didn't want to do an [auto]biography because he thought when he did an [auto]biography it would be the end of his life. In other words, your [auto]biography is your life from beginning to end ... and he was superstitious, highly superstitious.[85]

In 1973 Ellington's autobiography Music Is My Mistress *was published in New York by Doubleday & Co. It was his only book, and was written with the help of his friend and confident Stanley Dance. Ellington's previous excursions into the literary world included numerous ghost-written magazine articles under his name and introductions to books, including Willie 'The Lion' Smith's* Music On My Mind, *Leonard Feather's* Encyclopedia of Jazz *and Stanley Dance's* World of Duke Ellington.

THE VILLAGE VOICE: He tells his story and gives us just the facts he wants us to have. Hidden well inside, totally out of view, is the real, prime Duke.[86]

THE NEW YORK TIMES REVIEW OF BOOKS: His judgements of himself and his contemporaries are generous and restrained. He has chosen not to indulge in emotional self-revelation, not to record for posterity the daily inner tensions, the feuds and fusses that are the universal counterpoint to any effort of disciplined artistic creation.[87]

MERCER ELLINGTON: I liked the book. It's not his [auto]biography, it's a way to get $50,000 [the publisher's advance]. It's an anthology. He talks about everybody except himself, its an old trick of his![88]

RUTH ELLINGTON: When he was older, he became more withdrawn, in order to compose more music. In other words, he became closer to his music. In *Music Is My Mistress* he said, 'I'm like a hermit living with my mistress.' He said that. Just more concentrated on music, that's why he withdrew from his extra-curricular activities, to concentrate on music.[89]

COOTIE WILLIAMS: That last trip he was on. He was working night by night. And I know he was sick. He was just barely making it. He told Mercer don't take the bus too far away from him, that's when he left to come home.[90]

On 22 March 1974, Ellington returned to the apartment he shared with Evie Ellis at 140 West End Avenue, New York, after playing the Sturges-Young Auditorium, Sturgis, MI. After a couple of days at home, he entered the Harkness Pavilion of the Columbia Presbyterian Hospital on 168th Street in New York.

DUKE ELLINGTON: Vooraes–Lympi. Braun–Exploration. Austin–Lung Penetration. King–Lung Penetration. Rielly–Barium.[91]

BOB UDKOFF: When Ellington was sick, Ruth, Ellington's sister, called me, and said she would like – Sinatra had tremendous power, he had more power than the Pope – and she wanted Sinatra to have Ellington's doctors checked out, he was at the Columbia-Presbyterian. So she asked me if I would call him, and I knew him slightly, I didn't know him well, but I did call and talked to him and told him what Ruth's concerns were, and he says, 'OK'. He flew Dr Debakey, who is the great heart specialist from Houston, on his own plane to New York to talk to Ruth's doctors. And of course it was hopeless, he had lymphoma, couldn't do anything for him and the doctors he had were the best. And on his birthday, his 75th birthday just prior to his death, I was there (I [had] celebrated most of them – a good many of them, at least), and the hall was lined with baskets of fruit and flowers Sinatra sent. It must have cost $2,000–$3,000, it was a gesture of course, they gave all that stuff away. I remember that particular day Nixon called him, 29 April 1974, which was the day that Nixon went on television to divulge the transcripts of the Watergate case, so he must have had a lot on his mind, this is a redeeming feature about Nixon, he took the time to call Ellington and wish him Happy Birthday.[92]

DUKE ELLINGTON: Vertigo–Diabetes. Cob treat. Nurses off. Tumour stop shrinking. Hiccoughs. Cough. Hyman: Outlook. Blood in urine. Susceptibility. No Fertility. Disease to everything.[93]

DON GEORGE: When Duke was dying in the hospital, Evie came early in the mornings when no-one else was there. She brought some fancy ice cream or the strawberry cheesecake he liked, some manuscripts that he could run down on the piano he had installed ... Even though the intense sedation kept him alternating between periods of pain and euphoria, to the very end he called her two or three times every day to say to her, 'I love you, doll. Honest, I love you.'[94]

MERCER ELLINGTON: She had been visiting and sitting with him every day and she really did not want to tell him that she had cancer too.[95]

DUKE ELLINGTON: His ears rushing with echoes of his own crying and pleading, his spiritual nakedness felt only the rising caress of insecurity. So close to death he could smell it.[96]

RUTH ELLINGTON: The night that he was dying he called me in and said, 'Kisses, kisses.' I picked him up out of the bed and kissed him and put him down and he said, '*More* kisses.' And I picked him up and gave him *more* kisses, and then he looked at me as if he were taking my picture, because he was lying in bed and I was standing up and he said, 'Smile, kisses.' Fixed me with a smile for all eternity and then as I was leaving the room he picked up the cross on the chair I had given him, kissed it twice and that night he took flight.[97]

Duke Ellington died at 3.10 a.m. on 24 May 1974 in the Harkness Pavilion.

THE NEW YORK TIMES: Duke Ellington, Master of Music, Dies at 75.[98]

PRESIDENT RICHARD NIXON: The wit, taste, intelligence and elegance that Duke Ellington brought to his music have made him, in the eyes of millions of people both here and abroad, America's foremost composer.[99]

MERCER ELLINGTON: I know that it was only after the autopsy that the doctors really realized that the trouble was in the lymphatic gland, and that's why it spread throughout the blood system and it was so difficult to do anything about it at all.[100]

RUTH ELLINGTON: I think he had a very complicated mind, a very complicated mind, like in his book *Music Is My Mistress* he talked about music being his mistress and that she was 10,000 years old and as modern as tomorrow and that she was beyond time and mathematics. He talked like that, so therefore his music sounds like that. Unlimited.[101]

MERCER ELLINGTON: The first time I ever got to see financial figures dealing with Duke Ellington was after he passed away. I don't think he wanted me to know his earnings.[102]

Ellington's funeral was in the Cathedral of St John the Divine in New York City on 27 May 1974. Over 10,000 mourners filled the church, while the service was relayed to 2,500 outside. Ella Fitzgerald, for whom Ellington had once extravagantly promised to write a Broadway show, and a close friend since she started out in Chick Webb's band back in the 1930s, sang Ellington's 'Solitude' and a heart wrenching 'Just a Closer Walk With Thee'. Her failing eyesight meant she read the lyrics, printed in two-inch capital letters, from a lectern in front of her. Later she said she was so upset she froze while singing and could not remember whether she had sung the words correctly. A tape recording featuring Johnny Hodges and Alice Babs, taken from the Second Sacred Concert, which Ellington had once said was his most important work, was played over the public address. His long-time friend Stanley Dance gave the Funeral Address.

STANLEY DANCE: It is Memorial Day, when those who died for the free world are properly remembered. Duke Ellington never lost faith in this country and he served it well. His music will go on serving it for years to come.[103]

COOTIE WILLIAMS: It was a very beautiful funeral. It brought me back to the time we played the concert there. He was the greatest guy I ever met in my life. Musician and man.[104]

PAUL GONSALVES: Duke was certainly my idol from the start. He did something for jazz. He gave it *class*.[105]

EPILOGUE

On 8 October 1974, Ellington's longtime confidant Harry Carney died; many said his end was hastened by a broken heart. It seemed for all the world as if the long, coded conversations he and Ellington shared as they drove from gig to gig together across America would now be pursued beyond the grave. Ellington had never been told that Paul Gonsalves had passed away in London on 15 May 1974. Two years later, after a long and painful battle against cancer, Beatrice 'Evie' Ellis died on 7 April 1976 and was laid to rest alongside Ellington in Woodlawn Cemetery.

As a young man, Duke Ellington had recorded with the Washingtonians in 1924, but it was not until 1926 that he recorded under his own name to form an unbroken thread through the history of jazz until his death. The development of Ellington the composer, arranger, piano player and bandleader was unique. He created his own orbit, adjacent to, but not part of, the jazz mainstream: his early records had characteristics in common with early jazz and later recordings displayed elements from the Swing Era and modern jazz. But the evolution of Ellington as an artist did not mirror early jazz, the Swing Era or modern jazz that followed. Ellington followed his own path and remained true to himself as a creative artist, yet he never influenced the course of jazz history in the way other jazz greats did, but instead created a body of work universally acclaimed, both inside and outside jazz, for its variety, originality and excellence. Throughout it was his voice as a composer and arranger that predominated, expressed through the unique instrumental personalities that comprised his big band. Ultimately, perhaps Ellington's greatness lay in the fact that at almost any point in his long career the best of his recorded legacy always represented some of the finest performed, most adventurously crafted and emotionally serious work in jazz and of twentieth-century music.

NOTES

FOREWORD

1   The Smithsonian Institution Ellington Oral History Project: Interview with Mercer Ellington, September 1990, conducted by Dr Marcia M. Greenlee. Courtesy Archives Center, NMAH, Smithsonian Institution, Washington D.C. Also, *Duke Ellington . . . and his Famous Orchestra*, BBC-TV. Courtesy the National Sound Archive, the British Library.
2   A felicitous phrase I have borrowed from a witty Max Harrison review in the *IAJRC* Journal (Winter 1995, p. 76) in a context not too far removed from my text.

PAGE XXI

1   Library of Congress Voice of America Recordings. WB 357. Interview with Howard Boxer at the Howard Theatre, Washington D.C., on 26 April 1962.

PROLOGUE

1   The 1870 and 1880 Censuses are consistent in indicating 1840 as the year of James Ellington's birth, but the 1900 Census shows his year of birth as 1838. Note that there is no entry for an Ellington in either North or South Carolina in *Free Negro Heads of Families in the United States in 1830* by Carter G. Woodson (The Association for the Study of Negro Life and History, Inc., Washington D.C., 1925), suggesting the strong possibility that James Ellington was born into slavery.

2   *The People*, 18 June 1933. In an interview with Hannen Swaffer, following his London Palladium debut, Duke Ellington confirms he knew his 'great-grandfather was a slave'. Courtesy Dr L. M. Newman, curator, The Jack Hylton Collection: The Library, Lancaster University.

3   In *Ellington: The Early Years* by Mark Tucker (Bayou Press, Oxford 1991), Daisy's date of birth is shown as 4 January 1879; see p. 19.

CHAPTER ONE:
FLAMING YOUTH

1   Duke Ellington interview by Michael Parkinson on *The Parkinson Show*, BBC TV, 1973, Courtesy The National Sound Archive, The British Library.

2   An edited talk between Duke Ellington and Henry Whiston of the Canadian Broadcasting Company, published in *Jazz Journal*, February 1967, p. 4.

3   Carter Harman Interview Collection: 1964 #8. Courtesy Archives Center, NMAH, Smithsonian Institution, Washington D.C.

4   *The New York Times Magazine*, 12 September 1965, p. 66.

5   *Music Is My Mistress* by Duke Ellington (W. H. Allen, London 1974), p. 12.

6   Carter Harman Interview Collection: Las Vegas 1956 #3. Courtesy Archives Center, NMAH, Smithsonian Institution, Washington D.C.

7   The Smithsonian Institution Ellington Oral History Project: Interview with Ruth Boatwright-Ellington, August 1989, conducted by Dr Marcia M. Greenlee, Tape 1. Courtesy Archives Center, NMAH, Smithsonian Institution, Washington D.C.

8   Carter Harman Interview Collection: 1964. Courtesy Archives Center, NMAH, Smithsonian Institution, Washington D.C.

9   Carter Harman Interview Collection: 1964 #8. Courtesy Archives Center, NMAH, Smithsonian Institution, Washington D.C.

10   Carter Harman Interview Collection: 1964 #8. Courtesy Archives Center, NMAH, Smithsonian Institution, Washington D.C.

11   The Smithsonian Institution Ellington Oral History Project: Interview with Ruth Boatwright-Ellington, August 1989, conducted by Dr Marcia M. Greenlee, Tape 1. Courtesy Archives Center, NMAH, Smithsonian Institution, Washington D.C.

12 Carter Harman Interview Collection: 1964 #1. Courtesy Archives Center, NMAH, Smithsonian Institution, Washington D.C.
13 Carter Harman Interview Collection: 1964 #2. Courtesy Archives Center, NMAH, Smithsonian Institution, Washington D.C.
14 Carter Harman Interview Collection: Las Vegas 1956 #3. Courtesy Archives Center, NMAH, Smithsonian Institution, Washington D.C.
15 Carter Harman Interview Collection: Las Vegas 1956 #3. Courtesy Archives Center, NMAH, Smithsonian Institution, Washington D.C.
16 Carter Harman Interview Collection: 1964 #2. Courtesy Archives Center, NMAH, Smithsonian Institution, Washington D.C.
17 The Smithsonian Institution Ellington Oral History Project: Interview with Ruth Boatwright-Ellington, August 1989, conducted by Dr Marcia M. Greenlee, Tape 1. Courtesy Archives Center, NMAH, Smithsonian Institution, Washington D.C.
18 *Music Is My Mistress* by Duke Ellington (W. H. Allen, London 1974), p. 17.
19 *Music Is My Mistress* by Duke Ellington (W. H. Allen, London 1974), p. 16.
20 An edited talk between Duke Ellington and Henry Whiston of the Canadian Broadcasting Company, published in *Jazz Journal*, February 1967, p. 4.
21 *The Bronzeman*, August 1932, p. 20.
22 *Never Whistle in a Dressing Room* by Maurice Zolotow (E. P. Dutton & Co, New York 1944), p. 297. Zolotow extensively interviewed Ellington in the early 1940s, and his proselytizing journalism on his behalf included 'The Duke of Hot' that appeared in the *Saturday Evening Post* in 1943. This magazine article was later expanded and revised and appeared as the chapter 'The Duke of Hot' in the above book.
23 *The Bronzeman*, August 1932, p. 20.
24 *Never Whistle in a Dressing Room* by Maurice Zolotow (E. P. Dutton & Co, New York 1944), p. 297.
25 *The Bronzeman*, August 1932, p. 21.
26 An edited talk between Duke Ellington and Henry Whiston of the Canadian Broadcasting Company, published in *Jazz Journal*, February 1967, p. 4. **Note:** Ellington gives a good demonstration of 'Soda Fountain Rag' on Carter Harman Interview Collection: 1956 #3 (Courtesy Archives Center, NMAH, Smithsonian Institution, Washington D.C.). This version is one of just a very few examples we have

of Ellington playing this tune. The best known performances are on *Duke Ellington Live at the Whitney* (Impulse IMP 11732) and an even briefer snippet from ABC News of Ellington at Carnegie Hall in 1972.

27 Duke Ellington's handwritten notes for his autobiography *Music is My Mistress*. This section was written on the notepaper of the Waldorf-Astoria, New York. The Duke Ellington Collection #301 Series 5 (Box #5, Folder 6), Courtesy Archives Center, NMAH, Smithsonian Institution, Washington D.C.

28 BBC Radio interview with Duke Ellington, 1963. Taken from a 2:30 min. extract (remainder not kept by BBC). Courtesy The National Sound Archive, The British Library.

29 *The Bronzeman*, August 1932, p. 21.

30 An edited talk between Duke Ellington and Henry Whiston of the Canadian Broadcasting Company, published in *Jazz Journal*, February 1967, p. 4.

31 The Smithsonian Institution Ellington Oral History Project: Interview with Ruth Boatwright-Ellington, August 1989, conducted by Dr Marcia M. Greenlee, Tape 1. Courtesy Archives Center, NMAH, Smithsonian Institution, Washington D.C.

32 Carter Harman Interview Collection: 1964 #8. Courtesy Archives Center, NMAH, Smithsonian Institution, Washington D.C.

33 Carter Harman Interview Collection: 1964 #8. Courtesy Archives Center, NMAH, Smithsonian Institution, Washington D.C.

34 The Smithsonian Institution Ellington Oral History Project: Interview with Ruth Boatwright-Ellington, August 1989, conducted by Dr Marcia M. Greenlee, Tape 2. Courtesy Archives Center, NMAH, Smithsonian Institution, Washington D.C.

35 Interview with Otto Hardwick, 29 April 1964, conducted by Felix Grant, Radio WMAL, Washington D.C. Courtesy Donald L. McCathran.

36 *Ebony*, March 1959, p. 134.

37 Carter Harman Interview Collection: 1964 #8. Courtesy Archives Center, NMAH, Smithsonian Institution, Washington D.C.

38 'Music is "Tops" to You and Me ... and Swing is a Part of It' by Edward Kennedy 'Duke' Ellington. Magazine feature from 1938, vertical clippings file 1936–8, Institute of Jazz Studies, Rutgers.

39 *Crescendo*, April 1964, p. 6.

40 'Music is "Tops" to You and Me ... and Swing is a Part of It' by

Edward Kennedy 'Duke' Ellington. Magazine feature from 1938, vertical clippings file 1936–8, Institute of Jazz Studies, Rutgers.

41 *Boy Meets Horn* by Rex Stewart (Bayou Press, Oxford 1991), p. 4.

42 Duke Ellington talks to Stanley Dance, BBC Radio 1971. Courtesy The National Sound Archive, The British Library.

43 Carter Harman Interview Collection: 1964 #4. Courtesy Archives Center, NMAH, Smithsonian Institution, Washington D.C.

44 *Christian Science Monitor*, 13 December 1930. Republished in *The Duke Ellington Reader* edited by Mark Tucker (Oxford University Press, New York 1993), p. 42.

45 'Music is "Tops" to You and Me ... and Swing is a Part of It' by Edward Kennedy 'Duke' Ellington. Magazine feature from 1938, vertical clippings file 1936–8, Institute of Jazz Studies, Rutgers.

46 Carter Harman Interview Collection: 1964 #4. Courtesy Archives Center, NMAH, Smithsonian Institution, Washington D.C.

47 Library of Congress Voice of America Recordings. Press conference, 29 April 1962.

48 *Jazz Masters of the '30s* by Rex Stewart (Macmillan, New York 1972), pp. 81 & 82.

49 Carter Harman Interview Collection: 1964 #5. Courtesy Archives Center, NMAH, Smithsonian Institution, Washington D.C.

50 Carter Harman Interview Collection: 1964 #1. Courtesy Archives Center, NMAH, Smithsonian Institution, Washington D.C.

51 *Music Is My Mistress* by Duke Ellington (W. H. Allen, London 1974), p. 10.

52 *Ebony*, March 1959, p. 132.

53 Carter Harman Interview Collection: Las Vegas 1956 #1. Courtesy Archives Center, NMAH, Smithsonian Institution, Washington D.C.

54 Carter Harman Interview Collection: Las Vegas 1956 #1. Courtesy Archives Center, NMAH, Smithsonian Institution, Washington D.C.

55 *Swing*, May 1940, p. 10.

56 *Jazz Masters of the '30s* by Rex Stewart (Macmillan, New York 1972), p. 81.

57 Carter Harman Interview Collection: Las Vegas 1956 #3. Courtesy Archives Center, NMAH, Smithsonian Institution, Washington D.C.

58 Carter Harman Interview Collection: Courtesy Archives Center, NMAH, Smithsonian Institution, Washington D.C.

59 *Ebony*, March 1959, p. 134.

60 Carter Harman Interview Collection: May 1964. Courtesy Archives Center, NMAH, Smithsonian Institution, Washington D.C.

61 *Ebony*, March 1959, p. 134.

62 Interview with Otto Hardwick, 29 April 1964, conducted by Felix Grant, Radio WMAL, Washington D.C. Courtesy Donald L. McCathran.

63 *Swing*, May 1940, p. 10.

64 Interview with Otto Hardwick, 29 April 1964, conducted by Felix Grant, Radio WMAL, Washington D.C. Courtesy Donald L. McCathran.

65 *Swing*, May 1940, p. 10.

66 Interview with Otto Hardwick, 29 April 1964, conducted by Felix Grant, Radio WMAL, Washington D.C. Courtesy Donald L. McCathran.

67 *Swing*, May 1940, p. 10.

68 *Jazz*, March 1963, p. 11.

69 *Swing*, March 1940, p. 32.

70 *Boy Meets Horn* by Rex Stewart (Bayou Press, Oxford 1991), pp. 172 & 173.

71 *Jazz*, March 1963, p. 11.

72 Carter Harman Interview Collection: Courtesy Archives Center, NMAH, Smithsonian Institution, Washington D.C.

73 *Swing*, May 1940, p. 10.

74 *Crescendo*, April 1964, p. 6.

75 *Downbeat*, 13 July 1967, p. 21.

76 *Swing*, May 1940, p. 10.

77 The Smithsonian Institution Jazz Oral History Project: Interview with William 'Sonny' Greer, January 1979, conducted by Stanley Crouch. Courtesy The Institute of Jazz Studies, Rutgers.

78 Interview with Otto Hardwick, 29 April 1964 conducted by Felix Grant, Radio WMAL, Washington D.C. Courtesy Donald L. McCathran.

79 The Smithsonian Institution Jazz Oral History Project: Interview with William 'Sonny' Greer, January 1979, conducted by Stanley Crouch. Courtesy The Institute of Jazz Studies, Rutgers.

80 Duke Ellington interview by Michael Parkinson on *The Parkinson Show*, BBC TV, 1973. Courtesy The National Sound Archive, The British Library.

81 Ruth Ellington interview on *Duke Ellington ... and his Famous*

Orchestra, BBC-TV. Courtesy The National Sound Archive, The British Library.

82 *Swing*, May 1940, p. 10.

83 The Smithsonian Institution Jazz Oral History Project: Interview with Juan Tizol, November 1978, conducted by Patricia Willard. Courtesy The Institute of Jazz Studies, Rutgers.

84 *Jazz*, March 1963, p. 11.

85 Carter Harman Interview Collection: Las Vegas 1956 #1. Courtesy Archives Center, NMAH, Smithsonian Institution, Washington D.C.

86 *Jazz*, March 1963, p. 11.

87 *Crescendo*, April 1964, p. 6.

88 *Jazz*, March 1963, p. 11.

89 An edited talk between Duke Ellington and Henry Whiston of the Canadian Broadcasting Company, published in *Jazz Journal*, February 1967, p. 4.

90 *Jelly Roll, Jabbo, and Fats* by Whitney Balliett (Oxford University Press, New York 1983), p. 60.

91 *Duke Ellington In Person* by Mercer Ellington with Stanley Dance (Hutchinson, London 1978), p. 8.

92 *Boy Meets Horn* by Rex Stewart (Bayou Press, Oxford 1991), pp. 33 & 35.

93 *Swing*, May 1940, p. 10.

94 *Swing*, May 1940, p. 23.

95 Carter Harman Interview Collection: 1964 #1. Courtesy Archives Center, NMAH, Smithsonian Institution, Washington D.C.

96 *Treat It Gentle* by Sidney Bechet (Twayne, New York 1960), p. 140.

97 *Swing*, May 1940, p. 10.

98 *Swing*, May 1940, p. 10.

99 Carter Harman Interview Collection: Las Vegas 1956 #1. Courtesy Archives Center, NMAH, Smithsonian Institution, Washington D.C.

100 *Swing*, May 1940, p. 10.

101 Carter Harman Interview Collection: 1964 #1. Courtesy Archives Center, NMAH, Smithsonian Institution, Washington D.C.

102 The Smithsonian Institution Ellington Oral History Project: Interview with Mercer Ellington, September 1990, conducted by Dr Marcia M. Greenlee, Tape 2. Courtesy Archives Center, NMAH, Smithsonian Institution, Washington D.C.

103 Carter Harman Interview Collection: 1964 #1. Courtesy Archives Center, NMAH, Smithsonian Institution, Washington D.C.

104 Carter Harman Interview Collection: 1964 #1. Courtesy Archives Center, NMAH, Smithsonian Institution, Washington D.C.

CHAPTER TWO:
JUNGLE NIGHTS IN HARLEM

1 Carter Harman Interview Collection: May 1964. Courtesy Archives Center, NMAH, Smithsonian Institution, Washington D.C.
2 The Smithsonian Institution Jazz Oral History Project: Interview with William 'Sonny' Greer, January 1979, conducted by Stanley Crouch. Courtesy The Institute of Jazz Studies, Rutgers.
3 *Swing*, May, 1940 p. 23.
4 Willie 'The Lion' Smith interview, date unknown. Courtesy Leonard Malone, The Leonard Malone Collection.
5 *Music on My Mind: The Memoirs of an American Pianist* by Willie 'The Lion' Smith with George Hoeffer (The Jazz Book Club, London 1966), p. x. From the foreword written by Duke Ellington.
6 *Faces of Jazz*. Programme Number 6 (1972). Courtesy Danmarks Radio, Copenhagen.
7 *Music on My Mind: The Memoirs of an American Pianist* by Willie 'The Lion' Smith with George Hoeffer (The Jazz Book Club, London 1966), p. x. From the foreword written by Duke Ellington.
8 *Music on My Mind: The Memoirs of an American Pianist* by Willie 'The Lion' Smith with George Hoeffer (The Jazz Book Club, London 1966), pp. 149–150.
9 Carter Harman Interview Collection: Las Vegas 1956 #3. Courtesy Archives Center, NMAH, Smithsonian Institution, Washington D.C.
10 *Swing*, May 1940, p. 23.
11 *Faces of Jazz*. Programme Number 6 (1972). Courtesy Danmarks Radio, Copenhagen.
12 *Music on My Mind: The Memoirs of an American Pianist* by Willie 'The Lion' Smith with George Hoeffer (The Jazz Book Club, London 1966), p. 150.
13 *Swing*, May 1940, p. 23.
14 *Faces of Jazz*. Programme Number 6 (1972). Courtesy Danmarks Radio, Copenhagen.
15 Carter Harman Interview Collection 1964 #3. Courtesy Archives Center, NMAH, Smithsonian Institution, Washington D.C.

16 *Voices of the Jazz Age* by Chip Deffaa (Bayou Press, Oxford 1990), p. 16.
17 Carter Harman Interview Collection: Las Vegas, 1956 #3. Courtesy Archives Center, NMAH, Smithsonian Institution, Washington D.C.
18 The Smithsonian Institution Ellington Oral History Project: Interview with Mercer Ellington, September 1990, conducted by Dr Marcia M. Greenlee, Tape 4. Courtesy Archives Center, NMAH, Smithsonian Institution, Washington D.C.
19 Carter Harman Interview Collection: 1964 #1. Courtesy Archives Center, NMAH, Smithsonian Institution, Washington D.C.
20 *Swing*, May 1940, p. 23.
21 *New Yorker*, 8 July 1944.
22 *Swing*, May 1940, p. 23.
23 *Duke Ellington Talks to Max Jones and Humphrey Lyttelton*, BBC Radio 1964. Courtesy The National Sound Archive, The British Library.
24 *Boy Meets Horn* by Rex Stewart (Bayou Press, Oxford 1991), p. vi.
25 *Swing*, June 1940, p. 11.
26 'Schiefe' was the surname of either Arthur Whetsol's father or his stepfather. Whetsol was sometimes called by the nickname 'Chief'.
27 *Jazz from the Beginning* by Garvin Bushell as told to Mark Tucker (Bayou Press, Oxford 1988), pp. 45–7.
28 *Swing*, June 1940, p. 11.
29 *Metronome*, November 1944, p. 26.
30 Carter Harman Interview Collection: May 1964. Courtesy Archives Center, NMAH, Smithsonian Institution, Washington D.C.
31 *Metronome*, November 1944, p. 26.
32 Carter Harman Interview Collection: Las Vegas 1956 #1. Courtesy Archives Center, NMAH, Smithsonian Institution, Washington D.C.
33 Carter Harman Interview Collection: 1964 #8. Courtesy Archives Center, NMAH, Smithsonian Institution, Washington D.C.
34 *Ebony*, March 1959, p. 134.
35 The Smithsonian Institution Ellington Oral History Project: Interview with Mercer Ellington, September 1990, conducted by Dr Marcia M. Greenlee, Tape 1. Courtesy Archives Center, NMAH, Smithsonian Institution, Washington D.C.
36 *Ebony*, March 1959, p. 134.
37 *Duke Ellington In Person* by Mercer Ellington with Stanley Dance (Hutchinson, London 1978), p. 16.
38 *Music on My Mind: The Memoirs of an American Pianist* by Willie

'The Lion' Smith with George Hoeffer (The Jazz Book Club, London 1966), p. 150.

39 Carter Harman Interview Collection: 1964 #3. Courtesy Archives Center, NMAH, Smithsonian Institution, Washington D.C.

40 *Hear Me Talkin' to Ya* compiled by Nat Shapiro and Nat Hentoff (Holt, Rinehart & Winston Inc., New York 1955), p. 224.

41 Mercer Ellington interview on *Duke Ellington ... and his Famous Orchestra*, BBC-TV. Courtesy The National Sound Archive, The British Library.

42 *Ebony*, March 1959, p. 134.

43 *Swing*, June 1940, p. 11.

44 The Smithsonian Institution Jazz Oral History Project: Interview with William 'Sonny' Greer, January 1979, conducted by Stanley Crouch. Courtesy The Institute of Jazz Studies, Rutgers.

45 *Swing*, June 1940, p. 11.

46 The Smithsonian Institution Jazz Oral History Project: Interview with William 'Sonny' Greer, January 1979, conducted by Stanley Crouch. Courtesy The Institute of Jazz Studies, Rutgers.

47 Duke Ellington's handwritten notes for his autobiography *Music is My Mistress*. This section was written on the notepaper of the Waldorf-Astoria, New York. The Duke Ellington Collection #301, Series 5 (Box #5, Folder 6), Courtesy Archives Center, NMAH, Smithsonian Institution, Washington D.C.

48 *Swing*, June 1940, p. 11.

49 *Swing*, June 1940, p. 11.

50 The Smithsonian Institution Jazz Oral History Project: Interview with Tom Whaley, March 1980, conducted by Milt Hinton. Courtesy The Institute of Jazz Studies, Rutgers.

51 *Downbeat*, 13 July 1967, p. 21.

52 *Swing*, June 1940, p. 11.

53 The Smithsonian Institution Jazz Oral History Project: Interview with William 'Sonny' Greer, January 1979, conducted by Stanley Crouch. Courtesy The Institute of Jazz Studies, Rutgers.

54 *Downbeat*, 17 April 1969, p. 16.

55 The Smithsonian Institution Jazz Oral History Project: Interview with William 'Sonny' Greer, January 1979, conducted by Stanley Crouch. Courtesy The Institute of Jazz Studies, Rutgers.

56 *Music on My Mind: The Memoirs of an American Pianist* by Willie

'The Lion' Smith with George Hoeffer (The Jazz Book Club, London 1966), p. 183.

57 *Good Morning Blues: The Autobiography of Count Basie* as told to Albert Murray (Heinemann, London 1986), pp. 83–4.

58 *Swing*, June 1940, p. 11.

59 *Clipper*, 23 November 1923, p. 12. Also reproduced in full in *The Duke Ellington Reader* edited by Mark Tucker (Oxford University Press, New York 1993), p. 22.

60 *Downbeat*, 17 April 1969, p. 16.

61 *Metronome*, November 1944, p. 17.

62 Duke Ellington talks to Stanley Dance, BBC Radio 1971. Courtesy The National Sound Archive, The British Library.

63 *Metronome*, November 1944, p. 17.

64 The Smithsonian Institution Jazz Oral History Project: Interview with William 'Sonny' Greer, January 1979, conducted by Stanley Crouch. Courtesy The Institute of Jazz Studies, Rutgers.

65 *Downbeat*, 17 April 1969, p. 16.

66 *Swing*, June 1940, p. 11.

67 *Downbeat*, 13 July 1967, p. 22.

68 Duke Ellington's handwritten notes for his autobiography *Music is My Mistress*. This section was written on the notepaper of the Ambassador Hotel, Chicago. Ellington's emphasis in using capital letters has been preserved. The Duke Ellington Collection #301, Series 5 (Box #5, Folder 6), Courtesy Archives Center, NMAH, Smithsonian Institution, Washington D.C.

69 Carter Harman Interview Collection: 1964 #8. Courtesy Archives Center, NMAH, Smithsonian Institution, Washington D.C.

70 Carter Harman Interview Collection: 1964 #6. Courtesy Archives Center, NMAH, Smithsonian Institution, Washington D.C.

71 *Swing*, June 1940, pp. 11 & 22. Note that, in both Ellington's handwritten notes for his autobiography *Music is My Mistress* and in the book itself, he describes how the music publisher of *Chocolate Kiddies*, Jack Robbins, had to pawn his wife's engagement ring to pay a $500 advance to Ellington and Trent.

72 Carter Harman Interview Collection: 1964 #3. Courtesy Archives Center, NMAH, Smithsonian Institution, Washington D.C.

73 *Voices of the Jazz Age* by Chip Deffaa (Bayou Press, Oxford 1990), pp. 14–20.

74 Copy of programme courtesy of Jens Lindgren, Svenskt Visarkiv, Stockholm.
75 Carter Harman Interview Collection: 1964 #3. Courtesy Archives Center, NMAH, Smithsonian Institution, Washington D.C.
76 *Swing*, June 1940, p. 11.
77 *Metronome*, November 1944, pp. 17 & 26.
78 *Downbeat*, 7 June 1962, p. 14.
79 The Smithsonian Institution Jazz Oral History Project: Interview with Lawrence Brown, July 1976, conducted by Patricia Willard. Courtesy The Institute of Jazz Studies, Rutgers.
80 The Smithsonian Institution Jazz Oral History Project: Interview with William 'Sonny' Greer, January 1979, conducted by Stanley Crouch. Courtesy The Institute of Jazz Studies, Rutgers.
81 Carter Harman Interview Collection: 1964 #8. Courtesy Archives Center, NMAH, Smithsonian Institution, Washington D.C.
82 Original advertisment in negative form, taken from *Variety*, 27 October 1926. Courtesy Archives Center, NMAH, Smithsonian Institution, Washington D.C.
83 Carter Harman Interview Collection: May 1964. Courtesy Archives Center, NMAH, Smithsonian Institution, Washington D.C.
84 *New Yorker*, 8 July 1944.
85 The Smithsonian Institution Jazz Oral History Project: Interview with William 'Sonny' Greer, January 1979, conducted by Stanley Crouch. Courtesy The Institute of Jazz Studies, Rutgers.
86 Duke Ellington's handwritten notes for his autobiography *Music is My Mistress*. The Duke Ellington Collection #301, Series 5 (Box #5, Folder 6), Courtesy Archives Center, NMAH, Smithsonian Institution, Washington D.C. This section, quoted in its entirety, was written on the notepaper of the Hotel Muehlebach, Kansas City (undated). Note that the passage in parentheses beginning 'Forsook his 1st violin etc' has a line through it, although in a different pen to Ellington's own. With this (surprisingly) fulsome tribute to Paul Whiteman one cannot help but speculate that a little of Paul Whiteman may have rubbed off onto the impressionable young twenty-four-year-old bandleader.
87 The Smithsonian Institution Jazz Oral History Project: Interview with William 'Sonny' Greer, January 1979, conducted by Stanley Crouch. Courtesy The Institute of Jazz Studies, Rutgers.
88 *Ebony*, March 1959, p. 134.

89 *Duke Ellington In Person* by Mercer Ellington and Stanley Dance (Hutchinson, London 1978), p. 18.

90 *Music on My Mind: The Memoirs of an American Pianist* by Willie 'The Lion' Smith with George Hoeffer (The Jazz Book Club, London 1966), p. 173.

91 *Variety*, 14 October 1925. Review by Abel (Green). Courtesy Archives Center, NMAH, Smithsonian Institution, Washington D.C.

92 Carter Harman Interview Collection: 1964 #8. Courtesy Archives Center, NMAH, Smithsonian Institution, Washington D.C.

93 *Metronome*, February 1945, p. 17.

94 *Downbeat*, 7 June 1962, p. 14.

95 The Smithsonian Institution Jazz Oral History Project: Interview with Lawrence Brown, July 1976, conducted by Patricia Willard. Courtesy The Institute of Jazz Studies, Rutgers.

96 *Metronome*, February 1945, pp. 17 & 26.

97 Carter Harman Interview Collection: 1964 #5. Courtesy Archives Center, NMAH, Smithsonian Institution, Washington D.C.

98 *Metronome*, February 1945, p. 17.

99 Carter Harman Interview Collection: 1964 #4. Courtesy Archives Center, NMAH, Smithsonian Institution, Washington D.C.

100 Carter Harman Interview Collection: 1964 #1. Courtesy Archives Center, NMAH, Smithsonian Institution, Washington D.C.

101 Carter Harman Interview Collection: 1964 #4. Courtesy Archives Center, NMAH, Smithsonian Institution, Washington D.C.

102 Interview with Otto Hardwick, 29 April 1964, conducted by Felix Grant, Radio WMAL, Washington D.C. Courtesy Donald L. McCathran.

103 Carter Harman Interview Collection: 1964 #4. Courtesy Archives Center, NMAH, Smithsonian Institution, Washington D.C.

104 The Smithsonian Institution Jazz Oral History Project: Interview with William 'Sonny' Greer, January 1979, conducted by Stanley Crouch. Courtesy The Institute of Jazz Studies, Rutgers.

105 Carter Harman Interview Collection: 1964 #4. Courtesy Archives Center, NMAH, Smithsonian Institution, Washington D.C. Ellington is insistent in several interviews among this collection that Bechet was with him during most of 1926.

106 The Smithsonian Institution Jazz Oral History Project: Interview with William 'Sonny' Greer, January 1979, conducted by Stanley Crouch. Courtesy The Institute of Jazz Studies, Rutgers.

107 *Downbeat*, 7 June 1962, p. 15.

108 *Chicago Defender*, 27 August 1927. Republished in *The Duke Ellington Reader* edited by Mark Tucker (Oxford University Press, New York 1993), pp. 24 & 25. The article makes it clear Ellington had been touring New England during the summer months since 1925.

109 *Treat It Gentle* by Sidney Bechet (Twayne, New York 1960), pp. 141–2 & 143.

110 Duke Ellington talks to Stanley Dance, BBC Radio 1971. Courtesy The National Sound Archive, The British Library.

111 *Downbeat*, 13 July 1967, p. 22.

112 Carter Harman Interview Collection: 1964 #7. Courtesy Archives Center, NMAH, Smithsonian Institution, Washington D.C.

113 The Smithsonian Institution Jazz Oral History Project: Interview with Juan Tizol, November 1978, conducted by Patricia Willard. Courtesy The Institute of Jazz Studies, Rutgers.

114 *Swing*, June 1940, p. 22.

115 Duke Ellington's handwritten notes for his autobiography *Music is My Mistress*. This section was written on the notepaper of the Downtowner Motor Inns. The Duke Ellington Collection #301, Series 5 (Box #5, Folder 6) Courtesy Archives Center, NMAH, Smithsonian Institution, Washington D.C.

116 *Music on My Mind: The Memoirs of an American Pianist* by Willie 'The Lion' Smith with George Hoeffer (The Jazz Book Club, London 1966), p. 174.

117 Carter Harman Interview Collection: 1964 #3. Courtesy Archives Center, NMAH, Smithsonian Institution, Washington D.C.

118 *Metronome*, February 1945, p. 17.

119 *Swing*, March 1940, p. 32.

120 *Downbeat*, 13 July 1967, p. 22.

121 Carter Harman Interview Collection: 1964 #5. Courtesy Archives Center, NMAH, Smithsonian Institution, Washington D.C.

122 *Downbeat*, 13 July 1967, p. 22.

123 *Swing*, June 1940, p. 11.

CHAPTER THREE:
COTTON CLUB STOMP

1 *Irving Mills Documentary*. Interview with Irving Mills on 23 October 1984 from a work in progress produced and directed by Don Mc-Glynn. Courtesy Don McGlynn. Grateful thanks to Don, who allowed me to use whatever material I needed from his fascinating film, as yet unfinished because of funding problems. Is there anyone out there who wants to help complete this valuable jazz documentary?

2 *Swing*, June 1940, p. 11.

3 Carter Harman Interview Collection: 1964 #8. Courtesy Archives Center, NMAH, Smithsonian Institution, Washington D.C.

4 From the film documentary *A Duke Named Ellington* (1988). Courtesy Leonard Malone, writer and co-producer. The Leonard Malone Collection.

5 *Irving Mills Documentary*. Interview with Irving Mills (1984) from a work in progress produced and directed by Don McGlynn. Courtesy Don McGlynn.

6 Carter Harman Interview Collection: 1964 #8. Courtesy Archives Center, NMAH, Smithsonian Institution, Washington D.C.

7 *New York Age*, 18 November 1927.

8 *Downbeat*, 17 April 1969, p. 16.

9 *Amateur Night at the Apollo: Ralph Cooper Presents Five Decades of Great Entertainment* by Ralph Cooper with Steve Dougherty (HarperCollins, New York 1990), pp. 53 & 54.

10 The Smithsonian Institution Jazz Oral History Project: Interview with William 'Sonny' Greer, January 1979, conducted by Stanley Crouch. Courtesy The Institute of Jazz Studies, Rutgers.

11 *Swing*, June 1940, p. 22.

12 *Irving Mills Documentary*. Interview with Irving Mills (1984) from a work in progress produced and directed by Don McGlynn. Courtesy Don McGlynn.

13 Magazine article circa 1970, 'Duke's Big Night' by Jimmy McHugh. Vertical file: Duke Ellington 1968–70. Courtesy The Institute of Jazz Studies, Rutgers.

14 The Smithsonian Institution Jazz Oral History Project: Interview with William 'Sonny' Greer, January 1979, conducted by Stanley Crouch. Courtesy The Institute of Jazz Studies, Rutgers.

15 *Variety*, 7 December 1927.

16 Duke Ellington talks to Stanley Dance, BBC Radio 1971. Courtesy The National Sound Archive, The British Library.

17 The Smithsonian Institution Jazz Oral History Project: Interview with Barney Bigard, July 1976, conducted by Patricia Willard. Courtesy The Institute of Jazz Studies, Rutgers.

18 Carter Harman Interview Collection: 1964 #5. Courtesy Archives Center, NMAH, Smithsonian Institution, Washington D.C.

19 The Smithsonian Institution Jazz Oral History Project: Interview with Barney Bigard, July 1976, conducted by Patricia Willard. Courtesy The Institute of Jazz Studies, Rutgers.

20 Interview with Otto Hardwick, 29 April 1964, conducted by Felix Grant, Radio WMAL, Washington D.C. Courtesy Donald L. McCathran.

21 *Downbeat*, 13 July 1967, p. 22.

22 *Metronome*, February 1945, p. 17.

23 *Jazz Journal*, December 1966, p. 21.

24 *Voices of the Jazz Age* by Chip Deffaa (Bayou Press, Oxford 1990), pp. 39–40. A battle of bands between Ellington and Johnson at the Rockland Palace on Easter Monday, 1 April 1929, was reported by *Variety*. A breakfast dance that began at 3.30 a.m. and lasted 'until 8 that morning' saw Johnson, 'acclaimed winner by witnesses to the battle of music'.

25 *Hear Me Talkin' to Ya* compiled by Nat Shapiro and Nat Hentoff (Holt, Rinehart & Winston Inc., New York 1955), p. 235.

26 *Irving Mills Documentary*. Interview with Irving Mills (1984) from a work in progress produced and directed by Don McGlynn. Courtesy Don McGlynn. From an interview 23 October 1984, conducted by Leonard Feather, Don McGlynn and Bob Udkoff.

27 *Hear Me Talkin' to Ya* compiled by Nat Shapiro and Nat Hentoff (Holt, Rinehart & Winston Inc., New York 1955), p. 234.

28 *Second Movement* by Spike Hughes (Museum Press Ltd, London 1951), p. 230.

29 *Irving Mills Documentary*. Interview with Irving Mills (1984) from a work in progress produced and directed by Don McGlynn. Courtesy Don McGlynn.

30 Carter Harman Interview Collection: 1964 #7. Courtesy Archives Center, NMAH, Smithsonian Institution, Washington D.C.

31 *Second Movement* by Spike Hughes (Museum Press Ltd, London 1951), p. 230.

32 The Smithsonian Institution Jazz Oral History Project: Interview with William 'Sonny' Greer, January 1979, conducted by Stanley Crouch. Courtesy The Institute of Jazz Studies, Rutgers.

33 *Jazz Journal*, June 1990, p. 13.

34 *Swing*, June 1940, p. 22.

35 From the accompanying booklet for *The Ellington Era 1927–1940: Duke Ellington & his Famous Orchestra Volume One* (Columbia C3L 27).

36 The Smithsonian Institution Jazz Oral History Project: Interview with William 'Sonny' Greer, January 1979, conducted by Stanley Crouch. Courtesy The Institute of Jazz Studies, Rutgers.

37 From the film documentary *A Duke Named Ellington* (1988). Courtesy Leonard Malone, writer and co-producer. The Leonard Malone Collection: originally used in *Faces of Jazz* (1972).

38 Carter Harman Interview Collection: 1964 #5. Courtesy Archives Center, NMAH, Smithsonian Institution, Washington D.C.

39 From the film documentary *A Duke Named Ellington* (1988). Courtesy Leonard Malone, writer and co-producer. The Leonard Malone Collection, originally used in *Faces of Jazz* (1972).

40 From the film documentary *A Duke Named Ellington* (1988). Courtesy Leonard Malone, writer and co-producer. The Leonard Malone Collection, originally used in *Faces of Jazz* (1972).

41 Interview with Otto Hardwick, 29 April 1964, conducted by Felix Grant, Radio WMAL, Washington D.C. Courtesy Donald L. McCathran.

42 *Faces of Jazz*. Programme Number 7 (1972). Courtesy Danmarks Radio, Copenhagen.

43 *Irving Mills Documentary*. Interview with Irving Mills (1984) from a work in progress produced and directed by Don McGlynn. Courtesy Don McGlynn.

44 Carter Harman Interview Collection: May 1964. Courtesy Archives Center, NMAH, Smithsonian Institution, Washington D.C.

45 *Variety*, 21 March 1928, p. 69.

46 Carter Harman Interview Collection: May 1964. Courtesy Archives Center, NMAH, Smithsonian Institution, Washington D.C.

47 *Second Movement* by Spike Hughes (Museum Press Ltd, London 1951), pp. 231 & 232.

48 *From Satchmo to Miles* by Leonard Feather (Quartet Books, London 1974), p. 52.

49 The Smithsonian Institution Jazz Oral History Project: Interview with William 'Sonny' Greer, January 1979, conducted by Stanley Crouch. Courtesy The Institute of Jazz Studies, Rutgers.

50 The Smithsonian Institution Jazz Oral History Project: Interview with Barney Bigard, July 1976, conducted by Patricia Willard. Courtesy The Institute of Jazz Studies, Rutgers.

51 *Jazz Journal*, December 1966, p. 21.

52 *Faces of Jazz.* Programme Number 6 (1972). Courtesy Danmarks Radio, Copenhagen.

53 The Smithsonian Institution Ellington Oral History Project: Interview with Mercer Ellington, September 1990, conducted by Dr Marcia M. Greenlee, Tape 4. Courtesy Archives Center, NMAH, Smithsonian Institution, Washington D.C.

54 The Smithsonian Institution Jazz Oral History Project: Interview with Barney Bigard, July 1976, conducted by Patricia Willard. Courtesy The Institute of Jazz Studies, Rutgers.

55 *Irving Mills Documentary.* Interview with Irving Mills (1984) from a work in progress produced and directed by Don McGlynn. Courtesy Don McGlynn.

56 The Smithsonian Institution Jazz Oral History Project: Interview with William 'Sonny' Greer, January 1979, conducted by Stanley Crouch. Courtesy The Institute of Jazz Studies, Rutgers.

57 *Hear Me Talkin' to Ya* compiled by Nat Shapiro and Nat Hentoff (Holt, Rinehart & Winston Inc., New York 1955), p. 235.

58 Duke Ellington interview by Michael Parkinson on *The Parkinson Show*, BBC-TV, 1973. Courtesy The National Sound Archive, The British Library.

59 The Smithsonian Institution Jazz Oral History Project: Interview with William 'Sonny' Greer, January 1979, conducted by Stanley Crouch. Courtesy The Institute of Jazz Studies, Rutgers.

60 *Jazz Journal*, June 1990, p. 13.

61 *Talking Jazz* by Max Jones (Macmillan, London 1987), p. 10.

62 Interview with Otto Hardwick, 29 April 1964, conducted by Felix Grant, Radio WMAL, Washington D.C. Courtesy Donald L. McCathran.

63 *Jazz Journal*, December 1966, p. 21.

64 *Music is My Mistress* by Edward Kennedy Ellington (W. H. Allen, London 1974), p. 54.

65 *Metronome*, February 1945, p. 17.

66 Carter Harman Interview Collection: 1964 #5. Courtesy Archives Center, NMAH, Smithsonian Institution, Washington D.C.

67 The Smithsonian Institution Jazz Oral History Project: Interview with Barney Bigard, July 1976, conducted by Patricia Willard. Courtesy The Institute of Jazz Studies, Rutgers.

68 Carter Harman Interview Collection: 1964 #5. Courtesy Archives Center, NMAH, Smithsonian Institution, Washington D.C.

69 *Boy Meets Horn* by Rex Stewart (Bayou Press, Oxford 1991), p. 204.

70 The Smithsonian Institution Ellington Oral History Project: Interview with Mercer Ellington, September 1990, conducted by Dr Marcia M. Greenlee, Tape 6. Courtesy Archives Center, NMAH, Smithsonian Institution, Washington D.C.

71 *Downbeat*, 7 June 1962, p. 20.

72 *Swing*, March 1940, p. 32.

73 Duke Ellington's handwritten notes for his autobiography *Music is My Mistress*. This section was written on the notepaper of the Steigenberger Park Hotel, Düsseldorf. The Duke Ellington Collection #301, Series 5 (Box #5, Folder 6), Courtesy Archives Center, NMAH, Smithsonian Institution, Washington D.C.

74 *Downbeat*, 7 June 1962, p. 20.

75 *Jazz Journal*, January 1966, p. 8.

76 *Jazz Journal*, August 1964, p. 19.

77 *Crescendo*, March 1964, p. 17.

78 *Metronome*, February 1945, p. 17.

79 *Storyville*, April/May 1973, p. 129.

80 The Smithsonian Institution Jazz Oral History Project: Interview with William 'Sonny' Greer, January 1979, conducted by Stanley Crouch. Courtesy The Institute of Jazz Studies, Rutgers.

81 *Storyville*, April/May 1973, p. 125.

82 *Metronome*, February 1945, p. 26.

83 The Smithsonian Institution Jazz Oral History Project: Interview with Lawrence Brown, July 1976, conducted by Patricia Willard. Courtesy The Institute of Jazz Studies, Rutgers.

84 *Swing*, July 1940, p. 9.

85 Carter Harman Interview Collection: 1964 #3. Courtesy Archives Center, NMAH, Smithsonian Institution, Washington D.C.

86 *Irving Mills Documentary*. Interview with Irving Mills (1984) from a work in progress produced and directed by Don McGlynn. Courtesy Don McGlynn.

87 *Variety*, 20 March 1930.

88 *Swing*, June 1940, p. 11.

89 Mercer Ellington interview on *Duke Ellington ... and his Famous Orchestra*, BBC-TV documentary. Courtesy The National Sound Archive, The British Library.

90 The Smithsonian Institution Jazz Oral History Project: Interview with Cootie Williams, May 1976, conducted by Helen Dance. Courtesy The Institute of Jazz Studies, Rutgers.

91 *Jazz Spoken Here* by Wayne Enstice and Paul Rubin (Louisiana State University Press, Baton Rouge 1992), p. 119.

92 The Smithsonian Institution Jazz Oral History Project: Interview with Cootie Williams, May 1976, conducted by Helen Dance. Courtesy The Institute of Jazz Studies, Rutgers.

93 *Swing*, March 1940, p. 32.

94 *Pittsburgh Courier*, 4 May 1929, pp. 2 & 3.

95 *Boy Meets Horn* by Rex Stewart (Bayou Press, Oxford 1991), p. 118.

96 *Duke Ellington In Person* by Mercer Ellington and Stanley Dance (Hutchinson, London 1978), p. 47.

97 *Irving Mills Documentary*. Interview with Irving Mills (1984) from a work in progress produced and directed by Don McGlynn. Courtesy Don McGlynn.

CHAPTER FOUR:

HIGH LIFE

1 Carter Harman Interview Collection: May 1964. Courtesy Archives Center, NMAH, Smithsonian Institution, Washington D.C.

2 *Storyville*, April/May 1973, p. 130.

3 Carter Harman Interview Collection: Las Vegas 1956 #1. Courtesy Archives Center, NMAH, Smithsonian Institution, Washington D.C.

4 *Storyville*, April/May 1973, p. 129.

5 Duke Ellington's handwritten notes for his autobiography *Music is My Mistress*. This section was written on the notepaper of the Sheraton Towers, Boston. The Duke Ellington Collection #301,

Series 5 (Box #5, Folder 6). Courtesy Archives Center, NMAH, Smithsonian Institution, Washington D.C.

6 Unprovenanced clipping showing part of Ziegfeld's answer to Bob Garland's (*Telegram*) review of *Show Girl* that appeared in a three-column article in that paper. Reproduced in *Duke Ellington Day by Day and Film By Film* by Dr Klaus Stratemann (Jazzmedia ApS, Denmark 1992), p. 4. It also quotes the *Chicago Defender* (10 August 1929), '[The Ellington band] play the early part of the evening with Ziegfeld's *Show Girl* after which they play the rest of the night at the famous Cotton Club.'

7 The Smithsonian Institution Jazz Oral History Project: Interview with William 'Sonny' Greer, January 1979, conducted by Stanley Crouch. Courtesy The Institute of Jazz Studies, Rutgers.

8 Carter Harman Interview Collection: May 1964. Courtesy Archives Center, NMAH, Smithsonian Institution, Washington D.C.

9 *Metronome*, February 1945, p. 26.

10 Carter Harman Interview Collection: 1964 #5. Courtesy Archives Center, NMAH, Smithsonian Institution, Washington D.C.

11 The Smithsonian Institution Jazz Oral History Project: Interview with Juan Tizol, November 1978, conducted by Patricia Willard. Courtesy The Institute of Jazz Studies, Rutgers.

12 The Smithsonian Institution Jazz Oral History Project: Interview with Barney Bigard, July 1976, conducted by Patricia Willard. Courtesy The Institute of Jazz Studies, Rutgers.

13 *Lyrics on Several Occasions* by Ira Gershwin (Omnibus Press, London 1978), p. 152.

14 The Smithsonian Institution Ellington Oral History Project: Interview with Mercer Ellington, September 1990, conducted by Dr Marcia M. Greenlee, Tape 3. Courtesy Archives Center, NMAH, Smithsonian Institution, Washington D.C.

15 Fredi Washington may have been the star, but Ellington had an affair with her, something that trombonist Lawrence Brown, who was married to her from 1933–48, never forgave him for.

16 *Billboard*, 9 November 1929, p. 24.

17 *Evening Graphic*, 18 June 1932.

18 *Ebony*, March 1959, p. 134.

19 *Duke Ellington in Person* by Mercer Ellington and Stanley Dance (Hutchinson, London 1978), pp. 47–8.

20 The Smithsonian Institution Jazz Oral History Project: Interview with

Lawrence Brown, July 1976, conducted by Patricia Willard. Courtesy The Institute of Jazz Studies, Rutgers.

21 The Smithsonian Institution Jazz Oral History Project: Interview with Barney Bigard, July 1976, conducted by Patricia Willard. Courtesy The Institute of Jazz Studies, Rutgers.

22 *Duke Ellington in Person* by Mercer Ellington and Stanley Dance (Hutchinson, London 1978), pp. 17–18.

23 The Smithsonian Institution Jazz Oral History Project: Interview with Barney Bigard, July 1976, conducted by Patricia Willard. Courtesy The Institute of Jazz Studies, Rutgers.

24 *Ebony*, March 1959, pp. 134 & 138.

25 Carter Harman Interview Collection: 1964 #8. Courtesy Archives Center, NMAH, Smithsonian Institution, Washington D.C.

26 Carter Harman Interview Collection: Las Vegas 1956 #3. Courtesy Archives Center, NMAH, Smithsonian Institution, Washington D.C.

27 The Smithsonian Institution Ellington Oral History Project: Interview with Ruth Boatwright-Ellington, August 1989, conducted by Dr Marcia M. Greenlee, Tape 1. Courtesy Archives Center, NMAH, Smithsonian Institution, Washington D.C.

28 Carter Harman Interview Collection: 1964 #8. Courtesy Archives Center, NMAH, Smithsonian Institution, Washington D.C.

29 *Jazz Journal*, June 1990, p. 12.

30 Carter Harman Interview Collection: 1964 #8. Courtesy Archives Center, NMAH, Smithsonian Institution, Washington D.C.

31 The Smithsonian Institution Ellington Oral History Project: Interview with Mercer Ellington, September 1990, conducted by Dr Marcia M. Greenlee, Tape 2. Courtesy Archives Center, NMAH, Smithsonian Institution, Washington D.C.

32 Carter Harman Interview Collection: 1964 #8. Courtesy Archives Center, NMAH, Smithsonian Institution, Washington D.C.

33 *The New York Times*, 29 March 1981. Arts and Leisure, p. 6.

34 Carter Harman Interview Collection: May 1964. Courtesy Archives Center, NMAH, Smithsonian Institution, Washington D.C.

35 The Smithsonian Institution Jazz Oral History Project: Interview with William 'Sonny' Greer, January 1979, conducted by Stanley Crouch. Courtesy The Institute of Jazz Studies, Rutgers.

36 Duke Ellington talks to Stanley Dance, BBC Radio 1971. Courtesy The National Sound Archive, The British Library.

37 *Herald Tribune* review by Howard Barnes included a full-page ad in

Variety, Wednesday, 2 April 1930, highlighting Ellington's recent successful engagement at the Fulton Theatre with Chevalier. Also included in Irving Mills' spread were rave reviews by *Daily News*, *Daily Mirror*, *Evening World* and *Evening Sun*. Reproduced in *Duke Ellington Day by Day and Film By Film* by Dr Klaus Stratemann (Jazzmedia ApS, Denmark 1992), p. 28.

38 The Smithsonian Institution Ellington Oral History Project: Interview with Mercer Ellington, September 1990, conducted by Dr Marcia M. Greenlee, Tape 3. Courtesy Archives Center, NMAH, Smithsonian Institution, Washington D.C.

39 Duke Ellington talks to Stanley Dance, BBC Radio 1971. Courtesy The National Sound Archive, The British Library.

40 *Swing*, June 1940, p. 22.

41 Carter Harman Interview Collection: 1964 #4. Courtesy Archives Center, NMAH, Smithsonian Institution, Washington D.C.

42 *Storyville*, April/May 1973, p. 131.

43 *Swing*, June 1940, p. 22.

44 *Duke Ellington talks to Max Jones and Humphrey Lyttelton*, BBC Radio 1964. Courtesy The National Sound Archive, The British Library.

45 Magazine feature in the series *Bandstand Personalities*, 1945, p. 43, source unknown. 'The Duke of Jazzdom' by Gretchen Weaver. Vertical clippings file 1943–5, Institute of Jazz Studies, Rutgers.

46 *With Louis and Duke* by Barney Bigard (Macmillan, London 1986), p. 89.

47 *Swing*, June 1940, p. 22.

48 *With Louis and Duke* by Barney Bigard (Macmillan, London 1986), p. 89.

49 *Variety*, 21 May 1930, p. 35.

50 The Smithsonian Institution Ellington Oral History Project: Interview with Ruth Boatwright-Ellington, August 1989, conducted by Dr Marcia M. Greenlee, Tape 1. Courtesy Archives Center, NMAH, Smithsonian Institution, Washington D.C.

51 *Irving Mills Documentary*. Interview with Irving Mills (1984) from a work in progress produced and directed by Don McGlynn. Courtesy Don McGlynn.

52 Carter Harman Interview Collection: May 1964. Courtesy Archives Center, NMAH, Smithsonian Institution, Washington D.C.

53 *Of Minnie the Moocher and Me* by Cab Calloway and Bryant Rollins (Crowell, New York 1976), pp. 86 & 87.

54 *Storyville*, April/May, 1973, p. 130.

55 Duke Ellington Interview with Jack Cullen, Radio CKNW, Vancouver. Recorded 1962. Courtesy Leonard Malone Collection.

56 The Smithsonian Institution Jazz Oral History Project: Interview with William 'Sonny' Greer, January 1979, conducted by Stanley Crouch. Courtesy The Institute of Jazz Studies, Rutgers.

57 The Smithsonian Institution Jazz Oral History Project: Interview with Juan Tizol, November 1978, conducted by Patricia Willard. Courtesy The Institute of Jazz Studies, Rutgers.

58 The Smithsonian Institution Ellington Oral History Project: Interview with Ruth Boatwright-Ellington, August 1989, conducted by Dr Marcia M. Greenlee, Tape 1. Courtesy Archives Center, NMAH, Smithsonian Institution, Washington D.C.

59 *Storyville*, April/May 1973, p. 131.

60 Carter Harman Interview Collection: 1964 #8. Courtesy Archives Center, NMAH, Smithsonian Institution, Washington D.C.

61 Carter Harman Interview Collection: 1964 #8. Courtesy Archives Center, NMAH, Smithsonian Institution, Washington D.C.

62 Carter Harman Interview Collection: May 1964. Courtesy Archives Center, NMAH, Smithsonian Institution, Washington D.C.

63 Carter Harman Interview Collection: 1964 #5. Courtesy Archives Center, NMAH, Smithsonian Institution, Washington D.C.

64 An edited talk between Duke Ellington and Henry Whiston of the Canadian Broadcasting Company, published in *Jazz Journal*, February 1967, p. 4.

65 The Smithsonian Institution Jazz Oral History Project: Interview with William 'Sonny' Greer, January 1979, conducted by Stanley Crouch. Courtesy The Institute of Jazz Studies, Rutgers.

66 The Smithsonian Institution Jazz Oral History Project: Interview with William 'Sonny' Greer, January 1979, conducted by Stanley Crouch. Courtesy The Institute of Jazz Studies, Rutgers.

67 Carter Harman Interview Collection: 1964 #5. Courtesy Archives Center, NMAH, Smithsonian Institution, Washington D.C.

68 *Boy Meets Horn* by Rex Stewart (Bayou Press, Oxford 1991), p. 178.

69 *Downbeat*, 15 July 1942, p. 31.

70 Carter Harman Interview Collection: 1964 #8. Courtesy Archives Center, NMAH, Smithsonian Institution, Washington D.C.

71 *Irving Mills Documentary*. Interview with Irving Mills (1984) from a

work in progress produced and directed by Don McGlynn. Courtesy Don McGlynn.

72 *Cleveland Press*, 12 June 1932.

73 *Irving Mills Documentary*. Interview with Irving Mills (1984) from a work in progress produced and directed by Don McGlynn. Courtesy Don McGlynn. From an interview 23 October 1984 conducted by Leonard Feather, Don McGlynn and Bob Udkoff.

74 The Smithsonian Institution Jazz Oral History Project: Interview with William 'Sonny' Greer, January 1979, conducted by Stanley Crouch. Courtesy The Institute of Jazz Studies, Rutgers.

75 *Irving Mills Documentary*. Interview with Irving Mills (1984) from a work in progress produced and directed by Don McGlynn. Courtesy Don McGlynn.

76 *Washington D.C. News*, 2 October 1931.

77 *Beyond Category: The Life and Genius of Duke Ellington* by James Edward Hasse (Simon & Schuster, New York, 1993), p. 151. Hasse says the meeting with President Hoover was cancelled because the man who set it up, C. L. Skinner had a police record.

78 Carter Harman Interview Collection: 1964 #5. Courtesy Archives Center, NMAH, Smithsonian Institution, Washington D.C.

79 The Smithsonian Institution Jazz Oral History Project: Interview with Lawrence Brown, July 1976, conducted by Patricia Willard. Courtesy The Institute of Jazz Studies, Rutgers.

80 Carter Harman Interview Collection: 1964 #5. Courtesy Archives Center, NMAH, Smithsonian Institution, Washington D.C.

81 The Smithsonian Institution Ellington Oral History Project: Interview with Mercer Ellington, September 1990, conducted by Dr Marcia M. Greenlee, Tape 1. Courtesy Archives Center, NMAH, Smithsonian Institution, Washington D.C.

82 The Smithsonian Institution Jazz Oral History Project: Interview with Lawrence Brown, July 1976, conducted by Patricia Willard. Courtesy The Institute of Jazz Studies, Rutgers.

83 *The World of Duke Ellington* by Stanley Dance (Macmillan, London 1971), p. 56.

84 Carter Harman Interview Collection: 1964 #5. Courtesy Archives Center, NMAH, Smithsonian Institution, Washington D.C.

85 The Smithsonian Institution Jazz Oral History Project: Interview with Lawrence Brown, July 1976, conducted by Patricia Willard. Courtesy The Institute of Jazz Studies, Rutgers.

86 The Smithsonian Institution Jazz Oral History Project: Interview with Lawrence Brown, July 1976, conducted by Patricia Willard. Courtesy The Institute of Jazz Studies, Rutgers.

87 *Talking Jazz* by Max Jones (Macmillan, London 1987), p. 60.

88 Carter Harman Interview Collection: Las Vegas 1956. Courtesy Archives Center, NMAH, Smithsonian Institution, Washington D.C.

89 The Smithsonian Institution Jazz Oral History Project: Interview with Barney Bigard, July 1976, conducted by Patricia Willard. Courtesy The Institute of Jazz Studies, Rutgers.

90 *Storyville*, April/May 1973, p. 131.

91 *Hear Me Talkin' to Ya* compiled by Nat Shapiro and Nat Hentoff (Holt, Rinehart & Winston Inc., New York 1955), p. 236.

92 *Irving Mills Documentary*. Interview with Irving Mills (1984) from a work in progress produced and directed by Don McGlynn. Courtesy Don McGlynn.

93 *Jazz Spoken Here* by Wayne Enstice and Paul Rubin (Louisiana State University Press, Baton Rouge 1992), p. 119.

94 The Smithsonian Institution Ellington Oral History Project: Interview with Ruth Boatwright-Ellington, August 1989, conducted by Dr Marcia M. Greenlee, Tape 1. Courtesy Archives Center, NMAH, Smithsonian Institution, Washington D.C.

95 The Smithsonian Institution Ellington Oral History Project: Interview with Mercer Ellington, September 1990, conducted by Dr Marcia M. Greenlee, Tape 3. Courtesy Archives Center, NMAH, Smithsonian Institution, Washington D.C.

96 The Smithsonian Institution Jazz Oral History Project: Interview with Barney Bigard, July 1976, conducted by Patricia Willard. Courtesy The Institute of Jazz Studies, Rutgers.

97 *Jazz Spoken Here* by Wayne Enstice and Paul Rubin (Louisiana State University Press, Baton Rouge 1992), p. 118.

98 The Smithsonian Institution Jazz Oral History Project: Interview with Lawrence Brown, July 1976, conducted by Patricia Willard. Courtesy The Institute of Jazz Studies, Rutgers.

99 *Irving Mills Documentary*. Interview with Irving Mills (1984) from a work in progress produced and directed by Don McGlynn. Courtesy Don McGlynn. From an interview 23 October 1984 conducted by Leonard Feather, Don McGlynn and Bob Udkoff.

100 *Downbeat*, 13 July 1967, p. 22.

101 *Irving Mills Documentary*. Interview with Irving Mills (1984) from a

work in progress produced and directed by Don McGlynn. Courtesy Don McGlynn. From an interview 23 October 1984 conducted by Leonard Feather, Don McGlynn and Bob Udkoff.

102 The Smithsonian Institution Jazz Oral History Project: Interview with Lawrence Brown, July 1976, conducted by Patricia Willard. Courtesy The Institute of Jazz Studies, Rutgers.

103 *Hot Jazz and Jazz Dance: Roger Pryor Dodge Collected Writings 1929–1964*, Pryor Dodge ed. (Oxford University Press, New York 1995), pp. 84, 86 & 103.

104 *Evening Graphic*, 18 June 1932.

105 The Smithsonian Institution Jazz Oral History Project: Interview with Lawrence Brown, July 1976, conducted by Patricia Willard. Courtesy The Institute of Jazz Studies, Rutgers.

106 Interview with Otto Hardwick, 29 April 1964, conducted by Felix Grant, Radio WMAL, Washington D.C. Courtesy Donald L. McCathran.

107 *Talking Jazz* by Max Jones (Macmillan, London 1987), p. 11.

108 Carter Harman Interview Collection: Las Vegas, 1956. Courtesy Archives Center, NMAH, Smithsonian Institution, Washington D.C.

109 The Smithsonian Institution Jazz Oral History Project: Interview with Juan Tizol, November 1978, conducted by Patricia Willard. Courtesy The Institute of Jazz Studies, Rutgers.

110 *Boy Meets Horn* by Rex Stewart (Bayou Press, Oxford 1991), pp. 153–4.

111 The Smithsonian Institution Jazz Oral History Project: Interview with Juan Tizol, November 1978, conducted by Patricia Willard. Courtesy The Institute of Jazz Studies, Rutgers.

112 *Hear Me Talkin' to Ya* compiled by Nat Shapiro and Nat Hentoff (Holt, Rinehart & Winston Inc., New York 1955), p. 235.

113 *Irving Mills Documentary*. Interview with Irving Mills (1984) from a work in progress produced and directed by Don McGlynn. Courtesy Don McGlynn. From an interview 23 October 1984 conducted by Leonard Feather, Don McGlynn and Bob Udkoff.

114 The Smithsonian Institution Jazz Oral History Project: Interview with William 'Sonny' Greer, January 1979, conducted by Stanley Crouch. Courtesy The Institute of Jazz Studies, Rutgers.

115 *Alberta Hunter: A Celebration in Blues* by Frank C. Taylor and Gerald Cook (McGraw-Hill, New York 1987).

116 *New Yorker*, 8 July 1944.

CHAPTER FIVE:
THE DUKE STEPS OUT

1 *Pittsburgh Courier*, 31 December 1931, p. 2.

2 *Evening Graphic*, 18 June 1932.

3 *Swing*, September 1940, p. 9.

4 *Irving Mills Documentary*. Interview with Irving Mills (1984) from a work in progress produced and directed by Don McGlynn. Courtesy Don McGlynn. From an interview 23 October 1984 conducted by Leonard Feather, Don McGlynn and Bob Udkoff.

5 *The Melody Maker*, 3 June 1933. 'Standing Room Only for "MM" Concert, Jack Hylton Booking Extra Dates.' Courtesy Dr Lindsay M. Newman, The Library, Lancaster University.

6 *Swing*, September 1940, p. 9.

7 *Talking Jazz* by Max Jones (Macmillan, London 1987), p. 11.

8 *Swing*, September 1940, p. 9.

9 Interview with Otto Hardwick, 29 April 1964, conducted by Felix Grant, Radio WMAL, Washington D.C. Courtesy Donald L. McCathran.

10 *The People*, 18 June 1933. 'Hannen Swaffer Listens to the Soul of a Negro.' Courtesy Dr Lindsay M. Newman, The Library, Lancaster University.

11 *Swing*, September 1940, p. 9.

12 *News of the World*, 11 June 1933. 'A Negro Band's Debut In England.' Courtesy Dr Lindsay M. Newman, The Library, Lancaster University.

13 *Swing*, September 1940, p. 9.

14 The Smithsonian Institution Jazz Oral History Project: Interview with Juan Tizol, November 1978, conducted by Patricia Willard. Courtesy The Institute of Jazz Studies, Rutgers.

15 *Swing*, September 1940, p. 9.

16 The Smithsonian Institution Jazz Oral History Project: Interview with William 'Sonny' Greer, January 1979, conducted by Stanley Crouch. Courtesy The Institute of Jazz Studies, Rutgers.

17 *The People*, 18 June 1933. 'Hannen Swaffer Listens to the Soul of a Negro.' Courtesy Dr Lindsay M. Newman, The Library, Lancaster University.

18 Programme notes: *A Concert of the Music of Duke Ellington presented by The Melody Maker*, 25 June 1933, p. 23.

19 Carter Harman Interview Collection: Las Vegas 1956. Courtesy Archives Center, NMAH, Smithsonian Institution, Washington D.C.

20 *The People*, 18 June 1933. 'Hannen Swaffer Listens to the Soul of a Negro.' Courtesy Dr Lindsay M. Newman, The Library, Lancaster University.

21 *Gramophone*, July 1933, p. 67.

22 *Swing*, September 1940, p. 9.

23 Carter Harman Interview Collection: 1964 #8. Courtesy Archives Center, NMAH, Smithsonian Institution, Washington D.C.

24 *Irving Mills Documentary*. Interview with Irving Mills (1984) from a work in progress produced and directed by Don McGlynn. Courtesy Don McGlynn. From an interview 23 October 1984 conducted by Leonard Feather, Don McGlynn and Bob Udkoff.

25 *Swing*, September 1940, p. 9.

26 The Smithsonian Institution Jazz Oral History Project: Interview with William 'Sonny' Greer, January 1979, conducted by Stanley Crouch. Courtesy The Institute of Jazz Studies, Rutgers.

27 *Swing*, September 1940, p. 9.

28 *Swing*, September 1940, p. 9.

29 *Swing*, September 1940, pp. 9 & 24.

30 Probably *New York Times*, dated 9 August 1933. Duke Ellington file, Lincoln Center for Performing Arts, New York.

31 *Daily Mail*, 4 September 1998, p. 11. 'What is the Truth About George's Death?' by Ross Benson.

32 *Swing*, September 1940, p. 24.

33 *Daily Mail*, 31 July 1933.

34 *Swing*, September 1940, p. 24.

35 *The Melody Maker*, 12 August 1933, p. 11; 19 August 1933, p. 13.

36 Carter Harman Interview Collection: 1964 #5. Courtesy Archives Center, NMAH, Smithsonian Institution, Washington D.C.

37 *The Melody Maker*, 12 August 1933, p. 11; 19 August 1933, p. 13.

38 *Swing*, September 1940, p. 24.

39 *The Melody Maker*, 12 August 1933, p. 11; 19 August 1933, p. 13.

40 *Jazz Spoken Here* by Wayne Enstice and Paul Rubin (Louisiana State University Press, Baton Rouge 1992), p. 118.

41 *The Melody Maker*, 1 July 1933.

42 Duke Ellington talking to Percy Mathison Brooks, 14 July 1933. Alternate (previously unissued) version of a 'Recorded Souvenir Of

Duke Ellington's First Visit To England In 1933'; courtesy the National Sound Archive, The British Library.

43 *Swing*, September 1940, p. 24.

44 *Downbeat*, 25 April 1974, p. 16.

45 The Smithsonian Institution Jazz Oral History Project: Interview with William 'Sonny' Greer, January 1979, conducted by Stanley Crouch. Courtesy The Institute of Jazz Studies, Rutgers.

46 Interview with Otto Hardwick, 29 April 1964, conducted by Felix Grant, Radio WMAL, Washington D.C. Courtesy Donald L. McCathran.

47 The Smithsonian Institution Jazz Oral History Project: Interview with William 'Sonny' Greer, January 1979, conducted by Stanley Crouch. Courtesy The Institute of Jazz Studies, Rutgers.

48 *Irving Mills Documentary*. Interview with Irving Mills (1984) from a work in progress produced and directed by Don McGlynn. Courtesy Don McGlynn. From an interview 23 October 1984 conducted by Leonard Feather, Don McGlynn and Bob Udkoff.

49 *Of Minnie the Moocher and Me* by Cab Calloway and Bryant Rollins (Crowell, New York 1976), pp. 106 & 120.

50 *Irving Mills Documentary*. Interview with Irving Mills (1984) from a work in progress produced and directed by Don McGlynn. Courtesy Don McGlynn. From an interview 23 October 1984 conducted by Leonard Feather, Don McGlynn and Bob Udkoff.

51 *Irving Mills Presents Duke Ellington by Irving Mills: Advertising Manual*. Compiled by the Irving Mills office in 1934 and sent to managers of theatres and ballrooms to assist in their publicity campaigns promoting an appearance by Duke Ellington and his Famous Orchestra. Courtesy Don McGlynn.

52 *Irving Mills Documentary*. Interview with Irving Mills (1984) from a work in progress produced and directed by Don McGlynn. Courtesy Don McGlynn. From an interview 23 October 1984 conducted by Leonard Feather, Don McGlynn and Bob Udkoff.

53 *Downbeat*, 17 April 1969, p. 17.

54 *Irving Mills Documentary*. Interview with Irving Mills (1984) from a work in progress produced and directed by Don McGlynn. Courtesy Don McGlynn.

55 The Smithsonian Institution Jazz Oral History Project: Interview with Lawrence Brown, July 1976, conducted by Patricia Willard. Courtesy The Institute of Jazz Studies, Rutgers.

56 *Irving Mills Documentary*. Interview with Irving Mills (1984) from a work in progress produced and directed by Don McGlynn. Courtesy Don McGlynn. From an interview 23 October 1984 conducted by Leonard Feather, Don McGlynn and Bob Udkoff.

57 Carter Harman Interview Collection: 1964 #8. Courtesy Archives Center, NMAH, Smithsonian Institution, Washington D.C.

58 *Swing*, September 1940, p. 24.

59 The Smithsonian Institution Jazz Oral History Project: Interview with Juan Tizol, November 1978, conducted by Patricia Willard. Courtesy The Institute of Jazz Studies, Rutgers.

60 *Irving Mills Documentary*. Interview with Irving Mills (1984) from a work in progress produced and directed by Don McGlynn. Courtesy Don McGlynn. From an interview 23 October 1984 conducted by Leonard Feather, Don McGlynn and Bob Udkoff.

61 The Smithsonian Institution Jazz Oral History Project: Interview with William 'Sonny' Greer, January 1979, conducted by Stanley Crouch. Courtesy The Institute of Jazz Studies, Rutgers.

62 Carter Harman Interview Collection: 1964 #5. Courtesy Archives Center, NMAH, Smithsonian Institution, Washington D.C.

63 The Smithsonian Institution Jazz Oral History Project: Interview with William 'Sonny' Greer, January 1979, conducted by Stanley Crouch. Courtesy The Institute of Jazz Studies, Rutgers.

64 The Smithsonian Institution Jazz Oral History Project: Interview with Lawrence Brown, July 1976, conducted by Patricia Willard. Courtesy The Institute of Jazz Studies, Rutgers.

65 Carter Harman Interview Collection: 1964 #5. Courtesy Archives Center, NMAH, Smithsonian Institution, Washington D.C.

66 The Smithsonian Institution Jazz Oral History Project: Interview with Barney Bigard, July 1976, conducted by Patricia Willard. Courtesy The Institute of Jazz Studies, Rutgers.

67 The Smithsonian Institution Jazz Oral History Project: Interview with William 'Sonny' Greer, January 1979, conducted by Stanley Crouch. Courtesy The Institute of Jazz Studies, Rutgers.

68 *Storyville*, April/May 1973, p. 131.

69 The Smithsonian Institution Jazz Oral History Project: Interview with Juan Tizol, November 1978, conducted by Patricia Willard. Courtesy The Institute of Jazz Studies, Rutgers.

70 Duke Ellington talks to Stanley Dance, BBC Radio 1971. Courtesy The National Sound Archive, The British Library.

71 Carter Harman Interview Collection: 1956 #5. Courtesy Archives Center, NMAH, Smithsonian Institution, Washington D.C.

72 Duke Ellington interview by Michael Parkinson on *The Parkinson Show*, BBC-TV, 1973. Courtesy The National Sound Archive, The British Library.

73 Carter Harman Interview Collection: Las Vegas 1956 #3. Courtesy Archives Center, NMAH, Smithsonian Institution, Washington D.C.

74 The Smithsonian Institution Jazz Oral History Project: Interview with William 'Sonny' Greer, January 1979, conducted by Stanley Crouch. Courtesy The Institute of Jazz Studies, Rutgers.

75 The Smithsonian Institution Ellington Oral History Project: Interview with Mercer Ellington, September 1990, conducted by Dr Marcia M. Greenlee, Tape 2. Courtesy Archives Center, NMAH, Smithsonian Institution, Washington D.C.

76 The Smithsonian Institution Ellington Oral History Project: Interview with Ruth Boatwright-Ellington, August 1989, conducted by Dr Marcia M. Greenlee, Tape 2. Courtesy Archives Center, NMAH, Smithsonian Institution, Washington D.C.

77 *Irving Mills Documentary*. Interview with Irving Mills (1984) from a work in progress produced and directed by Don McGlynn. Courtesy Don McGlynn. From an interview 23 October 1984 conducted by Leonard Feather, Don McGlynn and Bob Udkoff.

78 *Swing*, September 1940, p. 24.

79 *Los Angeles Daily News*, 21 April 1934, p. 14.

80 Interview with author, 24 July 1998.

81 Radio interview from *Paul Worth presents A Portrait of Duke Ellington*. Courtesy Don McGlynn collection.

82 The Smithsonian Institution Jazz Oral History Project: Interview with Barney Bigard, July 1976, conducted by Patricia Willard. Courtesy The Institute of Jazz Studies, Rutgers.

83 The Smithsonian Institution Jazz Oral History Project: Interview with Juan Tizol, November 1978, conducted by Patricia Willard. Courtesy The Institute of Jazz Studies, Rutgers.

84 Carter Harman Interview Collection: 1964 #5. Courtesy Archives Center, NMAH, Smithsonian Institution, Washington D.C.

85 *Boy Meets Horn* by Rex Stewart (Bayou Press, Oxford 1991), p. 150.

86 *New Theater*, December 1935, p. 6. Jerry Valburn Duke Ellington collection, Box #1. Courtesy Library of Congress, Washington D.C.

87 *New York Amsterdam News*, unprovenanced cutting, probably late 1935, courtesy Schomberg Institute of Black Studies, Harlem.

88 Carter Harman Interview Collection: 1964 #8. Courtesy Archives Center, NMAH, Smithsonian Institution, Washington D.C.

89 *New Yorker*, 8 July 1944.

90 Carter Harman Interview Collection: 1964 #8. Courtesy Archives Center, NMAH, Smithsonian Institution, Washington D.C.

91 *Duke Ellington In Person* by Mercer Ellington with Stanley Dance (Hutchinson, London 1978), pp. 68–9

92 *The New York Amsterdam News*, 15 June 1935, p. 11.

93 *Duke Ellington In Person* by Mercer Ellington with Stanley Dance (Hutchinson, London 1978), pp. 68–9.

94 *New Yorker*, 8 July 1944.

95 *Variety*, provenance unknown. Courtesy Institute of Jazz Studies, Rutgers.

96 *American Music-Lover*, provenance unknown. Courtesy Institute of Jazz Studies, Rutgers.

97 *Esquire*, provenance unknown. Courtesy Institute of Jazz Studies, Rutgers.

98 *New Yorker*, provenance unknown. Courtesy Institute of Jazz Sudies, Rutgers.

99 *Washington Post*, provenance unknown. Courtesy Institute of Jazz Studies, Rutgers.

100 *Swing*, September 1940, p. 24.

101 *Jazz Journal*, May 1966, p. 13.

102 *Swing*, September 1940, p. 24.

103 *Downbeat*, 22 April 1965, p. 21. Reprinted in *Jazz Masters of the '30s* by Rex Stewart (Macmillan, New York 1972).

104 *Swing*, September 1940, p. 24.

105 *Soap Box* by Adam Clayton Powell Jr, dated 1936. Probably from *New York Age* or *New York Amsterdam News*. Vertical clippings file, 1935–8, Institute of Jazz Studies, Rutgers.

106 The Smithsonian Jazz Oral History Project: Interview with Lawrence Brown, July 1976, conducted by Patricia Willard. Courtesy The Institute of Jazz Studies, Rutgers.

107 Interview with Otto Hardwick, 29 April 1964, conducted by Felix Grant, Radio WMAL, Washington D.C. Courtesy Donald L. McCathran.

108 *Irving Mills Documentary*. Interview with Irving Mills (1984) from a work in progress produced and directed by Don McGlynn. Courtesy Don McGlynn. From an interview 23 October 1984 conducted by Leonard Feather, Don McGlynn and Bob Udkoff.
109 Carter Harman Interview Collection: 1964 #8. Courtesy Archives Center, NMAH, Smithsonian Institution, Washington D.C.
110 *Duke Ellington In Person* by Mercer Ellington and Stanley Dance (Hutchinson, London 1978), pp. 53–4.
111 *The Afro-American*, 30 May 1936.
112 The Smithsonian Institution Ellington Oral History Project: Interview with Mercer Ellington, September 1990, conducted by Dr Marcia M. Greenlee, Tape 1. Courtesy Archives Center, NMAH, Smithsonian Institution, Washington D.C.
113 *Downbeat*, 22 April 1965, p. 21. Reprinted in *Jazz Masters of the '30s* by Rex Stewart (Macmillan, New York 1972).
114 The Smithsonian Institution Jazz Oral History Project: Interview with Barney Bigard, July 1976, conducted by Patricia Willard. Courtesy The Institute of Jazz Studies, Rutgers.
115 *Music Maker*, August 1967. Republished in *Jazz Masters of the '30s* by Rex Stewart (Macmillan, New York 1972).
116 *The New York Times Magazine*, 12 September 1965, p. 76.
117 'Music is "Tops" to You and Me ... and Swing is a Part of It' by Edward Kennedy 'Duke' Ellington. Magazine feature from 1938, vertical clippings file 1936–8, Institute of Jazz Studies, Rutgers.

CHAPTER SIX:

STEPPIN' INTO SWING SOCIETY

1 *Variety*, 29 January 1936, p. 45.
2 'Music is 'Tops' to You and Me ... and Swing is a Part of It' by Edward Kennedy 'Duke' Ellington. Magazine feature from 1938, vertical clippings file 1936–8, Institute of Jazz Studies, Rutgers.
3 *The Call*, 18 December 1937.
4 *Swing*, September 1940, p. 24.
5 *Metronome*, June 1937. Reprinted in *Simon Says: The Sights and*

Sounds of the Swing Era by George T. Simon (Arlington House, New York 1971), pp. 83 & 84.

6 *Swing*, September 1940, p. 24.

7 Liner notes *Duke Ellington The Duke's Men: Small Groups Vol. 1* (Columbia/Legacy 468618–2), p. 11.

8 The Smithsonian Institution Jazz Oral History Project: Interview with Juan Tizol, November 1978, conducted by Patricia Willard. Courtesy The Institute of Jazz Studies, Rutgers.

9 Liner notes *Duke Ellington The Duke's Men: Small Groups Vol. 1* (Columbia/Legacy 468618–2), p. 15.

10 Carter Harman Interview Collection: 1964 #4. Courtesy Archives Center, NMAH, Smithsonian Institution, Washington D.C.

11 Carter Harman Interview Collection: 1964 #3. Courtesy Archives Center, NMAH, Smithsonian Institution, Washington D.C.

12 *Faces of Jazz*. Programme Number 8 (1972). Courtesy Danmarks Radio, Copenhagen.

13 *Downbeat*, 13 July 1967, p. 22.

14 *Metronome*, April 1937. Reprinted in *Simon Says: The Sights and Sounds of the Swing Era* by George T. Simon (Arlington House, New York 1971), pp. 402 & 403.

15 Carter Harman Interview Collection: 1964 #8. Courtesy Archives Center, NMAH, Smithsonian Institution, Washington D.C.

16 *New Yorker*, 8 July 1944. Richard O. Boyer authored a three-part 'Profile' of Ellington (24 June, 1 July and 8 July issues) called *The Hot Bach* after several extended interviews with Ellington during a second extended run at New York's Hurricane Club (opening 30 March and closing 7 June).

17 The Smithsonian Institution Jazz Oral History Project: Interview with Juan Tizol, November 1978, conducted by Patricia Willard. Courtesy The Institute of Jazz Studies, Rutgers.

18 The Smithsonian Institution Jazz Oral History Project: Interview with Barney Bigard, July 1976, conducted by Patricia Willard. Courtesy The Institute of Jazz Studies, Rutgers.

19 *FBI File 100–434443: Edward Kennedy (Duke) Ellington.* In response to a request received from the Educational Exchange Service on 25 March 1953, a response was sent citing several instances of Ellington's alleged involvement with 'communist front' organizations, which the FBI apparently construed as any organization involved in racial equality or

overseas humanitarian causes. The contents were again cited in a letter dated 22 July 1955, repeated in slightly modified form in a letter under the signature of John Edgar Hoover, Director of the Federal Bureau of Investigation, dated 5 June 1957 and again on 22 May 1964.

20 *Metronome*, April 1937.

21 The Smithsonian Institution Jazz Oral History Project: Interview with Juan Tizol, November 1978, conducted by Patricia Willard. Courtesy The Institute of Jazz Studies, Rutgers.

22 Carter Harman Interview Collection. Courtesy Archives Center, NMAH, Smithsonian Institution, Washington D.C.

23 'Music is "Tops" to You and Me . . . and Swing is a Part of It' by Edward Kennedy 'Duke' Ellington. Magazine feature from 1938, vertical clippings file 1936–8, Institute of Jazz Studies, Rutgers.

24 *Boy Meets Horn* by Rex Stewart (Bayou Press, Oxford 1991), p. 209.

25 Carter Harman Interview Collection: 1964 #4. Courtesy Archives Center, NMAH, Smithsonian Institution, Washington D.C.

26 The Smithsonian Institution Jazz Oral History Project: Interview with Lawrence Brown, July 1976, conducted by Patricia Willard. Courtesy The Institute of Jazz Studies, Rutgers.

27 Interview with author, 24 July 1998.

28 Liner notes *Duke Ellington: The Duke's Men: Small Groups Vol 1* (Columbia/Legacy 468618–2), p. 12.

29 The Smithsonian Institution Jazz Oral History Project: Interview with Barney Bigard, July 1976, conducted by Patricia Willard. Courtesy The Institute of Jazz Studies, Rutgers.

30 *Storyville*, April/May 1973, p. 124.

31 The Smithsonian Institution Jazz Oral History Project: Interview with Barney Bigard, July 1976, conducted by Patricia Willard. Courtesy The Institute of Jazz Studies, Rutgers.

32 *Swing*, September 1940, p. 24.

33 Carter Harman Interview Collection: Courtesy Archives Center, NMAH, Smithsonian Institution, Washington D.C.

34 Ed Anderson interview on *Duke Ellington . . . and his Famous Orchestra*, BBC-TV. Courtesy The National Sound Archive, The British Library.

35 The Smithsonian Institution Jazz Oral History Project: Interview with Barney Bigard, July 1976, conducted by Patricia Willard. Courtesy The Institute of Jazz Studies, Rutgers.

36 *Jazz Journal*, October 1976, p. 7.

37 *The Real Duke Ellington* by Don George (Robson Books, London 1982), p. 137.

38 Ed Anderson interview on *Duke Ellington . . . and his Famous Orchestra*, BBC-TV. Courtesy The National Sound Archive, The British Library.

39 *The Real Duke Ellington* by Don George (Robson Books, London 1982), p. 138.

40 *Storyville*, April/May 1973, p. 132.

41 Carter Harman Interview Collection: 1964 #1. Courtesy Archives Center, NMAH, Smithsonian Institution, Washington D.C.

42 The Smithsonian Institution Jazz Oral History Project: Interview with Cootie Williams, May 1976, conducted by Helen Dance. Courtesy The Institute of Jazz Studies, Rutgers.

43 The Smithsonian Institution Ellington Oral History Project: Interview with Ruth Boatwright-Ellington, August 1989, conducted by Dr Marcia M. Greenlee, Tape 1. Courtesy Archives Center, NMAH, Smithsonian Institution, Washington D.C.

44 *Downbeat*, 26 December 1956, p. 25.

45 Interview with author, 24 July 1998.

46 *The New York Times Magazine*, 17 January 1943, p. 10.

47 *Swing*, September 1940, p. 24.

48 Duke Ellington interview by Michael Parkinson on *The Parkinson Show*, BBC-TV, 1973. Courtesy The National Sound Archive, The British Library.

49 Billy Strayhorn interview on Danish Radio, provenance unknown. Courtesy Leonard Malone.

50 Duke Ellington interview by Michael Parkinson on *The Parkinson Show*, BBC-TV, 1973. Courtesy The National Sound Archive, The British Library.

51 Carter Harman Interview Collection: 1964 #8. Courtesy Archives Center, NMAH, Smithsonian Institution, Washington D.C.

52 *Downbeat*, 5 November 1952, p. 10.

53 The Smithsonian Institution Jazz Oral History Project: Interview with William 'Sonny' Greer, January 1979, conducted by Stanley Crouch. Courtesy The Institute of Jazz Studies, Rutgers.

54 The Smithsonian Institution Jazz Oral History Project: Interview with Juan Tizol, November 1978, conducted by Patricia Willard. Courtesy The Institute of Jazz Studies, Rutgers.

55 The Smithsonian Institution Jazz Oral History Project: Interview with

Lawrence Brown, July 1976, conducted by Patricia Willard. Courtesy The Institute of Jazz Studies, Rutgers.

56 Interview with author, 24 July 1998.

57 *Downbeat*, 7 June 1962, p. 22.

58 Carter Harman Interview Collection: 1964 #8. Courtesy Archives Center, NMAH, Smithsonian Institution, Washington D.C.

59 Carter Harman Interview Collection: 1964 #5. Courtesy Archives Center, NMAH, Smithsonian Institution, Washington D.C.

60 *Swing*, September 1940, p. 24.

61 The Smithsonian Institution Jazz Oral History Project: Interview with William 'Sonny' Greer, January 1979, conducted by Stanley Crouch. Courtesy The Institute of Jazz Studies, Rutgers.

62 *Boy Meets Horn* by Rex Stewart (Bayou Press, Oxford 1991), p. 187.

63 *Jazz Journal*, September 1967, p. 6.

64 Magazine feature in the series 'Bandstand Personalities', 1945, p. 43, source unknown. 'The Duke of Jazzdom' by Gretchen Weaver. Vertical clippings file, 1943–5, Institute of Jazz Studies, Rutgers.

65 The Smithsonian Institution Jazz Oral History Project: Interview with William 'Sonny' Greer, January 1979, conducted by Stanley Crouch. Courtesy The Institute of Jazz Studies, Rutgers.

66 *Swing*, September 1940, p. 24.

67 The Smithsonian Institution Jazz Oral History Project: Interview with William 'Sonny' Greer, January 1979, conducted by Stanley Crouch. Courtesy The Institute of Jazz Studies, Rutgers.

68 *Boy Meets Horn* by Rex Stewart (Bayou Press, Oxford 1991) p. 189.

69 Carter Harman Interview Collection: 1964 #8. Courtesy Archives Center, NMAH, Smithsonian Institution, Washington D.C.

70 *Swing*, September 1940, p. 24.

71 *Melody Maker*, 6 May 1939, p. 1.

72 *John Hammond on Record: An Autobiography with Irving Townsend* (Penguin Books, London 1981), p. 139.

73 Interview with author, 24 July 1998.

74 Carter Harman Interview Collection: 1964 #8. Courtesy Archives Center, NMAH, Smithsonian Institution, Washington D.C.

75 *Downbeat*, 5 November 1952, p. 6.

76 *Boy Meets Horn* by Rex Stewart (Bayou Press, Oxford 1991), p. 189.

77 *Downbeat*, 7 June 1962, p. 22.

78 Duke Ellington interview by Michael Parkinson on *The Parkinson*

Show, BBC-TV, 1973. Courtesy The National Sound Archive, The British Library.

79 Carter Harman Interview Collection: 1964 #5. Courtesy Archives Center, NMAH, Smithsonian Institution, Washington D.C.

80 Carter Harman Interview Collection: 1964 #8. Courtesy Archives Center, NMAH, Smithsonian Institution, Washington D.C.

81 The Smithsonian Institution Jazz Oral History Project: Interview with Lawrence Brown, July 1976, conducted by Patricia Willard. Courtesy The Institute of Jazz Studies, Rutgers.

82 Carter Harman Interview Collection: 1964 #8. Courtesy Archives Center, NMAH, Smithsonian Institution, Washington D.C.

83 *Downbeat*, 7 June 1962, p. 23.

84 *More Dialogues in Swing* by Fred Hall (Pathfinder Publishing, Ventura, Calif. 1991), p. 104.

85 Duke Ellington's handwritten notes for his autobiography *Music is My Mistress*. This section was written on the notepaper of the Rice Hotel, Houston. The Duke Ellington Collection #301, Series 5 (Box #5, Folder 6), Courtesy Archives Center, NMAH, Smithsonian Institution, Washington D.C.

86 *Variety*, 21 February 1940, p. 34.

CHAPTER SEVEN:
IN A MELLOTONE

1 *Swing*, September 1940, p. 24.

2 The Smithsonian Institution Jazz Oral History Project: Interview with William 'Sonny' Greer, January 1979, conducted by Stanley Crouch. Courtesy The Institute of Jazz Studies, Rutgers.

3 Carter Harman Interview Collection: 1964 #5. Courtesy Archives Center, NMAH, Smithsonian Institution, Washington D.C.

4 The Smithsonian Institution Jazz Oral History Project: Interview with Lawrence Brown, July 1976, conducted by Patricia Willard. Courtesy The Institute of Jazz Studies, Rutgers.

5 *Downbeat*, 30 May 1956, p. 25.

6 *Jazz Journal*, September 1967, p. 5.

7 From the film documentary *A Duke Named Ellington* (1988). Courtesy Leonard Malone, writer and co-producer. The Leonard Malone Collection: Originally used in *Faces of Jazz*.

8 From the film documentary *A Duke Named Ellington* (1988). Courtesy Leonard Malone, writer and co-producer. The Leonard Malone Collection. Originally used in *Faces of Jazz.*

9 *Jazz Anecdotes* by Bill Crow (Oxford University Press, London 1990), p. 249.

10 *Talking Jazz* by Max Jones (Macmillan, London 1987), p. 83.

11 The Smithsonian Institution Ellington Oral History Project: Interview with Mercer Ellington, September 1990, conducted by Dr Marcia M. Greenlee, Tape 4. Courtesy Archives Center, NMAH, Smithsonian Institution, Washington D.C.

12 *Talking Jazz* by Max Jones (Macmillan, London 1987), pp. 83–4.

13 From the film documentary *A Duke Named Ellington* (1988). Courtesy Leonard Malone, writer and co-producer. The Leonard Malone Collection: Originally used in *Faces of Jazz.*

14 The Smithsonian Institution Ellington Oral History Project: Interview with Mercer Ellington, September 1990, conducted by Dr Marcia M. Greenlee, Tape 5. Courtesy Archives Center, NMAH, Smithsonian Institution, Washington D.C.

15 The Smithsonian Institution Jazz Oral History Project: Interview with Lawrence Brown, July 1976, conducted by Patricia Willard. Courtesy The Institute of Jazz Studies, Rutgers.

16 *Downbeat*, 1 June 1967, p. 20. Reprinted in *Jazz Masters of the '30s* by Rex Stewart (Macmillan, New York 1972).

17 The Smithsonian Institution Jazz Oral History Project: Interview with William 'Sonny' Greer, January 1979, conducted by Stanley Crouch. Courtesy The Institute of Jazz Studies, Rutgers.

18 *Jazz Journal*, September 1967, p. 5.

19 Interview with Mercer Ellington on *Sounds of Surprise: Ben Webster – the Brute and the Beautiful*. BBC-TV. Courtesy The National Sound Archive, The British Library.

20 *Jazz Journal*, September 1967, pp. 5–6.

21 Interview with Herb Jeffries on *Omnibus: Reminiscing in Tempo – Part 2: 'Riding on a Blue Note'*. BBC-TV. Courtesy The National Sound Archive, The British Library.

22 The Smithsonian Institution Ellington Oral History Project: Interview with Mercer Ellington, September 1990, conducted by Dr Marcia M. Greenlee, Tape 1. Courtesy Archives Center, NMAH, Smithsonian Institution, Washington D.C.

23 *Downbeat*, 1 June 1967, p. 23. Reprinted in *Jazz Masters of the '30s* by Rex Stewart (Macmillan, New York 1972).

24 The Smithsonian Institution Jazz Oral History Project: Interview with Barney Bigard, July 1976, conducted by Patricia Willard. Courtesy The Institute of Jazz Studies, Rutgers.

25 The Smithsonian Institution Jazz Oral History Project: Interview with Cootie Williams, May 1976, conducted by Helen Dance. Courtesy The Institute of Jazz Studies, Rutgers.

26 *The World of Duke Ellington* by Stanley Dance (Macmillan, London 1971), p. 128.

27 The Smithsonian Institution Jazz Oral History Project: Interview with Lawrence Brown, July 1976, conducted by Patricia Willard. Courtesy The Institute of Jazz Studies, Rutgers.

28 *Downbeat*, 21 May 1964, reprinted in the January 1998 issue, p. 34.

29 *Duke Ellington His Life and Music* edited by Peter Gammond (Roy Publishers, New York 1958), p. 176 & 177.

30 The Smithsonian Institution Jazz Oral History Project: Interview with Tom Whaley, March 1980, conducted by Milt Hinton. Courtesy The Institute of Jazz Studies, Rutgers.

31 Carter Harman Interview Collection: 1964 #4. Courtesy Archives Center, NMAH, Smithsonian Institution, Washington D.C.

32 Carter Harman Interview Collection: 1964 #5. Courtesy Archives Center, NMAH, Smithsonian Institution, Washington D.C.

33 *More Dialogues in Swing* by Fred Hall (Pathfinder Publishing, Ventura, Calif. 1991), p. 105.

34 Duke Ellington Interview on Danish Radio. Provenance unknown. Courtesy Leonard Malone.

35 *Off the Record: An Oral History of Popular Music* by Joe Smith, edited by Mitchell Fink (Sidgwick & Jackson, London 1989), p. 29.

36 *American Popular Music Business in the 20th Century* by Russell Sanjek and Davis Sanjek (Oxford University Press, New York 1991), p. 64.

37 *Downbeat*, 1 November 1940, p. 16.

38 *The World of Duke Ellington* by Stanley Dance (Macmillan, London 1971), p. 29.

39 Carter Harman Interview Collection: 1964 #5. Courtesy Archives Center, NMAH, Smithsonian Institution, Washington D.C.

40 *Lush Life* by David Hajdu (Farrar Straus Giroux, New York 1996), pp. 83–4.

41 *Downbeat*, 30 May 1956.

42 Carter Harman Interview Collection: 1964 #5. Courtesy Archives Center, NMAH, Smithsonian Institution, Washington D.C.

43 From the film documentary *A Duke Named Ellington* (1988). Courtesy Leonard Malone, writer and co-producer. The Leonard Malone Collection: Originally used in *Faces of Jazz*.

44 The Smithsonian Institution Jazz Oral History Project: Interview with Lawrence Brown, July 1976, conducted by Patricia Willard. Courtesy The Institute of Jazz Studies, Rutgers.

45 The Smithsonian Institution Ellington Oral History Project: Interview with Ruth Boatwright-Ellington, August 1989, conducted by Dr Marcia M. Greenlee, Tape 1. Courtesy Archives Center, NMAH, Smithsonian Institution, Washington D.C.

46 Duke Ellington talks to Stanley Dance, BBC Radio 1971. Courtesy The National Sound Archive, The British Library.

47 *FBI File 100–434443: Edward Kennedy (Duke) Ellington.* In response to a request received from the Educational Exchange Service on 25 March 1953, a response was sent citing several instances of Ellington's alleged involvement with 'communist front' organizations, which the FBI apparently construed as any organization involved in racial equality or overseas humanitarian causes. The contents were again cited in a letter dated 22 July 1955, repeated in slightly modified form in a letter under the signature of John Edgar Hoover, Director of the Federal Bureau of Investigation, dated 5 June 1957 and again on 22 May 1964.

48 Duke Ellington talks to Stanley Dance, BBC Radio 1971. Courtesy The National Sound Archive, The British Library.

49 Interview with author, 24 July 1998.

50 Interview with Sid Kuller on *Omnibus: Reminiscing in Tempo – Part 2: 'Riding on a Blue Note'*. BBC-TV. Courtesy The National Sound Archive, The British Library.

51 Carter Harman Interview Collection: 1964 #5. Courtesy Archives Center, NMAH, Smithsonian Institution, Washington D.C.

52 Interview with author, 24 July 1998.

53 The Smithsonian Institution Ellington Oral History Project: Interview with Mercer Ellington, September 1990, conducted by Dr Marcia M. Greenlee, Tape 3. Courtesy Archives Center, NMAH, Smithsonian Institution, Washington D.C.

54 Carter Harman Interview Collection: 1964 #7. Courtesy Archives Center, NMAH, Smithsonian Institution, Washington D.C.

55 *Metronome*, October 1941. Reprinted in *Simon Says: The Sights and Sounds of the Swing Era* by George T. Simon (Arlington House, New York 1971), pp. 263 & 264.

56 An edited talk between Duke Ellington and Henry Whiston of the Canadian Broadcasting Company, published in *Jazz Journal*, February 1967, p. 5.

57 Carter Harman Interview Collection: Las Vegas 1956. Courtesy Archives Center, NMAH, Smithsonian Institution, Washington D.C.

58 *More Dialogues in Swing* by Fred Hall (Pathfinder Publishing, Ventura, Calif. 1991), p. 110.

59 Interview with Sid Kuller on *Omnibus: Reminiscing in Tempo – Part 2: 'Riding on a Blue Note'*. BBC-TV. Courtesy The National Sound Archive, The British Library.

60 Duke Ellington Interview by Orson Welles, 8 June 1970. American TV Show. Courtesy Leonard Malone.

61 An edited talk between Duke Ellington and Henry Whiston of the Canadian Broadcasting Company, published in *Jazz Journal*, February 1967, p. 6. When Ellington related the same story on the Orson Welles television show, 8 June 1970, on American TV (courtesy Leonard Malone, Leonard Malone Collection), the essential detail remained the same, albeit in much truncated form. However, in this later interview and in his introduction to Leonard Feather's *Encyclopedia of Jazz*, Ellington says he was on a retainer of $1,000 per week.

62 The Smithsonian Institution Ellington Oral History Project: Interview with Mercer Ellington, September 1990, conducted by Dr Marcia M. Greenlee, Tape 4. Courtesy Archives Center, NMAH, Smithsonian Institution, Washington D.C.

63 *Jazz Journal*, December 1981, pp. 11 & 12.

64 *Downbeat*, 5 November 1952.

65 *Boy Meets Horn* by Rex Stewart (Bayou Press, Oxford 1991), p. 198.

66 The Smithsonian Institution Jazz Oral History Project: Interview with Tom Whaley, March 1980, conducted by Milt Hinton. Courtesy The Institute of Jazz Studies, Rutgers.

67 Carter Harman Interview Collection: 1964 #5. Courtesy Archives Center, NMAH, Smithsonian Institution, Washington D.C.

68 *Boy Meets Horn* by Rex Stewart (Bayou Press, Oxford 1991), p. 192.

69 *More Dialogues in Swing* by Fred Hall (Pathfinder Publishing, Ventura, Calif. 1991), p. 109.

70 The Smithsonian Institution Jazz Oral History Project: Interview with Juan Tizol, November 1978, conducted by Patricia Willard. Courtesy The Institute of Jazz Studies, Rutgers.

71 *Boy Meets Horn* by Rex Stewart (Bayou Press, Oxford 1991), pp. 192 & 214.

72 The Smithsonian Institution Jazz Oral History Project: Interview with Barney Bigard, July 1976, conducted by Patricia Willard. Courtesy The Institute of Jazz Studies, Rutgers.

73 The Smithsonian Institution Jazz Oral History Project: Interview with Lawrence Brown, July 1976, conducted by Patricia Willard. Courtesy The Institute of Jazz Studies, Rutgers.

74 Carter Harman Interview Collection: 1964 #5. Courtesy Archives Center, NMAH, Smithsonian Institution, Washington D.C.

75 *Duke Ellington His Life and Music* edited by Peter Gammond (Roy Publishers, New York 1958), p. 182.

76 The Smithsonian Institution Jazz Oral History Project: Interview with Lawrence Brown, July 1976, conducted by Patricia Willard. Courtesy The Institute of Jazz Studies, Rutgers.

77 *From Birdland to Broadway* by Bill Crow (Oxford University Press, New York 1992), p. 142.

78 The Smithsonian Institution Ellington Oral History Project: Interview with Mercer Ellington, September 1990, conducted by Dr Marcia M. Greenlee, Tape 5. Courtesy Archives Center, NMAH, Smithsonian Institution, Washington D.C.

79 *The New York Times*, 28 May 1943.

80 *Downbeat*, 1943. Vertical clippings file, Institute of Jazz Studies, Rutgers.

81 Carter Harman Interview Collection: 1964 #8. Courtesy Archives Center, NMAH, Smithsonian Institution, Washington D.C.

82 *FBI File 100–434443: Edward Kennedy (Duke) Ellington.* In response to a request received from the Educational Exchange Service on 25 March 1953, a response was sent citing several instances of Ellington's alleged involvement with 'communist front' organizations, which the FBI apparently construed as any organization involved in racial equality or overseas humanitarian causes. The contents were again cited in a letter dated 22 July 1955, repeated in slightly modified form in a letter under the signature of John Edgar Hoover, Director of the

Federal Bureau of Investigation, dated 5 June 1957 and again on 22 May 1964.

83 Carter Harman Interview Collection: 1964 #8. Courtesy Archives Center, NMAH, Smithsonian Institution, Washington D.C.

84 *Variety*, 20 January 1943, p. 43.

85 *Jazz Journal*, July 1974, p. 8.

86 The Smithsonian Institution Jazz Oral History Project: Interview with William 'Sonny' Greer, January 1979, conducted by Stanley Crouch. Courtesy The Institute of Jazz Studies, Rutgers.

87 The Smithsonian Institution Jazz Oral History Project: Interview with Lawrence Brown, July 1976, conducted by Patricia Willard. Courtesy The Institute of Jazz Studies, Rutgers.

88 Carter Harman Interview Collection: Las Vegas 1956. Courtesy Archives Center, NMAH, Smithsonian Institution, Washington D.C.

89 *New York Herald Tribune*, 25 January 1943.

90 *World Telegram*, 25 January 1943.

91 *New York Sun*, 25 January 1943.

92 *Downbeat*, 15 February 1943, p. 12.

93 Duke Ellington interview by Michael Parkinson on *The Parkinson Show*, BBC-TV, 1973. Courtesy The National Sound Archive, The British Library.

94 *Downbeat*, 15 February 1943, p. 12.

95 Library of Congress, Voice of America Recordings WB357. Duke Ellington interviewed by Howard Boxer at the Howard Theatre, Washington D.C., 26 April 1962.

96 *Music Is My Mistress* by Duke Ellington (W. H. Allen, London 1974), p. 103.

97 Carter Harman Interview Collection: Las Vegas, 1956. Courtesy Archives Center, NMAH, Smithsonian Institution, Washington D.C.

98 *Jazz Spoken Here* by Wayne Enstice and Paul Rubin (Louisiana State University Press, Baton Rouge 1992), p. 121.

99 *Downbeat*, 13 July 1967, p. 22.

100 Duke Ellington talks to Stanley Dance, BBC Radio 1971. Courtesy The National Sound Archive, The British Library.

101 Carter Harman Interview Collection: 1964 #8. Courtesy Archives Center, NMAH, Smithsonian Institution, Washington D.C.

102 Library of Congress Voice of America Recordings. Press conference, 29 April 1962.

103 Carter Harman Interview Collection 1964 #3. Courtesy Archives Center, NMAH, Smithsonian Institution, Washington D.C.

104 Carter Harman Interview Collection: May 1964. Courtesy Archives Center, NMAH, Smithsonian Institution, Washington D.C.

105 From the film documentary *A Duke Named Ellington* (1988). Courtesy Leonard Malone, writer and co-producer. The Leonard Malone Collection.

106 Duke Ellington's handwritten notes for his autobiography *Music is My Mistress*. This section was written on the notepaper of the Steigenberger Park Hotel, Düsseldorf. The Duke Ellington Collection #301, Series 5 (Box #5, Folder 6), Courtesy Archives Center, NMAH, Smithsonian Institution, Washington D.C.

107 Al Hibbler interview on *Duke Ellington . . . and his Famous Orchestra*, BBC-TV. Courtesy The National Sound Archive, The British Library.

108 From the film documentary *A Duke Named Ellington* (1988). Courtesy Leonard Malone, writer and co-producer. The Leonard Malone Collection.

109 Al Hibbler interview on *Duke Ellington . . . and his Famous Orchestra*, BBC-TV. Courtesy The National Sound Archive, The British Library.

110 From the film documentary *A Duke Named Ellington* (1988). Courtesy Leonard Malone, writer and co-producer. The Leonard Malone Collection. Originally used in *Faces of Jazz*.

111 Carter Harman Interview Collection: 1964 #5. Courtesy Archives Center, NMAH, Smithsonian Institution, Washington D.C.

112 Carter Harman Interview Collection: 1964 #4. Courtesy Archives Center, NMAH, Smithsonian Institution, Washington D.C.

113 *Variety*, 15 December 1943, p. 41.

114 *Variety*, 5 January 1944, p. 1.

115 *New Yorker*, 8 July 1944.

CHAPTER EIGHT:
THINGS AIN'T WHAT THEY USED TO BE

1 Carter Harman Interview Collection: 1964 #8. Courtesy Archives Center, NMAH, Smithsonian Institution, Washington D.C.

2 *FBI File 100–434443: Edward Kennedy (Duke) Ellington.* In response to a request received from the Educational Exchange Service on 25 March 1953, a response was sent citing several instances of Ellington's

alleged involvement with 'communist front' organizations, which the FBI apparently construed as any organization involved in racial equality or overseas humanitarian causes. The contents were again cited in a letter dated 22 July 1955, repeated in slightly modified form in a letter under the signature of John Edgar Hoover, Director of the Federal Bureau of Investigation, dated 5 June 1957 and again on 22 May 1964.

3   *FBI File 100–434443: Edward Kennedy (Duke) Ellington.* In response to a request received from the Educational Exchange Service on 25 March 1953, a response was sent citing several instances of Ellington's alleged involvement with 'communist front' organizations, which the FBI apparently construed as any organization involved in racial equality or overseas humanitarian causes. The contents were again cited in a letter dated 22 July 1955, repeated in slightly modified form in a letter under the signature of John Edgar Hoover, Director of the Federal Bureau of Investigation, dated 5 June 1957 and again on 22 May 1964.

4   *FBI File 100–434443: Edward Kennedy (Duke) Ellington.* In response to a request received from the Educational Exchange Service on 25 March 1953, a response was sent citing several instances of Ellington's alleged involvement with 'communist front' organizations, which the FBI apparently construed as any organization involved in racial equality or overseas humanitarian causes. The contents were again cited in a letter dated 22 July 1955, repeated in slightly modified form in a letter under the signature of John Edgar Hoover, Director of the Federal Bureau of Investigation, dated 5 June 1957 and again on 22 May 1964.

5   The Smithsonian Institution Jazz Oral History Project: Interview with Juan Tizol, November 1978, conducted by Patricia Willard. Courtesy The Institute of Jazz Studies, Rutgers.

6   The Smithsonian Institution Jazz Oral History Project: Interview with Lawrence Brown, July 1976, conducted by Patricia Willard. Courtesy The Institute of Jazz Studies, Rutgers.

7   *Metronome*, July 1944. Reprinted in *Simon Says: The Sights and Sounds of the Swing Era* by George T. Simon (Arlington House, New York 1971), pp. 458 & 459.

8   The Smithsonian Institution Ellington Oral History Project: Interview with Mercer Ellington, September 1990, conducted by Dr Marcia M.

Greenlee, Tape 4. Courtesy Archives Center, NMAH, Smithsonian Institution, Washington D.C.

9 *FBI File 100–434443: Edward Kennedy (Duke) Ellington.* In response to a request received from the Educational Exchange Service on 25 March 1953, a response was sent citing several instances of Ellington's alleged involvement with 'communist front' organizations, which the FBI apparently construed as any organization involved in racial equality or overseas humanitarian causes. The contents were again cited in a letter dated 22 July 1955, repeated in slightly modified form in a letter under the signature of John Edgar Hoover, Director of the Federal Bureau of Investigation, dated 5 June 1957 and again on 22 May 1964.

10 Magazine feature in the series *Bandstand Personalities*, 1945, p. 43, source unknown. 'The Duke of Jazzdom' by Gretchen Weaver. Vertical clippings file 1943–5, Institute of Jazz Studies, Rutgers.

11 *New Yorker*, 24 June 1944.

12 Carter Harman Interview Collection: 1964 #8. Courtesy Archives Center, NMAH, Smithsonian Institution, Washington D.C.

13 *Nat King Cole* by Maria Cole with Louie Robinson (W. H. Allen & Co Ltd, London 1972, p. 15.

14 The Smithsonian Institution Jazz Oral History Project: Interview with William 'Sonny' Greer, January 1979, conducted by Stanley Crouch. Courtesy The Institute of Jazz Studies, Rutgers.

15 The Smithsonian Institution Jazz Oral History Project: Interview with Jimmy Jones, February 1978, conducted by Patricia Willard. Courtesy The Institute of Jazz Studies, Rutgers.

16 The Smithsonian Institution Jazz Oral History Project: Interview with Lawrence Brown, July 1976, conducted by Patricia Willard. Courtesy The Institute of Jazz Studies, Rutgers.

17 Carter Harman Interview Collection: 1964 #5. Courtesy Archives Center, NMAH, Smithsonian Institution, Washington D.C.

18 *Jazz Journal*, February 1963, p. 6.

19 Carter Harman Interview Collection: 1964 #5. Courtesy Archives Center, NMAH, Smithsonian Institution, Washington D.C.

20 From the film documentary *A Duke Named Ellington* (1988). Courtesy Leonard Malone, writer and co-producer. The Leonard Malone Collection.

21 The Smithsonian Institution Jazz Oral History Project: Interview with

Lawrence Brown, July 1976, conducted by Patricia Willard. Courtesy The Institute of Jazz Studies, Rutgers.

22 Carter Harman Interview Collection: 1964 #5. Courtesy Archives Center, NMAH, Smithsonian Institution, Washington D.C.

23 *FBI File 100–434443: Edward Kennedy (Duke) Ellington.* In response to a request received from the Educational Exchange Service on 25 March 1953, a response was sent citing several instances of Ellington's alleged involvement with 'communist front' organizations, which the FBI apparently construed as any organization involved in racial equality or overseas humanitarian causes. The contents were again cited in a letter dated 22 July 1955, repeated in slightly modified form in a letter under the signature of John Edgar Hoover, Director of the Federal Bureau of Investigation, dated 5 June 1957 and again on 22 May 1964.

24 Carter Harman Interview Collection: 1964 #8. Courtesy Archives Center, NMAH, Smithsonian Institution, Washington D.C.

25 The Smithsonian Institution Jazz Oral History Project: Interview with Tom Whaley, March 1980, conducted by Milt Hinton. Courtesy The Institute of Jazz Studies, Rutgers.

26 The Smithsonian Institution Jazz Oral History Project: Interview with Juan Tizol, November 1978, conducted by Patricia Willard. Courtesy The Institute of Jazz Studies, Rutgers.

27 *Billboard*, 23 November 1946, p. 43.

28 The Smithsonian Institution Jazz Oral History Project: Interview with Lawrence Brown, July 1976, conducted by Patricia Willard. Courtesy The Institute of Jazz Studies, Rutgers.

29 The Smithsonian Institution Jazz Oral History Project: Interview with William 'Sonny' Greer, January 1979, conducted by Stanley Crouch. Courtesy The Institute of Jazz Studies, Rutgers.

30 *Django Reinhardt* by Charles Delaunay (Da Capo, New York 1981), pp. 138 & 139.

31 The Smithsonian Institution Jazz Oral History Project: Interview with William 'Sonny' Greer, January 1979, conducted by Stanley Crouch. Courtesy The Institute of Jazz Studies, Rutgers.

32 *Django Reinhardt* by Charles Delaunay (Da Capo, New York 1981), pp. 137 & 138.

33 An edited talk between Duke Ellington and Henry Whiston of the Canadian Broadcasting Company, published in *Jazz Journal*, February 1967, p. 5.

34 George Abbot, as interviewed by David Hajdu from *Lush Life: A Biography of Billy Strayhorn* by David Hajdu (Farrar Straus Giroux, New York 1996), p. 102.

35 *Downbeat*, 15 January 1947.

36 *Variety*, 28 May 1947, p. 52.

37 Carter Harman Interview Collection: 1964 #8. Courtesy Archives Center, NMAH, Smithsonian Institution, Washington D.C.

38 *FBI File 100–434443: Edward Kennedy (Duke) Ellington.* In response to a request received from the Educational Exchange Service on 25 March 1953, a response was sent citing several instances of Ellington's alleged involvement with 'communist front' organizations, which the FBI apparently construed as any organization involved in racial equality of overseas humanitarian causes. The contents were again cited in a letter dated 22 July 1955. It was again repeated in slightly modified form in a letter under the signature of John Edgar Hoover, Director of the Federal Bureau of Investigation, dated 5 June 1957 and again on 22 May 1964.

39 The Smithsonian Institution Jazz Oral History Project: Interview with Lawrence Brown, July 1976, conducted by Patricia Willard. Courtesy The Institute of Jazz Studies, Rutgers.

40 Carter Harman Interview Collection: 1964 #8. Courtesy Archives Center, NMAH, Smithsonian Institution, Washington D.C.

41 Carter Harman Interview Collection: 1964 #8. Courtesy Archives Center, NMAH, Smithsonian Institution, Washington D.C.

42 An edited talk between Duke Ellington and Henry Whiston of the Canadian Broadcasting Company, published in *Jazz Journal*, February 1967, p. 6.

43 Carter Harman Interview Collection: 1964 #8. Courtesy Archives Center, NMAH, Smithsonian Institution, Washington D.C.

44 *Melody Maker*, 26 June 1948, p. 1.

45 *Jazz at Ronnie Scott's*, Number 114, p. 20.

46 Panel discussion, Ellington '97.

47 Panel discussion, Ellington '97.

48 *Jazz at Ronnie Scott's*, Number 114, p. 20.

49 Panel discussion, Ellington '97.

50 *Jazz at Ronnie Scott's*, Number 114, p. 20.

51 *Melody Maker*, 10 July 1948.

52 *Crescendo*, March 1964, p. 17.

53 Jimmy Hamilton interview on *Duke Ellington ... and his Famous*

Orchestra, BBC-TV. Courtesy The National Sound Archive, The British Library.

54 *Downbeat*, 8 September 1948, p. 1.
55 Carter Harman Interview Collection: May 1964. Courtesy Archives Center, NMAH, Smithsonian Institution, Washington D.C.
56 The Smithsonian Institution Jazz Oral History Project: Interview with Lawrence Brown, July 1976, conducted by Patricia Willard. Courtesy The Institute of Jazz Studies, Rutgers.
57 *Downbeat*, 17 June 1949, pp. 1 & 12.
58 *Metronome*, September 1952. Reprinted in *Simon Says: The Sights and Sounds of the Swing Era* by George T. Simon (Arlington House, New York 1971), p. 36.
59 The Smithsonian Institution Ellington Oral History Project: Interview with Mercer Ellington, September 1990, conducted by Dr Marcia M. Greenlee, Tape 8. Courtesy Archives Center, NMAH, Smithsonian Institution, Washington D.C.
60 The Smithsonian Institution Ellington Oral History Project: Interview with Mercer Ellington, September 1990, conducted by Dr Marcia M. Greenlee, Tape 2. Courtesy Archives Center, NMAH, Smithsonian Institution, Washington D.C.
61 Carter Harman Interview Collection: 1964 #4. Courtesy Archives Center, NMAH, Smithsonian Institution, Washington D.C.
62 An edited talk between Duke Ellington and Henry Whiston of the Canadian Broadcasting Company, published in *Jazz Journal*, February 1967, p. 7.
63 Carter Harman Interview Collection: 1964 #8. Courtesy Archives Center, NMAH, Smithsonian Institution, Washington D.C.
64 Carter Harman Interview Collection: 1964 #8. Courtesy Archives Center, NMAH, Smithsonian Institution, Washington D.C.
65 Carter Harman Interview Collection: 1964 #6. Courtesy Archives Center, NMAH, Smithsonian Institution, Washington D.C.
66 The Smithsonian Institution Jazz Oral History Project: Interview with Lawrence Brown, July 1976, conducted by Patricia Willard. Courtesy The Institute of Jazz Studies, Rutgers.
67 *FBI File 100–434443: Edward Kennedy (Duke) Ellington.* In response to a request received from the Educational Exchange Service on 25 March 1953, a response was sent citing several instances of Ellington's alleged involvement with 'communist front' organizations, which the FBI apparently construed as any organization involved in racial equality

or overseas humanitarian causes. The contents were again cited in a letter dated 22 July 1955, repeated in slightly modified form in a letter under the signature of John Edgar Hoover, Director of the Federal Bureau of Investigation, dated 5 June 1957 and again on 22 May 1964.

68 The Smithsonian Institution Ellington Oral History Project: Interview with Mercer Ellington, September 1990, conducted by Dr Marcia M. Greenlee, Tape 3. Courtesy Archives Center, NMAH, Smithsonian Institution, Washington D.C.

69 *Crescendo*, March 1964, pp. 21 & 22.

70 The Smithsonian Institution Jazz Oral History Project: Interview with Lawrence Brown, July 1976, conducted by Patricia Willard. Courtesy The Institute of Jazz Studies, Rutgers.

71 *Crescendo*, March 1964, p. 23.

72 The Smithsonian Institution Jazz Oral History Project: Interview with Lawrence Brown, July 1976, conducted by Patricia Willard. Courtesy The Institute of Jazz Studies, Rutgers.

73 *Jazz Anecdotes* by Bill Crow (Oxford University Press, London 1990), pp. 247–8.

74 Interview with Mercer Ellington on *Omnibus: Reminiscing in Tempo – Part 2: 'Riding on a Blue Note'*. BBC-TV. Courtesy The National Sound Archive, The British Library.

75 *The Real Duke Ellington* by Don George (Robson Books, 1982), p. 81.

76 The Smithsonian Institution Jazz Oral History Project: Interview with Barney Bigard, July 1976, conducted by Patricia Willard. Courtesy The Institute of Jazz Studies, Rutgers.

77 The Smithsonian Institution Jazz Oral History Project: Interview with William 'Sonny' Greer, January 1979, conducted by Stanley Crouch. Courtesy The Institute of Jazz Studies, Rutgers.

78 Carter Harman Interview Collection: 1964 #8. Courtesy Archives Center, NMAH, Smithsonian Institution, Washington D.C.

79 *Downbeat*, 13 July 1967, p. 21.

80 *Crescendo International*, May 1983, p. 24.

81 The Smithsonian Institution Jazz Oral History Project: Interview with Lawrence Brown, July 1976, conducted by Patricia Willard. Courtesy The Institute of Jazz Studies, Rutgers.

82 *Crescendo*, March 1964, p. 17.

83 Cue Hodges, as interviewed by David Hajdu from *Lush Life: A Biography of Billy Strayhorn* by David Hajdu (Farrar Straus Giroux, New York 1996), p. 140.

84 Carter Harman Interview Collection: May 1964. Courtesy Archives Center, NMAH, Smithsonian Institution, Washington D.C.

85 The Smithsonian Institution Jazz Oral History Project: Interview with Juan Tizol, November 1978, conducted by Patricia Willard. Courtesy The Institute of Jazz Studies, Rutgers.

86 *Barney, Bradley, and Max* by Whitney Balliett (Oxford University Press, New York 1989), pp. 208 & 209.

87 The Smithsonian Institution Jazz Oral History Project: Interview with Barney Bigard, July 1976, conducted by Patricia Willard. Courtesy The Institute of Jazz Studies, Rutgers.

88 *Crescendo International*, May 1983, p. 24.

89 *Melody Maker*, 15 May 1951. 'Drummer Bellson Makes the New Ellington Band Rock' by Leonard Feather.

90 Carter Harman Interview Collection: 1964 #8. Courtesy Archives Center, NMAH, Smithsonian Institution, Washington D.C.

91 *Barney, Bradley, and Max* by Whitney Balliett (Oxford University Press, New York 1989), p. 209.

92 The Smithsonian Institution Jazz Oral History Project: Interview with Lawrence Brown, July 1976, conducted by Patricia Willard. Courtesy The Institute of Jazz Studies, Rutgers.

93 Mercer Ellington interview on *Duke Ellington ... and his Famous Orchestra*, BBC-TV. Courtesy The National Sound Archive, The British Library.

94 *Metronome*, September 1952. Reprinted in *Simon Says: The Sights and Sounds of the Swing Era* by George T. Simon (Arlington House, New York 1971), p. 36.

95 *Jazz Journal*, December 1986, p. 11.

96 Carter Harman Interview Collection: 1964 #6. Courtesy Archives Center, NMAH, Smithsonian Institution, Washington D.C.

97 From the film documentary *A Duke Named Ellington* (1988). Courtesy Leonard Malone, writer and co-producer. The Leonard Malone Collection.

98 The Smithsonian Institution Jazz Oral History Project: Interview with Cootie Williams, May 1976, conducted by Helen Dance. Courtesy The Institute of Jazz Studies, Rutgers.

99 *Jazz Journal*, December 1986, p. 11.

100 *Metronome*, September 1952. Reprinted in *Simon Says: The Sights and Sounds of the Swing Era* by George T. Simon (Arlington House, New York 1971), p. 36.

101 *Crescendo*, June 1977, p. 21.

102 *The Afro-American*, 3 November 1951, p. 3.

103 Carter Harman Interview Collection: 1964 #2. Courtesy Archives Center, NMAH, Smithsonian Institution, Washington D.C.

104 *The Afro-American*, 24 November 1951, p. 7.

105 Carter Harman Interview Collection: 1964 #3. Courtesy Archives Center, NMAH, Smithsonian Institution, Washington D.C.

106 The Smithsonian Institution Ellington Oral History Project: Interview with Mercer Ellington, September 1990, conducted by Dr Marcia M. Greenlee, Tape 3. Courtesy Archives Center, NMAH, Smithsonian Institution, Washington D.C.

107 *The Afro-American*, 1 December 1951, p. 5.

108 *The Afro-American*, 1 December 1951, p. 5.

109 *Jazz Journal*, June 1990, p. 13.

110 The Smithsonian Institution Ellington Oral History Project: Interview with Mercer Ellington, September 1990, conducted by Dr Marcia M. Greenlee, Tape 7. Courtesy Archives Center, NMAH, Smithsonian Institution, Washington D.C.

111 From the film documentary *A Duke Named Ellington* (1988). Courtesy Leonard Malone, writer and co-producer. The Leonard Malone Collection.

112 The Smithsonian Institution Ellington Oral History Project: Interview with Mercer Ellington, September 1990, conducted by Dr Marcia M. Greenlee, Tape 1. Courtesy Archives Center, NMAH, Smithsonian Institution, Washington D.C.

113 Carter Harman Interview Collection: 1964 #8. Courtesy Archives Center, NMAH, Smithsonian Institution, Washington D.C.

114 The Smithsonian Institution Jazz Oral History Project: Interview with William 'Sonny' Greer, January 1979, conducted by Stanley Crouch. Courtesy The Institute of Jazz Studies, Rutgers.

115 *Beneath the Underdog* by Charles Mingus (Penguin, London 1975), p. 233.

116 The Smithsonian Institution Jazz Oral History Project: Interview with Juan Tizol, November 1978, conducted by Patricia Willard. Courtesy The Institute of Jazz Studies, Rutgers.

117 *Ebony*, May 1954, pp. 105 & 106. 'Sex Is No Sin' by Duke Ellington. 'Suave Bandleader Says Wholesome Sex Is One Of God's Finest Creations.'

118 Letter from President Dwight D. Eisenhower to Duke Ellington, 12

March 1955. Vertical file 1953–5. Courtesy The Institute of Jazz Studies, Rutgers.

119 Panel discussion, Ellington '97.

120 Carter Harman Interview Collection: Las Vegas 1956 #1. Courtesy Archives Center, NMAH, Smithsonian Institution, Washington D.C.

121 Duke Ellington's handwritten notes. The Duke Ellington Collection #301, Series 5 (Box #6, Folder 1), Courtesy Archives Center, NMAH, Smithsonian Institution, Washington D.C.

122 *Lush Life* by David Hajdu (Farrar Straus Giroux, New York 1996), p. 193.

123 *Jazz Journal*, January 1967, p. 7.

124 *Duke Ellington Talks to Max Jones and Humphrey Lyttelton*, BBC Radio 1964. Courtesy The National Sound Archive, The British Library.

125 *Metronome*, September 1952. Reprinted in *Simon Says: The Sights and Sounds of the Swing Era* by George T. Simon (Arlington House, New York 1971), p. 36.

126 The Smithsonian Institution Ellington Oral History Project: Interview with Mercer Ellington, September 1990, conducted by Dr Marcia M. Greenlee, Tape 7. Courtesy Archives Center, NMAH, Smithsonian Institution, Washington D.C.

127 *Duke Ellington His Life and Music* edited by Peter Gammond (Roy Publishers, New York 1958), p. 187.

128 Carter Harman Interview Collection: 1964 #8. Courtesy Archives Center, NMAH, Smithsonian Institution, Washington D.C.

129 The Smithsonian Institution Ellington Oral History Project: Interview with Clark Terry, October 1990, conducted by Dr Marcia M. Greenlee. Courtesy Archives Center, NMAH, Smithsonian Institution, Washington D.C.

130 *Downbeat*, 26 December 1956, p. 25.

131 The Smithsonian Institution Ellington Oral History Project: Interview with Mercer Ellington, September 1990, conducted by Dr Marcia M. Greenlee, Tape 6. Courtesy Archives Center, NMAH, Smithsonian Institution, Washington D.C.

132 Carter Harman Interview Collection: Courtesy Archives Center, NMAH, Smithsonian Institution, Washington D.C.

133 *Jazz Anecdotes* by Bill Crow (Oxford University Press, London 1990), pp. 110–11.

134 *Crescendo*, March 1964, p. 17.
135 *Christian Science Monitor*, 3 April 1956.

CHAPTER NINE:
NEWPORT UP

1 Carter Harman Interview Collection: Las Vegas 1956 #1. Courtesy Archives Center, NMAH, Smithsonian Institution, Washington D.C.
2 Interview with George Wein on *Omnibus: Reminiscing in Tempo – Part 2: 'Riding on a Blue Note'*. BBC-TV. Courtesy The National Sound Archive, The British Library.
3 *Jazz Journal*, October 1976, p. 4.
4 *Downbeat*, 6 August 1958, p. 20.
5 *Newport Jazz Festival: The Illustrated History* by Burt Goldblatt (The Dial Press, New York 1977), p. 28.
6 Carter Harman Interview Collection: Las Vegas, 1956 #1. Courtesy Archives Center, NMAH, Smithsonian Institution, Washington D.C.
7 *Newport Jazz Festival: The Illustrated History* by Burt Goldblatt (The Dial Press, New York 1977), pp. 28–29.
8 Clark Terry interview on *Duke Ellington . . . and his Famous Orchestra*, BBC-TV. Courtesy The National Sound Archive, The British Library.
9 *Crescendo*, March 1964, p. 23.
10 Duke Ellington talks to Stanley Dance, BBC Radio 1971. Courtesy The National Sound Archive, The British Library.
11 *Newport Jazz Festival: The Illustrated History* by Burt Goldblatt (The Dial Press, New York 1977), p. 29.
12 From the film documentary *A Duke Named Ellington* (1988). Courtesy Leonard Malone, writer and co-producer. The Leonard Malone Collection.
13 Carter Harman Interview Collection: 1964 #6. Courtesy Archives Center, NMAH, Smithsonian Institution, Washington D.C.
14 *Time*, 20 August 1956, p. 54.
15 Carter Harman Interview Collection: Courtesy Archives Center, NMAH, Smithsonian Institution, Washington D.C.
16 *Crescendo*, March 1964, p. 23.
17 *Jazz Journal*, October 1977, p. 35.
18 Carter Harman Interview Collection: 1964 #8. Courtesy Archives Center, NMAH, Smithsonian Institution, Washington D.C.

19 *Jazz Journal*, October 1976, p. 5.
20 Duke Ellington interview by Michael Parkinson on *The Parkinson Show*, BBC-TV, 1973. Courtesy The National Sound Archive, The British Library.
21 Billy Strayhorn interview on Danish Radio, provenance unknown. Courtesy Leonard Malone, the Leonard Malone Collection.
22 From the film documentary *A Duke Named Ellington* (1988). Courtesy Leonard Malone, writer and co-producer. The Leonard Malone Collection.
23 *Downbeat*, 27 June 1957, p. 18.
24 *Jazz Journal*, January 1966, p. 9.
25 *Downbeat*, 26 December 1956, p. 25.
26 *Boy Meets Horn* by Rex Stewart (Bayou Press, Oxford 1991), p. 203.
27 *The New York Times Magazine*, 12 September 1965, p. 70.
28 Jimmy Hamilton interview on *Duke Ellington ... and his Famous Orchestra*, BBC-TV. Courtesy The National Sound Archive, The British Library.
29 *Duke Ellington His Life and Music* edited by Peter Gammond (Roy Publishers, New York 1958), p. 183.
30 *Jazz Journal*, January 1967, p. 7.
31 *Jazz Journal*, January 1967, p. 7.
32 From the film documentary *A Duke Named Ellington* (1988). Courtesy Leonard Malone, writer and co-producer. The Leonard Malone Collection.
33 *Downbeat*, November 1979, p. 36.
34 *Downbeat*, 18 November 1965, p. 23.
35 *Jazz Journal*, November 1963, p. 18.
36 *Lush Life* by David Hajdu (Farrar Straus Giroux, New York 1996), p. 168.
37 From the film documentary *A Duke Named Ellington* (1988). Courtesy Leonard Malone, writer and co-producer. The Leonard Malone Collection.
38 Billy Strayhorn interview on Danish Radio, provenance unknown. Courtesy Leonard Malone, The Leonard Malone Collection.
39 The Smithsonian Institution Ellington Oral History Project: Interview with Mercer Ellington, September 1990, conducted by Dr Marcia M. Greenlee, Tape 6. Courtesy Archives Center, NMAH, Smithsonian Institution, Washington D.C.
40 *Downbeat*, 30 May 1956.

41 From the film documentary *A Duke Named Ellington* (1988). Courtesy Leonard Malone, writer and co-producer. The Leonard Malone Collection.

42 Radio interview from *Paul Worth presents A Portrait of Duke Ellington*. Courtesy Don McGlynn Collection.

43 An edited talk between Duke Ellington and Henry Whiston of the Canadian Broadcasting Company, published in *Jazz Journal*, February 1967, p. 7.

44 An edited talk between Duke Ellington and Henry Whiston of the Canadian Broadcasting Company, published in *Jazz Journal*, February 1967, p. 7.

45 *Jazz Anecdotes* by Bill Crow (Oxford University Press, London 1990), pp. 126–7.

46 *Jazz*, October 1962, p. 9.

47 The Smithsonian Institution Jazz Oral History Project: Interview with Jimmy Jones, February 1978, conducted by Patricia Willard. Courtesy The Institute of Jazz Studies, Rutgers.

48 *Jazz Anecdotes* by Bill Crow (Oxford University Press, London 1990), p. 249.

49 An edited talk between Duke Ellington and Henry Whiston of the Canadian Broadcasting Company, published in *Jazz Journal*, February 1967, p. 5.

50 Duke Ellington talks to Stanley Dance, BBC Radio 1971. Courtesy The National Sound Archive, The British Library.

51 From the film documentary *A Duke Named Ellington* (1988). Courtesy Leonard Malone, writer and co-producer. The Leonard Malone Collection.

52 From the film documentary *A Duke Named Ellington* (1988). Courtesy Leonard Malone, writer and co-producer. The Leonard Malone Collection.

53 Duke Ellington interview by Michael Parkinson on *The Parkinson Show*, BBC-TV, 1973. Courtesy The National Sound Archive, The British Library.

54 Interview with author, 24 July 1998.

55 *Melody Maker*, 26 April 1969, p. 21.

56 *Jazz Journal*, October 1976, p. 6.

57 The Smithsonian Institution Ellington Oral History Project: Interview with Mercer Ellington, September 1990, conducted by Dr Marcia M.

Greenlee, Tape 8. Courtesy Archives Center, NMAH, Smithsonian Institution, Washington D.C.

58 Mercer Ellington interview on *Duke Ellington ... and his Famous Orchestra*, BBC-TV. Courtesy The National Sound Archive, The British Library.

59 The Smithsonian Institution Ellington Oral History Project: Interview with Mercer Ellington, September 1990, conducted by Dr Marcia M. Greenlee, Tape 5. Courtesy Archives Center, NMAH, Smithsonian Institution, Washington D.C.

60 *Jazz Journal*, March 1991, p. 10.

61 Duke Ellington interview by Michael Parkinson on *The Parkinson Show*, BBC-TV, 1973. Courtesy The National Sound Archive, The British Library.

62 The Smithsonian Institution Ellington Oral History Project: Interview with Mercer Ellington, September 1990, conducted by Dr Marcia M. Greenlee, Tape 4. Courtesy Archives Center, NMAH, Smithsonian Institution, Washington D.C.

63 *The New York Times Magazine*, 12 September 1965, p. 76.

64 *Jazz*, October 1962, p. 8.

65 An edited talk between Duke Ellington and Henry Whiston of the Canadian Broadcasting Company, published in *Jazz Journal*, February 1967, p. 4.

66 *FBI File 100–43443: Edward Kennedy (Duke) Ellington.* Correspondence from J. Edgar Hoover, FBI Director to Legal Attaché, American Embassy, Paris, 29 December 1960. The Department of State had previously alerted the FBI in a memo dated 21 November 1960, marked 'Confidential'. The following page was withheld, the reason given: 'Specifically authorized under criteria established by an Executive order to be kept secret in the interest of national defense or foreign policy and are in fact properly classified pursuant to such Executive order.'

67 An edited talk between Duke Ellington and Henry Whiston of the Canadian Broadcasting Company, published in *Jazz Journal*, February 1967, p. 4.

68 Interview with author, 24 July 1998.

69 Carter Harman Interview Collection: 1964 #2. Courtesy Archives Center, NMAH, Smithsonian Institution, Washington D.C.

70 *Jazz Journal*, July 1990, p. 13.

71 *The New York Times Magazine*, 12 September 1965, p. 76.

72 *New York Post*, 15 February 1961.

73 *Duke Ellington In Person* by Mercer Ellington and Stanley Dance (Hutchinson, London 1978), p. 132.

74 Duke Ellington's handwritten notes for his autobiography *Music is My Mistress*. This section was written on the notepaper of the Holiday Inn, Pittsburgh. The Duke Ellington Collection #301, Series 5 (Box #5, Folder 6), Courtesy Archives Center, NMAH, Smithsonian Institution, Washington D.C.

75 Liner notes to *Clark Terry featuring Paul Gonsalves: Daylight Express* (Chess GRP 181192).

76 Duke Ellington interview by Michael Parkinson on *The Parkinson Show*, BBC-TV, 1973. Courtesy The National Sound Archive, The British Library.

77 The Smithsonian Institution Ellington Oral History Project: Interview with Mercer Ellington, September 1990, conducted by Dr Marcia M. Greenlee, Tape 5. Courtesy Archives Center, NMAH, Smithsonian Institution, Washington D.C.

78 The Smithsonian Institution Ellington Oral History Project: Interview with Mercer Ellington, September 1990, conducted by Dr Marcia M. Greenlee, Tape 5. Courtesy Archives Center, NMAH, Smithsonian Institution, Washington D.C.

79 An edited talk between Duke Ellington and Henry Whiston of the Canadian Broadcasting Company, published in *Jazz Journal*, February 1967, p. 6.

80 *Jazz Journal*, May 1961, p. 19.

81 Carter Harman Interview Collection: 1964 #7. Courtesy Archives Center, NMAH, Smithsonian Institution, Washington D.C.

82 Carter Harman Interview Collection: 1964 #7. Courtesy Archives Center, NMAH, Smithsonian Institution, Washington D.C.

83 Carter Harman Interview Collection: 1964 #7. Courtesy Archives Center, NMAH, Smithsonian Institution, Washington D.C.

84 Carter Harman Interview Collection: 1964 #7. Courtesy Archives Center, NMAH, Smithsonian Institution, Washington D.C.

85 The Smithsonian Institution Jazz Oral History Project: Interview with Jimmy Jones, February 1978, conducted by Patricia Willard. Courtesy The Institute of Jazz Studies, Rutgers.

86 Carter Harman Interview Collection: 1964 #8. Courtesy Archives Center, NMAH, Smithsonian Institution, Washington D.C.

87 The Smithsonian Institution Jazz Oral History Project: Interview with

Jimmy Jones, February 1978, conducted by Patricia Willard. Courtesy The Institute of Jazz Studies, Rutgers.

88 *Marshall Royal: Jazz Survivor* by Marsall Royal with Claire P. Gordon (Cassell, London 1996), p. 122.

89 Carter Harman Interview Collection. Courtesy Archives Center, NMAH, Smithsonian Institution, Washington D.C.

90 Panel discussion, Ellington '97

91 *Jazz*, October 1962, p. 8.

92 An edited talk between Duke Ellington and Henry Whiston of the Canadian Broadcasting Company, published in *Jazz Journal*, February 1967, p. 7.

93 *Jazz Journal*, March 1991, p. 10.

94 *Jazz*, October 1962, p. 9.

95 *Jazz Journal*, March 1991, p. 10.

96 An edited talk between Duke Ellington and Henry Whiston of the Canadian Broadcasting Company, published in *Jazz Journal*, February 1967, p. 6.

97 Duke Ellington's handwritten notes for his autobiography *Music is My Mistress*. This section was written on the notepaper of the Ambassador Hotel, Chicago. The Duke Ellington Collection #301, Series 5 (Box #5, Folder 6), Courtesy Archives Center, NMAH, Smithsonian Institution, Washington D.C.

98 Interview with author, 30 December 1997.

99 *Jazz Spoken Here* by Wayne Enstice and Paul Rubin (Louisiana State University Press, Baton Rouge 1992), p. 124.

100 Duke Ellington's handwritten notes for his autobiography *Music is My Mistress*. This section was written on the notepaper of the Ambassador Hotel, Chicago. The Duke Ellington Collection #301, Series 5 (Box #5, Folder 6), Courtesy Archives Center, NMAH, Smithsonian Institution, Washington D.C.

101 An edited talk between Duke Ellington and Henry Whiston of the Canadian Broadcasting Company, published in *Jazz Journal*, February 1967, p. 6.

102 *What a Wonderful World* by Bob Thiele and Bob Golden (Oxford University Press, New York 1995), pp. 125–6.

103 The Smithsonian Institution Ellington Oral History Project: Interview with Ruth Boatwright-Ellington, August 1989, conducted by Dr Marcia M. Greenlee, Tape 1. Courtesy Archives Center, NMAH, Smithsonian Institution, Washington D.C.

104 From the film documentary *A Duke Named Ellington* (1988). Courtesy Leonard Malone, writer and co-producer. The Leonard Malone Collection: Originally used in *Faces of Jazz*.

105 The Smithsonian Institution Ellington Oral History Project: Interview with Mercer Ellington, September 1990, conducted by Dr Marcia M. Greenlee, Tape 5. Courtesy Archives Center, NMAH, Smithsonian Institution, Washington D.C.

106 *Jazz Journal*, July 1990, p. 13.

107 *The New York Times Magazine*, 12 September 1965, p. 76.

108 Interview with author, 24 July 1998.

109 The Smithsonian Institution Ellington Oral History Project: Interview with Mercer Ellington, September 1990, conducted by Dr Marcia M. Greenlee, Tape 4. Courtesy Archives Center, NMAH, Smithsonian Institution, Washington D.C.

110 The Smithsonian Institution Jazz Oral History Project: Interview with Jimmy Jones, February 1978, conducted by Patricia Willard. Courtesy The Institute of Jazz Studies, Rutgers.

111 Interview with author, 24 July 1998.

112 Jimmy Hamilton interview on *Duke Ellington ... and his Famous Orchestra*, BBC-TV. Courtesy The National Sound Archive, The British Library.

113 Carter Harman Interview Collection: Courtesy Archives Center, NMAH, Smithsonian Institution, Washington D.C.

114 *Faces of Jazz*, Programme Number 8 (1972). Courtesy Danmarks Radio, Copenhagen.

115 Cootie Williams interview on *Duke Ellington ... and his Famous Orchestra*, BBC-TV. Courtesy The National Sound Archive, The British Library.

116 *Faces of Jazz*, Programme Number 8 (1972). Courtesy Danmarks Radio, Copenhagen.

117 Carter Harman Interview Collection: Courtesy Archives Center, NMAH, Smithsonian Institution, Washington D.C.

118 Carter Harman Interview Collection: Courtesy Archives Center, NMAH, Smithsonian Institution, Washington D.C.

119 Library of Congress Voice of America Recordings. WB 357: Interview with Howard Boxer at the Howard Theatre, Washington D.C., on 26 April 1962.

CHAPTER TEN:
SERIOUS SERENADE

1 Library of Congress Voice of America Recordings. Press conference, 29 April 1962.

2 The Smithsonian Institution Jazz Oral History Project: Interview with Tom Whaley, March 1980, conducted by Milt Hinton. Courtesy The Institute of Jazz Studies, Rutgers.

3 Carter Harman Interview Collection: 1964 #3. Courtesy Archives Center, NMAH, Smithsonian Institution, Washington D.C.

4 The Smithsonian Institution Jazz Oral History Project: Interview with Jimmy Jones, February 1978, conducted by Patricia Willard. Courtesy The Institute of Jazz Studies, Rutgers.

5 *Variety*, 17 July 1963, p. 20.

6 *Variety*, 4 September 1963, p. 20.

7 *Duke Ellington Talks to Max Jones and Humphrey Lyttelton*, BBC Radio 1964. Courtesy The National Sound Archive, The British Library.

8 The Smithsonian Institution Ellington Oral History Project: Interview with Mercer Ellington, September 1990, conducted by Dr Marcia M. Greenlee, Tape 5. Courtesy Archives Center, NMAH, Smithsonian Institution, Washington D.C.

9 Interview with Marian Logan on *Omnibus: Reminiscing in Tempo – Part 2: 'Riding on a Blue Note'*. BBC-TV. Courtesy The National Sound Archive, The British Library.

10 The Smithsonian Institution Ellington Oral History Project: Interview with Mercer Ellington, September 1990, conducted by Dr Marcia M. Greenlee, Tape 3. Courtesy Archives Center, NMAH, Smithsonian Institution, Washington D.C.

11 *Duke: A Portrait of Duke Ellington* by Derek Jewell (Elm Tree Books, London 1977), pp. 116–17.

12 Interview with Marian Logan on *Omnibus: Reminiscing in Tempo – Part 2: 'Riding on a Blue Note'*. BBC-TV. Courtesy The National Sound Archive, The British Library.

13 Carter Harman Interview Collection: 1964 #3. Courtesy Archives Center, NMAH, Smithsonian Institution, Washington D.C.

14 *The Real Duke Ellington* by Don George (Robson Books, London 1982), p. 115.

15 Carter Harman Interview Collection: Courtesy Archives Center, NMAH, Smithsonian Institution, Washington D.C.

16 *Variety*, 28 August 1963, p. 56.
17 The Smithsonian Institution Jazz Oral History Project: Interview with Lawrence Brown, July 1976, conducted by Patricia Willard. Courtesy The Institute of Jazz Studies, Rutgers. According to Ellington's FBI file (100–434443), the White House were furnished with his file on 19 February 1963.
18 *Jazz*, November/December 1963, p. 27.
19 Duke Ellington interview by Michael Parkinson on *The Parkinson Show*, BBC-TV, 1973. Courtesy The National Sound Archive, The British Library.
20 *Jazz*, November/December 1963, p. 27.
21 Carter Harman Interview Collection: 1964 #2. Courtesy Archives Center, NMAH, Smithsonian Institution, Washington D.C.
22 The Smithsonian Institution Jazz Oral History Project: Interview with Lawrence Brown, July 1976, conducted by Patricia Willard. Courtesy The Institute of Jazz Studies, Rutgers.
23 Carter Harman Interview Collection: 1964 #8. Courtesy Archives Center, NMAH, Smithsonian Institution, Washington D.C.
24 *Jazz: A Biography of Billy Strayhorn*, November/December 1963, p. 27.
25 Dr Arthur Logan, as interviewed by David Hajdu from *Lush Life: A Biography of Billy Strayhorn* by David Hajdu (Farrar Straus Giroux, New York 1996), p. 230.
26 *Jazz*, November/December 1963, p. 27.
27 The Smithsonian Institution Jazz Oral History Project: Interview with Lawrence Brown, July 1976, conducted by Patricia Willard. Courtesy The Institute of Jazz Studies, Rutgers.
28 The Smithsonian Institution Jazz Oral History Project: Interview with Lawrence Brown, July 1976, conducted by Patricia Willard. Courtesy The Institute of Jazz Studies, Rutgers.
29 Marian Logan, as interviewed by David Hajdu from *Lush Life: A Biography of Billy Strayhorn* by David Hajdu (Farrar Straus Giroux, New York 1996), p. 231.
30 From the film documentary *A Duke Named Ellington* (1988). Courtesy Leonard Malone, writer and co-producer. The Leonard Malone Collection.
31 *Jazz Journal*, January 1966, p. 9.
32 Liner notes, *Far East Suite* (Bluebird/BMG ND87640).
33 Carter Harman Interview Collection: 1964 #1. Courtesy Archives Center, NMAH, Smithsonian Institution, Washington D.C.

34 *Melody Maker*, 22 February 1964, p. 3.
35 *Jazz at Ronnie Scott's*, Number 114, p. 21.
36 *Melody Maker*, 26 April 1969, p. 21.
37 The Smithsonian Institution Ellington Oral History Project: Interview with Mercer Ellington, September 1990, conducted by Dr Marcia M. Greenlee, Tape 4. Courtesy Archives Center, NMAH, Smithsonian Institution, Washington D.C.
38 *Daily Mail*, 20 April 1964.
39 Perry Watkins, as interviewed by David Hajdu from *Lush Life: A Biography of Billy Strayhorn* by David Hajdu (Farrar Straus Giroux, New York 1996), p. 233.
40 Marian Logan, as interviewed by David Hajdu from *Lush Life: A Biography of Billy Strayhorn* by David Hajdu (Farrar Straus Giroux, New York 1996), p. 233.
41 Billy Strayhorn, as interviewed by David Hajdu from *Lush Life: A Biography of Billy Strayhorn* by David Hajdu (Farrar Straus Giroux, New York 1996), p. 233.
42 Carter Harman Interview Collection: 1964 #4. Courtesy Archives Center, NMAH, Smithsonian Institution, Washington D.C.
43 *Music Maker*, August 1967. Reprinted in *Jazz Masters of the '30s* by Rex Stewart (Macmillan, New York 1972).
44 *Jazz*, October 1962, p. 8.
45 *Jazz Journal*, March 1991, p. 10.
46 *Jazz Journal*, January 1966, p. 9.
47 Interview with author, 24 July 1998.
48 *Jazz Journal*, January 1966, p. 9.
49 *The New York Times*, 29 March 1981.
50 The Smithsonian Institution Ellington Oral History Project: Interview with Mercer Ellington, September 1990, conducted by Dr Marcia M. Greenlee, Tape 4. Courtesy Archives Center, NMAH, Smithsonian Institution, Washington D.C.
51 *Jazz Spoken Here* by Wayne Enstice and Paul Rubin (Louisiana State University Press, Baton Rouge 1992), pp. 127–8.
52 The Smithsonian Institution Ellington Oral History Project: Interview with Mercer Ellington, September 1990, conducted by Dr Marcia M. Greenlee, Tape 5. Courtesy Archives Center, NMAH, Smithsonian Institution, Washington D.C.
53 *The New York Times*, 29 March 1981.
54 The Smithsonian Institution Ellington Oral History Project: Interview

with Mercer Ellington, September 1990, conducted by Dr Marcia M. Greenlee, Tape 1. Courtesy Archives Center, NMAH, Smithsonian Institution, Washington D.C.

55 Carter Harman Interview Collection: May 1964. Courtesy Archives Center, NMAH, Smithsonian Institution, Washington D.C.

56 *New York Post*, May 1965. Courtesy The Institute of Jazz Studies, Rutgers.

57 *New York Times Magazine*, 12 September 1965, p. 64.

58 Duke Ellington interview by Michael Parkinson on *The Parkinson Show*, BBC-TV, 1973. Courtesy The National Sound Archive, The British Library.

59 Carter Harman Interview Collection: 1964 #3. Courtesy Archives Center, NMAH, Smithsonian Institution, Washington D.C.

60 Duke Ellington interview, Radio CJRT FM, Radio Canada 1970. Courtesy Leonard Malone.

61 Duke Ellington Interview by Orson Welles, 8 June 1970. American TV Show. Courtesy Leonard Malone, The Leonard Malone Collection.

62 *Jazz Spoken Here* by Wayne Enstice and Paul Rubin (Louisiana State University Press, 1992), p. 120.

63 *Barney, Bradley, and Max* by Whitney Balliett (Oxford University Press, New York 1989), p. 209.

64 Ruth Ellington interview on *Duke Ellington ... and his Famous Orchestra*, BBC-TV. Courtesy The National Sound Archive, The British Library.

65 Mercer Ellington interview on *Duke Ellington ... and his Famous Orchestra*, BBC-TV. Courtesy The National Sound Archive, The British Library.

66 *Dizzy, Duke, The Count and Me* by Jimmy Lyons with Ira Kamin (A California Living Book, San Francisco 1978), p. 53.

67 *Duke Ellington In Person* by Mercer Ellington with Stanley Dance (Hutchinson, London 1978), p. 127.

68 Carter Harman Interview Collection: Courtesy Archives Center, NMAH, Smithsonian Institution, Washington D.C.

69 The Smithsonian Institution Ellington Oral History Project: Interview with Ruth Boatwright-Ellington, August 1989, conducted by Dr Marcia M. Greenlee, Tape 1. Courtesy Archives Center, NMAH, Smithsonian Institution, Washington D.C.

70 *The Real Duke Ellington* by Don George (Robson Books, London 1982), p. 138.

71 *Jazz Masters of the '30s* by Rex Stewart (Collier Macmillan Ltd, London 1972), p. 93.

72 Duke Ellington's handwritten notes on the notepaper of the Sir John Hotel, Miami, Florida. This reflection was written in sections, with arrows and passages marked 'insert', and has hopefully been assembled as Ellington envisaged. The Duke Ellington Collection #301, Series 5 (Box #5, unnumbered folder), Courtesy Archives Center, NMAH, Smithsonian Institution, Washington D.C.

73 The Smithsonian Institution Ellington Oral History Project: Interview with Mercer Ellington, September 1990, conducted by Dr Marcia M. Greenlee, Tape 2. Courtesy Archives Center, NMAH, Smithsonian Institution, Washington D.C.

74 *The Real Duke Ellington* by Don George (Robson Books, London 1982), pp. 141–2.

75 Carter Harman Interview Collection: 1964 #3. Courtesy Archives Center, NMAH, Smithsonian Institution, Washington D.C.

76 Interview with author, 14 February 1997.

77 The Smithsonian Institution Jazz Oral History Project: Interview with Jimmy Jones, February 1978, conducted by Patricia Willard. Courtesy The Institute of Jazz Studies, Rutgers.

78 Duke Ellington talks to Stanley Dance, BBC Radio 1971. Courtesy The National Sound Archive, The British Library.

79 *Jazz Journal*, January 1966, p. 8.

80 *The New York Times Magazine*, 12 September 1965, p. 76.

81 The Smithsonian Institution Ellington Oral History Project: Interview with Mercer Ellington, September 1990, conducted by Dr Marcia M. Greenlee, Tape 4. Courtesy Archives Center, NMAH, Smithsonian Institution, Washington D.C.

82 *Duke Ellington talks to Max Jones and Humphrey Lyttelton*, BBC Radio 1964. Courtesy The National Sound Archive, The British Library.

83 The Smithsonian Institution Jazz Oral History Project: Interview with Jimmy Jones, February 1978, conducted by Patricia Willard. Courtesy The Institute of Jazz Studies, Rutgers.

84 *It Wasn't All Velvet* by Mel Tormé (Robson Books, London 1989), pp. 233–6.

85 The Smithsonian Institution Jazz Oral History Project: Interview with Jimmy Jones, February 1978, conducted by Patricia Willard. Courtesy The Institute of Jazz Studies, Rutgers.

86 Ed Anderson interview on *Duke Ellington . . . and his Famous*

Orchestra, BBC-TV. Courtesy The National Sound Archive, The British Library.

87 *FBI File 100–434443*. Letter dated 19 February 1968, updating file details sent to the White House, 26 May 1965, at the request of Mrs Mildred Stegall, White House Staff.

88 Duke Ellington's typewritten notes: 'The Race For Space' by Duke Ellington. The Duke Ellington Collection #301, Series 5 (Box #6, Folder 2), Courtesy Archives Center, NMAH, Smithsonian Institution, Washington D.C.

89 The Smithsonian Institution Ellington Oral History Project: Interview with Ruth Boatwright-Ellington, August 1989, conducted by Dr Marcia M. Greenlee, Tape 2. Courtesy Archives Center, NMAH, Smithsonian Institution, Washington D.C.

90 Carter Harman Interview Collection: 1964 #2. Courtesy Archives Center, NMAH, Smithsonian Institution, Washington D.C.

91 Carter Harman Interview Collection: 1964 #2. Courtesy Archives Center, NMAH, Smithsonian Institution, Washington D.C.

92 Carter Harman Interview Collection: 1964 #3. Courtesy Archives Center, NMAH, Smithsonian Institution, Washington D.C.

93 *Ebony*, March 1967, pp. 46–7, courtesy Schomberg Institute of Black Studies, Harlem, New York.

94 The Smithsonian Institution Ellington Oral History Project: Interview with Mercer Ellington, September 1990, conducted by Dr Marcia M. Greenlee, Tape 5. Courtesy Archives Center, NMAH, Smithsonian Institution, Washington D.C.

95 Interview with author, 24 July 1998.

96 Lena Horne, as interviewed by David Hajdu from *Lush Life: A Biography of Billy Strayhorn* by David Hajdu (Farrar Straus Giroux, New York 1996), p. 252.

97 Marian Logan, as interviewed by David Hajdu from *Lush Life: A Biography of Billy Strayhorn* by David Hajdu (Farrar Straus Giroux, New York 1996), p. 253.

98 Interview with author, 24 July 1998.

99 Duke Ellington interview by Michael Parkinson on *The Parkinson Show*, BBC-TV, 1973. Courtesy The National Sound Archive, The British Library.

100 Marian Logan, as interviewed by David Hajdu from *Lush Life: A Biography of Billy Strayhorn* by David Hajdu (Farrar Straus Giroux, New York 1996), p. 254.

101 Liner notes, *And His Mother Called Him Bill* (Bluebird/BMG ND86287).

102 Mercer Ellington, as interviewed by David Hajdu from *Lush Life: A Biography of Billy Strayhorn* by David Hajdu (Farrar Straus Giroux, New York 1996), p. 259.

103 The Smithsonian Institution Jazz Oral History Project: Interview with Lawrence Brown, July 1976, conducted by Patricia Willard. Courtesy The Institute of Jazz Studies, Rutgers.

104 Interview with Mercer Ellington on *Omnibus: Reminiscing in Tempo – Part 2: 'Riding on a Blue Note'*. BBC-TV. Courtesy The National Sound Archive, The British Library.

105 *The White Plains Reporter Dispatch*, 28 June 1968. Also quoted in *Lush Life* by David Hajdu (Farrar Straus Giroux, New York 1996), p. 261.

106 The Smithsonian Institution Ellington Oral History Project: Interview with Mercer Ellington, September 1990, conducted by Dr Marcia M. Greenlee, Tape 4. Courtesy Archives Center, NMAH, Smithsonian Institution, Washington D.C.

107 The Smithsonian Institution Jazz Oral History Project: Interview with Jimmy Jones, February 1978, conducted by Patricia Willard. Courtesy The Institute of Jazz Studies, Rutgers.

108 Carter Harman Interview Collection: 1964 #4. Courtesy Archives Center, NMAH, Smithsonian Institution, Washington D.C.

109 The Smithsonian Institution Ellington Oral History Project: Interview with Mercer Ellington, September 1990, conducted by Dr Marcia M. Greenlee, Tape 2. Courtesy Archives Center, NMAH, Smithsonian Institution, Washington D.C.

110 *Jazz Spoken Here* by Wayne Enstice and Paul Rubin (Louisiana State University Press, Baton Rouge 1992), p. 128.

111 Duke Ellington interview by Michael Parkinson on *The Parkinson Show*, BBC-TV, 1973. Courtesy The National Sound Archive, The British Library.

112 *Jazz Journal*, August 1968, p. 3.

113 The Smithsonian Institution Jazz Oral History Project: Interview with Cootie Williams, May 1976, conducted by Helen Dance. Courtesy The Institute of Jazz Studies, Rutgers.

114 Liner notes, *Second Sacred Concert* (Prestige PCD 24045–2).

115 Duke Ellington's handwritten note. The Duke Ellington Collection #301, Series 5 (Box #6, Folder 1), Courtesy Archives Center, NMAH, Smithsonian Institution, Washington D.C.

CHAPTER ELEVEN:

HALF THE FUN

1   Interview with author, 24 July 1998.

2   The Smithsonian Institution Ellington Oral History Project: Interview with Mercer Ellington, September 1990, conducted by Dr Marcia M. Greenlee, Tape 5. Courtesy Archives Center, NMAH, Smithsonian Institution, Washington D.C.

3   *Jazz Journal*, December 1985, p. 9.

4   The Smithsonian Institution Jazz Oral History Project: Interview with Lawrence Brown, July 1976, conducted by Patricia Willard. Courtesy The Institute of Jazz Studies, Rutgers.

5   The Smithsonian Institution Ellington Oral History Project: Interview with Mercer Ellington, September 1990, conducted by Dr Marcia M. Greenlee, Tape 3. Courtesy Archives Center, NMAH, Smithsonian Institution, Washington D.C.

6   Liner notes, *Latin American Suite* (Fantasy OJCCD 469–2).

7   Carter Harman Interview Collection: 1964 #1. Courtesy Archives Center, NMAH, Smithsonian Institution, Washington D.C.

8   The Smithsonian Institution Ellington Oral History Project: Interview with Mercer Ellington, September 1990, conducted by Dr Marcia M. Greenlee, Tape 2. Courtesy Archives Center, NMAH, Smithsonian Institution, Washington D.C.

9   The Smithsonian Institution Jazz Oral History Project: Interview with Jimmy Jones, February 1978, conducted by Patricia Willard. Courtesy The Institute of Jazz Studies, Rutgers.

10 Carter Harman Interview Collection: Las Vegas 1956 #1. Courtesy Archives Center, NMAH, Smithsonian Institution, Washington D.C.

11 Carter Harman Interview Collection: Las Vegas 1956 #1. Courtesy Archives Center, NMAH, Smithsonian Institution, Washington D.C.

12 Carter Harman Interview Collection: Las Vegas 1956 #1. Courtesy Archives Center, NMAH, Smithsonian Institution, Washington D.C.

13 The Smithsonian Institution Ellington Oral History Project: Interview with Ruth Boatwright-Ellington, August 1989, conducted by Dr

Marcia M. Greenlee, Tape 1. Courtesy Archives Center, NMAH, Smithsonian Institution, Washington D.C.

14 Interview with author, 24 July 1998.

15 *New York Times*, 30 April 1969.

16 Interview with author, 24 July 1998.

17 *Jazz Journal*, October 1990, p. 17.

18 Duke Ellington talks to Stanley Dance, BBC Radio 1971. Courtesy The National Sound Archive, The British Library.

19 Interview with author, 24 July 1998.

20 Interview with Bob Udkoff on *Omnibus: Reminiscing in Tempo – Part 2: 'Riding on a Blue Note'*. BBC-TV. Courtesy The National Sound Archive, The British Library.

21 The Smithsonian Institution Ellington Oral History Project: Interview with Mercer Ellington, September 1990, conducted by Dr Marcia M. Greenlee, Tape 8. Courtesy Archives Center, NMAH, Smithsonian Institution, Washington D.C.

22 Interview with author, 24 July 1998.

23 The Smithsonian Institution Ellington Oral History Project: Interview with Mercer Ellington, September 1990, conducted by Dr Marcia M. Greenlee, Tape 8. Courtesy Archives Center, NMAH, Smithsonian Institution, Washington D.C.

24 *Jazz Journal*, June 1986, p. 13.

25 Duke Ellington interview by Michael Parkinson on *The Parkinson Show*, BBC-TV, 1973. Courtesy The National Sound Archive, The British Library.

26 The Smithsonian Institution Ellington Oral History Project: Interview with Mercer Ellington, September 1990, conducted by Dr Marcia M. Greenlee, Tape 6. Courtesy Archives Center, NMAH, Smithsonian Institution, Washington D.C.

27 Panel discussion, Ellington '97

28 Panel discussion, Ellington '97.

29 *Talking Jazz* by Max Jones (Macmillan, London 1987), pp. 227–8.

30 *The Canadian Composer*, October 1970, p. 12.

31 *Music Is My Mistress* by Duke Ellington (W. H. Allen, London 1974), p. 4.

32 *Downbeat*, 21 January 1971, p. 20.

33 *Jazz Journal*, June 1986, p. 13.

34 *Boy Meets Horn* by Rex Stewart (Bayou Press, Oxford 1991), p. 209.

35 The Smithsonian Institution Jazz Oral History Project: Interview with Cootie Williams, May 1976, conducted by Helen Dance. Courtesy The Institute of Jazz Studies, Rutgers.

36 The Smithsonian Institution Jazz Oral History Project: Interview with Jimmy Jones, February 1978, conducted by Patricia Willard. Courtesy The Institute of Jazz Studies, Rutgers.

37 Duke Ellington's handwritten notes on the notepaper of the Ramada Inn, Greensboro, North Carolina. The Duke Ellington Collection #301, Series 5 (Box #6, Folder 1), Courtesy Archives Center, NMAH, Smithsonian Institution, Washington D.C.

38 *The Canadian Composer*, October 1970, p. 14.

39 The Smithsonian Institution Ellington Oral History Project: Interview with Mercer Ellington, September 1990, conducted by Dr Marcia M. Greenlee, Tape 1. Courtesy Archives Center, NMAH, Smithsonian Institution, Washington D.C.

40 Interview with author, 24 July 1998.

41 *Jazz Spoken Here* by Wayne Enstice and Paul Rubin (Louisiana State University Press, Baton Rouge 1992), pp. 119–20.

42 From the film documentary *A Duke Named Ellington* (1988). Courtesy Leonard Malone, writer and co-producer. The Leonard Malone Collection.

43 *The Canadian Composer*, October 1970, p. 14.

44 *New York Times*, 14 September 1971.

45 Interview with author, 24 July 1998.

46 The Smithsonian Institution Ellington Oral History Project: Interview with Ruth Boatwright-Ellington, August 1989, conducted by Dr Marcia M. Greenlee, Tape 1. Courtesy Archives Center, NMAH, Smithsonian Institution, Washington D.C.

47 Interview with author, 24 July 1998.

48 *Duke Ellington in Person* by Mercer Ellington with Stanley Dance (Hutchinson, London 1978), p. 177.

49 Duke Ellington interview by Michael Parkinson on *The Parkinson Show*, BBC-TV, 1973. Courtesy The National Sound Archive, The British Library.

50 *Jazz Spoken Here* by Wayne Enstice and Paul Rubin (Louisiana State University Press, Baton Rouge 1992), p. 124.

51 Interview with author, 24 July 1998.

52 Duke Ellington interview by Michael Parkinson on *The Parkinson*

Show, BBC-TV, 1973. Courtesy The National Sound Archive, The British Library.

53 *Vogue*, 1 February 1972.

54 Duke Ellington talks to Stanley Dance, BBC Radio 1971. Courtesy The National Sound Archive, The British Library.

55 *Downbeat*, 13 April 1972, p. 14.

56 *Downbeat*, 13 April 1972, p. 15.

57 *Downbeat*, 23 December 1971, p. 36.

58 Duke Ellington Press Conference, Japan 1964. Courtesy Leonard Malone, Leonard Malone Collection.

59 The Smithsonian Institution Ellington Oral History Project: Interview with Mercer Ellington, September 1990, conducted by Dr Marcia M. Greenlee, Tape 3. Courtesy Archives Center, NMAH, Smithsonian Institution, Washington D.C.

60 The Smithsonian Institution Jazz Oral History Project: Interview with Barney Bigard, July 1976, conducted by Patricia Willard. Courtesy The Institute of Jazz Studies, Rutgers.

61 Duke Ellington's handwritten notes written on the notepaper of the Hotel Pontchartrain, Detroit. The Duke Ellington Collection #301, Series 5 (Box #6, Folder 1), Courtesy Archives Center, NMAH, Smithsonian Institution, Washington D.C.

62 The Smithsonian Institution Jazz Oral History Project: Interview with Barney Bigard, July 1976 conducted by Patricia Willard. Courtesy The Institute of Jazz Studies, Rutgers.

63 The Smithsonian Institution Jazz Oral History Project: Interview with Barney Bigard, July 1976, conducted by Patricia Willard. Courtesy The Institute of Jazz Studies, Rutgers.

64 The Smithsonian Institution Ellington Oral History Project: Interview with Mercer Ellington, September 1990, conducted by Dr Marcia M. Greenlee, Tape 1. Courtesy Archives Center, NMAH, Smithsonian Institution, Washington D.C.

65 The Smithsonian Institution Jazz Oral History Project: Interview with Cootie Williams, May 1976, conducted by Helen Dance. Courtesy The Institute of Jazz Studies, Rutgers.

66 The Smithsonian Institution Ellington Oral History Project: Interview with Ruth Boatwright-Ellington, August 1989, conducted by Dr Marcia M. Greenlee, Tape 2. Courtesy Archives Center, NMAH, Smithsonian Institution, Washington D.C.

67 Duke Ellington's handwritten notes on the notepaper of the Spanish Trail, Tucson, Arizona. The Duke Ellington Collection #301, Series 5 (Box #6, Folder 1), Courtesy Archives Center, NMAH, Smithsonian Institution, Washington D.C.

68 The Smithsonian Institution Ellington Oral History Project: Interview with Mercer Ellington, September 1990, conducted by Dr Marcia M. Greenlee, Tape 1. Courtesy Archives Center, NMAH, Smithsonian Institution, Washington D.C.

69 *Jazz Masters of the '30s* by Rex Stewart (Collier-Macmillan Ltd, London 1972), p. 88.

70 The Smithsonian Institution Ellington Oral History Project: Interview with Mercer Ellington, September 1990, conducted by Dr Marcia M. Greenlee, Tape 2. Courtesy Archives Center, NMAH, Smithsonian Institution, Washington D.C.

71 *Jazz Journal*, December 1985, p. 9.

72 *Jazz Spoken Here* by Wayne Enstice and Paul Rubin (Louisiana State University Press, Baton Rouge 1992), p. 125.

73 The Smithsonian Institution Ellington Oral History Project: Interview with Ruth Boatwright-Ellington, August 1989, conducted by Dr Marcia M. Greenlee, Tape 1. Courtesy Archives Center, NMAH, Smithsonian Institution, Washington D.C.

74 *Jazz Journal*, October 1976, p. 7.

75 *The Real Duke Ellington* by Don George (Robson Books, London 1982), p. 243.

76 The Smithsonian Institution Ellington Oral History Project: Interview with Mercer Ellington, September 1990, conducted by Dr Marcia M. Greenlee, Tape 8. Courtesy Archives Center, NMAH, Smithsonian Institution, Washington D.C.

77 Duke Ellington's handwritten notes on the notepaper of The Detroit Hilton, Detroit, Michigan. The Duke Ellington Collection #301, Series 5 (Box #6, Folder 1), Courtesy Archives Center, NMAH, Smithsonian Institution, Washington D.C.

78 The Smithsonian Institution Ellington Oral History Project: Interview with Mercer Ellington, September 1990, conducted by Dr Marcia M. Greenlee, Tape 2. Courtesy Archives Center, NMAH, Smithsonian Institution, Washington D.C.

79 *Jazz Journal*, July 1974, p. 8.

80 Interview with George Wein on *Omnibus: Reminiscing in Tempo* –

Part 2: 'Riding on a Blue Note'. BBC-TV. Courtesy The National Sound Archive, The British Library.

81 Duke Ellington interview by Michael Parkinson on *The Parkinson Show*, BBC-TV, 1973. Courtesy The National Sound Archive, The British Library.

82 Duke Ellington's handwritten notes on the notepaper of Holiday Inn of St. Louis – Downtown, St. Louis, Missouri. The Duke Ellington Collection #301, Series 5 (Box #6, Folder 1), Courtesy Archives Center, NMAH, Smithsonian Institution, Washington D.C.

83 Duke Ellington talks to Stanley Dance, BBC Radio 1971. Courtesy The National Sound Archive, The British Library.

84 Both a typed outline and cast breakdown for 'Queenie Pie' form part of The Duke Ellington Collection #301, Series 5 (Box #3, Folders 3 & 4), Courtesy Archives Center, NMAH, Smithsonian Institution, Washington D.C.

85 The Smithsonian Institution Ellington Oral History Project: Interview with Mercer Ellington, September 1990, conducted by Dr Marcia M. Greenlee, Tape 1. Courtesy Archives Center, NMAH, Smithsonian Institution, Washington D.C.

86 *The Village Voice*, 13 December 1973, p. 44.

87 *The New York Times Review of Books*, 18 August 1974, p. 6.

88 The Smithsonian Institution Ellington Oral History Project: Interview with Mercer Ellington, September 1990, conducted by Dr Marcia M. Greenlee, Tape 2. Courtesy Archives Center, NMAH, Smithsonian Institution, Washington D.C.

89 The Smithsonian Institution Ellington Oral History Project: Interview with Ruth Boatwright-Ellington, August 1989, conducted by Dr Marcia M. Greenlee, Tape 2. Courtesy Archives Center, NMAH, Smithsonian Institution, Washington D.C.

90 The Smithsonian Institution Jazz Oral History Project: Interview with Cootie Williams, May 1976, conducted by Helen Dance. Courtesy The Institute of Jazz Studies, Rutgers.

91 Duke Ellington's handwritten note written on the notepaper of the Presbyterian Hospital in the City of New York at the Columbia-Presbyterian Medical Center, Harkness Pavilion, 180 Fort Washington Avenue, New York. The Duke Ellington Collection #301, Series 5 (Box #3, Folders 3 & 4), Courtesy Archives Center, NMAH, Smithsonian Institution, Washington D.C.

92 Interview with author, 24 July 1998.

93 Duke Ellington's handwritten note written on the notepaper of the Presbyterian Hospital in the City of New York at the Columbia-Presbyterian Medical Center, Harkness Pavilion, 180 Fort Washington Avenue, New York. The Duke Ellington Collection #301, Series 5 (Box #3, Folders 3 & 4), Courtesy Archives Center, NMAH, Smithsonian Institution, Washington D.C.

94 *The Real Duke Ellington* by Don George (Robson Books, London 1982), p. 141.

95 *Duke Ellington In Person* by Mercer Ellington with Stanley Dance (Hutchinson, London 1978), p. 202.

96 Duke Ellington's handwritten notes written on the notepaper of the Baur au Lac, Zurich. The Duke Ellington Collection #301, Series 5 (Box #6, Folder 1), Courtesy Archives Center, NMAH, Smithsonian Institution, Washington D.C.

97 The Smithsonian Institution Ellington Oral History Project: Interview with Ruth Boatwright-Ellington, August 1989, conducted by Dr Marcia M. Greenlee, Tape 2. Courtesy Archives Center, NMAH, Smithsonian Institution, Washington D.C.

98 *The New York Times*, 25 May 1974, p. 1.

99 *The New York Times*, 25 May 1974, p. 1.

100 *Jazz Spoken Here* by Wayne Enstice and Paul Rubin (Louisiana State University Press, Baton Rouge 1992), p. 125.

101 The Smithsonian Institution Ellington Oral History Project: Interview with Ruth Boatwright-Ellington, August 1989, conducted by Dr Marcia M. Greenlee, Tape 1. Courtesy Archives Center, NMAH, Smithsonian Institution, Washington D.C.

102 The Smithsonian Institution Ellington Oral History Project: Interview with Mercer Ellington, September 1990, conducted by Dr Marcia M. Greenlee, Tape 7. Courtesy Archives Center, NMAH, Smithsonian Institution, Washington D.C.

103 *Jazz Journal*, July 1974, p. 15. Dance, a longtime associate and close friend of Duke Ellington, delivered the eulogy at Ellington's funeral, of which this was the final, and apposite, paragraph.

104 The Smithsonian Institution Jazz Oral History Project: Interview with Cootie Williams, May 1976, conducted by Helen Dance. Courtesy The Institute of Jazz Studies, Rutgers.

105 *Crescendo*, March 1964, p. 22.

A DISCOGRAPHY

Courtesy of The Institute of Jazz Studies, Rutgers

This discography, kindly prepared by John Clement of the Institute of Jazz Studies, Rutgers University, is intended as a guide to Ellington on compact disc and long playing recordings. It makes no claims to completeness; indeed, the twilight world of bootleg reissues, pirated broadcasts and the like makes this a thankless and probably impossible task. It is designed as an aid to the interested reader and a starting point for a novice Ellington fan to begin exploring the sheer breadth of Ellington's recorded work.

A Guide to Duke Ellington on Compact Disc

Label	Issue	Title	Anth
ABC	836188	Hot Town – Jazz Classics In Digital Stereo	Y
ABC	836198	Great Original Performances 1928–1934	N
ABC	836201	Swing Big Bands 1929–1936	Y
ABC	838437	Swing Vol 2 1930–1938	N
Affinity	1	Message – 14 Jazz Masterpieces	Y
Affinity	777	Live In Paris 1959	N
Affinity	1000	'65 Revisited	N
ASV Living Era	5200	Rexatious 1926–1941	N
Atlantic	90043	Recollections of the Big Band Era	N
Bandstand	1509	European Tour	N
Bandstand	1523	Live at the Blue Note	N
BBC	590	Jazz Classics In Digital Stereo Vol 3 New York	N

A DISCOGRAPHY

Label	Issue	Title	Anth
BBC Music	1	Jazz – Classic Cuts From 80 Years Of Jazz 1918–1977	Y
BBC	643	1927–1934	N
BBC	686	Swing: 1930 to 1938	N
Bethlehem	30202	Presents 19??	N
Black Lion	760123	Feeling Of Jazz	N
Blue Note	5023	Lullabies For Lovers 19??	Y
Blue Note	5024	Twilight Jazz Time 19??	Y
Blue Note	30082	Togo Brava Suite	N
Blue Note	32746	70th Birthday Concert (2 CD)	N
Blue Note	53016	Ahora Jazz (2 CD)	Y
Blue Note	96582	Blue Vocals Vol 1	Y
Blue Note	96904	Blue Piano Vol 2	Y
Blue Note	46398	Money Jungle w/Mingus, Roach	N
Bluebell	5	Far Away Star	Y
Bluebird	5659	The Blanton-Webster Band (3 CD)	N
Bluebird	6641	Black, Brown & Beige (3 CD)	N
Bluebird	87640	Far East Suite	N
Bluebird	2178	Duke Ellington: Solos, Duets, and Trios	N
Bluebird	2192	Bluebird Sampler 1990	Y
Bluebird	2499	Jungle Nights In Harlem 1927–1932	N
Bluebird	1532	Jubilee Stomp	N
Bluebird	6287	And His Mother Called Him Bill	N
Bluebird	6751	Great Ellington Small Units	Y
Bluebird	6754	Classic Jazz Piano	Y
Bluebird	6755	Women: Classic Female Jazz Artists 1939–1952	Y
Bluebird	6852	Early Ellington 1927–34	N
Bluebird	8337	Bluebird Sampler '88	Y
Bluebird	9583	Early Black Swing: The Birth Of Big Band Jazz, 1927–1934	Y
Bluebird	9683	Three Great Swing Saxophones	Y
Bluebird	61109	Masters Of The Big Bands 1939–1976	Y
Bluebird	66071	Masters Of The Big Bands – The Vocalists 1936–1947	Y
Bluebird	66084	RCA Victor Jazz – The 20's–60's (5 CD – No Booklet)	Y

Label	Issue	Title	Anth
Bluebird	66531	1952 Seattle Concert	N
Bluebird	66551	Far East Suite – Special Mix	N
Capitol	21090	Oscillatin Rhythm 1953–1962	Y
Capitol	98931	Capitol Jazz (3 CD)	Y
CDS	611	Battle Of The Big Bands	Y
Circle	101	Orchestra Vol 1 1943 – World B'casts	N
Circle	102	Orchestra Vol 2 1943 – World B'casts	N
Circle	103	Orchestra Vol 3 1943 & 1945 – World B'casts	N
Circle	104	Orchestra Vol 4 1945 – World B'casts	N
Circle	105	Orchestra Vol 5 1945 – World B'casts	N
Classics	539	Chronological 1924–27	N
Classics	542	Chronological 1927–28	N
Classics	550	Chronological 1928	N
Classics	559	Chronological 1928–29	N
Classics	569	Chronological 1929	N
Classics	577	Chronological 1929–30	N
Classics	596	Chronological 1930 Vol 2	N
Classics	605	Chronological 1930–1931	N
Classics	637	Chronoligical 1933	N
Classics	675	Chronological 1937	N
Classics	700	Chronological 1938	N
Classics	717	Chronological 1938 Vol 2	N
Classics	726	Chronological 1938 Vol 3	N
Classics	747	Chronological 1938–1939	Y
Columbia	7708	This Is Jazz Sampler	Y
Columbia	37340	It Don't Mean A Thing	N
Columbia	47732	Ellington, Buck Clayton All Stars at Newport 1956	N
Columbia	45037	Jazz Masters (2 CD)	Y
Columbia	45143	Jazz Arranger	Y
Columbia	46177	Okeh Ellington (2 CD)	N
Columbia	46825	Three Suites (Nutcracker, Peer Gynt & Sweet Thursday)	N
Columbia	46995	Ellington – The Duke's Men: Small Groups Vol 1 (2 CD)	Y
Columbia	48654	Reminiscing In Tempo	N

A DISCOGRAPHY

Label	Issue	Title	Anth
Columbia	48835	Duke's Men Vol 2 1938–1939 (2 CD)	N
Columbia	52454	Tribute To Black Entertainers (2 CD)	Y
Columbia	52862	Swing Time – Fabulous Big Band Era 1925–1955 (3 CD)	Y
Columbia	53407	Stars Of The Apollo (2 CD) (No Booklet?)	Y
Columbia	53584	Live At Newport 1958 (2 CD)	N
Columbia	57901	16 Most Requested Songs	N
Columbia	65326	Music Of Prohibition	Y
Columbia	75041	Jazz Into TV CM & Screen	Y
Columbia	64274	Black, Brown and Beige	N
Columbia	450509	First Time (with Count Basie)	N
Columbia	462959	The Essential	N
Columbia	450986	At Newport (1956)	N
Columbia	460059	Jazz Party	N
Columbia	460823	Blues In Orbit	N
Columbia	460830	Uptown	N
Columbia	463342	Indigos	N
Columbia (Portrait)	465464	Braggin' In Brass 1938 Years (2 CDs)	N
Columbia	468402	Festival Session	N
Columbia	468403	Midnight In Paris	N
Columbia	468404	Piano in the Background	N
Columbia	468436	Newport '58	N
Columbia	469136	At the Bal Masque	N
Columbia	469137	Anatomy of a Murder	N
Columbia	496138	All American Jazz	N
Columbia	469139	The Girls Suite/The Perfume Suite	N
Columbia	469140	Such Sweet Thunder	N
Columbia	469407	Masterpieces by Ellington	N
Columbia	469409	Liberian Suite	N
Columbia	471319	Jazz at the Plaza Vol 2	N
Columbia	471320	Drum is a Woman	N
Columbia	472083	The Cosmic Scene	N
Columbia	472084	Unknown Session	N
Columbia	472354	Grieg: Peer Gynt Suites	N
Columbia	472356	The Nutcracker Suite	N
Columbia	474930	Piano in the Foreground	N

A DISCOGRAPHY

Label	Issue	Title	Anth
DA Music	3701	Original Jazz Masters Vol 1–5 (5 CD)	Y
Decca	629	Anthology Of Big Band Swing 1930–1955 (2 CD)	Y
Decca	639	Piano Anthology	Y
Decca	640	Early Ellington – Complete Bruns/Voc Recs 1926–1931 (3 CD)	N
Decca	641	Black Legends Of Jazz (2 CD)	Y
Decca	42325	Brunswick Era Vol 1 – 1926–29	N
Decca	42348	Jungle Band Vol 2 1929–1931	N
Discovery	71002	Afro-Bossa	N
Discovery	71003	Symphonic Ellington	N
Echo Jazz	4	Duke Ellington Orchestra	N
Emarcy	842071	Live! (1959 Newport Jazz Festival)	N
Emporio	571	Jazz After Hours	Y
ENJA	9309	Morning In Paris	N
EPM Musique	158002	Jazz Violin 1926–1942	Y
Europe 1	1503	En Concert – Theatre Des Champs Elysees 29 Jan 1965 (2 CD)	N
Famous Music	7	Duke Ellington – Beyond Category (3 CD Box)	Y
Fantasy	OJCCD645	The Afro-Eurasian Eclipse	N
Fantasy	OJCCD469	Latin American Suite	N
Fantasy	OJCCD664	Yale Concert	N
FMCG	46	Dinner Jazz	Y
Fremeaux & Associes	11	Swing Piano Bar 1921–1941	Y
Fremeaux & Associes	37	Jazz Dance Music 1923–1941	Y
Fremeaux & Associes	41	Jazz Vocal Groups 1927–1944 (2 CD)	Y
GRP	9796	Joy Of Christmas Past	Y
Hindsight	410	22 Original Big Band Recordings	N
Hindsight	501	World Famous Orchestra 1946–1947 (3 CD Box)	N
Hot 'N Sweet	5104	Birth Of A Band Vol 1	N
Hot 'N Sweet	5111	Vol 2 Black and Tan Fantasy	N
Hot 'N Sweet	5112	Vol 3 Black Beauty 1927–28	N
IAJRC	1005	First Annual Connecticut Jazz Festival 1956	Y

A DISCOGRAPHY

Label	Issue	Title	Anth
Impulse	101	Impulse Jazz – 30 Year Celebration (2 CD Box)	Y
Impulse	162	Duke Ellington Meets Coleman Hawkins	N
Impulse	166	Duke Ellington & John Coltrane	N
Impulse	173	Live At The Whitney	N
Impulse	8881	Act On Impulse! – Can You Dig It?!	Y
Impulse	39103	Duke Ellington & John Coltrane	N
Jazz Anthology	550022	Ellington/Basie Boston 1940	N
Jazz Anthology	550292	Blue Chicago 1952	N
Jazz CD	JZCD301	The Essential V Discs	N
Jazz CD	JZCD335	Cotton Club: The Legendary Broadcasts	N
Jazz Heritage	512999	Jazz Collection Vol 2	Y
Jazz Heritage	523584	Great Chicago Concerts 1946 (2 CD)	N
Jazz Unlimited	2036	At Birdland 1952	N
Jazz Up	305	Live In Italy 1967 Vol 1	N
Jazz Up	306	Live In Italy 1967 Vol 2	N
Jazz Up	322	Live At Carnegie Hall 1964	N
Jazzterdays	102401	In The Mood	Y
JMY	1011	Standards – Live At The Salle Pleyel 1969	N
JSP	2	Hoagy Carmichael Vol Two 1929–1932	Y
JSP	335	Playing With The Strings 1925–30	Y
Kaz	501	The Private Collection Vol 1	N
Kaz	502	The Private Collection Vol 2	N
Kaz	503	The Private Collection Vol 3	N
Kaz	504	The Private Collection Vol 4	N
Kaz	505	The Private Collection Vol 5	N
Kaz	506	The Private Collection Vol 6	N
Kaz	507	The Private Collection Vol 7	N
Kaz	508	The Private Collection Vol 8	N
Kaz	509	The Private Collection Vol 9	N
Kaz	510	The Private Collection Vol 10	N
Laserlight	15314	Kings Of Swing	Y
Laserlight	15753	Orchestra	N
Laserlight	15782	Cool Rock	N
Laserlight	15783	Happy Birthday Duke Vol 1	N

Label	Issue	Title	Anth
Laserlight	15784	Happy Birthday Duke Vol 2	N
Laserlight	15785	Happy Birthday Duke Vol 3	N
Laserlight	15786	Happy Birthday Duke Vol 4	N
Laserlight	15787	Happy Birthday Duke Vol 5	N
Laserlight	15954	Jazz Piano Anthology (5 CD)	Y
LMR	83001	Dance Concerts – California 1958	N
LMR	83004	Suites – New York, 1968 & 1970	N
Magic	37	Live In New York 1955–56	N
Magnetic	119	Live Concerts In Paris 1958	N
Masters Of Jazz	8	Complete Edition Vol 1 1924–1926	N
Masters Of Jazz	9	Complete Edition Vol 2 1926–1927	N
Masters Of Jazz	23	Complete Edition Vol 2 1931–1933	N
Masters Of Jazz	25	Complete Edition Vol 3 1927–1928	Y
Masters Of Jazz	30	Complete Edition Vol 4 1928	Y
Masters Of Jazz	32	Complete Edition Vol 3 1934–1937	N
Masters Of Jazz	52	Complete Edition Vol 5 1928	N
Masters Of Jazz	69	Complete Edition Vol 6 1929	N
Masters Of Jazz	88	Complete Edition Vol 7 1929	N
Masters Of Jazz	101	Complete Edition Vol 8 1929	N
Masters Of Jazz	123	Complete Edition Vol 9 1929–1930	N
Masters Of Jazz	801	Anthology of Scat Singing Vol 1 1924–1929	Y
Masters Of Jazz	802	Anthology of Scat Singing Vol 2 1929–1933	Y
Masters Of Jazz	804	Anthology of Jazz Drumming Vol 1 1904–1928	Y
MCA	42318	Orchestral Works	N
Memphis Archives	7002	Saturday Night Swing Club 1937 (2 CD)	Y
Memphis Archives	7015	Piano Wizards 1927–1939	Y
Memphis Archives	7018	Oriental Illusions 1922–1938	Y
Moon	61	Carnegie Hall '64 Volume One	N
Moon	68	Carnegie Hall '64 Volume Two	N
Mosaic	160	Complete Capitol Recordings (5 CD)	N
Music & Arts	616	1956 Stratford Festival	N
Musica Jazz	1088	Don Byas	Y
Musica Jazz	1089	Il Contrabasso Nel Jazz	Y

A DISCOGRAPHY

Label	Issue	Title	Anth
Musica Jazz	1091	Great Duke Ellington – Milano 21 Feb 1963	N
Musica Jazz	1099	Live in Europe	N
Musica Jazz	1101	Echoes of Harlem	Y
Musica Jazz	1104	La Fisarmonica Nel Jazz (Accordion)	Y
Musica Jazz	OMMCD 1	Il Flauto Nel Jazz	Y
Musicmasters	5041	Never Before Released Recordings 1965–1972	N
Musicmasters	60176	Four Symphonic Works by Duke Ellington	N
Musicmasters	65106	Great London Concerts 1963–1964	N
Musicmasters	65110	Great Chicago Concerts (1946) (2 CD)	N
Musicmasters	65114	Cornell University Concert	N
Musicmasters	844401	The Great Chicago Concerts	N
Musicraft	70052	Happy-Go-Lucky-Local (The Complete Musicraft Sides)	N
N2K	10004	Instrumental History Of Jazz 1916–1992 (2 CD)	Y
Natasha Imports	4016	Stereo Reflections in Ellington	N
Novus	3017	Radio Days – Soundtrack	Y
Novus	61083	Jazz Pizazz	Y
Novus	63150	Jazz Pizazz – Novus Celebrates 5 Years	Y
Pablo	5304	Berlin '65 and Paris '67	N
Prestige	24045	Second Sacred Concert	N
Radiex Music	1000	In Hamilton (2 CD)	N
RCA	51364	In A Mellotone 1940–1942	N
RCA	61142	RCA Records Label – 1st Note In Black Music (3 CD)	Y
RCA	66443	Corrina Corrina – Motion Picture Soundtrack	Y
RCA	66471	Indispensable & Small Groups 1940–46 (2 CD)	N
RCA	68705	Popular	N
RCA	68779	RCA Victor 80th Anniversary Vol 3 1940–1949	Y
Reader's Digest	9	Uptown Saturday Night 1937–1993 (3 CD)	Y

Label	Issue	Title	Anth
Reader's Digest	311	Dance Band Days (6 CD)	Y
Red Baron	48631	Hot Summer Dance	N
Red Baron	52759	Duke Ellington's My People	N
Red Baron	53821	Red Baron Jazz Sampler	Y
Red Baron	64602	What A Wonderful World	Y
Rhino	71131	Blues Masters Vol 13 New York City Blues	Y
Rhino	71786	Jingle Bell Jam – Jazz Christmas Classics	Y
Rhino	72245	Cabin In The Sky – Soundtrack	Y
Rhino	72468	Masters Of Jazz Vol 1 Traditional Jazz Classics	Y
Rhino	72470	Masters Of Jazz Vol 3 Big Bands Of The 30's & 40's	Y
Rhino	72471	Masters Of Jazz Vol 4 Big Bands Of The 50's & 60's	Y
Rhino	72472	Masters of Jazz – Female Vocal Classics	Y
RND	1302	Cotton Club Stars	Y
Roulette	28637	Live At The Blue Note (2 CD)	N
Ryko	76	Steal This Disc 2	Y
Ryko	10713	Paris Blues Soundtrack	N
Saja	91041	Studio Sessions Chicago 1956 Vol 1	N
Saja	91042	The Suites New York 1968, 1970 Vol 2	N
Saja	91043	Studio Sessions New York 1962 Vol 3	N
Saja	91044	Studio Sessions New York 1963 Vol 4	N
Saja	91045	Dance Date California 1958 Vol 5	N
Saja	91230	Dance Dates California 1958 Vol 6	N
Saja	91231	Studio Sessions 1957 & 1962 Vol 7	N
Saja	91232	Studio Sessions 1957 1965 1966 1967 SF Chicago NY Vol 8	N
Saja	91233	Studio Sessions 1968 New York Vol 9	N
Saja	91234	Studio Sessions 1965 1966 1971 New York Chicago Vol 10	N
Signature	40030	Happy Reunion	N
Smithsonian	30	Big Band Jazz (4 CD)	Y
Smithsonian	33	Smithsonian Collection Of Classic Jazz (5 CD)	Y

A DISCOGRAPHY

Label	Issue	Title	Anth
Smithsonian	39	Jazz Piano (4 CD Box)	Y
Smithsonian	100	We'll Meet Again – Love Songs Of World War II (2 CD)	Y
Smithsonian	102	Swing That Music!	Y
Smithsonian	104	Beyond Category (2 CD)	N
Smithsonian	107	I Got Rhythm – Music Of George Gershwin (4 LP)	Y
Smithsonian	108	Big Band Renaissance	Y
Smithsonian	Digital 33	Smithsonian Collection Of Classic Jazz 1916–1981 (5 CD)	Y
Spectrum Music	552644	Strike Up The Band	Y
Status	1008	Live At Monterey 1960	N
Status	1009	Live At Monterey 1960	Y
Status	1013	Live At The Greek Theatre Los Angeles 1966	N
Swing	8444	Harlem Comes To London	Y
Swing	8453	Ridin' In Rhythm #1	Y
Timeless	4	1926–1932	Y
V Disc	139	Songs That Went To War – WWII 50th Anniversary (2 CD)	Y
Verve	846	Verve – Introducing Jazz Masters	Y
Verve	1551	Introducing Jazz Masters	Y
Verve	516338	Jazz Masters 4	N
Verve	517953	Compact Jazz – Ella and Duke	N
Verve	519853	Introducing the Jazz Masters	Y
Verve	521007	Playboy's 40th Anniversary 1953–1993 (4 CD)	Y
Verve	521404	Back To Back 1959	N
Verve	521661	Jazz Scene (2 CD)	Y
Verve	521737	Verve Story (4 CD)	Y
Verve	527223	Day Dream – Best Of The Duke Ellington Songbook	N
Verve	529700	Ella At Duke's Place	N
Verve	529908	Lush Life – The Billy Strayhorn Songbook	Y
Verve	531932	Best Of Jazz Round Midnight	Y
Verve	539030	Ella & Duke At The Cote D'Azur 1966 (2 CD)	N

Label	Issue	Title	Anth
Verve	539033	Cote D'Azur Concerts 1966 (8 CD)	N
Verve	821578	Side By Side	N
Verve	823637	Back To Back	N
Verve	833281	Compact Jazz – Best Of The Big Bands	Y
Verve	833291	Compact Jazz	Y
Verve	837035	Ella Fitzgerald Sings The Duke Ellington Song Book (3 CD)	N
Verve	849357	Verve Jazz Box (7 CD)	Y
Verve	SACDVER 7	Verve New Releases July 1997	Y
Victor Jazz	68516	Sophisticated Lady	N
VJC	1002	Those Sensational Swinging Sirens Of The Silver Screen	N
VJC	1003	Take The A Train – Standard Transcriptions	N
VJC	1011	Live 1947–1948	N
VJC	1015	I'll Be Seeing You – Sarah Vaughan Memorial Album	N
VJC	1016	Christmas Jubilee	Y
VJC	1019	Fargo, North Dakota, November 7, 1940 (2 CD)	N
VJC	1024	Carnegie Hall Nov 13 1948 (2 CD)	N
Vogue	655004	Lamplighter's All Star Jazz	Y
Warner Bros	46703	Monterey Jazz Festival 40 Legendary Years 1958–1996	Y
WEA	30953	I Capolavori Di Duke Ellington 19??	N
West Hill	1017	American Pop: An Audio History 1893–1946 (9 CD)	Y

A Guide To Duke Ellington on Long Playing Recordings

Allegro Elite	4014	Duke Ellington Plays	N
Allegro Elite	4038	Duke Ellington Plays	N
Allegro Elite	4119	Let's Dance Hit Parade	Y
Brunswick	58002	Ellingtonia Volume One	N
Brunswick	58012	Ellingtonia Volume Two	N

Label	Issue	Title	Anth
Brunswick	58024	Harlem Jazz 1930	Y
Capitol	440	Premiered By Ellington	N
Capitol	477	Duke Plays Ellington	N
Clef	1	Jazz Scene	Y
Clef	2	Jazz Scene	Y
Columbia	2522	Duke's Mixture	N
Columbia	2562	Here's The Duke	N
Columbia	6024	Mood Ellington	N
Columbia	6073	Liberian Suite	N
Jazz Panorama	1802	Duke Ellington Vol 1	N
Jazz Panorama	1811	Braggin' In Brass	N
Jazz Panorama	1816	Reminiscing In Tempo	N
London	3551	Duke 1926	N
Mercer	1001	Billy Strayhorn Trio	N
Palm Club	11	Duke Ellington (NC As Issued)	N
RCA	LEJ 4	RCA Victor Encyclopedia Of Recorded Jazz 4	Y
RCA	LPM 3067	Plays The Blues	N
RCA	LPT 1	Theme Songs	Y
RCA	LPT 2	Dance Band Hits	Y
RCA	LPT 4	Keyboard Kings Of Jazz	Y
RCA	LPT 27	Great Tenor Sax Artists	Y
RCA	LPT 31	Modern Jazz Piano	Y
RCA	LPT 3017	This Is Duke Ellington	N
RCA	STD Groove 16006	Popular Selections – Program Transcriptions	N
RCA	STD Groove 16007	Popular Selections – Program Transcriptions	N
Royale	18143	Duke Ellington And His Orchestra And Others	Y
Tax	5	Duke Ellington	N
Tax	8	Mills' Ten Blackberries (NC)	N
Triton	14	Duke Ellington And His Orchestra Volume 1	N
X	3037	Early Recordings Volume 1	N
AAMCO	301	Royal Concert Vol 1	N
AAMCO	313	Royal Concert Vol 2	N

A DISCOGRAPHY

Label	Issue	Title	Anth
ABC	38266	New York – Jazz Classics In Digital Stereo	Y
Ace of Clubs	1176	Music of Duke Ellington	Y
Ace of Hearts	23	Cotton Club Days	N
Ace of Hearts	47	Duke In Harlem 1926–1930	N
Ace of Hearts	89	Cotton Club Days Vol 2	N
AFE	13	Original Cotton Club Orchestras (3 LP)	Y
Affinity	3010	Live Vol 2	N
Affinity	9	Live Volume One	N
Affinity	34	Live Volume Two	N
Affinity	57	Paris Jazz Party	N
Aircheck	4	Duke Is On The Air – Blue Note Chicago Illinois	N
Aircheck	29	On The Air Vol 2	N
Ajazz	523	At The Music Hall	N
Alamac	2404	Duke Ellington – 1941 Classics	N
Alamac	2416	Duke Ellington And His Orchestra 1939–40	N
Alamac	2439	Duke Ellington And His Famous Orchestra	N
Allegro	1591	Duke Ellington	N
Allegro Elite	3074	Duke Ellington	N
Alto	710	He's Mr Edward Kennedy	N
American Rec Society	419	Jazz Scene	Y
Archive of F&J Music	221	Early Duke Ellington	Y
Archive of F&J Music	249	Duke Ellington Vol 2 The Early Years	N
Archive of F&J Music	266	Duke Ellington Vol 3	N
Archive of Jazz	101571	Duke Ellington And His Orchestra 1928–33	N
Ariston	12028	Black Brown and Beige	N
Ariston	12029	F.D.R. Memorial	N
Ariston	12031	Duke's Fabulous Recordings	N
ASV Living Era	5017	Runnin' Wild	Y
Atlantic	304	Great Paris Concert (2 LP)	N
Atlantic	1580	New Orleans Suite	N
Atlantic	1665	Recollections Of The Big Band Era	N
Atlantic	1688	Jazz Violin Session	N

A DISCOGRAPHY

Label	Issue	Title	Anth
Atlantic	50403	New Orleans Suite	N
Atlantic	81704	Mainstream	Y
Atlantic	90043	Recollections Of The Big Band Era	N
Atlantic	2	Concert At Carnegie Hall (2 LP)	Y
Audiofidelity	3	Don't Explain (3 LP Box)	N
Audiofidelity	13	Original Cotton Club Orchestras (3 LP)	Y
Bandstand	7128	Highlights of the 1930's–40's	Y
Bethlehem	60	Historically Speaking – The Duke	N
Bethlehem	6005	Duke Ellington Presents	N
Bethlehem	6037	Big Band Contrast	Y
Bethlehem	EXLP 1	George Gershwin's Porgy And Bess (3 LP)	Y
Bethlehem	EXLP 2	Bethlehem's Grab Bag – Now Everybody Wins For Only $1.98	Y
Bethlehem	FCP 4009	Bethlehem's Finest Vol 9	Y
Bethlehem	FCP 4014	Bethlehem's Finest Vol 14	Y
Bethlehem	New 1	Porgy And Bess (3 LP Box – Revised Edn)	Y
Bethlehem	New 6013	Bethlehem Years Vol 1	N
Bethlehem	6805	Bethlehem Years Vol 2	N
Big Band Archives	1217	Suddenly It Jumped	N
Big Band Archives	2203	Big Band Christmas (2 LP)	Y
Big Band Archives	2204	Big Bottom Scene . . . And All That Jazz (2 LP)	Y
Big Band Landmarks	20	Duke Ellington And His Orchestra 1959	N
Biograph	M 2	Band Shorts – Black & Tan, Bundle Of Blues, Symphony In Black	N
Black Lion	52001	Serenade To Sweden	N
Black Lion	52011	Magenta Haze	N
Blu-Disc	1001	Unheard And Seldom Heard Ellington Vol 1	N
Blu-Disc	1003	Unheard And Seldom Heard Ellington Vol 2	Y
Blue Note	85129	Money Jungle	N
Bluebird	5659	Blanton-Webster Band (4 LP Box)	N
Bluebird	6641	Black Brown & Beige – 1944–46 Band Recordings (4 LP Box)	N

A DISCOGRAPHY

Label	Issue	Title	Anth
Bluebird	6754	Classic Jazz Piano 1927–1957	Y
Bluebird	6852	Early Ellington 1927–1934	N
Bluebird	7640	Far East Suite	N
Bluebird	8337	Bluebird Sampler '88	Y
Bluebird	9583	Early Black Swing – Birth of Big Band Jazz 1927–1934	Y
Bluebird	9683	Three Great Swing Saxophones	Y
Book Of The Month	5622	Duke Ellington At Fargo 1940 (3 LP)	N
Boulevard	4025	And Their Orchestras	Y
Broadway	118	Early Transcripts And Rare Recordings	N
Brunswick	54007	Early Ellington	N
Brunswick	87094	Golden Book Of Classic Swing Vol 2	Y
Brunswick	88002	Best Of The King Of Swing	Y
Bulldog	2021	20 Golden Pieces	N
BYG	529071	Duke Ellington	N
BYG	529081	Duke Ellington	N
Camay	3043	Hail To The Duke	N
Camden	328	Great Jazz Pianists	Y
Camden	459	Duke Ellington At The Cotton Club	N
Camden	6001	Historia Del Jazz	Y
Camden	New 152	Mood Indigo (2 LP)	N
Capitol	477	Duke Plays Ellington	N
Capitol	521	Ellington '55	N
Capitol	637	Dance To The Duke!	N
Capitol	667	Battle Of The Big Bands	Y
Capitol	679	Ellington Showcase	N
Capitol	795	History Of Jazz Vol 3 Everybody Swings	Y
Capitol	796	History Of Jazz Vol 4 Enter The Cool	Y
Capitol	926	Hi-Fi Drums	Y
Capitol	1602	Best Of Duke Ellington	N
Capitol	1970	Esquire's World Of Jazz (2 LP)	Y
Capitol	2109	Jazz Story (5 LP Box)	Y
Capitol	2139	Jazz Story Vol 3	Y
Capitol	2140	Jazz Story Vol 4 Big Bands	Y
Capitol	6040	Jazz In The Making – Collectors Item	Y
Capitol	6718	Plaza House Presents The Greatest Hits Of The 50s/50s (2 LP)	Y

A DISCOGRAPHY

Label	Issue	Title	Anth
Capitol	7636	Very Best Of The Big Bands (6 LP Box)	Y
Capitol	11058	Piano Reflections	N
Capitol	16172	Best of Duke Ellington	N
Capitol	240814	Ellington '55	N
Capitol	New 293	Big Bands (6 LP)	Y
Caracol	422	Duke Ellington And His Orchestra	N
Caracol	430	Duke Ellington's Jazz Group	N
Caracol	433	Date With The Duke June 9 1945 Toledo	N
Caracol	434	Date With The Duke June 16 & 23 1945	N
Caracol	435	Date With The Duke – Hurricane Club NYC 1943–44	N
Caracol	436	Carnegie Hall Concert 1948 (2 LP)	N
Caracol	438	Date With The Duke 1945	N
Carras	0	Carras Vintage Jazz – Critics Choice	Y
CBS	26306	Duke 56–62 Vol 3	N
CBS	62614	At Newport	Y
CBS	62686	Liberian Suite – Tone Parallel To Harlem	N
CBS	62993	Primping For The Prom	N
CBS	63363	Black Brown & Beige	N
CBS	63564	Monologue	N
CBS	63838	Masterpieces By Ellington	N
CBS	64703	Cosmic Scene	N
CBS	66607	Complete Duke Ellington 1947–1952 (6 LP Box)	N
CBS	67252	Piano In The Foreground – Background (2 LP)	N
CBS	67264	Complete Vol 1 1925–1928 In Chronological Order (2 LP)	Y
CBS	68275	Complete Vol 2 1928–1930 (Note: One Record Missing)	N
CBS	82819	Unknown Session	N
CBS	84418	Piano In The Background	N
CBS	84419	Piano In The Foreground	N
CBS	88035	Complete Vol 4 1932 In Chronological Order (2 LP)	N

Label	Issue	Title	Anth
CBS	88082	Complete Vol 5 1932–1933 In Chronological Order (2 LP)	N
CBS	88137	Complete Vol 6 1933–1936 In Chronological Order (2 LP)	N
CBS	88140	Complete Vol 7 1936–1937 In Chronological Order (2 LP)	N
CBS	88185	Complete Vol 8 1937 In Chronological Order (2 LP)	N
CBS	88210	Complete Vol 9 1937 In Chronological Order (2 LP)	N
CBS	88220	Complete Vol 10 1937–1938 In Chronological Order (2 LP)	Y
CBS	88242	Complete Vol 11 1938 In Chronological Order (2 LP)	Y
CBS	88451	Complete Vol 12 1938 In Chronological Order (2 LP)	Y
CBS	88518	Complete Vol 13 1938–1939 In Chronological Order (2 LP)	Y
CBS	88521	Complete Vol 14 1939 In Chronological Order (2 LP)	Y
CBS	88522	Complete Vol 15 1939–1940 In Chronological Order (2 LP)	Y
CBS	88563	Duke 56–62 Vol 1 (2 LP)	N
CBS	88564	Duke 56–62 Vol 2 (2 LP)	N
CBS	450341	Jazz A Tous Les Etages	Y
CBS	450967	Jazz A Tous Les Etages Vol 2	Y
CBS Sony	1452	NJF At Newport	Y
Century	1003	Century Of American Music Vol 3	Y
Century	5503	Duke Ellington In Concert (Picture Disc)	N
Circle	101	Duke Ellington 1943	N
Circle	102	Duke Ellington Vol 2 1943	N
Circle	103	Duke Ellington Vol 3 1943	N
Circle	104	Duke Ellington Vol 4 1943	N
Circle	105	Duke Ellington Vol 5 1943–1945	N
Circle	106	Duke Ellington Vol 6 1945	N
Circle	107	Duke Ellington Vol 7 1945	N
Circle	108	Duke Ellington Vol 8 1945	N

A DISCOGRAPHY

Label	Issue	Title	Anth
Circle	109	Duke Ellington Vol 9 1945	N
Classic Jazz Masters	1	Harlem Jazz 1921–1931	Y
Clef	674	Jazz Scene	Y
Collector's Classics	4	Perfect Era	N
Collector's Classics	16	At Southland – At The Cotton Club	N
Columbia	27	Ellington Era Vol 1 (3 LP)	N
Columbia	31	Outstanding Jazz Compositions Of The 20th Century (2 LP)	Y
Columbia	35	Original Sound Of The Twenties (3 LP)	Y
Columbia	39	Ellington Era – Vol 2 (3 LP)	N
Columbia	236	Columbia Basic Library Of Great Jazz (3 LP)	Y
Columbia	558	Music Of Duke Ellington	N
Columbia	663	Blue Light	N
Columbia	777	$64000 Jazz	Y
Columbia	825	Masterpieces By Ellington	N
Columbia	830	Hi-Fi Ellington Uptown	N
Columbia	848	Liberian Suite – Tone Parallel To Harlem	N
Columbia	872	Blue Rose	N
Columbia	933	At Newport (Jazz Festival)	Y
Columbia	934	At Newport (Jazz Festival)	N
Columbia	951	Drum Is A Woman	N
Columbia	967	Dance Be Happy!	Y
Columbia	1020	Jazz Omnibus	Y
Columbia	1033	Such Sweet Thunder	N
Columbia	1036	Jazz Makers	Y
Columbia	1085	Ellington Indigos	N
Columbia	1162	Black Brown And Beige	N
Columbia	1198	Cosmic Scene	N
Columbia	1245	Newport 1958 Jazz Festival	N
Columbia	1282	Dance To Duke! (Bal Masque)	N
Columbia	1323	Ellington Jazz Party	N
Columbia	1360	Anatomy Of A Murder	N
Columbia	1400	Festival Session	N
Columbia	1445	Blues In Orbit	N
Columbia	1541	Nutcracker Suite	N
Columbia	1546	Piano In The Background	N

Label	Issue	Title	Anth
Columbia	1597	Peer Gynt Suites Nos 1&2 – Suite Thursday	N
Columbia	1610	Jazz Poll Winners	Y
Columbia	1715	First Time! – The Count Meets The Duke	N
Columbia	1765	Who's Who In The Swinging Sixties	Y
Columbia	1790	All American In Jazz	N
Columbia	1907	Midnight In Paris	N
Columbia	1970	Giants Of Jazz	Y
Columbia	2029	Piano In The Foreground	N
Columbia	2126	Jazz Critics' Choice	Y
Columbia	4418	Masterpieces By Ellington	N
Columbia	4639	Ellington Uptown	N
Columbia	6770	Blackbirds Of 1928	Y
Columbia	8166	Anatomy Of A Murder	N
Columbia	9629	Greatest Hits	N
Columbia	30009	Big Bands' Greatest Hits (2 LP)	Y
Columbia	30788	Stars Of The Apollo Theatre (2 LP)	Y
Columbia	31213	Big Bands Greatest Hits Volume 2 (2 LP)	Y
Columbia	32064	Duke Ellington Presents Ivie Anderson (2 LP)	N
Columbia	32355	Jazz Piano Anthology (2 LP)	Y
Columbia	32471	Jazz At The Plaza	N
Columbia	32564	World Of Duke Ellington (2 LP)	N
Columbia	32945	World Of Swing (2 LP)	Y
Columbia	33341	World Of Duke Ellington Volume 2 (2 LP)	N
Columbia	33402	Black Giants (2 LP)	Y
Columbia	33961	World of Duke Ellington Vol 3	N
Columbia	35342	Unknown Session	N
Columbia	36803	Jingle Bell Jazz (Christmas)	Y
Columbia	36807	Jazz Critics' Choice	Y
Columbia	36979	Festival Session	N
Columbia	37340	It Don't Mean A Thing If It Ain't Got That Swing	N
Columbia	38028	Girl's Suite And Perfume Suite	N
Columbia	38262	Newport – Live Unreleased Highlights From 1956 1958 1963	Y

A DISCOGRAPHY

Label	Issue	Title	Anth
Columbia	40474	Columbia Jazz Masterpieces – Sampler Volume 1	Y
Columbia	40586	First Time! – The Count Meets The Duke	N
Columbia	40587	Ellington At Newport (1956)	N
Columbia	40651	1930's Jazz – Big Bands	Y
Columbia	40712	Ellington Jazz Party	N
Columbia	40798	Columbia Jazz Masterpieces – Sampler Volume II	Y
Columbia	40799	1950's Jazz – The Singers	Y
Columbia	40836	Ellington Uptown	N
Columbia	40847	1930's Jazz – The Singers	Y
Columbia	40886	Columbia Jazz Masterpieces – Sampler Volume III	Y
Columbia	44051	Blues In Orbit	N
Columbia	44113	Columbia Jazz Masterpieces – Sampler Volume IV	Y
Columbia	44444	Indigos	N
Columbia	45037	Jazz Masters (2 LP)	Y
Columbia	45143	Jazz Arranger Vol 1	Y
Columbia	66639	Remember How Great . . .?	Y
Columbia	CB 4	Jazz At Columbia – Swing	Y
Columbia	CB 16	Jazz At Columbia – Collector's Items	Y
Columbia	CB 20	King The Count And The Duke	Y
Columbia	D 11	Music Time USA (5 LP Box) CL 1311–1315	Y
Columbia	GB 4	Winners' Circle	Y
Columbia	JJ 1	Columbia Jazz Festival	Y
Columbia	JS 1	Columbia Jazz Festival	Y
Columbia	JZ 1	I Like Jazz!	Y
Columbia	OL 6770	Blackbirds of 1928	Y
Columbia	XLP 36147	Ragtime To Cool	Y
Columbia Ltd Edition	10077	Bal Masque	N
Columbia Mus Treas	5122	Big Bands Revisited (7 LP)	Y
Columbia Mus Treas	5193	Best Of The Big Bands (2 LP #D403/404)	Y
Columbia Mus Treas	5267	Great Bands (2 LP #D448/449)	Y
Columbia Mus Treas	5618	Swing Years (2 LP #D817/818)	Y

A DISCOGRAPHY

Label	Issue	Title	Anth
Columbia Mus Treas	5620	Kings Of Swing (2 LP #D819/820)	Y
Columbia Mus Treas	5932	50 Years Of Jazz Greats (3 LP #D1043/1044/1045)	Y
Columbia Rec Prods	66640	Remember How Great . . .?	Y
Columbia Spec Prods	107	Hot Ones!	Y
Columbia Spec Prods	119	Cool & Carefree (Carrier)	Y
Columbia Spec Prods	206	Sounds That Swing	Y
Columbia Spec Prods	217	Jazz Set (Zenith)	Y
Columbia Spec Prods	276	When We're Together . . . With The Swinging Sounds	Y
Columbia Spec Prods	311	On Stage! Big Bands And All That Jazz (General Electric) 2 LP	Y
Columbia Spec Prods	558	Music Of Duke Ellington	N
Columbia Spec Prods	809	Big Beat Of Yesterday	Y
Columbia Spec Prods	825	Masterpieces By Ellington	N
Columbia Spec Prods	830	Hi-Fi Ellington Uptown	N
Columbia Spec Prods	951	Drum Is A Woman	N
Columbia Spec Prods	1033	Such Sweet Thunder	N
Columbia Spec Prods	1506	Great Big Bands	Y
Columbia Spec Prods	8015	Black Brown And Beige	N
Columbia Spec Prods	8072	Newport 58	N
Columbia Spec Prods	8127	Ellington Jazz Party	N
Columbia Spec Prods	8590	All American In Jazz	N
Columbia Spec Prods	10046	Body and Soul (3 LP Box)	Y
Columbia Spec Prods	13085	Blue Rose	N
Columbia Spec Prods	13153	Early Gold (4 LP)	Y
Columbia Spec Prods	13291	Greatest Hits	N
Columbia Spec Prods	13292	Primping For The Prom	N
Columbia Spec Prods	13293	Monologue	N
Columbia Spec Prods	13500	Festival Session	N
Columbia Spec Prods	13744	Black Bands – The Great Black Vocalists (4 LP)	Y
Columbia Spec Prods	13927	60 Of The Greatest Big Bands (6 LP Box)	Y
Columbia Spec Prods	14007	Fabulous Big Bands (6 LP)	Y
Columbia Spec Prods	14320	Echoes Of The Thirties (5 LP)	Y
Columbia Spec Prods	14926	We Love The Big Band Sound	Y

A DISCOGRAPHY

Label	Issue	Title	Anth
Columbia Spec Prods	15596	Big Bands Are Back (2 LP)	Y
Columbia Spec Prods	15949	Montreux – Detroit International Jazz Festival	Y
Columbia Spec Prods	15996	Brown Sugar (3 LP)	Y
Columbia Spec Prods	69450	When They Brought Down The House	Y
Columbia Spec Prods	82029	Swingin' Sound!	Y
Columbia Spec Prods	86088	Diamond Jubilee Showcase (2 LP)	Y
Contact	1	My People	N
Coral	100	Jazz Story (3 LP)	Y
Core	100	Jazz Salute To Freedom (2 LP)	Y
Coronet	276	Duke Ellington And His Orchestra	Y
D.E.T.S.	0	DETS Bonus – 400 Restaurant NYC 4/14/45; Blue Note 8/1/53	N
D.E.T.S.	1	Treasury Show #1 – April 7, 1945	N
D.E.T.S.	2	Treasury Show #2 – April 21, 1945	N
D.E.T.S.	3	Treasury Show #3 – April 28, 1945	N
D.E.T.S.	4	Treasury Show #4 – May 9, 1945	N
D.E.T.S.	5	Treasury Show #5 – May 12, 1945	N
D.E.T.S.	6	Treasury Show #6 – May 19, 1945	N
D.E.T.S.	7	Treasury Show #7 – May 26, 1945	N
D.E.T.S.	8	Treasury Show #8 – June 2, 1945	N
D.E.T.S.	10	Treasury Show #10 – June 16, 1945	N
D.E.T.S.	11	Treasury Show #11 – June 23, 1945	N
D.E.T.S.	12	Treasury Show #12 – June 30, 1945	N
D.E.T.S.	13	Treasury Show #13 – July 7, 1945	N
D.E.T.S.	14	Treasury Show #14 – July 14, 1945	N
D.E.T.S.	15	Treasury Show #15 – July 21, 1945	N
D.E.T.S.	16	Treasury Show #16 – July 28, 1945	N
D.E.T.S.	17	Treasury Show #17 – August 4, 1945	N
D.E.T.S.	18	Treasury Show #18 – August 11, 1945	N
D.E.T.S.	19	Treasury Show #19 – August 18, 1945	N
D.E.T.S.	20	Treasury Show #20 – August 25, 1945	N
D.E.T.S.	21	Treasury Show #21 – Sept. 1, 1945	N
D.E.T.S.	22	Treasury Show #22 – Sept. 8, 1945	N
D.E.T.S.	23	Treasury Show #23 – Sept. 15, 1945	N
D.E.T.S.	24	Treasury Show #24 – Sept. 22, 1945	N
D.E.T.S.	25	Treasury Show #25 – Oct. 13, 1945	N

A DISCOGRAPHY

Label	Issue	Title	Anth
D.E.T.S.	26	Treasury Show #26 – Oct. 13, 1945	N
D.E.T.S.	28	Treasury Show #27 & 28 – Oct. 20 and 27, 1945	N
D.E.T.S.	29	Treasury Show #28 and 29 – Oct. 27 and Nov. 3, 1945	N
D.E.T.S.	30	Treasury Show #29 and 30 – Nov. 3 and 10, 1945	N
D.E.T.S.	31	Treasury Show #30 and 31 – Nov. 10, 1945	N
D.E.T.S.	32	Treasury Show #31 and 32 – Nov. 17 and 24, 1945	N
D.E.T.S.	33	Civic Opera House Concert – Jan. 20, 1946	N
D.E.T.S.	34	Treasury Show #33 and 34 – April 20, 1946	N
D.E.T.S.	35	Treasury Show #35 – April 27, 1946	N
D.E.T.S.	36	Treasury Show #36 – May 4, 1946	N
D.E.T.S.	37	Treasury Show #37 and 38 – May 18 and 25, 1946	
D.E.T.S.	38	Treasury Show #39 – June 1, 1946	N
D.E.T.S.	39	Treasury Show #40 – June 8, 1946	N
D.E.T.S.	40	Treasury Show #41 – July 6, 1946	N
D.E.T.S.	41	Treasury Show #42 – July 27, 1946	N
D.E.T.S.	42	Treasury Show #43 – Aug. 3, 1946	N
D.E.T.S.	43	Treasury Show #44 – Aug. 17, 1946	N
D.E.T.S.	44	Treasury Show #45 – Aug. 24, 1946	N
D.E.T.S.	45	Treasury Show #46 – Aug. 31, 1946	N
D.E.T.S.	46	Treasury Show #47 – Oct. 5, 1946; Treasury Star Parade 231–3	N
D.E.T.S.	47	Blue Note, Chicago, June 24 and July 1, 1953	N
D.E.T.S.	48	Blue Note, Chicago, July 17 and 24, 1953	N
Decca	3214	Chronicle Of Music – The Age Of Jazz (Series G: No. 2)	Y
Decca	5069	North Of The Border In Canada	N
Decca	8398	Encyclopedia Of Jazz On Records Vol 1	Y

A DISCOGRAPHY

Label	Issue	Title	Anth
Decca	9224	Beginning Vol 1	N
Decca	9241	Hot In Harlem Vol 2	N
Decca	9247	Rockin' In Rhythm Vol 3	N
Decca	34313	Urban Sprawl & All That Jazz: A Musical Intro To Life's Year	Y
Decca	623579	Uncollected Vol 5	N
Decca	710176	Duke Ellington & Cincinnati Symphony Orchestra	N
Design	907	Three Of A Kind	Y
Discovery	841	Concert In The Virgin Islands	N
Doctor Jazz	39137	All Star Road Band (2 LP)	N
Doctor Jazz	40012	All Star Road Band Vol 2 (2 LP)	N
Doctor Jazz	40030	Happy Reunion	N
Doctor Jazz	40359	New Mood Indigo	N
Doctor Jazz	40706	Feel Good With The Good Music Of Doctor Jazz Vol 1	Y
Duke	1011	Goin' Up	N
Duke	1017	Hollywood Jam	N
Ellington '86	0	Stereo Excursion 1953–1973	N
Ellington '87	0	Concerts In Canada	N
Ellington '88	0	In London 1958 (2 LP)	N
Ellington '90	0	1949 Band Salutes Ellington '90	N
Ellington 88	0	In London 1958 (2 LP)	N
Ellington 90	0	1949 Band Salutes Ellington '90	N
Ember	2036	It's Duke Ellington	N
Encore	14359	Suite Thursday – Controversial Suite – Harlem Suite	N
Epic	201	Bing Crosby Story Vol 1 Early Jazz Years 1928–1932 (2 LP)	Y
Epic	22005	Duke's Men	Y
Epic	22006	Duke's Men	Y
Epitaph	4011	Duke Ellington 1899–1974 (2 LP)	N
Europa Jazz	1001	Armstrong – Fitzgerald – Ellington – Charles	Y
Europa Jazz	1010	Ellington – Hodges – Williams – Anderson	N
Europa Jazz	1022	Ellington – James – Pomeroy – Hendricks	Y
Europa Jazz	1039	Ellington – Jones – Dorham – McGhee	Y

A DISCOGRAPHY

Label	Issue	Title	Anth
Europa Jazz	1052	Basie – Williams – Ellington	Y
Everest	7	Legendary Duke Ellington (4 LP Box – One Missing)	N
Everybody's	3003	Live At The Apollo – Live Broadcasts	Y
Everybody's	3005	Reflections In Ellington: The 1932 Band In True Stereo	N
Evon	334	Jazz Stars	Y
Extreme Rarities	1002	Hot Jazz On Film Vol 1	Y
Extreme Rarities	1004	Hot Jazz On Film Vol 2	Y
Extreme Rarities	1008	Hot Jazz On Film Vol 4	Y
Fairmont	1001	Date With The Duke Vol 1 1945–46	N
Fairmont	1002	Date With The Duke Vol 2 1945–46	N
Fairmont	1003	Date With The Duke Vol 3 1945–46	N
Fairmont	1004	Date With The Duke Vol 4 1945–46	N
Fairmont	1007	Date With The Duke Vol 5 1945–46	N
Fairmont	1008	Date With The Duke Vol 6 1945–46	N
Fairmont	1009	Date With The Duke Vol 7 1945–46	N
Fairmont	1010	Date With The Duke Vol 8 1945–46	N
Fanfare	117	Saturday Night Swing Club Is On The Air	Y
Fanfare	135	Aquarium Restaurant NYC	N
Fantasy	8407	Second Sacred Concert (2 LP)	N
Fantasy	8419	Latin American Suite	N
Fantasy	9433	Yale Concert	N
Fantasy	9462	Duke Ellington The Pianist	N
Fantasy	9498	Afro-Eurasian Eclipse	N
Fantasy	9636	Featuring Paul Gonsalves	N
Fantasy	9640	Intimacy Of The Blues	N
FDC	1002	It Don't Mean A Thing	N
FDC	1003	Duke's Rare And Unissued Masters	N
FDC	1005	25th Anniversary Concert (2 LP)	Y
FDC	1011	Jazz Of The World War 2nd – Vol 2 1944–45	N
FDC	1013	Jazz Of The World War 2nd – Vol 3 1945–47	N
FDC	1015	Come And Have A Swing With Me P.S. I Love You Madly	N
FDC	1022	Duke's Unissued Masters Vol 2	N

A DISCOGRAPHY

Label	Issue	Title	Anth
Festival	130	Best Of Duke Ellington 1942–1946 (2 LP)	N
Festival	228	2 Great Concerts	N
Festival	237	Hollywood 1941 Classic Era (2 LP)	N
First Time	2501	Original Performances Of Big Band Themes On The Air (2 LP)	Y
Flutegrove	8	Piano Solos 1964	N
Flying Dutchman	166	It Don't Mean A Thing If It Ain't Got That Swing	N
Folkways	48	They All Played The Tiger Rag	Y
Folkways	67	Jazz 7 – New York 1922–1934	Y
Folkways	69	Jazz 8 – Big Bands 1924–1934	Y
Folkways	2807	Jazz Vol 7 New York 1922–1934	Y
Folkways	2808	Jazz Vol 8 Big Bands	Y
Folkways	2968	First Annual Tour Of The Pacific Northwest Spring 1952 (2 LP)	N
Follett	13	World Of Popular Music: Jazz (4 LP Box)	Y
Franklin Mint	5	Jazz Singers (4 LP Box #1)	Y
Franklin Mint	7	Jazz Singers (4 LP Box #3)	Y
Franklin Mint	8	Jazz Singers (4 LP Box #4)	Y
Franklin Mint	16	Jazz Masters Of The Sax (4 LP Box #4): Johnny Hodges	Y
Franklin Mint	21	Duke Ellington: Great Jazz Classics (4 LP Box #1)	N
Franklin Mint	22	Duke Ellington: Great Jazz Classics (4 LP Box #2)	N
Franklin Mint	23	Duke Ellington: Great Jazz Classics (4 LP Box #3)	Y
Franklin Mint	24	Duke Ellington: Great Jazz Classics (4 LP Box #4)	Y
Franklin Mint	35	Great Arrangers And Composers (4 LP Box #3)	Y
Franklin Mint	42	Bebop Legends (4 LP Box #2): Dizzy Gillespie	Y
Franklin Mint	70	Saxophone Stylists (4 LP Box #2) John Coltrane	Y
Franklin Mint	3001	Hidden Treasures Of The Big Band Era (2 LP)	Y

A DISCOGRAPHY

Label	Issue	Title	Anth
Franklin Mint	A 7	Greatest Recordings Of The Big Band Era (2 LP)	Y
Franklin Mint	A 55	Greatest Recordings Of The Big Band Era (2 LP)	Y
Franklin Mint	A 99	Greatest Recordings Of The Big Band Era (2 LP)	Y
Frog Box	100	Three Black Kings – World Premiere Recording (2 LP)	N
Galaxy	4807	Famous Orchestra And Soloists	N
Gaps	40	Duke Ellington And His Orchestra 1932–33	N
Gardenia	4001	1932–1936	N
Giants Of Jazz	1002	Jazz Giants	Y
Giants Of Jazz	1003	An Evening With The Duke	N
Giants Of Jazz	1008	Giants 3	Y
Giants Of Jazz	1018	Winners	Y
Giants Of Jazz	1020	Broadway Gala	N
Giganti Del Jazz	12	Ellington – Hodges – Williams – Anderson	N
Giganti Del Jazz	64	Ellington – Jones – Dorham – McGhee	Y
Giganti Del Jazz	2 LP 5	Jazz Giants (2 LP #s 1 & 27)	Y
Giganti Del Jazz	2 LP 7	Jazz Giants (2 LP #s 12 & 25)	N
GNP	9045	1953 Pasadena Concert	N
GNP	9049	1954 Los Angeles Concert	N
Golden Era	15062	Theme Songs Of The Big Bands Vol 2	Y
Goodyear	106657	Jazz Concert	Y
Guest Star	1425	Showcase Of Stars Vol 2	Y
Guest Star	1427	Original Big Band Sounds	Y
Guest Star	1486	Louis Armstrong	Y
Hall Of Fame	625	Immortal Duke Ellington Vol 1	N
Hall Of Fame	626	Immortal Duke Ellington Vol 2	N
Hall Of Fame	627	Immortal Duke Ellington Vol 3	N
Halo	50242	Jazz	Y
Harmony	7436	Ellington Fantasies	N
Harmony	11323	In My Solitude	N
Harmony	30566	Greatest Hits	N
Hindsight	125	Uncollected Duke Ellington And His Orchestra Vol 1 1946	N

Label	Issue	Title	Anth
Hindsight	126	Uncollected Duke Ellington And His Orchestra Vol 2 1946	N
Hindsight	127	Uncollected Duke Ellington And His Orchestra Vol 3 1946	N
Hindsight	128	Uncollected Duke Ellington And His Orchestra Vol 4 1947	N
Hindsight	129	Uncollected Duke Ellington And His Orchestra Vol 5 1947	N
Historia	621	Best Of Duke Ellington	N
Historical	33	Jazz From New York 1928–1932	Y
Hits	1001	Duke Ellington 1943–1946 Broadcasts	N
Hurricane	6001	Duke Ellington At The Hurricane Club – NYC Vol 1	N
Hurricane	6002	Duke Ellington At The Hurricane Club – NYC Vol 2	N
IAJRC	1	Jazz Collection Vol 1	Y
IAJRC	5	For The First Time	Y
IAJRC	11	Duke – Big Band And Small	Y
IAJRC	17	Swinging War Years – Radio Rhythm Vol 2	Y
IAJRC	30	Ben Webster – He Played It That Way	N
IAJRC	45	At The First Annual Connecticut Jazz Festival July 28, 1956	Y
IAJRC	51	V-Disc Stomp	Y
Impulse	26	Duke Ellington Meets Coleman Hawkins	N
Impulse	30	Duke Ellington & John Coltrane	N
Impulse	99	Definitive Jazz Scene Vol 1	Y
Impulse	5650	Duke Ellington Meets Coleman Hawkins	N
Impulse	8026	Best Of Impulse Vol 1	Y
Impulse	9256	Ellingtonia – Reevaluations: Impulse Years (2 LP)	Y
Impulse	9258	Reevaluations – The Impulse years (2 LP)	Y
Impulse	9284	Bass (3 LP Box)	Y
Impulse	9285	Ellingtonia Vol 2 (2 LP)	Y
Impulse	9350	Great Tenor Encounters	Y
J&B Rare Scotch	15441	Jazz & Beethoven	Y
Jazz Anthology	5103	Original Sessions 1943–1945	N

Label	Issue	Title	Anth
Jazz Anthology	5117	Carnegie Hall 1943	N
Jazz Anthology	5124	Live Sessions 1943–1945	N
Jazz Anthology	5135	Indiana Live Session June 1945	N
Jazz Anthology	5145	Jazz Group 1963	N
Jazz Anthology	5157	Great Jazz Music From The Southland Cafe Boston	Y
Jazz Anthology	5165	Original Sessions 1945–1946	N
Jazz Anthology	5168	Live Recording At The Cotton Club	N
Jazz Anthology	5169	Live Recording At The Cotton Club Vol 2	N
Jazz Anthology	5189	In Europe 1965	N
Jazz Anthology	5197	From The Blue Note Chicago 1952	N
Jazz Archives	12	Cotton Club 1938	N
Jazz Archives	13	Cotton Club 1938 Vol 2	N
Jazz Archives	15	Ben	Y
Jazz Archives	21	Collectors' Jackpot	Y
Jazz Archives	35	Ben And The Boys	N
Jazz Archives	40	Collector's Jackpot Vol 2	Y
Jazz Band	411	Live At Stuttgart Vol 1	N
Jazz Bird	2009	Meadowbrook To Manhattan	N
Jazz Bird	2010	West Coast Tour	N
Jazz Club	124	In Europe Vol 1	N
Jazz Connoisseur	4	Dance Date, Air Force USA March 1958	N
Jazz Guild	1002	Washington DC Armory Concert April 30, 1955	N
Jazz Guild	1004	Unusual Ellington	N
Jazz Guild	1006	Fargo Encores	N
Jazz Information	4001	Duke Ellington In Sweden	N
Jazz Moderne	3	Duke Ellington: Chicago, Detroit 1940	N
Jazz Panorama	1	Carnegie Hall Concert, Dec. 11, 1943	N
Jazz Panorama	2	Swing Era	Y
Jazz Panorama	6	Duke Ellington 1928–31	N
Jazz Panorama	12	Early Duke	N
Jazz Panorama	17	In Harlem	N
Jazz Society	501	Duke Ellington 1943–46	N
Jazz Society	520	Duke – Live From The Crystal Ballroom In Fargo, N.D. (2 LP)	N

A DISCOGRAPHY

Label	Issue	Title	Anth
Jazz Special	1	Count Basie & Duke Ellington	N
Jazz Supreme	102	Ellington 1928–1947	N
Jazz Vault	101	Orchestra (Sesac Reissue)	N
Jazz-Line	104	Duke Ellington (2 LP – Other LP Is Historia 631)	N
JJA	19777	Music Of Broadway 1930 (2 LP)	Y
Joker	3132	Greatest Esquire's Swing Sessions	N
Joker	3134	Jazz Of World War 2nd	N
Joker	3951	Blues Vol 5	Y
Joyce	1023	One Night Stand	N
Joyce	1053	One Night Stand At The Civic Opera (2 LP)	N
Joyce	1066	One Night Stand At The Club Zanzibar	N
Joyce	1071	One Night Stand Return To The Zanzibar	N
Joyce	1077	One Night Stand At The Steel Pier	N
Joyce	1079	One Night Stand At The Blue Note, Chicago	N
Joyce	1212	Tenderleaf Tea Show	N
Joyce	4014	Spotlight	N
Joyce	4015	Spotlight Back At Ciro's	N
Joyce	5013	Jubilee	N
Kaydee	7	Swinging Flicks Volume 1	Y
Kings Of Jazz	20030	50's Rare Of All Rarest Jazz Performances Vol 1	Y
Koala	14117	Nutcracker Suite	N
Koala	14157	Stardust	N
Laser	26012	Jump For Joy	N
LMR	10	Ellington Remembered	N
London	5034	Radio Transcriptions Vol 2	N
Longines	5112	Best Of Telephone Hour (5 LP Box)	Y
Macmillan Company	48987	Big Bands (3 LP Box – Includes De 34503, Longines & Col 661)	Y
Magic	19	Live In Paris	N
Max	1001	In Hollywood – On The Air	N
Max	1002	On The Air	N
Max	1003	On The Air 1940	N
MCA	1358	Beginning	N

Label	Issue	Title	Anth
MCA	1359	Hot In Harlem	N
MCA	1360	Rockin' In Rhythm	N
MCA	1374	Brunswick – Vocalion Rarities	N
MCA	2075	Beginning Vol 1 1926–1928	N
MCA	2077	Rockin In Rhythm Vol 3 1929–31	N
MCA	4061	Encyclopedia Of Jazz On Records Vols 1&2 (2 LP)	Y
MCA	39324	Irving Berlin 100th Anniversary Collection	Y
MCA	252315	Early Ellington	N
Melodiya	26781	1st Sacred Concert	N
Meritt	1	Various Artists 1927–1940	Y
Merritt	24	Jazz Potpourri Vol 2	Y
Merry Christmas	1005	Twenty From The Top Drawer	Y
MF	204	Popular Hits Ballets Extended Works & Jazz (5 LP Box)	N
MF Productions	2536	Duke Ellington 1899–1974 (5 LP Box)	N
MPS	21704	Collages	N
Murray Hill	56761	Big Bands Of The Swinging Years (4 LP)	Y
Murray Hill	61366	Spotlight On Drums (3 LP Box)	Y
Murray Hill	927942	Collectors History Of Classic Jazz (5 LP Box)	Y
Musica Jazz	1005	Live 1958	N
Musica Jazz	1021	Le Suites Sinfoniche	N
Musica Jazz	1055	Billy Strayhorn	N
Musica Jazz	1060	W.C. Handy	N
Musica Jazz	1061	Stan Getz	N
Musica Jazz	1068	Ben Webster	Y
Musica Jazz	1079	I Song Di Irving Berlin E Jerome Kern	Y
Musica Jazz	1082	Johnny Hodges	Y
Musicraft	2004	Carnegie Hall Concert (Musicraft 78S)	N
New World	216	Mirage – Avant-Garde And Third Stream Jazz	Y
New World	272	And Then We Wrote: American Composers & Lyricists Sing, Play	Y
New World	274	Jive At Five: The Stylemakers Of Jazz 1920s–1940s	Y

A DISCOGRAPHY

Label	Issue	Title	Anth
Nieman-Marcus	342	First Edition Second Series (4 LP Box)	Y
Nostalgia Book Club	1005	Echoes Of The Thirties (5 LP)	Y
Novus	3017	Radio Days – Soundtrack	Y
Odeon	144	Jungle Jamboree	N
Odeon	1154	Jungle Jamboree	N
Odeon	1195	Jazz In The Making	Y
Odyssey	32160252	Nutcracker – Peer Gynt Suites	N
Olympic	7129	Legendary	N
Opus Musicum	228	Jazz (3 LP Box)	Y
Ozone	12	Rare Broadcast Performances	Y
Pablo	2308242	Stockholm Concert, 1966	N
Pablo	2308245	Harlem	N
Pablo	2308247	In The Uncommon Market	N
Pablo	2310379	Norman Granz Presents Pablo Jazz In-Store Sampler Vol IV	Y
Pablo	2310703	Duke's Big 4	N
Pablo	2310721	This One's For Blanton	N
Pablo	2310762	Ellington Suites	N
Pablo	2310787	Intimate Ellington	N
Pablo	2310815	Up In Duke's Workshop	N
Pablo	2310845	Best	N
Pablo	2625704	Greatest Jazz Concert In The World (4 LP)	N
Palm 30	3	Fargo 7th Nov 1940 Vol 1	N
Palm 30	9	Fargo 7th Nov 1940 Vol 2	N
Palm 30	11	Fargo 7th Nov 1940 Vol 3	N
Palm 30	16	Second Esquire Jazz Concert	Y
Parlophone	1195	Jazz In The Making – Classic Era	Y
Parlophone	1222	Jazz In The Making Vol 2 The Swing Era	Y
Pathe	16029	Swing Sessions 1946–50	Y
Philips	7100	This Is Jazz No 1	Y
Philips	7338	Anatomy Of A Murder	N
Philips	7356	This Wonderful World Of Jazz	Y
Phontastic	5011	Far Away Star	N
Phontastic	7604	Hit Songs And Hot Songs	Y
Phontastic	7619	Tiger Rag 1931	Y
Phontastic	7647	Stormy Weather 1933	Y

A DISCOGRAPHY

Label	Issue	Title	Anth
Phontastic	7653	On The Sunny Side Of The Street 1934	Y
Phontastic	7658	These Foolish Things 1936	Y
Phontastic	7663	Rock It For Me 1937	Y
Phontastic	7667	Over The Rainbow 1939	Y
Pickwick	3033	Louis Armstrong & Duke Ellington	N
Pickwick	3390	We Love You Madly	N
Poljazz	673	Last Time	N
Portrait	44094	Back Room Romp	Y
Portrait	44395	Braggin' In Brass 1938 (2 LP)	N
Prestige	7645	Big Bands 1933	Y
Prestige	24029	Golden Duke (2 LP)	N
Prestige	24045	Second Sacred Concert (2 LP)	N
Prestige	24052	Piano Giants Vol 1 (2 LP)	Y
Prestige	24073	Carnegie Hall Concerts – December 1944 (2 LP)	N
Prestige	24074	Carnegie Hall Concerts – January 1946 (2 LP)	N
Prestige	24075	Carnegie Hall Concerts – December 1947 (2 LP)	N
Prestige	24103	Caravan (2 LP)	N
Prestige	34004	Duke Ellington Carnegie Hall Concert: #1 Jan. 23, 1943 (3 LP)	N
Prima	1	Chicago Civic Opera House Concert (2 LP)	N
Privateer	102	Duke Ellington At The Movies	N
Queen Disc	6	October 20 1945	N
Queen Disc	7	Jimmy Blanton Years	N
Queen Disc	18	At Carnegie Hall (Deep South Suite)	N
Queen Disc	49	At Tanglewood July 15 1956 Vol 1	N
Queen Disc	50	At Tanglewood July 15 1956 Vol 2	N
Quintessence	25091	Plays Duke Ellington	N
Quintessence	25101	Many Moods Of	N
Quintessence	25111	Things Ain't What They Used To Be	N
Radiola	1031	New Year's Radio Dancing Party 1945–1946	Y
Rare Records	3	At The Metropolitan Opera House	N
Rare Records	4	At The Metropolitan Opera House Vol 2	N

Label	Issue	Title	Anth
Raretone	5000	Live At Click Restaurant Philadelphia 1948	N
Raretone	5003	Live At Click Restaurant Vol 2	N
Raretone	5004	Live At Empire Hotel Hollywood	N
Raretone	5005	Live At Click Restaurant Vol 4	N
Raretone	23000	Study In Ellingtonia 1926–1931	N
Raretone	23001	Study In Ellingtonia 1932–1937	N
Raretone	23002	Study In Ellingtonia 1937	N
Raretone	23003	Study In Ellingtonia 1938	N
Raretone	23004	Study In Ellingtonia 1939	N
Rarities	22	Radio Remotes	Y
Rarities	29	His Famous Orchestra	N
Rarities	56	Fabulous Forties	N
Rarities	59	Fabulous Forties Vol 2	N
Rarities	70	Fabulous Forties Vol 3	N
RBF	3	History Of The New York Scene	Y
RBF	48	They All Played The Tiger Rag	Y
RCA	ABL1–ETC 785	Third Sacred Concert – Majesty Of God	N
RCA	ABL1–ETC 1023	Eastbourne Performance	N
RCA	ABL1–ETC 2086	Legendary Performer	N
RCA	ABL1–ETC 2811	Pure Gold	N
RCA	ABL1–ETC 4089	Sophisticated Duo	N
RCA	ABL1–ETC 4098	Sophisticated Ellington (2 LP)	N
RCA	LJM 1002	Seattle Concert	N
RCA	LJM 1008	Jazz For People Who Hate Jazz	Y
RCA	LM 6074	60 Years Of Music America Loves Best (2 LP)	Y
RCA	LM/LSC 2857	Duke At Tanglewood – Recorded Live	N
RCA	LM/LSC 6074	60 Years Of Music America Loves Best (2 LP)	Y
RCA	LPM/LSP 1092	Duke And His Men	N
RCA	LPM/LSP 1364	In A Mellotone	N
RCA	LPM/LSP 1393	Guide To Jazz	Y
RCA	LPM/LSP 1714	14 Blue Roads To St Louis (Blues)	Y
RCA	LPM/LSP 1715	At His Very Best	N
RCA	LPM/LSP 3499	Jazz Piano – Live Festival Recording	N
RCA	LPM/LSP 3576	Popular Duke Ellington	N

Label	Issue	Title	Anth
RCA	LPM/LSP 3582	Concert Of Sacred Music	N
RCA	LPM/LSP 3782	Far East Suite	N
RCA	LPM/LSP 3906	And His Mother Called Him Bill	N
RCA	LPM/LSP 6009	Indispensable (2 LP)	N
RCA	LPM/LSP 6702	Ten Great Bands (5 LP Box)	Y
RCA	LPT 1004	Duke Ellington's Greatest	N
RCA	LPV 506	Daybreak Express	N
RCA	LPV 517	Jumpin' Punkins	N
RCA	LPV 523	1928	Y
RCA	LPV 541	Johnny Come Lately	N
RCA	LPV 553	Pretty Woman	N
RCA	LPV 568	Flaming Youth	N
RCA	New 725	50 Of The Most Famous Records Ever Made No 3	Y
RCA	PR 111	Golden Anniversary Album (Chevrolet)	Y
RCA	PR 125	Music Of Life (5 LP)	Y
RCA	PRM 178	Barrett Presents Dixieland Swing And All That Jazz	Y
RCA	PRM 235	Symposium In Blues (NC)	Y
RCA	PRS 268	Sounds Terrific	Y
RCA	PRS 356	Sentimental Journey 30's–40's (2 LP)	Y
RCA	PRS 418	Lover's Concerto	Y
RCA	SPL–12 41	New Sensations In Jazz From RCA Victor (2 LP But 1/2 Missing)	Y
RCA	VPM 6042	This Is Duke Ellington (2 LP)	N
RCA	VPM 6043	This Is The Big Band Era (2 LP)	Y
RCA	436	Duke Ellington (Test Pressing – NC)	N
RCA	7002	Works Of Duke Integrale Vol 9	N
RCA	7047	Works Of Duke Integrale Vol 10	N
RCA	7072	Works Of Duke Integrale Vol 11	N
RCA	7094	Works Of Duke Integrale Vol 12	Y
RCA	7133	Works Of Duke Integrale Vol 13	Y
RCA	7134	Works Of Duke Integrale Vol 14	N
RCA	7135	Works Of Duke Integrale Vol 15	N
RCA	7143	History Of Jazz Piano (3 LP Box)	Y
RCA	7201	Works Of Duke Integrale Vol 16	Y
RCA	7217	Jazz Tribune (2 LP)	Y

Label	Issue	Title	Anth
RCA	7242	Mississippi Legend – The Music Of New Orleans (3 LP Box)	Y
RCA	7274	Works Of Duke Integrale Vol 17	Y
RCA	7301	Works Of Duke Integrale Vol 17	N
RCA	7302	Works Of Duke Vol 19	N
RCA	7303	Works Of Duke Integrale Vol 20	N
RCA	42039	Blues (3 LP Box)	Y
RCA	42047	Works Of Duke Integrale Vol 21	N
RCA	42397	Works Of Duke Integrale Vol 22	N
RCA	42415	Works Of Duke Integrale Vol 23	N
RCA	42852	Works Of Duke Integrale Vol 24 (Seattle Concert)	N
RCA	43259	Harlem – L'Age D'Or 1926–57 (3 LP Box)	Y
RCA	89166	And His Mother Called Him Bill	N
RCA	89506	Cotton Club Legend	Y
RCA	430206	Seattle Concert 25 Mar 1952	N
RCA	430227	Duke And His Men	N
RCA	731043	Works Of Duke Integrale Vol 1	N
RCA	741028	Works Of Duke Integrale Vol 2	N
RCA	741029	Works Of Duke Integrale Vol 3	N
RCA	741039	Works Of Duke Integrale Vol 4	N
RCA	741048	Works Of Duke Integrale Vol 5	N
RCA	741068	Works Of Duke Integrale Vol 6	N
RCA	741085	Works Of Duke Integrale Vol 7	N
RCA	741114	Works Of Duke Integrale Vol 8	N
RCA	90071	Seattle Concert	N
RCA	10041	La Storia Del Jazz – Blues	Y
RCA	10043	Storia Del Jazz – Swing	Y
RCA	RA 30	Story Vol 1 (6 LP Box)	N
RCA	RA 36	Story Vol 2 (9 LP Box)	Y
Reader's Digest	RD 25	Great Band Era (10 LP Box)	Y
Reader's Digest	RD 45	In The Groove With The Kings Of Swing (6 LP Box)	Y
Reader's Digest	RD4 44	Great Hits Of The Great Bands	Y
Reader's Digest	RDA 17	Reader's Digest All-Star Jazz Festival (8 LP No Notes)	Y

A DISCOGRAPHY

Label	Issue	Title	Anth
Reader's Digest	RDA 21	Swing Years (6 LP Box)	Y
Reader's Digest	RDA 25	Great Band Era (10 LP)	Y
Reader's Digest	RDA 49	Hear Them Again (10 LP Box)	Y
Reader's Digest	RDA 53	Remembering The '40s	Y
Reader's Digest	RDA 86	Golden Age Of Entertainment (10 LP)	Y
Reader's Digest	RDA 112	Big Bands Are Back Swinging Today's Hits	Y
Reader's Digest	RDA 158	Salute To American Music – Our First 200 Years	Y
Reader's Digest	RDA 206	Treasury Of Jazz Greats (8 LP Box)	Y
Regal	1038	Great Bands	Y
Relativity	8220	Singing Detective – Music From The BBC TV Serial	Y
Reprise	1024	Francis A. & Edward K.	N
Reprise	6069	Afro-Bossa	N
Reprise	6097	Symphonic Ellington	N
Reprise	6122	Ellington 65	N
Reprise	6141	Mary Poppins	N
Reprise	6154	Ellington '66	N
Reprise	6168	Will Big Bands Ever Come Back?	N
Reprise	6185	Concert In The Virgin Islands	N
Reprise	6234	Greatest Hits!	N
Riverside	11	History of Classic Jazz	Y
Riverside	115	Riverside History Of Classic Jazz Vol 7&8	Y
Riverside	129	Birth Of Big Band Jazz	Y
Riverside	475	Great Times!	N
Riverside	RB 5	Riverside History Of Classic Jazz (5 LP)	Y
Rondo	1766	In A Magenta Haze	N
Rondo	2017	Dance Band Greats	Y
Rondolette	7	Famous Orchestra And Soloists	N
Rose Boris	Desor 4481	Duke At Cornell Vol 1	N
Rose Boris	Enigma 1052	At A Dance In A Studio On Radio	N
Rose Boris	Montage 20	Mr Five By Five Live	Y
Rose Boris	Skata 502	Don't Worry Bout Me	N
Rose Boris	Sunburst 501	Rarest Style 1952	N
Rose Boris	Tetco 86801	Famed Fieldcup Concert Vol 1	N

A DISCOGRAPHY

Label	Issue	Title	Anth
Roulette	108	Echoes Of An Era	N
Roulette	155	Recording Together For The First Time (2 LP)	N
Roulette	52074	Louis Armstrong And Duke Ellington	N
Roulette	52103	Great Reunion	N
Roulette	671046	Complete Louis Armstrong & Duke Ellington Sessions	N
Saga	6902	His Most Important Second War Concert (NC)	N
Saga	6918	Volume 2 Lady Day	N
Saga	6925	Second Esquire Concert Vol 2	Y
Saga	6926	Vol 2	N
Sandy Hook	2029	At The Cotton Club 1938	N
Sandy Hook	2044	Hit-Of-The-Week Dance Date	Y
Sesac	PM 201	For Drive Time	Y
Session	107	Hooray For Duke Ellington	N
Session	125	Hooray For Esquire Jazz Concert	Y
Showcase	3301	Those Swingin' Days Of The Big Bands (3 LP)	Y
Smithsonian	11891	Smithsonian Collection Of Classic Jazz (6 LP Box)	Y
Smithsonian	R 3	1938 (2 LP)	N
Smithsonian	R 10	1939 (2 LP)	N
Smithsonian	R 13	1940 (2 LP)	N
Smithsonian	R 27	1941 (2 LP)	N
Smithsonian	R 30	Big Band Jazz – From The Beginnings To The Fifties (6 LP)	Y
Smithsonian	R 33	Smithsonian Collection Of Classic Jazz – Revised (7 LP Box)	Y
Smithsonian	R 35	Singers & Soloists Of The Swing Bands (6 LP Box)	Y
Smithsonian	R 37	Jump For Joy	Y
Solid State	19000	70th Birthday Concert (2 LP)	N
Soundcraft	1013	Saturday Night Swing Club Is On The Air	Y
Soundcraft	1014	Saturday Night Swing Club Is On The Air	Y
Sounds Great	8005	Mahogany Hall Stomp – Timex All Star Jazz Show	Y

Label	Issue	Title	Anth
Stanyan	10105	Ellington For Always	N
Stardust	124	All-Star Band	N
Stardust	201	Unique And Original Vol 1	N
Stardust	202	Unique And Original Vol 2	N
Stardust	203	Unique And Original Vol 3	N
Stardust	204	Unique And Original Vol 4	N
Stash	105	Early Viper Jive 1927–1933	Y
Stash	124	Cotton Club Stars (2 LP)	Y
Stash	125	Stash Christmas Album	Y
Storyville	243	And His Orchestra	Y
Storyville	4003	And His Orchestra	Y
Storyville	4106	Master Of Jazz	N
Sunbeam	5	Hodge Podge Of Off Beat Jazz Vol 2	Y
Sunbeam	214	Blackberry Jam 1943–45	Y
Sunbeam	219	Esquire's 2nd Annual All-American Jazz Concert (2 LP)	Y
Sunbeam	Bix 2	Sincerely Bix Beiderbecke Vol 2 (10 LP)	N
Super Majestic	2000	Blue Skies	N
Swing	8444	Harlem Comes To London	Y
Swing	8453	Ridin' In Rhythm (2 LP)	Y
Swing House	28	V.I.P.	N
Swing Treasury	104	Fickle Fling	N
Swing Treasury	105	Unbooted Character	N
Swing Treasury	110	Blue Skies	N
Swingfan	1001	Famous Orchestra Vol 1 1932–1938	N
Tax	8001	At The Cotton Club	N
Tax	8010	1936–1939	N
Tax	8012	Cotton Club Stomp	N
Tax	8037	Transcription Years Vol 1	N
Telestar	11100	Serenade To Sweden	N
Temple	550	Orchestra 1940–41	N
Temple	551	Ellington At Fargo Vol 1	N
Temple	552	Ellington At Fargo Vol 2	N
The Old Masters	2	Greatest Jazz Bands	Y
The Old Masters	10	Ellington Encore	N
The Old Masters	44	Opens The Cave Vol 1	N
The Old Masters	45	Opens The Cave Vol 2	N

A DISCOGRAPHY

Label	Issue	Title	Anth
Time Life	J 2	Giants Of Jazz (3 LP Box) Duke Ellington	Y
Time Life	J 12	Guitarists – Giants Of Jazz (3 LP Box)	Y
Time Life	J 19	Giants Of Jazz (3 LP Box) Johnny Hodges	Y
Time Life	J 21	Giants Of Jazz (3 LP Box) Ben Webster	Y
Time Life	STBB 5	Big Bands (2 LP Box) Duke Ellington	N
Time Life	STBB 16	Cotton Club Nights (2 LP Box)	N
Time Life	STBB 18	On The Road (2 LP Box)	Y
Time Life	STBB 20	Uptown! (2 LP Box)	Y
Time Life	STBB 28	World War II (2 LP Box)	Y
Tops	1766	In A Magenta Haze	N
Tops	9766	In A Magenta Haze	N
Trip	5816	Vintage Duke	N
Ultraphonic	50242	Jazz	Y
Unique Jazz	1	Hollywood Bowl Concert Aug 31 1947	N
Unique Jazz	3	Hollywood Bowl Concert Aug 31 1947 Vol 2	N
Unique Jazz	15	Rainbow Room Broadcasts 1967	N
Unique Jazz	16	Dance – Date Stereo 1958	N
Unique Jazz	27	Dance Date Air Force 1960	N
Unique Jazz	34	Stereo Air Force Date 1958 Vol 2	N
Unique Jazz	35	Duke Features Hodges	N
Unistar	111789	Great Sounds (4 LP)	Y
United Artists	90	Douglas Collection Radio Show (Sampler)	Y
United Artists	92	Togo Brava Suite (2 LP)	N
United Artists	274	Paris Blues	N
United Artists	3197	Original Motion Picture Hit Themes	Y
United Artists	4092	Paris Blues	N
United Artists	5632	Money Jungle	N
United Artists	14017	Money Jungle	N
United Artists	60032	English Concert (2 LP)	N
Up Front	144	Duke Ellington	N
Up-To-Date	2001	Undocumented Ellington 1946–1950	N
Up-To-Date	2002	Studio Recordings 1937–1947 Vol 1	N
Up-To-Date	2003	Studio Recordings Vol 2 1947–49	N

A DISCOGRAPHY

Label	Issue	Title	Anth
Up-To-Date	2004	Studio Recordings Vol 3 1926–52	N
Up-To-Date	2005	Studio Recordings Vol 4 1947–51	N
Up-To-Date	2006	Studio Recordings Vol 5 1929–1956	N
Up-To-Date	2007	Studio Series Vol 6 1930–1958	N
Up-To-Date	2008	Studio Series Vol 7 1929–1962	N
Up-To-Date	2009	Studio Series Vol 8 1933–67	N
USP	110488	Great Sounds (4 LP)	Y
V Disc	1002	Le Grandi Orchestre Vol 2	Y
V Disc	7196	V Disc Promotional LP	Y
Varese International	81007	Duke (An Interview)	N
Vee Jay	101	VJ Presents Narm '74 2 Record Sampler	Y
Vernon	502	Everlastin' Duke	N
Vernon	517	Inferno!	Y
Verve	2535	Duke Ellington Songbook (2 LP)	N
Verve	4008	Ella Fitzgerald Sings The Duke Ellington Song Book Vol 1 (2 LP)	N
Verve	4009	Ella Fitzgerald Sings The Duke Ellington Song Book Vol 2 (2 LP)	N
Verve	4010	Ella Fitzgerald Sings The Duke Ellington Song Book (4 LP Box)	N
Verve	4072	Ella & Duke At The Cote D'Azur (2 LP)	N
Verve	8317	Back To Back	N
Verve	8345	Side By Side	N
Verve	8701	Soul Call	N
Verve	8822	Blues Summit (2 LP)	N
Verve	2304417	Side By Side	N
Verve	2317073	Big Band Sound	N
Verve	2317101	Side By Side	N
VJM	VLP 71	Essential	N
VJM	VLP 72	Essential Mar 22 1927–Dec 19 1927	N
VJM	VLP 73	Essential Dec 29 1927–Oct 1 1928	N
VJM	VLP 74	Essential Oct 1 1928–Jan 8 1929	N
VJM	VLP 75	Essential Jan 8 1929–Apr 4 1929	N
Vogue	19	And The Ellingtonians	N
Warwick	2019	Jazz Legends	Y
William B. Williams	12	Make Believe Ballroom (4 LP–NC)	Y
World Record Club	160	Ellington In Concert	N

A DISCOGRAPHY

Label	Issue	Title	Anth
World Record Club	195	Ellington In Concert Vol 2	N
World Records	42	Ridin' In Rhythm (2 LP)	Y
World Records	265	Harlem Comes To London	Y
World's Greatest	2	Pop Jazz (10 LP Box) also 2A (5 LP) & 2B (5 LP)	Y

INDEX

INDEX

INDEX

INDEX

INDEX

INDEX

INDEX